BOB DYLAN DREAM

BOB DYLAN DREAM

MY LIFE WITH BOB

Roy Kelly

Pembury House Publishing

Published by Pembury House Publishing

5 Henwoods Mount, Pembury, Kent TN2 4BH

First published in Great Britain 2015

A CIP catalogue record for this book is available from the British Library

ISBN 9 780992 995683

For Jo and Louis
without whom
there would be no life.

Someday I'm going to write
The story of my life
I'll tell about the night we met
And how my heart can't forget
The way you smiled at me

The Story of My Life Bacharach/David
1958

PART ONE

AS I WAS ON MY WAY TO HIGH SCHOOL

LET ME FOLLOW YOU DOWN

> & discovering
>   that the ghost too
> is more than one person.
>   Bob Dylan

The spirit of the age
ageing,
looking back,
asleep and awake,

to see an ever-returning
absentee, always
here and gone:
the Village ghost,

catching an ancient
zeitgeist
with the lightning rod
of a guitar.

That cadet
mover and shaker

folk flake,
faking cute,

on the make
and taking it easy,
deadpanning,
jiving and planning,

prodigious rhymer
and embryo rake
focusing incandescent
volts of will

on the big break,
shucking everything
peripheral
for its sake.

A Greenwich wraith,
this apparition coolly regarding
a grandfather compelled
to haunt himself.

*We are talking of summer, summers, being young in the summertime, when
the girls wear clothes that are light and float and fall, and the air is warm
and kind, and the faces are alive with shining eyes and teeth, and the hair
is flowing and flying, and it's summer and they are all young in the kindly
warm air.*

CHAPTER ONE

ETERNAL CIRCLE

This is a story about Bob Dylan and me, and the times we shared. It's one I've been telling for over 40 years, and counting, and, like all stories repeated to people and oneself over a length of time, it becomes the kind of ballad Bob borrowed from the tradition, the ones he took up and made over into his own, the ballads that consist of scenes that may be momentarily clear but the connection between them is problematic, where the narrative has the not quite locatable quality that comes with trying to relate the plot of a dream or a film seen long ago. This is a story about telling a story, how we all figure ourselves into a continuing sequence that seems to have incidents but not much in the way of engineered twists and turns of plot. It's full of truth and the possibility of inaccurate facts. We tell ourselves stories from the past, from what we remember, what we believe we remember, and soon enough they float free of the reality they are supposed to be describing and become, like any song, a set of words you perform.

Everyone wonders how things will turn out, how the way they live will end. We have hopes for endings and want to choose them. We don't know for sure what will happen, no matter how trammelled our lives seem to be. Still, beginnings are as mysterious in their way. In the days when people made compilation tapes for one another the question of what was going to be first song heard detained me for hours sometimes. That beginning could determine whether people listened afterwards. It doesn't seem to apply in quite the same way with CDs because people can more easily start them wherever they please. In writing of course it still has the same kind of nagging but urgent quality. In life you get no choice at all. You had a personal and family history massing its crowd behind you, larger than Bob's oeuvre, as soon as you were born. So did he of course, stretching back to Lithuania and Odessa. Bob Dylan fans can investigate both, his and their own, blurring and comparing circumstances, journeys, progress, setbacks, the ages and landmarks he passes and measures out. Backwards and forwards the loom shuttle goes, and we come to temporary, tentative conclusions about ourselves. What is permanent and unchanging is how the songs and their singers that we absorbed as teenagers form a constituent element of our identity. Bob Dylan helps you to know where you come from and where you are. Beginnings are as arbitrary as endings. We all have a Hibbing that raised us.

A MATTER OF PUBLIC RECORD

Miles and miles of shelving
in hectares cubed at Kew,
there to provide conclusive proof
that the past has led to you.

Numberless numbered documents,
indexed in cyberspace,
exist to help expose the past
now buried in your face.

Parents double up and back
as far as farthest star;
a family tree spreads where you sit
and leaves you where you are.

When people ask where I'm from I tend to say Walsall, which always used to be Walsall, Staffs, but at some administrative point became Walsall, West Midlands; but really I come from outside the town, the outskirts, and when I think of it I think it's just as accurate to say I come from two places near Walsall. One is Blakenall, which was and is houses, a place where estates from different times and housing styles met, and didn't quite form a suburb, but a big spread out area of houses, streets, fields and a canal, north of the town itself. That's where the house was that I wasn't quite born in, but came to as soon as the hospital allowed, and where I lived until I was 21, becoming who I am. The other place I come from is Bloxwich, next door, down the road apiece, as the Stones and Chuck Berry say, which is a genuine small centre, smaller than a town, bigger than a village, and also where I went to school There are few things that define you more than that. I also come from the 1950s and 1960s, the time when I grew up in those places. As you get further away from them you see that place is an aspect of the time you knew it.

Bloxwich was a place and not just a collection of houses because, amongst other things, it had a market every Saturday. It was a small market on a tiny triangle of ground near the main road to Walsall, between the church and a police station. A dog leg of canvas-covered stalls went up, marking out the available space, and the ones I remember most are the stall where biscuits were sold in their deep square tins, slightly slanted forward to display the contents, and the stall of the man who sold eggs. He wore a dark blue beret, resolutely unstylish and never in any danger of being thought to have any allusion to jazz. He always wore a long shopkeeper's apron, green, and usually with a coat that suggested agricultural pursuits, the same dark blue as his beret, the cuffs bound with leather. His voice was the most striking thing about him, having a cracked yet continuous quality whose timbre to me was a representation of what the eggs seemed to be, something rural and of fields. I heard his voice and I could visualise the brown and white, almost terracotta, look of the eggs nestled in their grey, porous and geometric paper pulp hollows. Or I looked down at the rows of eggs, the friendly farmyard colours orderly across the stall, and I could hear his voice in my head. Edgar the egg man, long before I Am The Walrus, and that was the only name he needed. And what has this to do with Bob Dylan, with thinking about him for decades? I think it has to do with an idea of home, with who you are and where you come from always indissoluble, and with one of Bob Dylan's themes not only being endings, as Christopher Ricks points out, but also an idea of home as something you have to journey to find. Where you are from and the way it shapes you helps you recognise what your new place is. When I go back to Bloxwich now the market triangle is a flattened piece of asphalt and looks smaller than ever. Cars park on it. There's not been a market stall there for years. Edgar is long gone, except in my memory, where I see his beret and hear his yokel tones.

And that's why we all understand soon enough why you can't go home again. The world you interpret, that has meaning, is not simply the world you see but the world you understand, because it exists in the element of what you believe to be so. What you believe changes even when you think no change is going on. Bob Dylan pointed out a long time ago that everything passes, everything changes, in a song that he has been doing in every decade ever since the 1960s, with different voices, arrangements and bands to prove it. We can go back to the place where home used to be, and even if every building on every street was entirely unaltered it could never be the place we knew.

The place I knew was a housing estate where all the roads were named after rivers: Severn, Trent, Dee, Wye (which our accents always rendered as Wire and I never particularly noticed the sign telling me different), and of course Thames, which is the road I lived in, and which later, in one of those coincidences that make the theory of looking back so seductive, the river I lived near, and now cycle along most days to get to where I work, yards from Richmond Bridge. The Rivers Estate was made of houses like this:

created in their thousands all over the country to provide new homes for people after the war, in those austere years of rationing and shortages and expectations of a different world. People were going to have families in a new world, out of the cramped towns, where you could see the clouds in the sky, and the buildings still going up and the wooden fences. Men who'd been war time soldiers not that long before would hold their babies and feel England spreading out from that still point, and perhaps think that all over it houses and estates were being created that their babies would know as home, always, whatever happened.

These houses were prefabricated with breeze block on steel frames and had distinctive steel, square-edged, corrugated cladding, and went up quickly. We didn't think of them as prefabs in fact. That was a name with a specific meaning, and what it meant was the smaller one-storey houses, like bungalows. Those were the ones always identified as prefabs. Ours were called the steel houses. There were prefabs in a little angled row at the bottom of our street but they were swept away a couple of decades later by modernising forces. The steel houses are still there, though at different times they too have been improved. One of their difficulties was that the chimney consisted of what was essentially a metal tube going up the middle of the house. In some cases the accumulated clinker that attached itself to the tube from years of coal fires managed to catch light in some low level way, but high level enough to heat up the steel of the chimney tube until it glowed, making the airing cupboard and its contents, behind which it passed, catch light. Or at least that was the story we heard when a couple of houses did burn. The coal fire was a big part of my childhood. It heated the back boiler behind the fire, and every so often that required, for renewed efficiency, its tarry deposits to be chipped away using a hammer and a substitute chisel whose wooden handle was softened and mashed down at the end by repeated boiler-chipping hammering. You couldn't hit too hard for fear of damaging the miniature radiator-like heat exchanger, but it had to be enough to cause flakes of shiny carapace fall off. It was a satisfying experience, like an industrial nose-picking session. And sweeping the chimney was always a grubby sort of adventure too. There was the filthy sheet, never changed or washed, required to wrap around the grate, held up on the mantelpiece by flat irons, that prevented sooty clouds billowing into the room, and its rip in the front to allow the brush access, the wooden sticks added one by one, screwed together with brass ferrules and then pushed incrementally up the tube until you felt it go clear. Then there was the rushing out to see the triumph of the inadequate-looking bristle crown pushed through into the open air, three or four feet above the roof on its bamboo-style spindle. In Blakenall the Rivers Estate went up next to or near either earlier redbrick council houses from the 1930s, or, from the same time, those detached or semi-detached private houses that we know from Betjeman poems, or images of mythical suburban happy families in children's books, the kind of house that John Lennon's Aunt Mimi brought him up in and which most of us never went inside. They reminded me of the houses on the tins of Mansion House polish.

Everyone who becomes a fan of Bob Dylan tends to have a skewed relationship with time. Unless you actually knew him in Greenwich Village, or further back, Madison or Minneapolis or Hibbing already, you have to come across him when your time is right, often around your mid-teens. And when you've gone down to that symbolic crossroads, at that mythical midnight, you work your way backwards and forwards through his catalogue, which means through the years, comparing and contrasting where you were at and where he was at, and how this time is or isn't like that one, thinking in decades and chapters; and how lives progress or don't, and what progress could mean; and how he is in and out of your life, and what *that* could mean. You will look back on this later, and look forward to looking back, in whatever circumstance you find yourself.

When I say how I first came across the name of Bob Dylan, and which was the first album of his I owned, then I believe it to be so. It's certainly feels like the version I've told ever since I began telling it. But like children who have a clear picture – a memory, an imagination – of what used to be, what happened, I may be eligible to stand corrected by the equivalent of parents who can point out that what is being told is something that they told you, a scene at which you weren't present. You're too young to remember, they explain, what you're remembering is what we described. And now there's no-one around to do that, no-one I can verify the details with. I have to think of it, this ballad of Bob and me, like Barbara Allen, or more appropriately no doubt, Young But Daily Growing, the songs where every singer changes a verse or two along the way, and passes it on.

"At some point, probably in 1963, I saw Peter, Paul and Mary on Sunday Night At The London Palladium, and they mentioned the name Bob Dylan when introducing Blowing In The Wind," is the way my Bob Dylan story begins. In fact I now find I can't substantiate that. A cursory Google search tends to suggest that it was more likely to be summer 1964. That would tie in with when the trio were reported in the New Musical Express. This seems both a bit late, but also absolutely plausible. The only demur is that in my mind I think there's a suggestion that it was autumn when I saw them. I seem to remember darkness outside, and that wouldn't be the case with July. It's like trying to remember a dream. Things shift, nothing is definite. Except there is something definite about my mental picture of a black and white TV screen, and seeing them perform, and remembering the sound of the name Bob Dylan.

The truth seems to be that my becoming aware of Bob Dylan doesn't stand out in the same way that the actual appearance of The Beatles did. That was in the October of 1962, when their first single Love Me Do was released. Dave Powell, in our class, had a paper round, and that gave him access to one of those glossy A5 size magazines all about pop, or beat, music; the kind of publication that a year or so later became the Beatles own monthly magazine, chronicling their PR lives in a confection of words and pictures, put out by the same company, and worth 1/6 of anyone's pocket money. Before that there were other opportunist publications we rushed to be exploited by. Meet The Beatles, showing them, for unexplained reasons, larking in Victorian swimming costumes, but the larger format, stiff full colour cover made it seem worth the massive half a crown you had to part with to get it. This was around a time when even something so apparently ordinary as a press-stud tab collar on a tiny, gingham check shirt had enormous, almost other-worldly glamour and power. To have one, and to feel the way fashion could make you feel, was to experience something unjustifiable and out of everyday sense, the way I had once felt as a smaller child when a blue jumper with a roll collar had made me feel brilliantly special the first time I wore it and knocked on a neighbour's door. In his early magazine Dave showed us the advert for Love Me Do, accompanied by the disembodied heads of the Beatles, floating beside it in a column. We felt we'd never seen anything quite like this before. There was something about the hair, and the way at that stage they all looked similar, and not at all like previous groups, The Shadows for instance. We weren't so much impressed, though that might have been part of it, as amused in a slightly offended way. There was something challenging about them. I never forgot it and so I always date my knowledge of the Beatles to then, although I'd be just as much at sea as I am about Bob Dylan if I had to be precise about under what circumstances, on what radio programme, what show, what deejay, I first heard the record. Radio Luxemburg? Light Programme? Night? Day? Around that time is all the location I need. Five decades don't have to elapsed for you to feel that you've always known something. Once you knew about the Beatles you felt like they had been in your life forever, and also that they were completely yours and nothing to do with what parents might have liked or what went before. It takes time to realise that everything does connect to what went before.

So, at some point, perhaps in 1963, probably in 1964, Peter, Paul and Mary played Sunday Night At The London Palladium, the biggest entertainment deal there was in those days, and they sang Blowing In The Wind, and in the introduction they said the name of its writer in approximately reverential tones. I liked the sound of his name. I liked it very much and I didn't know why, and I don't know why. When they said songwriter I was thinking more of the people I thought of even then as songwriters, Irving Berlin, Rodgers and Hart, the world of musicals. Smart and neat though the folk trio was they meant something else it was clear. The sound of his name didn't make me think of Dylan Thomas specifically, not that I recall. I would have known his name then but not much of his work particularly well. There was though a romantic oddity to the word Dylan, which is more to do with the spelling than the sound, pleasing though the sound is. But here's another problem. If hearing them say it is one of my mainstays in how I came across him, how would I have an idea how his name was spelt? In that case I must have seen his name elsewhere, which is quite likely if they did appear in the July of 1964, or even if it was the autumn of 1963. Or am I overlaying the fact that I later knew what his name looked like with that memory of hearing them say it? I can't say for sure, but I've discovered that this is how memory works, with its palimpsests of scenes and experiences from different times laid over each other like transparencies, or computer windows, a version of visions in a patchwork partial collage.

So when did I hear him next, and what was the song, and was he widely played on the radio? Where did one hear him, living in that foreign country your own past, before the way radio is now arranged, before even pirate radio stations and their introduction of American practices? What I remember for sure, in the way a detail from a dream survives where everything around it blurs and drifts away, is that there was a little review in the Daily Express in the regular column by Anne Nightingale, (not then Annie, and some years from being a BBC radio dj.) We took the Daily Express because my

Dad preferred the racing coverage, where the great Peter O'Sullevan held sway, rather than through any political affiliation. Dad bet in tanners and he won in tanners, although there was always the background hope of half a crown. It was in the days before betting shops and the bookmaker was a one-armed man whose name was Knock, or at least that was the only name he was ever known by, who conducted business on a street corner. Usually he was dressed in a long tweedy overcoat and wore a cloth cap, and the overall effect was somehow American to me. It reminded me of scenes from Jimmy Cagney films where similar overcoats concealed guns of various sizes. Knock would hold a newspaper under his sleeved stump and dig into one of his deep pockets with the other hand to pay people out, or to take their stake. There were always a couple of punters flanking him and chatting or exchanging money. All it needed was an orchestra and they could have put on a Fugue For Tin Horns right there. Whenever I asked my dad if he made money backing horses he always said he more or less broke even over the long term. I doubt if he seriously kept a check. Winning or losing wasn't really the point, though it might have been nice to achieve a profit. If you bet in sixpences you know you are never going to haul away a fortune, even if the complicated roll ups and accumulators all come in at 50 to 1. The point was studying form, making your choices, deciding the stake and what sort of bet would be most effective, then walking down the street to Knock's corner to chat to the assembled race course enthusiasts who were assessing the going at every applicable practical or symbolic level.

Aside from dad's entertainment, having the Daily Express also allowed Rupert Bear to become part of my childhood, as he did Paul McCartney's, a 1920s and 30s suburban dream life that we never found odd despite it being enacted by clothed animals whose captions were in rhyming couplets. The appeal of the daily strip was enlarged by the Christmas annuals, with their lovely colours in which the orange of Chinese lanterns always featured prominently, and the origami printed diagrams with careful dotted lines and instructions that seemed so close to the illustrator's heart, none of which I ever attempted. I could name all of his friends for some time afterwards, and even if the others are more difficult to bring immediately to mind it seems that Algy the Pug, Edward Trunk and Freddy and Ferdy Fox will never leave me.

Less definite however is the date of Bob's tiny notice that I saw in passing sometime and somewhere between noticing Rupert and the James Bond strip that the Express had carried well before the Bond films were a reality, those Sixties emblems, the flip side of Steptoe and Son, and its taking some proprietorial interest in the appearance of whatever actor would embody the character. Interestingly their strip drawing did almost resemble Sean Connery. It's possible that it was early 1965 and Anne Nightingale was aware that he was about to tour and so was engaged in some kind of review catch up. Dates are always difficult when there's only memory to riffle through, and not some pre-existing list or chart. In fact memory is the most insubstantial, elusive and fugitive sense experience. Nothing exists inside your consciousness anything like as clear, vivid or precise as a Technicolor film in stereo sound, – or Gerald Durrell's enviably vulgar abundance – and yet there is something that seems to exist, this experience one appears to recall. The form may be imprecise, may resist definition, but a sequence of events and emotions can be carried around for years, forever, and one returns to them, not as one sees a film, and not as one reads a book, but in a way as immediate in that odd organ of perception, the mind's eye.

Then too there's the problem that whole areas of the past entirely disappear from what is remembered, as if they never were. All those days you know you went through, double French or maths, moment by moment, you know only because you recall saying those labels. Other times don't even have that incomplete access, time when your consciousness would have been just as full of you and the minute it was in as it is right now, as these words pass before it. There are times when you find by chance an old diary, or piece of writing, a poem completed, a play abandoned. It's in your hand quite recognisably and yet nothing of what it is or encapsulates seems anything to do with the person now reading it. What it is about or describes has been wiped entirely from the memory. The things we remember and mis-remember are all that has made some kind of impression on us. That's why they are still there. They're a tautology. We remember them because they are the kinds of things we remember. It's possible to feel some sort of understanding with Nazi war criminals, or possibly any criminals. They did what modern politicians are always enjoining people to do. They drew a line. They moved on. Lessons were learnt. They became involved with the present and new lives, and the details of what their old working lives entailed drifted away astern, moral enormities breaking up and vanishing like smoke. The days pass away and what do they leave behind? Every day that ever was, thousands of years, has led to this day and one consciousness perceiving it, and yet we are always in relationships with what has gone before.

What remains clear in this case is that this capsule characterisation by Anne Nightingale referred to his voice as the rasp of a file matched by his buzz saw harmonica. I was very struck by this. It was one of those times when the appeal of writing is made clear not by lessons in school, or great literature, but by journalism that is only trying to be short, snappy and attention catching. If you have a mind that is drawn to writing this is good news. It looks like the kind of thing you might be able to do. After all, it's about something in your ordinary, normal world, but it's making you think about it in a slightly different way. You see too that the writing is not only being accurate but being inaccurate too, making something more vivid than might be noticed in reality, being fanciful *and* true, which appealed to me greatly. It's the way people write about photographs also, attributing meaning and significance to elements within a representation of passing life, asserting something and linking it to a further assertion. Words could create a parallel world, one I wanted to try my hand at. There's an odd line, not always definable, between that state and falsification. It's not life, it's writing, trying to make something more interesting to read about than to experience, though the highest praise seemed to be for writing that readers knew they couldn't do themselves, but would make them say, "That's it, that's exactly like me and my life." All of this turned out to be relevant to Bob Dylan and how he fitted into lives like mine.

Anne Nightingale was describing Freewheelin', and it must have been around this time that I became a co-owner of the album. The other owner, the owner in residence, was someone else from school, who when I met him again at the only reunion our class ever had, a long, long time after Sixth Form, had become a successful businessman who ran a company, or possibly companies. This came as no surprise. He'd demonstrated his acumen early on by persuading me to pay half of the record's price, probably 32/6 which seemed to be the cost of an LP for years, even though I didn't at that point own a record player. I could go around his house and listen when it was convenient, he assured me. We weren't really that close friends, and he didn't encourage dropping in. I did it once, I don't remember more than that. His father watched us listening and me reading the back cover and gazing at the front. I remember his father as tall and stern, bald, or perhaps smaller and shy, bald certainly, seeming to give off, as I now think of it, alternating vibrations of despair, humour and tolerance. I don't think this had anything specifically to do with being Dutch so much as trying to understand what we could enjoy. "You think he can sing," he asked, "You like his singing? You like his voice?"

CHAPTER TWO
NOT FADE AWAY

I don't know what my co-owner thought. I don't recall now whether he went on to solo-buy other records, or if he stayed the course and was any kind of Bob fan later. *I* liked the singing, and the whole sound of how everything worked together, that voice, guitar and harmonica, and I liked everything about the record sleeve. He sang a song called Bob Dylan's Dream which began "While riding on a train going West." Everything about it was beguiling: his voice because it sounded a bit like a cowboy, and old and young, and the actual physical texture of it made words seem to mean something different in his mouth than other singers, with his small, entirely personal, pauses and emphases that no-one else would have made; the tune immediately appealing, a folk melody of course though I didn't know; that opening line which seemed to promise a novel in just a few words, and then went on to "I dreamed a dream," another folk borrowing that had an aura as ancient as a spell the way he sounded the Ds; and the title, because it contained the name of the singer and writer in an act of braggadocio that seemed normal, even modest, as well as having the word dream, always a mysterious word, the simple small sound of its blend of hard and soft, and what it symbolised about other worlds existing within the one we thought we knew that otherwise seemed so plain. Another song encapsulated this with the jokey but poetic notion, "I'll let you be in my dream if I can be in yours." And he sang most notably A Hard Rain's A'Gonna Fall. Occasionally, if I hear this by accident on the radio the surprise lets me get a slight flavour of that brand-new synaesthetic reaction when I heard it first. The combination of that flow of images, the sound of the guitar, and his voice was so unexpected to me, so enthralling. He has always been close to self parody, and all of the people who love his voice are aware of that, but the tremendous accomplishment is that the voice lets you shift in and out of such perception and never doubt the power and authenticity. That was then, and that's what moved us. All of it, what the record contained and what its appearance signified, was a peek at another world. These pleasures were curtailed when my mother found out the financial arrangement that had made these insights possible, the custody and access conditions. She insisted that despite my shoe sole toe-gripping, hot cheek embarrassment, I must have my money refunded and relinquish full ownership to the cunning monkey who now enjoyed nine points of it.

After that, an unrecorded not long after, my next Bob experience was all writing based. I came across, for reasons that remain entirely mysterious, the first two copies of the short-lived American magazine Hootenanny, edited by the Bob champion and pseudonymous first album sleeve note writer, Robert Shelton. One of them had a cover I don't recall; one had Bob and Joan at the 1963 Newport Folk Festival. Joan had her raven locks folksinger hair and was turned to look at him. He was staring ahead in profile, with his hair looking reasonably neat, his shirt flimsy, his nose curved, and his neck and Adam's apple very vulnerable. From the same session there is one where he is grinning, looking toothy and gummy at the same time, and she has turned to him with such ardent fondness, showing her white teeth, her face framed by long black hair, and looking so like the representative incarnation of exotic allure she could be a character in one of the traditional ballads she sang, the King of Spain's daughter perhaps. How these magazines ended up in England in a place where I could buy them was inexplicable then, and now has all the substance of a mirage. I don't remember seeing them in a newsagent's. Charity shops didn't exist as they now do, though second hand bookshops with magazines did. I'm guessing that's where I saw them and transported them to my bedroom, where Bob Dylan's column of free-form poetry, all Beats and Bob's, headed In The Wind, was read over and over. They used to rest for safety by the side of my bed, then moved to the wardrobe and then at some point, inevitably, left the building, the way we all do sooner or later. As far as I know he only wrote two columns for the magazine, and at that moment I had them both.

The second was a diatribe about a fake folk artist who offended his sensibilities because of the songs he sang, the way he sang them, and his dress sense, someone no better than a cabaret entertainer clearly. How terrible. He fantasises about stopping the performance to make him pay for these crimes, jumping up mid-song and shouting, "You're busted." It's funny, but too self-righteous, and also goes against the spirit of the first one, from the December 1963 issue. The later, and last, only remains in the more precarious memories of people like me, while the first still survives on the Internet in a couple of dedicated sites. In it, Bob in his most Guthrie manner, dropping ends of words and punctuation, shifting into phonetic spelling, falling in and out of rhyme, – so different from the snarled syntax and ampersands of his Festival programme notes only a year or so later, the Tarantula coded outpourings in waiting, – writes of folk music and its factions. His diagnosis, famously, was

> What's folk music an what aint's got nothin t do with the world
> It just aint healthy t let the music run yer life like that
> Yer life's gotta run the music
> You can't afford t let yer guitar own yer mind
> Yer mind's gotta own that guitar

and there's no hint of wanting to shout "Busted" at cabaret artistes who call themselves folk singers. More importantly he establishes his own folk credentials by giving a picture of life across America, with the nature lyric imagery that found its way into Lay Down Your Weary Tune, a sketch of the geographic panorama that spreads all the way over to the Pacific Ocean sands of Monterey, in a subliminal hint at claimed hobo qualifications; as well as indicating the teeming, building-crowded streets of New York City, and onto a speedy, name-dropping vignette of the art and music he was part of there.

I loved it unreservedly, uncritically, even though there are hokey aspects to it. It had the Holly Golightly quality of being an absolutely sincere fake, not that I could have identified that by name at the time. All I was tuned to receive was the apparent sincerity. Besides, most importantly, all of it, true or false, has the sense of a real person and the real sound of his thoughts, his voice, coming at you. A lot can be forgiven a writer if that requirement is met. I loved the lines about the sands waiting for your feet to be walking, and the con-jured visions of rain and snow up in the mountains, or clothes lines hung with shirts, and the sound of trains. What I didn't know then was that he was falling in with and acting out a received cultural idea that was already old in Greenwich Village and the folk culture. The idea is to do with authenticity and reality and what kind of life one can lead that is valuable. This blurs with the reality of America. The vastness of the geography, the amount and variety of terrain and landscape, sounding the names, blends with the working man and the kind of jobs he has. This goes back to Walt Whitman but con-nected too with all of the ideas that surrounded the Beat writers like heat haze. The cowboy and the West and the sense of moving towards the receding frontier were of the past, but a modern auto version seemed to exist in the moving across the country undertaken by Jack Kerouac and Neal Cassady, to drop in at the bars and clubs and dives of the cities with Beat-friendly districts studded across the States. The West and that figure both mythic and feared, the hobo, were fused in the Beat lonesome travellers, sustained by poetry and jazz. There was something intrinsically appealing about the sound of the word

Beat and all of its associations, and Bob Dylan fell for it along with his contemporaries. He was twice connected to Americana, ancient and modern.

Pete Seeger had actually travelled the country for real back in Woody Guthrie's time, a musical hobo despite coming from a cultured, educated background. And although genuine, sincere and brave in his commitment to ideals of the left, something of his background never allowed him to have that anti-glamour of the roughshod that Guthrie did, and his musical taste and style would never admit him to the cool or rock end of the spectrum. He was always involved in something idealistic, good for you and educational, with propagandist resonances. What Pete Seeger believed, along with the shifting collection of people he sang with, as well as John and Alan Lomax the father and son song collectors, was that there were songs out there that represented the didactic past. They had survived the centuries in some cases and were living artefacts to show how people had lived. Even if no-one around now actually sang them, if they were brought back to life and people were reconnected with them, lives could be made better. The context though always seems to place more people-value and authenticity on unions and manual labour, on hoboes and jumping freight trains. Suburbs and colleges and office workers don't seem to carry the same stamp of the genuine life, although, inconveniently, much of the folk audience was drawn from these areas, and so were many performers. It was these contradictions that suburban shop keeper's son and college drop-out Bobby Dylan was working through and encapsulating, embodying, over the next 18 months, while a suburban schoolboy and Dylan enthusiast read his school of Woody column. It ends with the injunction to live your life because the talkers will always be around and you won't; but before that he says, "An the time's a rollin' down every single street." And I could look out of the windows in my house, back and front, and see the wooden fences separating the back gardens where several streets looped together, a grassy semi-wasteland in a vast tract whose

separate ownership seemed notional in the summertime when the
gardens were at their most lush and savannah like; or the street at the
front, a bus route with small curved concrete lampposts, so that each
light looked like a fuchsia that came on by timed and comforting
magic, one of them right opposite my parent's bedroom, and watch
the time moving, and know that he wrote nothing but the truth.

Maybe I was happy when I was little, or maybe I was unhappy. A million other kids were the same way. What difference does it make?
Bob Dylan 1962

The time you are a child, – particularly the child you are from seven or eight and on into teenage years, when you have your own tastes and likes and dislikes, when books and magazines come into your orbit and you take notice of radio and television, and what you notice becomes absorbed into your consciousness, – all of that lasts such a short time, no longer than the gap now between one album and the next and the one after, par for the course for most acts these days. 1997, 2001, 2006, 9 years going on 10, Time Out Of Mind to Modern Times, and all the lovely boys likely now to be lunky guys thinking about what education will come next, and what work will follow. Perhaps the knowledge we all carry that once we were children and now we are not, is what makes reading theoretical discussions about what time is such a specifically vexing activity. That weaving of abstractions, whose claims to scientific objectivity relegate and diminish to anecdotal evidence every single person's intimate knowledge and experience of the subject, seems impenetrable and beside the point. Indeed, points of view are what it's all about, explains a kindly expert. Time is not a flow, offers his assistant, it might be more helpful to think of it as like space, being everywhere all the, as it might be, time. And let's not forget relativity and speed and perception and how going fast in one dimension makes you slow in another.

What we miss about childhood is the sense of being safe and looked after. Once when I was ill with some feverish cold a doctor was called out to see me, my dad's doctor, one he saw every week for the various tablets and ailments that required it. I was on the settee downstairs in the front room, the old settee with its parched brown leather, and its nails showing in the sides, nothing like leather furniture now with its air of faux-luxury. I was under my dad's Melton overcoat for warmth. It was belted, soft and dark-blue and I remember distinctly how it made me feel. Which of course was coddled and warm, safe and secure. Afterwards, when I saw it hanging from its hook in the hallway, it was never simply an everyday object for me because I remembered its physical presence as a kind of magic. When the doctor came in I moaned and grizzled, scared of his moustache perhaps, and his assessing eye. He said, quite reasonably I think now, but somewhat grumpily I believed then, "I've not touched you yet." He hadn't, but he probably disturbed that sense of all being well in the world, the enclosed world where everything was as it should be, even if I didn't feel well, simply by being a stranger from the outside. The time we feel most secure is when we sleep. That's why later if one is lucky enough to have a child, the routines of bedtime, and the way children look when asleep, arouse the most powerful emotions, the strongest evocation of how they are part of us. It's not restricted to children of course. Most sleeping mammals can occasion tender feelings of recognition. We see the elements we share. One of the things that changed about modern life is how much more there is of everything that goes into a house: furniture, tools, equipment, clothes, and bed linen; and how often we get tired of things, or believe them worn out, and buy afresh. As a child I think I had the same bed, eiderdown and bedspread forever. Despite this I don't recall what the eiderdown looked like, apart from its agreeable puffed up nature. Its colour must have been neutral and memory-resistant. I do remember the bedspread with its embossed yellow patterns and how it covered all of the bed and hung down the sides, and how when I raised my knees it changed the landscape that it seemed to be, a bedspread as big as Switzerland. That's what's missing from the street and house we might be able to go back to physically, but not in actuality, the place that used to be and the person, the child, we used to be in it. That reality is permanently unreal. And tenuous though it may seem this links to Bob Dylan and dreams too.

Dreams are not the wishes come true that they often seem to be taken as, or symbols of ease and happiness that some references suggest. The most memorable thing about a dream is the feeling that seems to be its character and purpose. Events in dreams, and their location, can be a series of elisions and scene changes, some of which seem to come from our life, or our past, or from nowhere we recognise at all. But what's always very clear is the atmosphere, the way one feels in the dream, the reality of emotion that can make you rouse exhausted with the effort of what something completely without physical presence has put you through. Dreams are always elusive and fading, and even when written down can't carry within the words the feeling and atmosphere that was so much of what the event of the dream was. Remembering things can be like that.

We all used to be children and now we are not. It doesn't need talk of how time can, on paper, be capable of travelling backwards and forwards, or how although wine glasses can be shattered one tends not to see them reassembling themselves, for anyone to see that though reading screeds and rolls and flows of text about time, its theories and speculation, might do to pass the time, one only has to look at photographs, or the orange fizz and flow of fireworks, or how the skin looks on the back of one's hand when you pluck it and let it fall, to understand the convincing argument of circumstantial evidence. How come we can't remember the future, ask people who speculate on the meaning of time. A question not about time of course, but language and meaning, about what words mean, about the meaning of meaning. You might as well enquire why we can't forget the future. Oddly, all of this can seem more relevant to Bob Dylan fans than a casual enquirer. When you are living in the days of childhood they seem as if they are all there is, and all there will ever be. No other kind of life will replace or supplant them and things will go on forever, just like this. Times change and things change and the only place they survive, enduring and intermittent, is in that elusive parallel world we all keep inside our memory, to which access cannot be guaranteed.

Childhood when read about or remembered, even in Bob Dylan's Chronicles, consists of summers and Christmases. All the other days merge or disappear it seems. The day after day of going to school and coming home, the arrival of the light and the drawing of the curtains, these days took place for me during the decade of the 1950s first of all. Unlike the idyllic plenty of Eisenhower America, the backdrop of what we came to see as the essentially American quality of life, mine was a time and space of making do and short measures. Rationing persisted until almost a decade after the war ended, so what seemed to be the over-there reality of consumer goods lining up to take their place in homes was entirely absent. I can't say that I knew anything about this. Like most children I inhabited what I took to be absolute normality. There wasn't a lot of money about, and there was even less in our house, where my mother had never gone out to work and my father received a dis-ability war pension. It was all absolute normality and a continuation of a previous time. When people died in our street there were still door to door collections to give to the family, even if the people lived some distance away and we didn't really know them, it being a long street. Curtains were drawn in that house until the funeral was over. Polio was around then and we benefited from the newly invented vaccine, but some children still caught it. A girl who lived in road at the end of ours, who went to my school, had to wear the soft leather wrappings and steel cal-liper leg brace that allowed stiffened, splayed mobility. In a photograph of that junior school class in 1959, at the end of the decade that gave the world rock 'n' roll in general and Elvis in particular, all of those children, whose names have now faded like biro on old compilation cassettes, could as easily be in 1939 going by clothes and haircuts, both boys and girls.

None of which prevented that rock and roll appearing in our lives, leaking through the Light Programme as best it could, allowing us the bonne chance of hearing the brilliant excitement that seemed to us absolutely new and unlike any entertainment or music that had gone before. This connected later with the Beatles and Bob Dylan. Younger than them by the crucial almost a decade, nevertheless I had still lived through and known the world before and after Elvis and the Everly Brothers, and all the others in that glorious first wave of rockers. Rock 'n' roll divided chronology the way BC and AD did. I understood those rockers were proof of a new way of arranging how things were. Hearing things in the right order, as they happen, day by merging, disappearing day, the curtains opening and closing, imparts the basic navigational skills required when faced later with the theme park developed on the site, "The Sixties", where time has become a mode of ever-present space, just as some theorists say.

CHAPTER THREE

DO YOU WANT TO KNOW
A SECRET

Everything is part of everything else when you're growing up. Everything co-exists without analysis. The absolute, unrecapturable strangeness of Jerry Lee Lewis with his semi-violent piano attacks, and sudden flop and swirl of heavy blond curls, a surprising fall of hair much longer than you expected, was happening at the same time as summer evenings spent running around streets, patting one's hip, pretending to be cowboys on horseback. At night we would morph from cowboys to a kind of commando, running about and hiding under the shrubs and bushes at the edge of people's gardens, feeling the air of that confinement as dark and green, moving in vibrations, the way shadows of heatwaves showed up on pavements or walls. Or we would play the game so tedious and annoying for householders, knocking on front doors and running away. We called it Red Apple. Elsewhere it's Knock Down Ginger, but it goes by many names, depending where you are. At the bottom of the street were garages, 4 or 5 only because cars were less plentiful then, with a tarmac area, a slight slope, in front of them. We used to play there, chasing games, those games that have also have topographical pseudonyms for it not counting when you are caught. With us it was tick off and tick on. Tick on and you were fair game. We played Tip It And Run, involving throwing a ball at bits of wood not unlike kindling arranged

against a wall, then scattering, but the details of the procedure and
the point have now dissolved. Right by the garages, at the side of
the pavement, was a sturdy green metal unit about as tall as us, and
holding, I'm assuming, telephone wiring. This was a focus for play
as well, often, when we were in imaginary cowboy mode, becoming
a stand-in for a horse, with us trying to leap up from the back of
it, vaulting onto the imagined saddle in the manner of the Range
Rider, who never used a stirrup to get on. He was the hero of one of
the Western series around then, along with his companion, always
billed as Dick West, All American Boy. The action, as I managed to
see it on neighbour's televisions, always involved him jumping onto
obligingly unflappable horses, often hanging under their necks at a
gallop while firing at the bad guys. In any kind of fracas the Range
Rider instantly became dishevelled because his buckskin shirt was
only tucked into his gunbelt. Any throwing of punches, and he was
always throwing punches when not leaping onto horseflesh, made it
break free. He was played by an actor called Jock Mahoney, who later
became a Tarzan briefly, and didn't have to remember to tuck in his
shirt at all.

The second half of the 1950s was the great age of the TV
Western. Something in the temper of the times and the subliminal
character of the Western form spoke, each to each. The rise of TV
owning masses, and the needs of the old film studios and new TV
production companies, conspired to turn out these lucrative products.
Stars were made. Comics and books were created to cash in on and
increase the appetite. All of this one discovers later. At the time what
I knew was that our street cleared on Monday nights when Wagon
Train was on, and I don't ever remember watching Hancock's Half
Hour. Michael Storey, a boy in my class in that last year of junior
school, had a photograph of Robert Horton that his mother had written off to the television company for. Horton played the scout Flint
McCullough and was the hit of the show. The photograph showed
him in the fringed buckskin which he managed to remove in most

episodes, and with his trademark, carefully arranged forelock. This caused quite a little phase of writing off for photographs, not because we were enamoured of him in a gay sense, but the object itself, the photograph, that it was possible to write off for to a company, staff in an office you would never see, and it would be sent to you, for nothing, seemed to hold some kind of magic. It wasn't simply the free aspect but in the photograph itself, and true only of that time and age we were. Having the photograph to own later would only have been a reminder of the power it once contained, an evoker of memory rather than a generator of spells. Horton also played Sunday Night At The London Palladium, years before Peter Paul and Mary, but being forced by the absence of horses and wagons to do something in a variety mode, turned out to be a not quite good enough singer of show tunes. His personal magic was at its lowest ebb then but this didn't affect the photograph's charge. I sometimes wonder what happened to it, knowing that the likely answer is that it was swapped or given away by me, or thrown out by a mother immune to its powers, and there was no-one around to explain them.

And on those winter days before Christmas, on Saturday afternoons in chill November, when tea means the Sporting Star – the Pink Un –, the radio's football results with their rote formula manipulating the rise and fall of sound, its rhythm, cadence and pauses indicating what the outcome was even if the scores weren't heard, and the smell of boiled ham and a celery stick, always to be dipped into a slight heap of salt on the side of the plate; on such winter afternoon when darkness comes early and the lights in the shops make old streets as unfamiliar and enticing as illustrations in children's stories, I used to go down the town with my mother, and we looked at the annuals in Smiths. I often found that physical sense of Christmas, of what one might call Christmasness, was particularly strong then. It was as if all of the feelings evoked by carols and readings closer to the day became as evident as a taste or an aroma. This aura enveloped what you thought and did, referring everything through an interior quality of an ideal Christmas, one never really experienced on the day itself to be honest. Its purity seemed more real and striking here, in the cold, in the dark and lights and crowded streets, and in their shops.

It was on an afternoon like this that I first saw Western Film and TV Annual 1959, edited by F. Maurice Speed, and though the book has been handed on and on into oblivion I will always have it in my heart, and remember the specificity of the excitement that stayed inside me like blood sugar, seeing the gloss of its coloured cover – Clint Walker as Cheyenne – the turn of the pages and the information and pictures they contained on series I'd seen and those I hadn't. Some of them simply weren't shown in our television area, Lew Grade's fiefdom ATV. Also we had only got a television that year, when the percentage of my Dad's pension was reassessed. This meant that he was less fit than originally judged, so he received more money and we joined the modern world with a TV. The first modern thing we saw was Fred Astaire singing to Ginger Rogers in studio snow, part way through the film that was there when we first switched on. Not that modern then. That film seemed very far away from where we were, joining contemporary Britain by acquiring a TV in 1959. It had been made all of 23 years before, such a short time, and that evening, in a sense always present to me, is a much older old-time movie now.

Previously, and even after we had our own TV set, on Sunday evenings we had all gone to my Uncle Lou's house, walking from our new estate to the older, red brick council houses of Booth Street, all of which had gone up for £200 each my dad assured me, though he didn't reveal his sources. We walked past the school, the newsagents, the bike shop and the Co-Op, where I had always admired the practised skill which the cheese counter assistants brought to the art of folding brown paper with tucks and triangles neat as geometry around the hunks of cheese we bought, and where I heard my mother's divi number, 78434, that remembers me more than I remember it, and will no doubt be one of the last things to fade when other more recent details disappear. Uncle Lou and Aunt Ethel's house was where we watched television on Sunday night, and where, therefore, we were able to share the late 50s splendour of Sunday Night At The London Palladium, the excitement of Beat The Clock and the farewell tiny roundabout with the star performers circling and waving to us that it never crossed my mind to think ridiculous. Before it there was usually a half hour police or detective show, sometimes with honorary American Robert Beatty, the Canadian actor and British resident, and for awhile it was a character called Mark Saber, a private eye with one arm. This too aroused no readings on the ridiculous meter. There was also, and more excitingly, Danger Man, Patrick McGoohan playing John Drake, first in half hour adventures, and then extended, perhaps less successfully, to an hour, but always proving why he should have been a prime James Bond candidate.

And on those evenings the same stories would come out in between the programmes. On Friday nights they came to us, on Sunday nights we went to them, and there was nothing new really that was said. The stories were like songs they performed, folk songs, traditional in form, the words the same from telling to telling, but the expression alive as if it were the first time. So Dad would say how he was coming back from shopping when he was about ten, a few coppers still held in his fist, and he came round a house at a street corner to find himself face to face with some boy who had crossed him, or the other way around, at some earlier time. And without pausing he hit him with his fist packed with loose change. Hard to believe looking at him then, small, a War Pensioner, deaf, mostly affable, but he had been a tough boy and nothing like me, never a likely candidate to smack someone's chops with a fistful of brown money. Or he told us about the dog they had who whined and barked, prevented from going down the street to follow his favourite boy, until he worked out how to run around the block from the other direction, (You could see the thought cross his mind, my dad reported) and thus find him.

And the time he was talking about could have been the time Woody Guthrie was a young man or a child, my dad and him being born almost the same year; or it could have been the time of the Cagney films we watched so fondly together. It was the past, and like children now who study as fixed rotation the Victorians and the Great War and the Romans it all might as well have happened in adjoining rooms. The past was what used to be and we were here, now, watching the summit of modern entertainment. It was the past, I thought later, that Bob Dylan fell for when he thought about Woody Guthrie and trains and hoboes, even though he had grown up in a small town to a family that sold electrical goods and ran the town's cinema. But that wasn't what he envisaged in his hopes and dreams:

> With my thumb out, my eyes asleep, my hat turned up
> an' my head turned on
> I's driftin' an' learnin' new lessons
> I was making my own depression

The key being that he thought the depression was romantic because it was part of the past that seemed to guarantee authenticity. I felt it was another world and the people who had come from it were a kind of visitor too, in the way angels were, but without necessarily any other angelic characteristics.

Bob Dylan wrote in his Guthrie style an apology for things he said at a civil rights award dinner, and a part of it is a remarkable honest, or so it seems to me, memory of where he comes from and what new place made him, and what the past seemed to mean.

> my country is the Minnesota-North Dakota territory that's
> where I was born an learned how t walk an
> it's where I was raised an went t school ... my
> youth was spent wildly among the snowy hills an
> sky blue lakes, willow fields an abandoned open

pit mines. contrary t rumors, I am very proud of
where I'm from an also of the many blood streams that
run in my roots. but I would not be doing what
I'm doing today if I hadn't come t New York. I was
given my direction from new york. I was fed in
new york. I was beaten down by new york an I was
picked up by new york. I was made t keep going on
by new york. I'm speakin now of the people I've met
who were strugglin for their lives an other peoples'
lives in the thirties an forties an the fifties
an I look t their times
I reach out t their times
an, in a sense, am jealous of their times

The way people, and we, were jealous of his Greenwich Village times, or the way teenagers now can imagine what they think the Sixties were. I used to ask my parents who had grown up not knowing television at all if they didn't think it amazing that it existed now, that they could watch it. Very patronising of me. After all, I didn't think it so amazing, I took it absolutely for granted, – the way children now do with computers – but I was suitably grateful when we finally had one in our own living room

Otherwise I'd seen things in friends' houses, or the next door neighbour, where I'd managed to watch 6-5 Special on a set that had a screen that was an exophthalmic 9" square and seemed slightly purple. At my friend Raymond's house, across the road in the houses that weren't steel, and which had lawns that sloped down, revealing that the street had houses built at different heights and we never even considered the implications of it, I'd seen the rather racier and more authentic looking Oh Boy, that made clear the difference between the restraint of the BBC and the spontaneity of ITV. Now on our own and bigger screen I could see the roster of shows detailed in the book. Laramie, one filmed, presciently, in colour, though we couldn't benefit from that, and featuring, amazingly, Hoagy Carmichael. Another of its cast, Robert Fuller, later popped up as a similar character with a different name, in Wagon Train, the market leader in Britain still, and along with its semi-clone Rawhide, not part of the Warner Brothers stable. Warner Bros, whose WB shield I found unaccountably appealing. I still do. (The same shield was on the deep red label of the Everly Brothers Cathy's Clown, serial number WB1, the first single on the label and their debut at the beginning of the 1960 decade, a brilliant tight drum recording in an almost martial roll, their unearthly voices, and the title phrase whose vocal texture and tune entered the consciousness like something already known, and remained, like knowing how to breathe.) Their voices and the sound of the records had been irresistible since Bye Bye Love, or the more weird and funny Bird Dog, but the appeal of Cathy's Clown was of a different order and caught on like a fever.

They also had the distinction of being the first pop band that I thought had really long hair. There was a music shop at the top end of Park Street, near to the cinema then called the Savoy, which became the ABC, and is now the site of the famous prize-winning Art Gallery. Park Street was, and is, the main road in the town, with W H Smiths and the railway station facing each other halfway down. The music shop had the proper, old-fashioned, turned wood framework, shapely and carved, holding curved glass windows like a wall around the entrance to the doorway. LP sleeves were displayed in a vertical line down the front of the window, and one of them was an Everlys record. It was a sideways on shot, the two of them looking off and grinning at a point past your right eye. And Phil, identifiable because he was the phair one, had hair that flew and feathered up from the side of his head way past his ear, looking bizarrely long, and piled up too on top of his head. I didn't notice the name of the record so taken was I with the hair, but a couple of decades later, having never forgotten the hair, I saw that it was Songs Our Daddy Taught Us, and was their versions of folk and traditional songs that musician father Ike had sung, made right in the middle of their first rock'n'roll success. This was another clue to how, though it seemed to come from outer space, rock music always had deep roots and connections with the past. The record contained a softened, tender Barbara Allen, which Bob Dylan may have heard since he was fond of them. He performed it a couple of years later, spellbindingly, in the Gaslight Café, one of the finest of his traditional interpretations in that great early voice, and fortunately recorded, a much more intense experience than the slow, decorous one they made. Like their album though it took me decades to come across this and have it enter my life. It had existed like a room behind a door I didn't know was there: Bob Dylan, where the past is always with us. But then, in the past, Cathy's Clown was of the moment and modern and absolutely now in the way Pop was supposed to be. (And thus to last your whole life, no matter if that takes a moment and its modernity to the end of the realm of decades.)

Maverick was a particular WB favourite. When it was shown on Sunday night and I was thought too young to stay up past bedtime to watch, having school the next day, I used to sneak from my bedroom and try to listen sitting at the bottom of the stairs. This was a hopeless way to try to follow a TV programme, and it didn't take long before I was caught and banned. It was shown at other times though. I remember, or think I remember, it being at some point on Sunday afternoons too. It's the past. Nothing is definite except I did see it, and the theme song permeated me permanently, jaunty and detailed with its tempo change, and the word pictures of the Mississippi and riverboats, New Orleans and playing cards, those jacks and queens. How can Bob Dylan have missed it, so much of the mythology is his, and now he dresses as if a paddle steamer would be his preferred mode of transport.

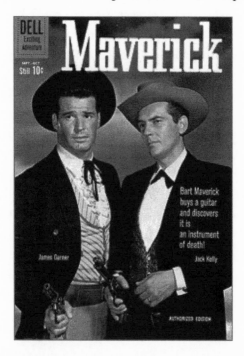

How great too that James Garner had such longevity, stepping from TV series to series, using the decades like stones. There were also from Warner Brothers Cheyenne, Bronco, Lawman, Sugarfoot. There was a name to ponder. I had no notion at the time that there had been an earlier film of the same name, or that there was a jazz tune, Sugarfoot Stomp. What did it mean? The theme song seemed to promise an explanation but didn't. There is something very appealing about the sound of the word. How do other languages manage when they have to use a different sound for "sugar"? Later, when it crossed channels from ITV to BBC, a fairly unusual move in those days, its title was

changed to Tenderfoot by means of an amateurish looking card supposed to be done in the same style as the original. It was a travesty of
sorts because any reader of Western annuals knew that a tenderfoot
was a different breed to the essentially James Stewart character, the
gentle talker who could do the tough stuff when required, that Will
Hutchins embodied here. So what if people didn't know the word
Sugarfoot? You don't change it to something else. The point is to
sound it, to hear the syllables sift and slide to a pleasing stop. It was
the same kind of well-meaning bone-headedness that transformed
Top Cat into Boss Cat without even changing channels, again with
a hand-made, afterthought aura about the inserted title card. The
original was too close to advertising cat food, was the conclusion
that someone intelligent and well-educated and capable of idiocy had
reached. I know the type well. I see it in the mirror too often.

The previous year my Christmas annual, along with the Rupert
perennial, had been Billy The Kid. The cover on that was a close
up of Robert Taylor in a presentation as stylised as costume drama:
colour co-ordinated in blue-black shirt, Stetson and eyebrows, and a
very long way from the reality of William Bonney, or Henry McCarty
as apparently The Kid's real name was.

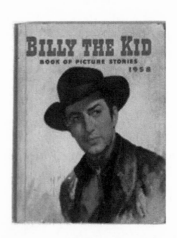

It wasn't until years afterwards that I knew this was a still from Taylor's 1941 film Billy The Kid, a lush MGM Technicolor addition to the romanticising, falsifying and mythologizing of Western characters, and then it puzzled me why more than a decade and a half, and a World War, after its release, a film born the same year as Bob Dylan could still be the source for English children's comics and annuals. Now I see it as a link in the chain, as Bob put it, following Pete Seeger and others. Pass it on boys, pass it on, says Hector in Alan Bennett's The History Boys. Bob Dylan was exposed to the same mythical West, its landscape and its characters, that I was, no matter that he actually lived in America. He was kissed by the times with their cowboy mouth. Actually growing up in the Walsall area gave anyone a connection with the Western, not one we made consciously I have to admit. Walsall was a centre for the leather trade for reasons that sound plausible enough when read about in histories (limestone, charcoal, iron, coal, hides) but actually are as mysterious as any other conjunction of elements that produces a result. And then another mystery is added when the leather trade that came from this combination, developed and grew, by reacting with various odd bits of metal manufacturing that also came into being via limestone, charcoal, iron, coal, into saddle making. Walsall became renowned, and still is, for the quality of its saddles, valuable exports all around the world. Its football team is called The Saddlers, though admittedly they are not so renowned. It's possible, if unlikely, that Walsall saddles may have travelled across the Wild West, like Billy The Kid.

CHAPTER FOUR
TOMORROW IS A LONG TIME

Around the same time as the Billy The Kid annual I used to spend hours completing, breaking up and returning to its box, and then the next week completing again, a jigsaw puzzle that one could get by sending away wrappers from Wagon Wheels, the chocolate-covered marshmallow biscuit that was always thinner and sweeter than you expected. I would sit on the floor near the window seat that all the steel houses had, (a miniature, low level, very slight resemblance to window seats in grand houses,) and fit the pieces together right next to those cold metal window frames that got even colder in winter time. There was something compulsive and soothing about doing this familiar thing, making something come out right, as it should, and you didn't know precisely how to do it just because you had done it before, but that certainly helped. The picture was a romantic Western scene with a wagon, a driver cracking a whip, and horses coming towards you out of a sagebrush desert landscape. The background buttes were orange, and the wagon cast dark shadows under clear Western skies. Except that I only know about the colour of the sky because for mad Internet reasons there is a little picture of the completed jigsaw out there on a site for those sad saps who remember doing that jigsaw near cold metal window frames and could now buy it if they thought it could return their childhood to them for £10, and rising. In my head, in my memory, in the unlocatable image that isn't quite a picture and somewhat more than words, the sky has some of the same majestic shades of red, purple and orange that the desert contains. It could be that clear as it is, – I see it now, – I'm confusing it with the background behind the head of the sailor on the front of Player's cigarettes, a packet I saw a lot when I was a little child but not later, not after my Dad's heart attack. The lesson committed to memory is that there's a truth that may not accord with facts. The point remains the same: all boys loved the American West then. A little earlier, before Wagon Wheels, it had been Davy Crockett, with his covetable, revenue-generating cap, another blatant commercial enterprise of whose base motives we remained innocent

Perhaps we absorbed by automatic osmosis the truth that Westerns, like Robin Hood, always fit the times they are made in and for. The past is most useful when it reflects present concerns. The look of Westerns, and how we want to design the past we imagine they took place in, is always decided by the conscious and subconscious motives of their current creators. That's why old Westerns are dressed so differently, realism always being a fluid concept. But Westerns have always been universal, while specifically American, by being about the oppositions we find in growing older, as we all must: rebellious pragmatism in contest with the conservative orthodoxy of settling down; the struggle between the internalised lawless desires and the constraints to be respectable; young gunslingers who, out to get the old guard, are fated to become the old guard; the difficulties of being laced with regret when you should be content. There's a frontier where anything goes, and there's civilisation. This fantasia of truth, untruth, legend and didactic drama, is the subtext to much of Bob Dylan's subject matter in general, as well as being specific to his songs with Western settings, like that vivid retelling of the plot of El Paso, Romance In Durango. You can hear it too in his liking for the sounds of place names, as well as more precisely in his attraction to Billy The Kid as a reference point in song words, and later a major Sam Peckinpah film, which when he was asked why he took part in it decades afterwards he said, "I guess I was just fond of Billy The Kid." Like Santa Fe it has something to do with the sound of words, at least it does for me, and in this case I don't think Bob Dylan is any different.

> With her picture books of the pyramid
> And her postcards of Billy The Kid,

> and Lincoln County Road or Armageddon

> and I wonder what Billy The Kid would answer to that kind of question?

> or the more surreal, and generally Western
> There's a definite number of Colt .45s that make up Marlene Dietrich

Westerns are always about how times change, and what that does to people. Times and people change whether we notice or not, whether we believe they have changed or not. People change appearance everyday but often only notice suddenly, unexpectedly. "The bum's gorn dear," says the former beauty queen, previously known for the outstanding pertness of her globular rear. Bob Dylan is now the man in the smart suit, best Stetson hat, and pencil moustache seen in the background of the saloon, holding a handful of cards and a poker face. Or perhaps you glimpsed him drifting to the rail of the riverboat at night, looking at the river falling back, watching its dark waters and shifting, glinting lights.

Fads and fashions arrive and depart. The Western had its day but for a while didn't know it. As Bob said about Woody Guthrie, "Everything happens in its own time. He was who he was because of the time he came along in." Police shows came in. We learned there were 8 million stories in the Naked City, and saw the hard, cold, black and white New York streets, and men in overcoats and trilby hats, the same kind of guys who had populated M Squad, Lee Marvin's series before he was quite Lee Marvin, back in half-hour TV world.. In another of those links and coincidences, around the time it was filmed and shown, that was Dylan's New York too. Plus there were the odd poetic titles for each episode, not that far from the kind of thing people might be saying in Village cafes and subterranean hangouts: The Sweetly Smiling Face Of Truth, Memory Of A Red Trolley Car, Make It Fifty Dollars and Add Love To Nona. And alongside the police were the doctors. Dr Kildare, that we did see every week, and Ben Casey, that we didn't, but knew about from Dell Comics, the way we picked up on a lot of what was popular. Dell shared newsstands with DC and Marvel and their roster of super heroes, but Dell contents were all drawings of TV characters, because it was the brand specialising in comic strip versions of TV shows. Oh, but how television marks us.

Oh Dr. Kildare, how I loved you and your programme,
back at the beginning of the 1960s,
when coffee served in a glass cup was the peak of glamour,
and toothsome Richard Chamberlain as unlined as an egg,
and the balance between the Beatles being unknown
and known was beginning to tip in everyone's favour.
Dr. Kildare with its stop-time credits, and the nurses

who sang carols around the wards at Christmas;
the lush Hollywood machine-tooled signature tune
whose orchestration everyone knew and liked
miles better than the words tacked on later
to generate a hit single for the company and the star,
though the title has a pleasing nursery quality yet.
Dr. Kildare with guest stars from the best of U.S. film and theatre,
old hands and new blood, like Zohra Lampert: dark hair,
sensuous mouth, bright teeth, a goofy American Greco
with an ambience of Beat, intense, funny and young.
Dear Zohra. It's possible I might be the only poet
this side of the Atlantic who would remember
her notable name and appearance, which is surely
nearing seventy now, should she be working, playing
wacky grandmas maybe on sitcoms that star kooky gals
as young and accomplished as she used to be
when I ate Weetabix, scrumpled and softened,
a supper bowl ingested with black and white television,
supported by a sofa of love and safety,
a land of warm milk and sugar thickly sprinkled
that tells a story, a story I believe to be true, a story
wholeheartedly in my favour, an imprinting forever
of entertainment and nurturing, the coincidence
delivering all the coincidences that conclude in me,
attempting to replicate a time that might as well
be as far away as Ancient Egypt, here at the breakfast table
that holds bits of paper and an actor's autobiography half-
read.

And along with those comforting, ritual, suppertime cereal bowls I
took in what television brought to us. The English police of Z Cars,
with its Beatles Liverpool association, and its anachronistic Dylan

connection of the Johnny Todd theme; as well as Bewitched, a glossy show about advertising and magic, what better conflation of the Sixties, which in its ways was a mini-Mad Men of its time, and quite unselfconsciously for real. Homage can be brilliantly achieved but the effect may be too layered for the heart to open as it does to guileless manipulation. I loved its credits and have always paid attention to the style of these, and the names that flow up, their familiarity making you believe that you know them almost as well as the actors you see. A similar effect came from the earlier in the evening, on a different day, Dick Van Dyke Show, where the clothes and the main leads were equally smart, casual and attractive, and the lines were sharp and funny. How could anyone not want to inhabit a suburbia like this? Why would anyone want to leave it? So comedy, police and doctors meshed together in the sofa evenings, as well as crusading journalists. Saints and Sinners, with Nick Adams, who was also Johnny Yuma, The Rebel, an actor pilloried in some column as having two expressions: hat on and hat off; and East Side/West Side with the redoubtable George C Scott. But the Westerns didn't quite go away, not recognising, as we all don't, when the times have changed, when your golden moment has receded. For awhile there was a series that I liked very much indeed called The Dakotas, where the writing was unusual and the stars were Chad Everett, whose hairstyle I envied, the wonderfully boss-eyed Jack Elam, who had been a supporting character in westerns on film and TV for years, and someone I had never heard of called Larry Ward. He later turned up for a few minutes being victimised by the craggy, fear-inducing Richard Boone, then being a most convincing villain against Paul Newman's tour de force of silence and stillness in the film Hombre. That was in 1967. At the end of the 1950s Richard Boone had been Paladin in the television western that spawned a thousand wordplays on its title, Have Gun – Will Travel, and had incarnated there an incorruptible, if eccentric, hero, and of course another Dell Comics candidate. He dressed in black and cultivated, though perhaps in a more lush fashion, the style of moustache now sported by Bob. Links and coincidences and all of it matters only because it entered my mind and stayed there.

In the 1950s when television was black and white and little, when I could only see it in the houses of neighbours or friends or relatives, the standard length for series was half an hour. The actual playing time was reduced by commercial breaks. All of those series that wove into children's lives, Lassie, Champion The Wonder Horse, Fury, (Pete, who cut his teeth on a branding iron) it's a wonder that they had time to accomplish any kind of story at all. Later the standard length began to be an hour. The routine of the Warner's corral of money makers had meant that it took six days at least to film an hour's show. If they were supplying them to a TV network on a weekly basis they were always running short of time. That's why Bret Maverick suddenly had a brother who could handle episodes all by himself, or Cheyenne was put into a triad rota with Bronco and Sugarfoot. They had to spread it out and grab the writing from wherever they could. Shakespeare's plots were re-worked. Old Maverick scripts had the names changed and ended up in The Alaskans, another series that never crossed the Atlantic. Stock footage the studio had filmed for routine second features years before was interpolated into the set bound creations that were so unexpectedly popular. With the western resurgence, however, series like The Virginian and The High Chaparral stretched to 90 minutes. Now they were cranking them out in colour at feature film length, every week. A treadmill for actors and writers alike so that anything good that emerges is always a bonus. Clint Walker, whose rise from obscurity to the mass appeal of Cheyenne didn't insulate him from not being paid enough, and not being creative enough, described the process as being like an animal pacing the cage in a zoo. It was something I couldn't confirm. When I was 10 or 11 none of the deficiencies of the sets or stories impinged on me in the slightest. I had to see it with a child's eyes. By the time the format had become such that I would notice, my interest had waned and instead music had become a constant background to thought.

Not that music isn't part of the appeal of any favourite television programme. The adverts I saw at friends and neighbour's houses at that time too, pre our own TV, stay in the memory banks. Some like Murray Mints the Too Good to Hurry Mints were catchy at the time and abide, always there to be called upon, ready to be catchy again. Whereas Shell with, We're going well, we're going Shell, you can be sure of Shell, in the voice of someone who might have been Bing, but could have been sound-alike Michael Holliday, wasn't only catchy but seemed to show a Britain and a life that you now knew existed and wondered if you would ever be part of. My friend Raymond's family with the telly also had a car, and I always associated the smooth, odd luxury of the occasional rides I had in it, such a notable, not to be taken for granted experience for a stranger to cars, with the casual affluence of that Shell Britain which was around when I was, but not quite around me. The Holliday/Bing voice with its easy, casual, tuneful cadence was an aural equivalent of the advert images, seeming to evoke the sensation of being transported in a car. Adverts and theme tunes to favourite programmes are embedded a long way down in the subconscious, around the same geological layers as nursery rhymes at a guess, and can be faithfully reproduced, word perfect, 50 years later, and months since they were even thought of.

Who of that era doesn't remember the snap, snap of 77 Sunset Strip, or the ersatz exotica of Hawaiian Eye, another Sunday evening favourite? The same years that generated the Warner Brothers Western success also saw the popularity of their detective series, with agencies, men in smart suits, and access to reach-me-down, corporate Beat speak. Everything connects to everything else; everything co-exists without requiring analysis. Bob Dylan liked James Dean enough when growing up to want to look like him in photographs, to be the rebel that Dean seemed to embody. He doesn't seem to have left any recorded views on Edd Kookie Byrnes, but speaking for myself there was a time when I was crazy about him with his like later man, dig, and his much-combed hair. This was when the plentiful combed-back surf of hair was popular, before the Beatles largely put paid to it, and Americans called it a pompadour, though we didn't. Ricky Nelson had it. I saw Ricky, later Rick, Nelson's face on the front of screen or teen magazines and envied him his hair and mouth and smoothness and sense of being who he was. I liked his voice too, also smooth and calm and sure of itself, an enviable creamy texture that sang Poor Little Fool or Travellin' Man, and not long after the bigger hit of Hello Mary Lou Once, as a class, we had to try to write a song and tape record it in the music lesson. All I could think of as a possible example to work from was a Rick Nelson song, perhaps It's Late, and it didn't help at all. It's a puzzle that having written poems intermittently almost ever since, I could come up with nothing at all that I considered to be worth presenting, all verbal possibilities seeming laughably inadequate, quite aside from the fact that a tune was more elusive than a lyric. It was an interesting glimpse though into how hard it is to be personal, to create something from within that you believe to have value, and break through taken for granted formal limitations. In following years, seeing how these restrictions were simply blown away or ignored by the Beatles and Bob Dylan I felt ashamed, remembering my smallness of resource, while admiring even more the example they gave and seeing how important confidence was, and how difficult to fake. At the time I ended up trying to look inconspicuous sitting beside the tape operator, hoping I wouldn't be called or even noticed, trying to look encouraging to classmates who had made the effort.

Another singer, entirely unknown here, aurally at least, called Fabian had the pompadour and the general cool American look of Ricky, but not his genuine voice and feel for a song. He was typical of the times too in that he had been plucked from the streets simply because of the way he looked, and long before boy bands he was pressed into the mould of a rock star, manufactured almost totally, with no discernible vocal skills at all. He did however look the part, as it was then conceived by management men trying to make money on a craze that might not last for long, as they saw it. Later he went into acting where he had more success, initially appearing in a sub-Elvis vehicle called Hound Dog Man. Despite a good cast and director the title tipped you off that it was a cynical cash-in on people who hadn't noticed that Elvis wasn't involved. All of this I only knew because of the movie magazines that somehow I ingested, the ones, like Modern Screen, that later, on the back of Bringing It All Back Home, Bob Dylan said people were ashamed to be seen looking at. I wasn't ashamed, and now I see it as sharing the world that Bob Dylan was part of but was about to leave, except then he was Bobby Zimmerman and had a snaggled version of the same pompadour. The universal nature within the entertainment business of Fabian's being lifted from obscurity became the subject of a cartoon later, which may have been in one of the Hootenanny magazines I owned, where a man in a car is calling over to a kid on a stoop. The caption was: "Hey you kid, the one that looks like a folksinger. C'mere."

Even the comic strips went for internal self-reference. One 77 Sunset Strip Dell story featured a car passing a billboard advertising Maverick, a crucial clue in tracking down a baddie later. It also proved quite a good working model for trying to draw Bret Maverick's face cartoon style. There was even a 77 Sunset Strip board game, a Cluedo knock-off, or homage, or folk-reworking and perfectly legitimate, as we would say these days, and I know I would only have wanted it because it had photographs on the box. We didn't play games at home, not even owning Monopoly, so there would have been no real reason to get it, but the marketing ethos was just as strong then as now, and what were the manufacturers to do before technology granted them Playstations? It was an object authenticated by the programme's magic. Luckily there were other photographs you could get for the price of a stamp once Robert Horton had shown us the way.

Because of a novelty hit, and an album trying to parlay that fluke into a further money-making venture, an album never released in England, Kookie had a record company presence here. Decca released Warner Brothers records then, and the publicity department sent you free photographs if you asked for them. This was not the postcard size of Wagon Train, but the traditional 8x10 publicity still. Even now I can get a slight taste of the excitement, some synaesthetic memory I felt receiving that photograph. There is something of the religious in being a fan, and that is what we need to beware of in ourselves. We like representations and images of one we deem special, different, holy perhaps. We like relics, the ordinary and everyday blessed by contact with the adored one, trying to absorb the magic by touching something that they touched: the cheeseburger plate, the hotel note-paper, the autographed scrap. We like sacred texts, interpretation, hidden meanings, instruction on how to live in the world. All of which proved such a trial for Bob Dylan.

CHAPTER FIVE
LITTLE BY LITTLE

As well as all the documentation and personal voodoo, we also like to dress how the special ones dress. Earlier, not that much earlier chronologically but an age in child time, the enviable head gear had been, as previously noted, Davy Crockett caps. That was another object lesson in the difference in consumerism, its expectations and realities. In photographs, in comics, on boxes containing Davy Crockett items, the fur-tailed cap looked a thing of splendour. The truth that existed outside of the ones constructed for the film was that they were cheap market knock-off replicas and they were *never* going to look right. The film itself was a cobbled-together attempt to make something useable out of a TV series. Its success, like so much popular culture, seems inexplicable out of its time and the net of reasons and belief that made us the way we were. No matter. Fess Parker, Davy's Fifties incarnation, and his furry cap, were a prehistoric era ago at the time Kookie had his wonderful white zip up jacket whose collar worked in tandem with his hair to transmit the look of cool sufficiency, that carriage through the world that told you here was a person at ease with the way he displaced the atmosphere. I never found one that I thought resembled its existential specifications, no matter how much I wished, or looked in gent's outfitters and tailors, the big chain ones like Burton down the town in Walsall, or the more individual, like Foster Brother's in

Bloxwich High Street between Harrison Street and Church Street, clothes for men and boys, with the old-fashioned glass-fronted drawers to keep socks or other items in, and the whole shop looking as if its mission was to keep the 1930s shopping experience alive. When I saw the front of Freewheelin' I recognised the same sensation of an individual's cool aura communicated through clothes and stance. Bob's blue jeans and cowboy boots, (the Western still not gone away; what else do Woody Guthrie and Ramblin' Jack Elliot evoke? Bob had come as far east as he could to ride that symbolic west-bound train), his brown suede jacket buttoned at the neck, only resembled Edd Byrnes at some deep Zen level and not at all in detail, – like the Chinese sage who can see a black horse and a white horse and not see a difference, making no distinction between the essential horsiness of each. That the West could still demonstrate absolutely contemporary cool had been proved recently in the person of Steve McQueen in the Magnificent Seven, who whatever his cowboy outfit had a jazz drummer's hip haircut, neat strong growth, very barbered, and the repose and confident stare that were all any of us understood about what constituted cool. This was reinforced coincidentally by me being bought my first pair of Y fronts the day I first saw The Magnificent Seven. The grown-up, stylish air I felt this lent me seemed to connect with the film, and I left the cinema the way boys carry themselves when exiting those aisles, their heads still full of pictures and attitudes, leaving the dark behind and finding themselves in a day. All of which makes me pause when I read that it's life and not art that influences people the most.

In their waste not, want not style Warners had earlier tried to cross-pollinate Kookie's appeal directly with the old West, having Edd and Clint Walker in their down time from series-making crank out a western called Yellowstone Kelly. Obviously this appealed to me on many levels. It had some pleasing scenery on the Warners back lot ranch, though Edd was shot through the chest with an arrow much too early in the proceedings to please his fans. Overall his hair didn't translate to the West. With Freewheelin' however one saw the hip, contemporary Kookie kind of relationship to the world, and felt the same envy, wanting to believe that if you dressed like that perhaps you could partake of that attitude. It's always easy to be a fan. More difficult to be a discerning or intelligent one, and not to grow too old for that. Looking back I see that all of my childhood prepared me to be a Sixties fan, and all of my sensibilities propelled me to write about it. I had an ability to fall for things – people's faces, the way things looked and sounded – and then want to say why, to myself as much as anyone else.

America had always been a real place and an imaginary land because of our cultural intake. We didn't realise that's how it was for Americans too. Alongside the TV Westerns and police series were magazines and comics. There were copies of True Detective, and similar publications, in the house, which must have been given to us by someone, we certainly wouldn't have bought them. That America, the one found in True Detective, was resolutely non-glamorous, composed of thousands of small towns where shabby brutalities occurred, and all the photographs had a sketched with charcoal quality. Another specialist magazine, and this was bought by our house, by me with pocket money, was The Ring, the monthly mag for boxing enthusiasts. I wasn't a boxing fan, but I was a Cassius Clay fan, along with most people who wouldn't have taken much of an interest in boxing at all. Thinking about it I must have known about Cassius Clay before I knew about Bob Dylan. He fought Henry Cooper in June of 1963, around the time the Beatles were riding high with She Loves You. There was always something appealing about him, his physical attractiveness yes, but also his fearless, amiable quality. As much as anything I loved the sound of his name: Cassius Marcellus Clay, suggesting Rome and Shakespeare. It seemed so unlikely that anyone could be called that, even in America. I became, like a lot of children, quite good at knowing the names and results of men, from paying The Ring close attention, who I would never have watched even if they had appeared on our television sports programmes, another example of reading's parallel world. The Ring was interesting for the language in which that kind of journal was written, the insider's column with its talk of ham 'n' eggers, those journeymen fighters who would always be at the bottom of the bill; the fact that there were bills and pecking orders, and such evocative names as Zora Folley and Ezard Charles, would finally get so little a return for practicing such a hard life. There was too the insight it gave into a little piece of American social history: the kind of fighter Floyd Patterson was, and how he differed from Sonny Liston, and how Cassius Clay was a larger, newer kind of personality and character, all of it demonstrating aspects of black people in America even if you weren't obviously thinking about it. It was another picture of a changing world, as much as reading about The Beatles was. My dad had spotted Cassius Clay in the 1960 Olympics when he was a light-heavyweight and young, so tall and so quick and on the way to winning a gold medal. Dad declared that he had class, which was really his highest praise for a sportsman, or anyone. It also confirmed him in another of his maxims: the good people in any activity always show it when they are young. All of this was background too only a year or so later, when Bob Dylan and Cassius Clay – separated by less than a year in age – seemed linked as embodiments of movements and changes, both of them exemplars, it seemed, for the society that raised them. Dylan also excoriated boxing, and most people associated with it, in his best foot on the bar rail singing style in the song Who Killed Davey Moore, and then had fun name-checking Cassius in one of his talking blues a little later, when he had become younger than that. What reading The Ring demonstrated was that Cassius Clay was bigger than the world he was in and came from. He felt like a star, a rock or pop star, a larger phenomenon than other boxers no matter how well known or good they were. He had a different meaning, he reverberated at a different frequency, and that too was a resemblance to Bob Dylan.

And then there were comics. Before Marvel Comics hit its stride, when it was still a schlock-fantasy/horror factory, and hadn't invented the roster of super heroes that 40 years later were to provide lucrative movie franchises – Spider Man, The Fantastic Four, The Hulk, Iron Man – the comics company we read and swapped was DC. This had been a comics producer since the 1940s, with popular heroes, and had a further run of success, another Golden Age, starting in the mid 1950s, by having the smart, almost post-modern idea, of reusing some of those same characters but updated, with the understanding that their forbears had had their adventures in a parallel universe. Sometimes to intensify the fun these different versions met up, one somehow bursting the barriers and ending up in the other world. There was something pleasing about the clean lines of DC Comics heroes. As well as the biggies, Superman and Batman, they also had the elegant lines of The Flash, Green Lantern, The Atom and their all-purpose collective the Justice League of America. The Flash looked wonderful with his skin tight red costume and yellow boots. And though adults look down on comics now as they did then, they are very useful introductions to some of the rules of art. They make you understand very quickly the differences between art and the real world. Any child who ever wears a super hero outfit to a birthday party, and experiences the loose, wrinkled, droopy nature of it, will understand what is superior and fantastic about illustration. The furls and foldings of Superman's cape, and his leg positions when landing and taking off, are at their best in lines on a page, rather than a big screen, no matter how brilliant and detailed modern computer generated imagery can be.

A friend of mine opened my eyes with the revelation that he bought or acquired comics he didn't particularly like so as to have swaps material, even taking something basically inferior or second rate like Aquaman, or the Blackhawks. I only ever wanted what I really wanted to own and read. The remnant of that attitude is my looking now on Amazon Marketplace or Bookfinder to see what price is being asked for something I own, knowing perfectly well I'm not going to sell it, wanting only its value to be confirmed. The friend with the open door comics policy was one I went to Rhyl with, his Mum and Dad kindly asking me along to the first holiday away from home I'd been on.

Somewhere in Rhyl we found a shop in an arcade that seemed like a storehouse of riches. It was here that there were carousels of comics, and Dell Comics were plentiful. There was a real appeal in seeing illustrated versions of the TV characters, with covers that featured posed set ups of the stars. It was here that I saw Have Gun – Will Travel at the height of its fame, a fame even more surprising since a lot of TV areas didn't show it.

5 years later I went to Rhyl again, this time on holiday with Jim and his family, and went looking for the shop again, expecting it, I suppose, to be unchanged, expecting probably to find some of

the same comics still there. I remember the disappointment at how inadequate it seemed compared to my memory, or what I believed my memory to be. Nothing of it matched up with the feeling it had previously drawn from me. Ah, the mechanics of feelings and chronology. It had all changed and wasn't as good and it was demonstrating what happened to the past in a way I hadn't thought about much previously. Places changed but America being an imagination was a constant. Another place we learned about it was from Mad magazine and its imitators, the illustrations again being versions of TV or films, but also parodies that alerted us to the ridiculousness of shows that away from Mad's influence we still gave our hearts to. Mort Drucker was one of their chief talents, and what, unlike Cassius Marcellus, could be more American than a name like that? As important as comics however in approaches to America was the local library.

The year before I was born a library had opened in Bloxwich, a refurbishment of a prefab building, two buildings in fact and now joined together, previously used as an ambulance station during the war, at that point closer than the gap between my two Rhyl visits. You could reach this building from various directions, but all of them had to be undertaken during the 1950s, something I was equipped to handle. You could think in terms of the long way round, or the shortest, though from our house it was all more or less the long way. The library was on a stretch of road called then and called now, The Pinfold, part of the main road from Bloxwich to Walsall. Not Pinfold, but always The Pinfold. It was standing in a crowd along The Pinfold once that I saw the Queen go by in a car on some kind of visit to the town, a small well-dressed woman whose face I could hardly see, passing through. Names are weird things, and perhaps even more weird in the West Midlands. Even as a child it struck me as slightly peculiar as a name for a road. It might have referred to an acute bend in the road if you thought, as I did, of a folded pin. All the road had however was a slight curve. Only now do I find that it was named after a much earlier association. A parish lock-up around that area centuries before had the same name. If you think of sheep and pens and holding areas it becomes to make more sense, as well as demonstrating how the past survives and changes, in language more than actuality.

One way to get to the library was to walk along Blakenall Lane and then take a right down something that was too small for a street, too wide and open for an alley, but was a walkway, alongside a school and the local playing fields. The school had the appealing name of The Sunshine School and the walk was called The Slang. This was even more mysterious than The Pinfold and again the definite article was always present. Anyone can look it up and find that it's an old word meaning a strip of land. This never occurred to us. If you walked down The Slang, past the school buildings with their iron fence and above-head-height privet, you came to the open spaces of the school yard and then the children's playground on the same side, with a slide, swings, and stands to leapfrog, and on the other the sports pitches for local football and cricket teams. It was here once out with my dad who had come to watch cricket I wandered off and, instead of looking for him, decided to find my way home again while he trailed around looking for me. When he made his miserable way back he was all set to give the worst news he could imagine and there I was, blithe and unaware. He didn't kill me. It took decades before I had any idea what he experienced, finding out how easily and quickly small children can disappear in plain sight.

After the playing fields you hooked a left and a right, along privet hedges with all of the green space below you, and children in the distance running around on the playground side. It was here, once, that some of us passed a bike leaning against the bushy leaves, just left there apparently. It was a notable bike because the bell was a Superman figure, a caped crusader in streamlined plastic reaching out beyond the handlebars. While we were looking at it, impressed, two lads came out from behind the end of the hedge and immediately the atmosphere shifted into panic. Run, someone shouted, and we did, though I wasn't clear why. The bike was a trap it seemed. But we weren't going to steal it. Why would they want to do anything to us? We were envying it, that was all. It didn't matter. They did chase us, and it had been a set up. It wasn't a fight and no-one got hit and it happened once probably 50 years ago and I remember it still. What does that mean? What does Bob Dylan always carry around with him from his childhood, unbidden and ever-present?

Coming out from this top end of the pitches, always associated with The Great Bike Ambush, brought you to Bloxwich Baths, where, aside from swimming, local bands played. It was managed by Bill Pickering, famous in Bloxwich and even beyond because he had swum the English Channel in record time. He also went on to swim the Wash, the Bristol Channel and the Firth of Forth. What made it more surprising is that he was a big fat man, proof that swimming and the fitness it encouraged had everything to do with endurance and willpower and nothing at all to do with being slim. In any case he was a name more than a presence. We went to Bloxwich Baths because it was the only one near to us, not because of a famous manager, and we didn't know it wasn't the latest thing in hygiene and facilities. The changing cubicles with their Western saloon-style doors were alongside the pool. Everything about you got damp and stayed damp when you went swimming, something that modernity will never be able to cure. At the entrance end there was hot Bovril and crisps for sale, and a Brylcream machine that for 1d squirted a perfumed, white, smooth gob into your palm that you rubbed into your not-dry hair to achieve that sought after styling perfection, as modelled by practically everyone, but certainly Kookie and Denis Compton. From the Baths, turning left, the prefabricated library was in plain view over the road, not that anyone ever went to both places in the same trip. The library is gone, the playing fields are different, and, now there's a new Leisure Centre in one corner. The privet itself has probably disappeared. All that remains is in my head in a form that only exists when it's called for, and yet will never go away. That's what the past is. And the person I am now, occasionally recalling it, can't remember anything much about that other person who experienced it at the time at all. I'm as much of a mystery as the thing that makes then different from now, the force that keeps changing us, all the things I think about when I consider Bob Dylan.

It was here in the altered ambulance station that I prowled around laying down the store of associations that, worryingly, never leaves. Like the Billy Bunter books I read, so removed from my life but addictive at a time when children can read any series, notice nothing about style at all, and want the same story and characters over and over, but with just enough difference so that they don't have to read the exact same title again unless they want to. That's why authors give us series and are shackled to success. With Frank Richards, and his other aliases, repetition with slight variations was what he was geared up to provide in industrial quantity. Biggles too was a staple then, also a one-man factory product from the rank-pulling Captain W. E. Johns, but here style did intrude. Even children noticed that Biggles found it hard simply to say something. He interjected, objected, queried, barked or on occasion ground out, but rarely said. There was another series, maybe not much regarded or even remembered now, that ignored school or the military and connected instead to the Western's appeal. A pseudonymous author named Rex Dixon, typical of lots of English children's writers in his productivity, turned out under various names different series, some science fiction and some not. His junior Western adventures featured a boy named Pocomoto. I loved these books and cannot now recall a word, but they fed into the general Western love that perhaps began with knowledge of Roy Rogers, after whom apparently I was not named, and his song A Four-Legged Friend, a frequent Uncle Mac favourite on Saturday morning Children's Favourites, a programme everyone listened to. A little later that liking for Westerns transferred to their exact adult library equivalent, (but read by between-agers), the shelves of diverting, forgettable books now largely vanished from modern libraries, more series, more Westerns, their titles as interchangeable as fridge magnet words, featuring heroes with names like Hogleg Bailey, chiefly written by English authors who with the aid of pseudonyms could generate 5 or 6 novels a year, year after year, and lived in places like Northampton or Ludlow and perhaps never went further west than Land's End.

I still look back slightly surprised at how much a part the library played in our lives. Neither my mother or father were educated beyond secondary school, which could have meant 14 in their time, but he always borrowed library books, and I grew up knowing that it was the thing to do. These days a boy who had free school meals, living in a council house, neither parent working, would not be seen as material to be a keen reader, or even perhaps an adequate student. And while it would be wrong to say I grew up in an intellectual household I did grow up in one where thought, enquiry and the reading of books were accepted as normal. This isn't a small thing in some sections of society. We listened, or at least I did, to The Critics, and was mightily surprised when they reviewed 'Til Death Us Do Part and found layers and issues in it that I had never noticed at all, rather expecting them to dismiss it. When we came across Bob on the back of Bringing It All Back Home wisely pointing out that some people were ashamed to be seen carrying Modern Screen magazine, I knew that some pupils had told teachers that they wouldn't want to be seen on their estate carrying a Sunday paper like the Observer in case of ridicule, or worse, they implied. Even my friend Jim, when an apprentice, had to think on his feet if in conversation he started to talk about something he might have read in one of the big Sundays, and another apprentice, puzzled, asked where Jim had seen that, because he knew it certainly hadn't made the People or the Sunday Mirror. Whereas we did take the Observer, and I sent off a postal order and for one year, the magic one of '65 to '66, subscribed to Private Eye. We also watched the Tonight programme where I admired most things about

Kenneth Allsop, particularly his hair style, and was very impressed to find out that the year before in interviewing John Lennon about his book he asked him why none of the wit and linguistic flair found there couldn't also be used in the songs he wrote, a minor revelation to Lennon which led, one could argue, to I Am The Walrus. Reading wove it all together, and the library allowed it take place.

CHAPTER SIX
EVERY LITTLE THING

In 1961, when Bob Dylan made his move and came to Greenwich Village, – which seems brave now, moving a thousand miles east, knowing no-one and with no place to stay, wanting to find the folk cafés and play in them – a new library opened in Bloxwich. The two events were more connected than they seemed. The library was moved and we moved with it, down the road from the Pinfold into Bloxwich proper, on a little side road with tall trees, a new purpose-built library, which eventually had a theatre attached and felt like modern times. In those mid 60s modern times, but linking back to the slightly earlier Beats, and not really connecting it to Kookie Byrnes, I read my way through Jack Kerouac books here, the way Bob Dylan had done elsewhere, working the seam along the shelf and trying more than just On The Road, as many as I could find. There were lots of things I liked about the sound of Kerouac's voice as it transmitted to you through the words on the page, though there was always a sad quality to the sound. Much later I learned that he had a lot to be sad about, but then I fell for the words, The Dharma Bums and Big Sur, and was particularly fond of Lonesome Traveller, with its short pieces and travel reflections on the railroad earth, and Desolation Angels, because I liked to read that co-joining of words and form a picture in my mind. It's actually just the sound of "angels". I wonder sometimes what word-sound other languages can possibly have for the same phenomenon that could carry a similar verbal effect. I know there will be none. There was also the idea of a man going up a mountain to watch for fires, and then writing about it, a mix of the American and Oriental which was the root of much Beat appeal, and something I could speculate about while knowing it would never be my lot, and besides would probably be hopeless at.

It was in this library too that I came across the writer who is perhaps an antithesis of Kerouac, and had the most affect on what I thought writing was and could do and became absolutely linked to my idea of America. I had subsequent English heroes and favourites, playwrights and poets among them, but S. J. Perelman was a first love at a time when I was at an age to look for models and notice the way sentences worked, (as distinct from gulping down stories, without noticing, being the reading equivalent of the Billy Bunter I read about.) I found Perelman I suppose because he was around on the same shelving as James Thurber, (humour) and I'd come across Thurber and worked my way along. I loved Thurber too, and read and re-read his pieces and stories, memorised his cartoon gag lines, but Perelman spoke directly to me in a way Thurber didn't quite. All of the things we like and their contradictions can be a mystery to us as much as anyone else. His anthology The Most of S. J. Perelman was what I read first, and that was a lucky break because it contained everything that was great about him to that point all in one go. He was a different kind of writer to Thurber, or any of those American humorists with whom it might be thought convenient to group him, and one that instantly appealed to me with his recondite vocabulary, ornate sentences, humour that came from an oscillation between a seeming modesty and clear immodesty, and his deadly eye for detail when engaged in either literary parody or a fantasy spun off a news item, a fantasy anatomising some modern absurdity. He also was very clued up on the artistic pretensions of the aspirant writers and creative spirits drawn to Greenwich Village, with or without talent, something that unknown to me but clear from him, had been going on decades before Dylan, or Woody Guthrie come to that, and this proved useful a couple of years later when reading the rhapsodies on folk's genesis and renaissance, when Bob Dylan's time there was already assuming the circumstantial imprecision of myth. It was S.J. Perelman's tone and insider knowledge of the Village faux bohemian scene in particular, the East Coast literary scene in general, and his familiarity with and contempt for the strata of Hollywood's industry that gave a new context for my naïve idolatry of things American. (Not that this stopped me from opening my heart to Bob's Hootenanny columns.) He also demonstrated mastery of the form and sound of a sentence, and if you want to be a writer that's the place to begin. Perelman had two great set pieces in the collection. One skewered all the commonplace clichés and tricks that were used by people in the trade to confect a scenario, and one did the same for the kind of writing that could be found in pulp, and other, would-be higher class, magazines. It was an education to see the merciless fun he could have with genres where readers don't actually notice the writing as such at all; as I hadn't in the prefab library. He was, in short, a stylist. Actually what he did wasn't dissimilar to what Bob Dylan was doing: he created a character and became it in performance, except his performance was on the page. And I fell for him a couple of years before the time, though I can't now be exact, that I started to know about Freewheelin'.

After my relinquishing of Freewheelin' because of the lack of a record player, – something I could see the sense of despite the awkward session with my mother, – a little way into the next year, on my birthday, my gift was the banishing of that lack. It wasn't the ubiquitous Dansette, the name synonymous with teenage bedroom players, but might as well have been. It looked the same as the evocative line illustrations on single record sleeves, with the lid that lifted and stayed open, the record spinning in plain sight, the silver grille speaker, and the desirable addition of a red light at the front to further prove it was on. The other distinguishing feature was a staticky buzz that started low but increased the longer it was on, until the music tended to sound as if it were being jammed by police car radios. It went back to the shop where it came from for the problem to be solved. This was the kind of shop that was really an electrical repair shop but sold a tiny number of TVs, record players, and even records, in a space not much bigger than a living room.

A few years previously, and hence a lifetime, the girl next door, who had the resonant name Gloria Dinsdale, some years older than me, had been given a record by us for a birthday (from me? my parents?) bought at this shop. It was by Jackie Dennis, who was a hit for about five minutes, a lad from Scotland who wore a kilt, and it would have been at Gloria's house that I saw him, his brief comet trail passing through 6-5 Special, the most exciting, and only show to feature teenage music until the superior, stylish Oh Boy appeared on ITV, losing the approved by Mum and Dad feel of the BBC effort, admirable though it was to have started it at all. Jackie Denis's trajectory coincided with another teenage falling star called Laurie London, whose big, and perhaps only, hit was a steal of the gospel song He's Got The Whole World In His Hands. I can still remember how special the record seemed, the feel and look of it, the paper sleeve it came in, and especially the smell of the plastic. Everything about it made it seem like a precious object, as if somehow it had dropped into this everyday world from a dimension altogether more wonderful. I can't honestly remember the song despite being able to check what its title was easily enough. La De Dah doesn't evoke any tune at all, though in my mind I can see a confident figure in a kilt, a little jacket, and a brushed-back, sticky-up hairdo. Gloria, and my older girl cousins, Jean and Maureen, read magazines like Valentine, Mirabelle and Romeo, and when I had the chance around them so did I. Valentine had comic strip romance stories whose titles were top selling singles of the time. It also featured a column called Ask Davey where readers asked questions about entertainment and someone, who might even have really been called Davey, gave out cheeky, chirpy information.

I liked all of this and almost inadvertently memorised most things whether I had an interest in the star or not, even then demonstrating a preference for the written word over reality. Years before Carry On films, stage stardom, and his American success reading Harry Potter books, the name Jim Dale was familiar, because every week there was a photograph of a cheery, good-natured, skiffling chap with his big wooden guitar. Just as familiar was a very similar picture of Lonnie Donegan, someone else synonymous then with skiffle though he had wandered in from trad jazz.

Skiffle was a craze like Davy Crockett had been, and seemed to be everywhere. Everyone knew Freight Train by Chas McDevitt, and almost no-one had heard of or heard Elizabeth Cotton whose song and guitar style it was. Skiffle sounded very English, although the songs were the American folk staples that also provided the repertoire of the polite collegiate folk groups that fuelled the slightly later American folk boom, and seemed to have so little to do with Woody Guthrie. Lonnie Donegan knew Guthrie and Leadbelly songs, and although the atmosphere that skiffle seemed to exist in was a willing amateurism, Donegan's voice had a yelping, vivacious intensity that had nothing to do with suburban kids dutifully plodding through an authentic text in order to achieve inauthenticity. Lonnie Donegan is a real link in the chain, as Bob Dylan put it later. The songs he did before he moved onto the novelty hits were the ones Bob Dylan would have taken up after he stumbled upon Odetta's work. And his voice in its attack and its energy, its not caring that it sounds like no-one else, was also a precursor of what we recognised when Bob Dylan became someone we knew. With Lonnie Donegan, and the groups that suddenly appeared with the name skiffle attached, boys could connect with the idea of playing guitars, being in groups, and getting immersed in music.

Aside from skiffle however, the record that perhaps meant most to me around then was pop, pure pop. Diana by Paul Anka, a precocious Canadian teen singer and songwriter, actually only a couple of months younger than Bob Dylan, couldn't have sounded more Fifties. It was like a style book for a 1957 pop record in every aspect, but Anka was smart enough to keep moving with the times, eventually writing for a range of people, and immortalising himself by providing the English words for the song that became My Way. In 1957 and just afterwards though, I would hang over the back of the sofa if he was on Two Way Family Favourites, or anything else that played pop, and think about a girl at school actually called Diane, but Diana seemed close enough, and everything about the tune and the way he sang the words connected with me. He was also casually demonstrating the difference between a genuine pop phenomenon, no matter how much it seemed of a piece with a novelty item, and the likes of Laurie London and Jackie Dennis.

Later, this electrical shop where our neighbourhood had to go to buy Jackie Dennis or Paul Anka if we didn't want to go to the trouble of catching the trolley down to Walsall, was caught in the consumer tides going in and out, that make people first want to buy and repair, then rent and service, then buy and throw away and buy again, and became a Granada TV Rental place. Renting a TV seems now as outlandish an idea as being able to choose from a range of them at a supermarket would have seemed then. The owner told my dad that the amount of money offered was so much he would have been a fool not to take it, clearly a better kind of offer that couldn't be refused than found in The Godfather. A few years prior to this windfall however, in response to my listening problem, he kept my record player for days before finally announcing success. A stray wire, he announced, had trapped itself where it shouldn't be, under a metal frame. That's what was causing all the trouble. Even to my limited knowledge this sounded unlikely, given the way the buzz developed steadily as playing time got longer. The problem was solved, he declared. Except it wasn't and it never did go away. From the point of view of parents it was an ideal self-regulating system to prevent excessive playing. The distraction always overpowered the music sooner or later. Nevertheless this was the means whereby I heard all of those mid-Sixties records I somehow acquired. I don't quite know how I did it. My parents didn't have much money, I'd only been a paperboy very briefly, and working on the Christmas post didn't come until later. We all ask, Who knows where the time goes; but looking back into an ill-defined past that's light on detail, its companion questions are, Where did the money come from, and how much was there?

Some of this mysterious money though, as soon as I possessed a record player, and despite my previous timeshare-ownership, went not on Freewheelin' but Another Side of Bob Dylan, at that point the latest Bob Dylan album you could buy. I read the back of Another Side Of with the same forensic attention I'd brought to the copies of Hootenanny, and tried to imagine what it was like to write that way, to live that life. It wasn't as easy to follow as the magazine, but had the same intensity of someone scrutinising himself and being honest about what he found. It wasn't poetry, just thoughts and words, images and anecdotes, dialogue. It wasn't written in the lines of the earlier material, which made an effort at an orthodox poetry layout, even if from a Beat context, but was more snarled up and jagged. Some worked very well, for me at least. Like this:

> "i could make you crawl
> if i was payin' attention"
> he said munchin' a sandwich
> in between chess moves
> "what d' you wanna make
> me crawl for?"
> "i mean i just could"
> "could make me crawl"
> "yeah, make you crawl!"
> "humm, funny guy you are"
> "no, i just play t' win,
> that's all"

"well if you can't win me,

then you're the worst player i ever played"

"what d' you mean?"

"i mean i lose all the time"

his jaw tightened an' he took

a deep breath

"hummm, now i gotta beat you"

which I got the point of immediately. I liked too the passing fancy of him in France saying that he must remember that he too plays the guitar, as if reminding himself how relative it is to be exotic; and also the word-picture of him pointing to a stubbly chin and saying, "The sea is very beautiful here," to a Greek lady who didn't understand English, let alone Kerouac gestures.

In my bedroom I played that album and read the sleeve and looked at the cover. He looked a bit meaner and older in the photograph, his hair cut down somewhat, jeans ragged and one knee sternly up. What surprised me much later seeing other photographs from this session, (the idea that there were other photographs from the session, and that they would be in colour, did not occur to me at the time), was that he was much more amiable there, larky and friendly. On this record cover he didn't have the sweetness that I thought I saw on Freewheelin', and lacked the wonderfully monochrome, detailed gravitas that seemed to comprehend all of suffering humanity, and in some sense to be it, of the Times They Are A' Changin' photograph, where the slimness of his neck with its tiny fuzz of hairs set against the inscribed curve of his collar had the declarative simplicity of a line in a poem. Overall one had to admit that this latest photograph didn't offer as much of a statement. Perhaps that was part of its point, in the accidental, intuitive, claimed later technique that analysis works, hindsight being a great assistance to theory. It's interesting that having imbued myself in a job-share way with the early and pure strains of a Bob politically aware, but also delivering tender love songs, where the playing and recording is impressively clear and warm, I now had by heart the album where he begins to repudiate that spokesman reputation. The title is a pun only if you know that Americans called an LP a side. The rest of us took the primary meaning that what he was offering were different kinds of songs, other aspects of his personality. The notes make that perfectly clear, as does their title, Some Other Kinds Of Songs. For someone whose reputation usually includes the description mysterious, inscrutable, secretive, all of these early writings, whether for his own or other people's album sleeves, are achingly personal and revelatory. What they are about is someone uncomfortable with who he is, or at least what's expected of him, and what he knows about himself.

The record shows this too. It's an odd jumble. Nothing has the impressive dexterous guitar work that was so evident on Don't Think Twice. The recording allows sloppiness and mistakes. There are songs that are throw backs to or jokey pastiches of talking blues, fun at first, but as tedious eventually as they would be to perform night after night. There is too the self-justifying and slightly dreary Ballad In Plain D, a song a capsule review in a copy of Time magazine that I saw later must have been referring to when it talked about his miles of sodden verse. What is also present though is a breakthrough to a more ambitiously personal style of writing, in Chimes Of Freedom, which made for such an unexpected, enthusiastic show in 1964 Newport, and also a bouncy, unrestrained, exciting kind of song and uninhibited singing, as on Spanish Harlem Incident, or even on the piano primitivism of Black Crow Blues. On It Ain't Me Babe you hear a voice just this side of raucous, but open and free and wholeheartedly intense on the chorus especially. His connection with his emotion and to the person listening was tremendously effective. I listened to this, and sometimes I went to a friend's house and listened to his copy of Times They Are A' Changin', and read that sleeve, and I thought about writing. I never did think of learning the guitar but I always thought about writing.

CHAPTER SEVEN
LONG TIME COMING

In part it was writing that I was seeking when I went down the town, to Walsall on a Saturday on the transport system masterminded by the wonderfully named R. Edgeley Cox, Walsall Corporation's bus Svengali, its trolleybuses and network of electric aerial cables covering miles and coming all the way out to Blakenall, where the wires curled round in their jointed, segmented progress and there was a bus stand, rather than stop, where they paused before beginning the return to Walsall. This was the place where urban myth had it that the bus drivers turned a key in a clock to signify journey times for some superior or other, and could then make a key-shaped mark on your hand in purple ink by pressing the key against it if you asked them. There had once been a clock there it was true, and boys used to gather around it, but I never saw a chronology tattoo. Later of course we all bear the marks.

The trolley buses weren't the only buses Walsall had, and not the only way to get to the town. Our own street, with its steel houses and brick houses and playing area garages and sloping lawns and fuchsia lampposts was also a bus route. This seems more and more unlikely to me the further away from it I get. The motor bus, blue and in the same livery as the trolley buses, went past our house following the 49 route, Bloxwich to Walsall. The trolley buses were number 15, Blakenall to Walsall. The 49 took what might be thought of as a

slightly more rural route, heading off as if going to the Barley Mow, but then swinging right, past Elkington's, along past a youth club once opened by tireless worker for youth, and British old-school show-biz Palladium staple, Frankie Vaughan, whose invigorating Tower of Strength was in the pop papers and charts around the time Bob Dylan was playing the ill-attended Carnegie Chapter Hall concert, then past Goscote Hospital, until, following a curve in the road, you could see the fields and the sweep of the canal cut into them. This area was evocatively called Coalpool, and also had a branch library I used, much tinier than Bloxwich and with irregular hours, which I often forgot, turning up to find doors locked, but the rest of the time its shelves yielded the Boardman American Bloodhound detective and thriller series, with their spine illustration of the trademark, a lugubrious hound in a deerstalker, the clue to identifying them on the shelves. These were also a crucial part of laying down an America of the mind in our house. When you were on the bus though, and looked out at the way the land was shaped, seeing geography as it might be in an illustration, you could believe for that moment in a rural England, an older England than the one we had to be in, one where farms and pasture might exist as they did in children's stories and the Tiger Tim and Rainbow Weekly children's comics I'd had only a few years before, where the word farm seemed to mean something different from its hard and physical reality. All of those days were vanished when I took that bus ride, as the days of the bus ride are gone now. History was always more immediate than we suspected. I'd like to say that when I first played Bob's Self Portrait LP a few years after that, and heard Days of 49, I thought of all this. It wouldn't be true, though now it is.

So there were a couple of ways to get to town and whichever one I took I ended up looking in Boots and Smiths and H. Taylor record departments, and writing as well as music could be investigated there. Taylor's was a specialist music shop with proper, dark wooden racks to hold the albums. It sold sheet music too and it was there that one could look in the book collections of songs, and see the chords and notes, which remained cryptic to us non-instrumentalists, but it also let us check the words. Sometimes there were other extras, like bits of interviews or photographs not on albums. This had a slightly diluted version of the appeal of the Hootenanny magazines where, in addition to examples of Bob free form poetry, there was a door opened into another culture. The small ads for guitars or songbooks or concerts were as important as the other articles in generating the atmosphere of that world so close by but already history. In Taylor's in a Paul Simon songbook I saw a short story called On Drums and Other Hollow Objects, one he has since suppressed perhaps, and no-one has posted to the Internet as yet. It was a further indication that this music and the people who made it was connected to writing, though Simon was operating in an area more orthodoxly creative writing class than Bob's school of Beat confessions. It was at Taylor's too that a friend and I saw the album Lightnin' Strikes – Lou Christie, and unkindly remarked, We hope; and where, under the influence not only of Bob Dylan but especially Brian Jones, and all of the groups that played their versions of the blues, I bought a harmonica, the wrong, child's kind at first, and eventually the right kind, the Hohner Echo Super Vamper, UK equivalent of Bob's own Marine Band. I had no idea what key to buy it in, or in fact that harmonicas came in keys. I blindly picked C, not knowing what its advantages or otherwise were, and over weeks stumbled into picking out Blowin' In The Wind, haltingly, and a phrase each of Love Me Do and Rolling and Tumbling, and later, much later, on a different harmonica but in the same key, almost all of Heart Of Gold, which I can still more or less do. I never as such learned to play it of course. I had to admit to myself quite early on that I liked possessing a harmonica rather more than trying to learn how to play. That proved to be a good deal more difficult than it sounded even though at one hallucinatory point I'd fantasized about sending off for a harmonica rack from the small columns at the back of Melody Maker. Another example of how image can be all, and how it vanquishes common sense.

In record shops then I read the back of Joan Baez In Concert Part 2 to get a glimpse of the child Bob Dylan, and connect to the snowy north he talks about in his Outlined Epitaphs. I liked the Joan Baez notes because they talk about pulling up the grass while being near his aunt's house, and watching the ore trains go by. I had an aunt with a train connection. My Aunt May, my mother's sister, visited us when I was around 5 or 6, and probably later, but that's the period I remember, or believe I remember. I was old enough to say, "A bopple of pop for me May," and the pop would be Vimto. That would have been in the summertime, because the summer was when they, and me, went to The Barley Mow, mow pronounced, in the Black Country way, to rhyme with cow, because that was down near the canal, and had a child-friendly field with a tree in it next to the outside tables and chairs. I fell out of that tree a few years later when trying to swing from a branch which promptly snapped. I wasn't hurt but was completely astounded about the sudden jump in time, and couldn't work out what had happened to the moments between one thing and the next. Why was I sitting on the ground looking bemused with no memory of getting there? May had had a more difficult life than my mother I think, having had a child when young and well before being married, but it was lovely to see them together. There is something comforting about being with your mother and your aunt when you are young, and seeing them laughing in each other's company, being sisters, knowing things you'll never know, and you are an only child eating Smiths crisps with their enclosed blue twist of salt that always puts too much in one place, and drinking Vimto with its purple-ish colour and fruit cordial taste, and burping. May had a funny, squinty eye and imperfect teeth, but had the attractiveness that some ugly features and a good heart can give. She liked to laugh about things like eating cauliflower and farting. "I was only laughing me one eye up," was her highest praise for something amusing, not a phrase I ever hear anymore, except when I say it.

She had married a Birmingham man who worked on the railway and she lived in Handsworth on the Soho Road (as in London's Soho, an almost equivalent of Greenwich Village, from certain artistic or musical perspectives, and being not quite the same sound as SoHo, also in New York, and near to the Village, and in any case another tiny element in that web of hindsight connections). Or rather she didn't live on Soho Road as such, but up a driveway gap between two lengths of large houses on that main road, and then tucked away in a railway worker's house in a terrace behind it, actually alongside a railway embankment. In fact, after the war and before the steel house estates gave people like my mother and father a place to be, they'd shared May's house, in the way married couples used to live in the parent's front parlour 20 years before. She lived far enough away from us for it to take two or three bus journeys. One of those journeys was notable because unlike any other bus trip you had to pay twice, as if you were enacting the bus conductor repartee, "Everybody paid? Anybody want to pay twice?", or were perhaps prefiguring lines in a Bob song yet to be written. The bus crossed an administrative boundary into another bus company area, and so people paid one fare to reach that point, and then another fare when they passed it. The ticket machines were different too, another point of exotic interest, the kind of thing you notice on holiday later in your life that distinguishes abroad from home. We had crossed a border in a way. On Walsall buses a silver grey machine with a milled wheel on top selected the price, and a side handle was turned to produce a little white or beige strip ticket printed with the fare you asked for. These strips, torn to size, were sometimes stuck across the warning printed at the front of buses upstairs: Please Retain Your Tickets For Inspection, so that "tickets" was amended to "tits". No detail too painstaking for successful comedy. The Birmingham or West Bromwich buses had flatter, wider machines with levers all across the front that were depressed to issue from a row of slots the same kind of variously coloured tickets that cinemas used, each representing different values. The skill here seemed to be for the conductor to select a variety of tickets to make up the fare price, and not use one roll excessively. I assumed that you needed the kind of calculating mind dart players were blessed with to do this well.

When we reached May's house I always liked the difference there was between her house and ours, how things were arranged. Everyone's house smells different to one's own, and everyone finds the way other people keep their spoons and cups and sugar slightly inexplicable. Uncle John was occasionally there, eating after returning from work, putting mustard on the side of his plate, which I found notable at the time, and, as it turned out, memorable. Did we even have mustard? I can't remember. Perhaps not as it made such an impression on me. Perhaps we did but didn't slide it onto the plate's edge in a moist, bright yellow heap, an adjunct to silent eating. John wasn't exactly hostile, but neither was he friendly. Silent and neutral seemed to be his setting. We were to do with May, not him, was the message, as he steadily chewed and sat in his railway shirt and trousers, nothing at all like Casey Jones. Actually, May's house was where I saw those half hours of Casey Jones, and Fury, and Champion and some of the others that were part of the TV world I was in and out of. The Cisco Kid was inexplicably popular, if looked at by today's standards, another film, like Billy The Kid, from the 1940s, but now transformed into half hour episodes, hundreds of them of which I saw maybe a handful, and all in a colour never transmitted to us. Cisco and Pancho, there they are still in DVD land, two senior character actors inviting us to come back to a mythical Old West California where they have their very short, innocuous adventures with horses and laughter and fake bad men, keeping TV studio executives and employees in business for six years, and preparing children like me for the blue jeans and cowboy boots to come.

May had a TV and we didn't, but aside from that the house was little and old-fashioned, and I don't remember ever going upstairs there. They had a downstairs outside lavatory. There was a scullery at the back of the house, scullery a word we never used at home, and that was where we always went in. The front door was not used by anyone as far as I could see. None of them seemed to be along that gloomy space with its little gardens, dark bricks and gravel. We always walked along the embankment and went in the back door, the scullery door, where it smelt of Palmolive soap. In the summer we could stand on the path alongside the railing fence, the rumpled path with its uneven, black Victorian tiny patterned inlay paving, and watch the grass on the slopes burn, spikes of orange and hanging smoke, grey and blue, dangerous and exciting. This view and this feeling were rural compared to the streets that the bus went through to get there. Something seedy and run down was what you felt on the main road, and it was summarized by a cinema poster I saw through the bus window once, Summer of The Seventeenth Doll, on a scruffy cinema I wouldn't have wanted to go inside. I didn't know what it was about, but the appearance and the sound of it, the way it was there in the street right in my vision, stood for the time I was in, and that was the late 1950s. Whereas there was still something of the 1940s, even the 1930s about Aunt May's house. The sink had a thick wooden furrowed block as a draining board. Once when we there a neighbour had left or found a pile of old Film Funs. They were musty and sad looking, with their cartoon strips of Laurel and Hardy, grey and not quite dry, like documents that had survived from an ancient kingdom. The dates on them said they were from the 1930s too, but they seemed much older than the Fred Astaire film of the same time, impossibly older too than the couple of decades they represented. Years had a different rate of exchange then. It was odd to see that the style of cartoons, and the kind of adventures the characters had was exactly the same as the comics still put out each week. Slightly unnerving though to feel so concretely what age could mean.

There were more exciting finds. We went there once and while we traveled to the boundary and then beyond it, my head was filled with the one hit sound of Marvin Rainwater, a fantastically, but apparently genuinely, named country singer with rock overtones who had also surfaced on the Palladium show, and briefly at the top of the charts with Whole Lotta Woman. My cousin Dorothy, Aunt May's earlier child, who was always called Aunt because she was an older generation, had a record player and I wondered if she would have bought it, even though I don't remember any conversations about music with her at all, and a more unlikely rock, or even country, fan you couldn't imagine than Aunt Dossie in her toothy and gawky but strong self-sufficiency, a natural spinster. And when we got there that day she did have it. A 78, on the MGM label, which meant it was a lovely yellow with the MGM lion on it. The other MGM record from around that time which tried to evoke an Elvis-style excitement was It's Only Make Believe, by another oddly, but not genuinely, named artiste, Conway Twitty. Bizarre though it was, this name was preferable to Harold Jenkins for a would-be rocker. Conway Twitty played Hibbing around the time I used to be familiar with the grass on Aunt May's embankment, and Bob and his friend John Bucklen went to see him, trying to pick up some of that Elvis magic. And that day in Aunt May's house, that one day, the presence of Whole Lotta Woman seemed like magic too. I half-believed that I had made it happen because I had wanted it so much. I still half-believe it, and later came to see that it does sometimes work out that way with things wanted achingly enough. Besides, it was a handy insight into Bob Dylan's methodology. He wished hard and worked harder to get what he wanted, and then had to learn to live with the fulfillment of wish lists. Also symbolic was my reading of his album sleeve poem to dwell upon details of his childhood, and then to be reminded of my own. This delayed reaction, reflections in a hallway of mirrors, has characterized much of my Bob experience down the decades we have shared.

All of the faults of style in that Baez album sleeve poem, and others from the same time, the faux hobo grammar and spelling, the desperately wanting to be someone other than a suburban Jewish boy from the freezing Mid West, were consumed and burnt away by what I took to be the sincerity behind the manner and mannerisms. The flaws were more or less invisible to me, in the way that a child reading deals with a story in the words that are before him, words that have no characteristics except to convey the narrative, achieving the enviable George Orwell standard of transparency in prose purely because that's all a child requires. What I thought Bob Dylan was, and meant, altered the way I could perceive his stylistic characteristics, excess or silliness (as an educated adult might see it.) At the same time what I took from that writing informed my belief about what he was and meant, another mirrored hallway. We're dealing with signals and frequencies and what one is tuned to receive. Which is exactly the process of being in a dream. An analogous process took place in the relationship between the kind of writing evident in his songs and this prose/poetry to be found elsewhere. The uniting factor was his voice. The sound of his voice gave it meaning, and if you look at the album sleeves what his poem typography was always trying to do, old-hat Beat though it may have then looked to the literati, (yuh gotta hand it t him, yuh got t, said the same Time put down review of the record) was to convey what his words would be like when spoken by him, moving from the public space of the album to the privacy of your mind. Whatever Bob Dylan seemed to be as a performer, the writing tried to tell us something else, or something more. Did I think, That's what I want to do? I think I did, and later I really did, though copying *his* style was as far from my mind as learning the guitar. Now here we were listening hard and open-hearted in our bedrooms with a couple of versions of Bob Dylan, both released in one year, heard in the next, and here was another about to enter the country for real.

CHAPTER EIGHT
TIME IS ON MY SIDE

1965. A pivotal time, the hinge of the decade, if you believe that decades are the ten years that begin with 0 and end in 9 and not something less tidy, something to do with a feeling in the air that's there and then, you notice, not there. Bob Dylan came to England in the Spring of 1965 for a tour, playing the town halls of sturdy provincial towns. Suddenly he was in papers and had a record in the charts. For reasons now that don't seem sensible I used to walk some distance before school to get a Melody Maker and walk home down the evocatively, and aptly, named Chantry Avenue – more of the substantial 1930s redbrick council houses and mature elms, near to the old-fashioned barbers with its wooden benches and queues, where we had read Reveille to find out what the 1950s were like, and current beat group hair aspirations bit the dust. On this walk I devoured the Melody Maker for news. I hadn't been a reader for his first visit. In 1963, in an odd happenstance and odder the more one considers it, he had been brought over to appear in a BBC television play. He was hired to act and sing through a combination of luck, chutzpah and his intrinsic attraction that caught the director's eye. He then turned up to announce that he couldn't act or learn other people's lines. He allowed that he could still sing. It's to everyone's credit that they worked around it, let him amble through and sing a couple of songs. That's one of the ways we know the past is a different place. So this concerned-young-people's Play For Today went out, and despite normally being a sure thing in our living room, a place where on the other channel we watched Armchair Theatre and its succession of innovatory TV plays of the moment by the likes of Pinter, as well as a little later back on BBC, Dennis Potter's Nigel Barton and Where The Buffalo Roam, we managed not to see it. Madhouse On Castle Street went unnoticed, and has since become unnoticeable, tapes destroyed, and all that exists are the memories of participants or viewers, a few still photographs, and some imperfect tapes of the songs. But then that's the way the past works, whether it's to do with Bob Dylan or not, blending incorporeal existence and fragmentary objective reality.

In 1964 at a higher level of acclaim he returned to England and played the Royal Festival Hall, something I think about every time we pass it to go to the Pizza Express on the other side of the road from there, the pavement dark and running with rain, or the air bright with shining heat. And after the small scale treat of pizzas and pudding and a single glass of red wine, (knowing that happiness comes from embracing limitation, especially when even somewhere as mass an eating experience as Pizza Express charges more for a glass than I would pay for a supermarket bottle) still happy we leave to walk back to Waterloo station, we can look out to its blue name, Royal Festival Hall, visible on the white wall opposite. I wonder what vantage point was there at that time to look over at the wall and its lettering where Pizza Express now is. The franchise didn't open its first branch until the next year. In any case in 1964 I knew nothing about pizzas, and was over a hundred miles away, not particularly aware of the Festival Hall or of Bob Dylan playing there. Luckily lots of important people were. Martin Carthy has mentioned often how impressed he was with Dylan's singing and writing of songs like Lonesome Death of Hattie Carroll, how his mastery of the form inspired him. Which was generous because on the previous TV play visit it was Martin Carthy who showed Bob the clubs that were rooms above pubs where he sampled

Guinness, and tried out his songs on audiences not so readily sympathetic, and from whom Bob soaked up English tunes and words to adapt and re-use later. Now he was in absolute artistic control at a major venue. And then along came 1965 where he was about to ratchet up this prestige to a wider audience.

Things divide into what I remember and what I don't remember. I don't remember how I got the money, or how much the ticket cost, or who I went with, (and I wouldn't have gone alone) or how I got there and back. Which is a lot not to remember. Or as I read in another context, "There's a lot that's still not fully unknown." I do remember the queue for the tickets when we, it must have been a we, bought them some time before, queueing around the solid, Greco-municipal, columnar architecture of Birmingham Town Hall, and seeing a boy carrying a copy of Another Side Of Bob Dylan as a badge of his credentials, although turning up to buy a ticket seemed proof enough of fan status to me. Still, I wasn't sure whether to deride him as ostentatious or regret the fact that I had nothing to carry myself. I remember too the show in wisps and fragments and scraps, although they have turned out to be quite tenacious over the years. I recall the size of him, the smallness and slightness, and, ridiculous though it sounds, the normal reality of him after an acquaintance based only on images and photographs on albums and elsewhere.

This wasn't quite a new experience. The previous year, around the same season as the Bob Festival Hall triumph I didn't attend, I had seen the Rolling Stones at the Gaumont in Wolverhampton, and had been similarly taken aback by their ordinariness combined with the special quality that making music on stage gave them. Keith Richard (not Richards then) did a gangling spider walk across the stage when playing a solo. Brian Jones was really small, leaning forward to sound his harmonica into the mike that looked about the same size as him, a vision of hair and a striped waistcoat. When the Stones appeared this same year on Top Of The Pops they looked as if they came from a different world. There were two appearances that stood out. One was when there was a film clip of them miming Not Fade Away on some shore somewhere, with Brian Jones all baggy eyes and a bell of hair. The other was when they appeared in the studio miming You Better Move On, a slow, moody song on an EP they had released, itself a notable event, being much more special than a single because of its photograph as well as the extra songs. This photograph had Keith Richard in a cloth cap, but one found trying one out that the result was not looking like urchin Keith Richard but a junior version of your dad, or someone else's dad not far away.. And they mimed and the song seemed part of the way they looked, surly and sulky, with that startling length of hair. The Beatles fringes at the front seemed to be what the Stones had at the back. How easy it seems to shock looking back, but growing hair that long wasn't something anyone could do. We couldn't for instance. Such a simple and definitive way to proclaim all kinds of different values; and then there were Mick Jagger's funny foot flips and shuffles, and obviously his lips. All of it separated them from ordinary groups, and certainly from us. I talked about this once with a girl called Athena Sanders, pronounced Saunders, and she too, like her name, seemed to come from a different world. It was her brother who told me about The Great Gatsby for the first time, and I started reading it, that book about infinite hope, sitting behind our house, facing the overgrown gardens and the paling fence, on a very hot day with a green wooden stool that we'd had since I was a toddler beside me, that used to look so big and now seemed insignificant, and the book made no sense to me. Everything happens in its own time, and my time didn't coincide with it until later, and then I couldn't understand how I had not seen how wonderful it was, and then I had to re-read it every year, as I still do.

And here was Bob Dylan, only a person, a little person, a touch taller than Brian, in ordinary clothes, a dark jacket, was it leather or not, blue trousers, smart casual as required in clubs and pubs and not at all like Freewheelin' or Times They Are A-Changin'. I had some recognition then of the power of photography, of how someone could look, or be arranged to look in the presentation of photographs, and how the sense you got from the reality of a person in front of you was quite distinct. Everything that came before, his past, everything that led up to this moment where he had to be before us on stage was gone, had no meaning. All that was going to exist would unfold into the moments to come; and that future was as unknown as the past had been. Whatever you knew or thought you knew or had read didn't signify now, even if you thought it did, because there was the actuality of someone being there. I was thinking of the face on the Times They Are A-Changin' cover and what it specifically evoked and how it was and wasn't there in that venue. You bring what you are to the show, and it necessarily changes what you see. Everything he meant was in the room, in what he was about to do, and what all of the consciousnesses in the separate heads watching would make of it.

It would be easy to check his programme of songs, there's not a set list of songs that hasn't been patiently transcribed and put out there now, but I want to go by what I remember and what I felt. He opened with Times They Are A-Changin', which seemed a nod to his unlikely chart success but now I know had been his opening number the previous year in American concerts, just letting people know what he was about. On record I had always liked the little extra twiddly bit in the harmonica solo, where he goes up a key, and I noticed he didn't do that. When you're familiar with a recorded version it makes it easy to miss what you know, but not to hear what you don't when someone is doing the song for real, live in front of you. Years afterwards I would play tapes of concerts I'd been to and not thought much of, and only get what he was trying to do hearing it again. Then again, later tapes might confirm the truth of a low opinion. You can only go by your senses but the tricky part is learning that they tell you conflicting things at different times. His opening song was not the only old song on display, old being used in the Bob sense of a year or two before. He also did Talking World War III Blues, which being based on a form derived from Woody Guthrie's 1930s model, always sounded old, but updated its contemporary quotient by working Donovan's name into it. The audience laughed, being easily pleased and flattered, as most audiences are. The point was, simply by being dressed as he was he demonstrated how far he had moved from the cover photograph on the album we knew the song from, in such a short time too, and thus how far he was from the man who created it. Involuntarily, automatically and artistically, he was demonstrating changing times before us.

The songs that made an impression were not the songs one knew, but the songs one didn't. He sang long, image-packed songs, full of rhymes and pictures, and not much like talking blues or what had been called protest. I remember Mr Tambourine Man because of the way it went on like a magician's ribbon pulled out of a sleeve, returning to the chorus and then setting sail again into another verse, a succession of scenes and pictures, and the audience hanging on, trying to hear the words and work out what it was about. It was Mr Tambourine Man and we'd never heard it before, we didn't know it, but we did know we'd heard nothing like it. Imagine never having heard Mr Tambourine Man, but of course we can't now even though we spent years in that state once. I heard the line about the diamond sky and one hand waving free and never forgot it. I didn't have to of course because in one way or another it's been played ever since, but I always know where I heard it first. There were other new long songs too: It's Alright Ma, Gates of Eden, It's All Over Now Baby Blue, and we listened as they unreeled and hung on and tried to make sense. And in the silence we listened to what broke the silence: his voice, his harmonica and his guitar.

"You think he can sing," he asked, *"You like his singing? You like his voice?"* The thing that's most difficult to people who aren't Bob Dylan fans is his voice, whereas someone who likes him is going to like him for lots of reasons, but the main one is always going to be his voice, or

was until these latter days. But the radio ensures the past is not only always with us but alive and well, and even someone whose collection is swollen with Bob product can be taken by surprise by the sound of his voice from decades ago, whatever he sounds like now. Trying to characterise the elements and quality of that sound can detain us for quite a time. One hears Times They Are A-Changin' and so much is present in the grain and texture of his voice, such a mixture of age and youth and confidence and assumed accent and genuine emotion that the words only render their full meaning when sung by him. That was why when hearing people say, kindly, patiently, that yes, they might grant he was a good songwriter, but he couldn't sing, and they always preferred to hear his songs when performed by other people, one response, immediately choked back and not acted upon, was to want to shout, "No, that's not it, that's not it at all." And hearing it again by chance on a kitchen radio while doing something else forty years later only confirms that view.

Watching the show I consciously tried to remember every detail, and felt that special atmosphere that we lazily but accurately call magic, of the gathering, being part of the crowd that had come to experience the same thing. I tried to remember everything and at different times have wondered if J. B. Priestly was right, and nothing you experience is really lost, it's all stored away and might be recalled if circumstances were right, if one was sufficiently susceptible to hypnosis. One looks back, forgetting and remembering what exists of someone who watched the show, that one tiny marker making that night special in a succession of nights, a dark parade that always comes around again, imagining looking back some time in the future, trying to recall every detail. And what of film, the indelible record, which with the elapse of time becomes a supplemented and amended indelibility, aside from any changes that a changed consciousness will bring. What if everything you had ever done in your life were recorded and you could bring it back, any time? Imagine inhabiting the present moment to the best of your ability, and then being years older and able to look back on all you had done. Doesn't everyone?

This delayed reaction, reflections in a hallway of mirrors, has characterized much of my Bob experience down the decades we have shared.

All of which might suggest that Bob Dylan was a major part of my perceptions then, and certainly the fact that I've written a lot since on my reactions to him and what he does tends to support that. But I look back and I know it's not true, not exclusively true. He was part, important but only one part, of something more that existed then, that was in the air and the age we were, like the atmosphere we inhabited. It came over the radio, and on television was present in Juke Box Jury and Thank Your Lucky Stars, (Oh Boy having died before the Sixties began). It could be read about in the girls' magazines of a helpful next door neighbour, Valentine and Mirabelle; and in Melody Maker, Disc, and the glossy, colourful monthly Rave, – the one that once had a front cover of John Lennon using a flower as a monocle, a while before flower power, acting out, unconsciously, *one eye open wide, one eye closed, so between the two the picture gets composed.* Everybody alive and of an age to understand it, every sentient being around, and of course everyone who wasn't even born but has come along since and read all about it, has a view of what the Sixties was and what it meant, and what everyone did then. Politics, – youth and its fiery political, revolutionary commitment, – is always believed to be an essential element of that brand, that franchise, now routinely and habitually called The Sixties, which again is not something it occurred to me to call them until afterwards, until they were almost gone. I must have missed the inaugural edition of the Observer colour magazine in 1962 which tried to assess who the Sixties people were, naming them as such, a bit precipitate and impressive so early in the game. I do know that the Sunday papers colour magazines were a crucial element in the perception of what it seemed to be part of that atmosphere and collective experience that was thought of as the

Sixties. My memory is of an American documentary that I am now unable to substantiate in any material way at all, narrated by someone who might have been Paul Newman, probably towards the end of 1969, and it looked back at a decade of events in entertainment, in sport, in politics, and its purpose was to explain that everything that had happened was part of this vast integrated cavalcade, everything was a facet of the same phenomenon. It all connected and demonstrated the same principles. It was all The Sixties. I recall a slight surprise at hearing the phrase. The Sixties. The Sixties? And yet what did I call the times I lived in, or at that time had lived through? I think I called them by the number of whatever year it happened to be. It's not that I was unaware of wider implications, but the meaning of meaning, particularly the retrospective meaning of meaning, is a tricky proposition.

There was a table in the back kitchen, which was the room next to the actual kitchen and in other circumstances might have been called the dining room, but not there and not then. On one side of it, along one wall, was a sideboard, clunky and shiny with dark wood and lighter speckles. It had the drawers with circular flat brassy handles where things were kept, important things like the bits of paper that accumulate, and the rent book. It also had the cupboards where one year when mooching I found hidden Christmas presents and my mother made my dad tell me off. That sideboard was there from the beginning and stayed there until the end and must have been a representative piece of immediate post-war furnishing, an example where design and sociology blended. In the winter, as well as the grey radiator near the door, on the opposite side there was an electric fire under the window, and in the summer there wasn't. I loved to watch the electric fire come on, the dark, curled wire, inert elements set in the white ceramic gradually heating up and going orange, then glowing red, becoming alive. In front of the fire, and in warmer weather in front of where the fire had been, we had a cat who had been a stray, a lost kitten, but after he wandered in from the long grass one day there had been a reciprocal adoption. He was taken in, fed, housed and looked after in a spirit of benign acceptance that didn't take too much sentimental notice of him. He was my mother's in so far as he was anyone's, but he wasn't anyone's really. We were chosen by him and the house felt better for his presence, a stray with his own place. He was never taken to the vet, and that seemed perfectly right, and like most cats he seemed fine up to the point he wasn't, and like most cats too his end was sad and unpleasant and came more quickly than we expected. I didn't realise then what a pretty and unusual colour he was, smokey blue and grey. The name we gave him was Billy, which was my mother's idea and nothing to do with The Kid, and Billy's place was outside or in the back kitchen That's where we had break-fast and listened to the radio before school, and that's where I came home for lunch and listened to the radio again, with the grass grow-ing long against the palings. When I was younger, every so often the breakfast cereal Shreddies included a free gift in its packet, and the gift was at least once, perhaps more, a little blue plastic frogman. If placed in a proper pop bottle, not the modern kind with a cap that screwed around the bottle neck, but the one that had a screw-in, roughly triangular top with a rubber washer, then the fact that he had tiny little holes, one in his face mask, one on his back, allowed air bubbles to form. Screwing down the bottle top exerted pressure (which is why it had to be the correct old-fashioned kind), inflating or reducing the bubbles so you could make him go up and down the bottle. That kitchen and back kitchen was where I put him through his paces. That's where I experienced childhood, and to a large extent that's where I experienced the Sixties that I didn't think of as the Sixties, in that room, at those times, and it all happened as I was on my way to High School. School and the Sixties are similar in that people tend to think of it as one long experience, but school at 11 is a different thing to school at 13, and different again from school at 16. The age you are alters the age you find yourself in. The Sixties has always meant different things and at the time I wasn't aware that what I thought and experienced, what I would remember, was also a product of sociology and design quite as much as that sideboard which was in for the long haul, sad and dignified, doing its work as best it could.

In the summer of 1962 then, well before, to remind us, people referred to anything as the Sixties, and before the Beatles were known to the world at large, on Sunday afternoons I listened to Pick Of The Pops. Sometimes I would listen on the outside roof that went across the coal shed at the side of the house. This roof was in corrugated sections of a thick, hard, whitish-grey fibrous material that was nonchalantly called asbestos, though I've been hoping ever since that it wasn't. Under it every month or so, sacks of coal were delivered, the sacks thick and substantial looking as if they were woven from coal dust and rope, the thump and rumble of the chunks of coal being tipped at the end of the shed where a floor level sliding wooden panel allowed access from the kitchen's back step. Once, I was in alone when they delivered and I didn't hear a thing. When my mother returned she was astonished and angry that I could be there and not know, not hear the coal going in. I was surprised too. I was absorbed in what I was doing, probably reading a book, or perhaps staring at the fire, and in any case being a child and unaware of adult duties. The coal men, usually two of them, had been known to my parents for years it seemed. Their faces were black with dust and their eyes were always startling, pale and red-rimmed in the middle of that skin darkness. They wore leather pads over the jackets to help cushion the weight of the bags, and caps inadequate to the task of keeping their heads clean, and always walked bent forward in a stoop to counter balance the load. Even when free of the coal they had a hunched tilt and both looked too small for the fierce physical demands of the job. They looked like the past, doing what they had always done, and the world was turning away from coal fires and the need to chip boilers free of gleaming tar casings.

Out there in the sun, above the dusty mineral dark of the coal-hole, with the end walls looking to a sufficiently imaginative eye like battlements, suggestions of castles and Robin Hood, I listened to the radio that I took out from the kitchen or the bedroom. It was a sturdy chunky transistor radio in maroon and white, plasticized cloth over wood, with white push buttons on top, and white notched round knobs, also on top, for volume and tuning, and I thought it looked about as modern as one could get, with just the right pleasing overtone of Americana. Like Kansas City in the musical Oklahoma it had gone about as fur as it could go. It was on this radio that I heard a couple of years before, intermittently and unplanned on Luxemburg, the Hollywood Argyles record Alley Oop, which linked to Kookie's beat speak – Like what's happening – and Stan Freburg's making fun of hipsters and fake folk, but was also a great record that seemed to show that America would always be superior. And what came over it now, amongst the Elvis and Everly Brothers, was Cliff, who had moved from the rock of Move It, to the family youth appeal of The Young Ones and Summer Holiday. There was too Poetry In Motion, and Picture Of You, the simple but pleasing hit by Joe Brown, who around then played on a bill in Liverpool higher than the Beatles, saw how good they were, and became George Harrison's friend, and decades later after George had died, sang at the concert to celebrate him I'll See You In My Dreams, to the accompaniment of the ukulele that George had come to love, the most moving song of the night, tears falling like rose petals. Alive in the present moment however that kind of future is not even a dream but simply blank, non-existent. What existed on the roof in the sunshine was Rambling Rose, It Might As Well Rain Until September, and Bobby Vee, not that long after being Bob Dylan's brief employer, another fact years from being generally known or being in any way relevant. All was pop and soft and not rock, part of the Sixties, the other Sixties. Those tunes had appeal because of the age we were, but also because hearing what came after, what was in fact being brewed up as I sat out there on that possibly unhealthy roof, one appreciated the jump cut change all the more.

The first change signalled by the Beatles, although they were part of something amazingly widespread, was that the wild energy and roughness of 1950s rock hadn't died out. It had gone underground, in some cases more literally than others. Hundreds of lads in towns across the UK seemed to have formed groups and they all shared a repertoire of songs that had been written and performed 4 or 5 years before, except now they sounded different. There was a sense of things being strange and new, and also completely expected and right. Here was a form of music that hadn't existed in quite the way it now did. Everyone knows the genealogy. Everyone can point to r&b, blues, country, all of the antecedents. None of it quite explains how rock music specifically tied to young people suddenly became such a part of the mid 1950s, and then almost as rapidly mutated into the fare I was hearing on the asbestos roof. Having Elvis go into the Army seemed to be part of it. Now it was back, at least for English ears.

The great songwriters operating in the teen hinterland between schlock, craft and canny art – symbolised by Lieber and Stoller, Pomus and Shuman and their permutations, – created that shared repertoire which worked in much the same way as floating sets of verses in blues lyrics. Everyone partook, and everyone imparted their own flavour. This outpouring of lads who weren't glamorous, who were of the provinces, who wanted to rock out in suits and ties with electric instruments and drums, who split up and reformed like so many amoeba, kept the spirit alive. In America the way songs were fed to acts was what caused problems. The Everly Brothers had wanted a wider choice, which caused break ups with publishing company and management. They wrote songs too, but they couldn't write enough. Elvis was such a sure-fire generator of money that the Colonel kept as tight a rein as possible on what was presented to his boy. Over here the lads played what they could and what they liked, and most people had a crack at, amongst others, Searchin', Yakety Yak, Fortune Teller, Poison Ivy, Some Other Guy, What'd I Say, I Got A Woman,

Sure To Fall, Money, Long Tall Sally. Even British first wave rockers like Marty Wilde and Billy Fury, the names telling you all you need to know about their origins, had written and recorded their own songs. Now these rough and ready beat groups were doing the same. Or at least one of them was. The Beatles weren't the first group to record songs that they wrote, Cliff's Shadows had done that; but they were always safe, good boys, even if Cliff had begun with a curled lip and enough grease to hold his hair like Elvis. The Beatles were the only ones, except for the Stones, (who were deemed r&b and thus didn't count in quite the same way), that sounded, – while recreating the power of rock's early days, – quite that kind of strange and new and wild, despite the suits and grins, their mesh of guitars and voices not really like other groups. They promised, and enacted, some kind of breaking loose. They mattered more than the Shadows, no matter that Hank B Marvin may have been responsible for at least one demographic cohort of teenage boys pestering their parents into getting them an electric guitar, and could you make it red please.

CHAPTER NINE
TELL ME WHAT YOU SEE

There are always links and always chains, and the Beatles, like many English would-be rockers, had taken Buddy Holly as a role model quite precisely. He wrote his own songs and operated a two guitars, bass and drums group. Cross-pollinate that with the Everly Brothers and John and Paul were on their way. But then Bob Dylan had loved Buddy Holly too. He had seen him in the big Duluth Armory on that last tour, the Winter Dance Party, 3 days before the plane crash, up there in the iron north that Bobby Zimmerman knew intimately and was so hard to get used to for someone from Texas, as mythically Western as anything in America. "And he *looked* at me," Bob Dylan said years later, pausing, seeming to mean so much by that simple phrase, remembering being three feet away from him. Buddy Holly created his own repertoire, and Bob Dylan intended to, and the Beatles were pouring it out. And in 1964 Bob Dylan hears the Beatles, and really hears them, "their chords were outrageous, just outrageous, but their harmonies made it all valid," he told Anthony Scaduto in an interview that appeared in Scaduto's biography of him. He was right. Musicologists have pointed out that the Beatles songs contain many more chords than is normal for pop songs, and they aren't chords that follow an expected sequence. The rest of us non-musicologists couldn't explain that, but we could hear it. Bob Dylan heard it, and the Beatles heard him and that changed some aspects of their song-making and singing. And on his English trips he hears all of it, the r&b in the charts, not tucked away in specialist late night radio shows, and it makes him think about the high school rock groups he had, none of which we knew about at the time. It also makes him think of something more. He hears the Animals record of House Of The Rising Sun, "in rock man, in rock," as he also told Scaduto, still amazed and pleased year afterwards. And right there he sees that there is a way to go that will fuse everything he loved and loves, from the tradition, all the traditions of folk, blues and rock and roll. He heard the groups, and they heard him, and I heard them all on that roof, and behind the steel cladding of the house in the bedroom a few feet from the roof, and in the living room and the back kitchen. It was 1962 and then 1965, and it was the Sixties which we never called them, and besides there were so many, some lasting for a very short time, and anyone there will describe something different, especially anyone who was on their way to High School.

Nelson Algren wrote once about Sinatra's bobby soxers (a different bobby obviously) screaming, "Spit on me Frankie, I'm in the front row," something he found puzzling as they were in the balcony. 1965. He looked at me and I looked at him and I wasn't in the front row. I was in the balcony too, and no one was screaming up there or anywhere. Someone did say that he thought a figure by the side of the stage, or the front of the stage, it wasn't clear, was Joan Baez. I nodded and couldn't tell who he was pointing at. It didn't matter. What our perceptions were pointing at was Bob Dylan, this person who used to be another person, or seemed to be. There are times when you can have a confidence about your place in the world, and what you know and what you have to do. It seems that the world has tipped in your favour and for a time everything seems to be right. It's one of the best feelings there is. He had it and we shared it. Despite the turmoil and anxieties about being a teenager, that feeling of being at one with your self, and your place in what you know, often seems to come then. There was a time when English rock stars were discovered by managers, by men in the business, doing what they did in a small time way but spotted as having the potential to make it big. Where they were discovered, for the most part it seemed in those 50s rocker days, was a coffee bar in Soho, the 2i's, a nascent I & I, although for the Beatles, despite the leg work undertaken in Hamburg, their place was a record store in Liverpool.

I think most teenagers expect that to happen to them in some indefinable way. I did. Knowing they don't play guitar, or perform in cafés, or in fact do much of anything at all doesn't seem to make too much difference to the background hope. Someone will see you in a shop or the street and see the something about you that is unique. There's a blinkered quality that is selfish and thoughtless, but also innocent. Teenagers have a certain confidence in their eligibility to be discovered; they expect their special qualities to be recognised by someone who will know them for what they are, and it's this that helps produce the heightened sense of involvement with the time whenever those teenage years happen to be. There's an obvious over-lap between this state of mind and what the world of entertainment offers, whether it's in acting or rock music. Anyone who performs, no matter how young they are, – your friends, your children even – will seem to become another person if they perform in a way that moves you. For that time and activity they are more than the person they have to be the rest of the time. People who become stars are stars because we treat them differently. They all start off as ordinary people, as ordinary as you and me, and it's this oscillation, this hav-ing to bear two things in mind, which causes problems. We want them to be better than us, to be our representative in some sense, but also to understand that they are subservient to us, because with-out an audience who would they be? Don't winners understand, we want to ask, that the word would be meaningless if their position wasn't defined by losers? Losers aren't nothing, they're essential to the scheme of things. How would a winner recognise himself without having a loser to be superior to?

But then the "stars" know quite well that, beneath the entourage and various protective HR layers, they are ordinary people too. Many try to tell us exactly this, and that most of the problems ordinary people have don't go away by their becoming well-known. No doubt money helps but in other ways other things can get worse. The life that you had is unreachable now because what you are, have become, affects the way anyone you meet reacts to you. There are all these strangers who think – because they have read everything about you – that they know you, with all of the pitfalls that entails. Bob Dylan once spoke matter-of-factly but movingly about looking into a pub or a restaurant through a lighted window, standing on the evening street outside. He could look in and see all the people unself-consciously doing what they do, enjoying themselves. That's as close as he could get. He knew that as soon as he went in through the door all that would change. There wouldn't be a natural state any more because he would have introduced an element that everyone had to take account of. Of course there's a major difference between the times when I was first becoming familiar with the idea of Bob Dylan, and when he was becoming familiar with Bob Dylan, and now. So much of that teenage sense of waiting to be recognised has shifted into a whole industry of television shows and the racks of almost identical gossip magazines that are in a symbiotic relationship with them. Now, deliberately ill-sorted, well-chosen people really can be discovered simply by putting themselves into a space where other people can watch them living, just living in a house, without having any ability as such at all, and where all personality defects only add to the value audiences derive from the process. Then their post-show lives can be messed up just like any other person who has become famous by more traditional means, and every subsequent stage of marriage, pregnancy, birth defect, weight gain, weight loss, drug dependency and illness unto death can be monitored and revealed to a grateful and condemnatory public. Audiences can mess up your life, but if you are a performer what are you to do? Are you strong enough to make your way once you have passed through the mirror?

We looked in the mirror of 1965 and heard the sound all around it. If you were a teenager you heard it. What puzzles me is where it came from, not in the sense of who made it, but how did we hear it. It had to be the radio but we're talking about a time when it was Home Service, Light Programme and the Third Programme. There was pirate radio with a station called Caroline North reaching us from its location off the Isle of Man where it began broadcasting in 1964, but exciting as it was I don't remember it as being everyday listening. Often I had to perch on the stairs with the rooftop transistor to try to make the best of the indifferent reception. What it did give us was programmes that only played pop, and also dj's who were young men rather than old, and who seemed only really to exist, even to themselves, when they were burbling behind a microphone. A lot of them affected the kind of voices called mid-Atlantic, where U.S. or Canadian flavours were laid across a provincial base. Once I heard one of them asking, "What are you dunking today, I'm dunking tomatoes in cocoa." This synthetic, ubiquitous, would-be zany vocal identity, aimlessly filling space/time between music, was accepted as the way to be a dj and spread like an infection, one we still suffer from today. Their major stroke of luck was in being able to be part of the music that had now begun to be created, and to have willing hordes of people exactly the right age, like us, to think it marvellous.

When one compares the paucity of what was available then with the roll call of station names that now scroll past on a digital display, having no idea what kind of thing they broadcast for the most part, it's a wonder how the sound of what was our modern world percolated through. But it did, and the sound was of guitars, guitars not as they had sounded even two years previously, but a sound that seemed to be part of the air around us, more entwining, more insidious, more seductive. Of course there were the Byrds and what was immediately dubbed their jingle-jangle guitar, slightly distorted and punctuating the songs, beginning with their first hit, Mr Tambourine Man which they had changed utterly, massively truncating it to one verse and a couple of choruses, changing the tune and, crucially according to Jim, later Roger, McGuinn, altering the tempo from 2/4 to 4/4, the way the Beatles played. It was different in kind rather than degree to the long unfolding we had heard in silence, spellbound and swallowed in Birmingham. The Byrds had made it pop and rock in short, and allowed those people always desperate to make labels to invent a new one: folk-rock. What they did seemed so new, although the Rickenbacker guitar used was as seen in A Hard Day's Night, the Beatles film that revealed to a whole swathe of American kids and folk-based musicians that being in a rock band was fun *and* creative; and the sound the Byrds made was not that dissimilar to that achieved by The Searchers in their string of hit singles in 1963 and 1964, another Liverpool group that seemed set fair for longevity. The Byrds took from England and England took it right back again. There was simultaneously the Beatles with the film Help. For all its importance I never saw A Hard Day's Night at the time. That was a treat for some decades later, over and over, when I had a child and he had come to love the Beatles too. But I did see Help when it came out and think of that change from the fake documentary, glowing black and white, of the first film, and the switch into the light and silliness and bright wash of colour of Help, its soundtrack slew of new songs, that difference in their sounds and appearance over one year; not forgetting its single, Ticket To Ride, with the rhythmic figure etched in guitar strings and drums. And in 1965 there was too, most importantly, the Kinks, who had begun the previous year with You Really Got Me, which has the distinction of really sounding nothing like anything else that had existed up to that point. Even now if you hear it, in a cinema say when they are playing soundtrack loops to amuse the sparse clientele before an early evening film begins, you can still get a homeopathic flavour of how strange and astounding its power was originally. And without the example of the Kinks how would the Who have had a starting place? And now all the groups seemed to be taking American forms, an English sensibility, and their personal idiosyncrasies to create something new under the sun. For awhile there everything under the sun seemed new.

1965 and all the Bob Dylans there ever were came over the air-waves, or were in the newspapers and magazines, and for a short time had been in the same country, and even the same room with some of us. In less than a year (following the path and progress he had made, but in a speedier, more compressed way) we had moved from the folk and blues and political awareness of Freewheelin', skipped to the more personal concerns and rushed-sounding Another Side of Bob Dylan, then backtracked to hear, but not at that point to buy, the much more socially focused Times They Are-A Changin' album. Now here was a record, Bringing It All Back Home, (and what did that title mean exactly?) that had electric guitar and a band. Not exactly a rock guitar or band it was true, but a shift in what was expected. And then there was the side without the band, with those long songs of words that made pictures, and the pictures were fused into the sound of his voice, and the sound of his voice is what people do or don't get about him. As with all of his albums we studied the covers, their pictures and words, and those pictures and words became part of the meaning the album would always carry, always associated with the living images and text of songs. What a dif-ference in appearance to the one-step-up-from-a-street-urchin that characterised Another Side of Bob Dylan. Here he wore a tailored jacket and a fancy shirt with purple cuff links. That alone showed you he had gone up in the world, and so did the setting, a room scat-tered with books, albums, and assorted cultural objects, as well as a cultural lady in a red dress. In Gates Of Eden he sang about a cow-boy angel and immediately fused the background Western legacy that folk always hinted at with Beat territory, Kerouac's desolation angels and Ginsberg's angel-headed hipsters. Mixing and matching, fusing and melding styles of the past with his present intent was what he was about, the album made clear, and in the voice that sounded really like no-one else.

Despite this, that spring and summer is when his sound and phrasing and elastic approach to the length of a line, (the same flexibility he brought to the measuring of time itself), or where it might require a breath to be taken, the unorthodoxy of his idiosyncratic, reckless way with a song, started to spread through pop. He had an attitude in how he stood next to a song, and other singers understood that. McGuinn said that he, quite deliberately, wanted to pitch his voice somewhere between Lennon and Dylan. He showed excellent taste but was fooling himself if he thought he ever sounded anything but slightly whiney. Lennon's is a wonderful voice for all aspects of rock, and the kind of music that wouldn't exist if the Beatles weren't creating it right then. But no-one could actually sound like him unless they'd suffered the life he had, the would-be hard man and the needy child you hear in his later, thin voice, not the thickened roughness of Twist and Shout, but the sharper textures of Strawberry Fields or Julia. The idea that style is not something you choose or adopt, but an outer expression of inner, involuntary characteristics and compulsions, wasn't one I was altogether familiar with then, but then neither, it seems, was Roger McGuinn.

That spring and on into the summer was the year of O Levels, which meant it was the kind of year that can shape your life, or at least encourage it in one direction or another. It had already shaped it by falling in with and amplifying interests I had. One of the O Level books was John Steinbeck's The Grapes of Wrath, which was absolutely of a piece with what I had learned about Woody Guthrie's life, and how that had cast its spell over the young Bob Dylan. Guthrie wrote his Ballad of Tom Joad not because of reading the book but after seeing the film based on it. But the book had a unique charge. Steinbeck's immensely detailed and realistic descriptions, based in a desire to document these things happening in America that some of its people might not want to think about, had a polemical but also a mystical purpose. That was to do with a reverence for democracy and decency and Ordinary People, subliminally capitalised in the same way that Pete Seeger always seemed to. It linked too with the historical movement west across America, with Whitman's reverence for the vastness of the land and the people, and had associations with Kerouac's later travels. The Okies weren't hoboes but to innocent romantics they might be confused. They weren't looking to find themselves, but to find a job. The bohemians and hobohemians wanted their lives to be more interesting or meaningful, and thought movement might make it so, also along the way confusing dirt and squalor with romance, romance too a prime factor in being meaningful, and squalor being a sign of that sought after authenticity. A lot of young people were prone to confusion. Perhaps thinking about exams and the future encouraged it.

Coming up for exams heightens everything, making you consider what will become of you, long and short term. What could be more intricately related to beginnings and endings? And the background to all of this was the sound of groups and guitars, and Bob Dylan's presence beneath them. No longer in the specialist area of folk music, with all of the cultural and social baggage that entailed, he was part of the scene, whatever he sang, the same context as the Beatles and the Stones, who knew him and admired him. He wasn't part of the same performing context, because who could imagine either of them doing a show that lasted as long as his, or being received in such attentive, dutiful silence, applause only breaking out at the end of a song. Both bands had already acknowledged his influence the previous year by writing and recording songs with flavours and traces of his style. Lennon produced I'm A Loser with just enough to let you know who he'd been listening to. The Stones did Good Times, Bad Times, with folky words and heartfelt harmonica as a B side to It's All Over Now, the first to really capture their interlocking dual guitars sound, chugging then urgent, shifting around as it kept moving forward. The Stones linked with him too because he had seen them on television, he tells us so right there on the back of Another Side of Bob Dylan, and they were English boys who had fallen for the blues, as he had done, trying their hand at selected Muddy Waters, Jimmy Reed and Howlin' Wolf songs. In the time-shift and retrospect that typifies being a Dylan fan it wasn't until year afterwards that one had proof of this. Listening to Freewheelin' I didn't know, and it certainly never crossed my mind in Birmingham Town Hall during the silence-buffered, image-littered unfolding of Mr Tambourine Man. Only with the appearance of bootlegs years after the fact did we get to hear Bob singing Smokestack Lightnin', with impassioned, self-possessed swoops and yodels. He was all of 20. He responded to his interviewer when she commented that he was brave to try a Howlin' song, "Yeah, Howlin' Wolf", with his dancing cadence emphasising Howlin' rather than Wolf, enclosing and conveying an amused approval that someone had the nerve to go by such an outlandish handle, almost as if he wished he had thought of it first. All of this was hidden around the angle of the decades when I heard it, almost as far forward from its first happening as the original 1920s bootleggers of booze were in the past from that radio interview, the 1920s, another decade that went under a label that broadened, mythologised and falsified reality, allowing us to carry a cartoon in our heads.

One of the advantages of being a teenager in the 1960s, I have always maintained, was of experiencing events and hearing records in the order they occurred, that are now claimed by people not born then or for decades afterwards, as their own, as a virtual reality. This means that those of us from that time don't have the perspective that comes with historical knowledge, where any element may be looked at in any order and related in whatever way one seems informative when patterns and theories as to why things happened suggest themselves. It also means that one is likely to be free of the sense, as I've heard it described, of having missed the biggest party in the world, and then having the burden of disappointment or envy or a need to be superior, knowing that it can't have been exactly as people say, but knowing too that you missed it. We know all this; we missed it even as we were there. It was just life, ordinary day to day life, but overarching it was a feeling that we part of something larger happening even when we did nothing special except know it existed for some people then, and except for the records that marked and illuminated months and seasons while our lives were disappearing into statistics and demography, the tables of morbidity and mortality where there are no individuals. Reality and illusion become part of each other, along with degrees of contemporary or subsequent revelation. For instance, what seemed to be the reality of the Beatles in their first stages, the cheeky, nutty moptops crowned by the Royal Varity Performance, immediately prior to their Fab incarnation that followed and overlapped it, is a world away from the photos that emerged of the Hamburg days, or the time they served in the Cavern. Then one feels something of what people born too late to be young in the Sixties get. They were the Beatles and not the Beatles. They were rowdy lads in leather jackets. One could read about and see that rougher reality even as one experienced A Hard Day's Night.

> They weren't the *Beatles* then.
> Who were they? A gang of lads.
> A bunch of scruffs who made a row
> with electric guitars. Just like now.
> Leather kids catching American fads
> like an illness, until they became one.

They had been like us, like people we knew on estates. Their estates were in Liverpool, but how different could Liverpool be from the streets and houses I knew? I can remember reading about John Lennon writing and drawing bits and pieces in Art College, and for the paper Mersey Beat, and his saying if he could collect the cigarette packets together there might be a book some day. That would be the cigarette packets we only stuck to the forks of bikes in order to jam them against the wheel spokes so that a satisfying noise would indicate increasing speed. But around this time it was clear he did assemble his bits and pieces because In His Own Write, a book of talismanic appeal, was published in blue and sepia, with him wearing the cap that could be associated with both Bob Dylan and Donovan. This didn't stop me thinking of, but rather allowed an imagining of the time he'd lived in before, when he did scribble and sketch on scraps, on cigarette packets and had no notion that anything would come of it, and I wondered how much it differed from my interior life.

Bob Dylan too had a previous life we were going to continue to find out about. In fact part of the future would be always occupied with analysing his past, and his past would grow at the rate ours did. Here at the top of the fountain of moments that brought us to this prominence, the Bob Dylan who had been on the front of Freewheelin', who had suffered on Times They Are-A Changin', been the refugee sheepherder in corduroy cap on his first album, was something else. Reconciling revelations, that's what living in the present has to mean. He was going to give us a lot of chances to do that. The background interrogation, the press conference we all carry around in our heads, has many questions, but one is, What did you know and when did you know it? Boundaries blur and dissolve. Was he ever a protest singer? What does protest mean anyway? What are you rebelling against Bobby, is the background hum in all the 1965 interviews. For Bob Dylan, with his apparent sense that only the present mattered, and his arbitrary idea of what can be considered ancient history, which fitted in so well then, it had become irrelevant.

1965 and during that spring and summer Donovan released his first single Catch The Wind, a pretty tune with words responsible for making many teenagers look at sunsets and think about ways they might be captured in words. I liked it very much but didn't think of buying it. Albums seemed to be a more substantial proposition. It sounded nothing like Blowing In The Wind, but, sharing a word with its title, was thought to be derivative anyway by showbiz reporters of the hard and red nose variety. Donovan didn't make things easy on himself, so denim clad from top to toe it suggested that even his underwear might come from Levi Strauss, he had at first seemed to be merely a Dylan surrogate, but with the songs coming through a British sensibility. He had a harmonica on a neck rack, he invoked Woody Guthrie with the inscription on his guitar, and at first he sang in accents derived from Dylan and Jack Elliot. Unusually he came to general attention by appearing on Ready Steady Go, the rock show that excited everyone on Friday nights, allowing us to know that the weekend started there. That is another example of how being immersed in the atmosphere of a particular time puts things under a spell. Seeing sliced up, re-packaged sections of Ready Steady Go years later, when owned by the shrewd Dave Clark, his fortune acquired when he ran the briefly Beatle-challenging Dave Clark Five, (challenging them, despite the clumping simplicity of Glad All Over, only in the States during that mad, heady, year that comprised the British Invasion, and the U.S. mags like Teen Beat ran entirely manufactured headlines like: "No Fair 5 Against 4, say Beatles," and herbal Herman's Hermits achieved a popularity they had never expected and never retained), you had to dwell on how all the excitement and wonder had withered and blown away. At the time though Donovan had taken a step out of a folkie anonymity and been given his chance, playing San Francisco Bay Blues, by Jesse Fuller, and couldn't have announced the roots he shared with Bob Dylan more clearly. Bob had sung one of Fuller's songs on his first album, and Fuller too was a one-man band artist with his neck-braced harmonica, kazoo and foot drum. Donovan made such a hit he was brought back in subsequent weeks

Aside from that shared American repertoire however Donovan had hung out with the English folk baroque crowd, including Bert Jansch, and was interested in playing the guitar in the way they did, interested too in the jazz that found its way into their technique.

Later it became clear that he'd fallen for the same things Bob Dylan had, as thousands of teenagers had, most noticeably kids who played guitar. He liked Whitman, Steinbeck, the Beats, and Kerouac, so rambling out of St. Albans he fell in with the London equivalent of a Greenwich Village life, except he also went to the seaside version down St. Ives way. It didn't mean he really wanted to be Bob Dylan however. He was part of the English scruff beatnik crowd really, the kind associated with university towns and CND, but with the added predilections of musicians, and although he was fresh out of the box he made an impression on the scene. You didn't have to make a choice between him and Bob Dylan despite superficial similarities. Even though he was only 24 Dylan was already a more experienced and tougher character it seemed, and though they shared stylistic starting points with Woody Guthrie, Jack Elliot and Jesse Fuller, they were already moving in different directions. Donovan's next single was Colours, with a banjo and reworked, traditional-type words about appreciating what he had in the morning, those everyday riches, when, punctual as daylight, he rose: the sun, the sky, the sparkling green corn, and the girl who made it complete. It was easy to deride as words, but then the effect a song has is always created by more than words. If you, a bookish, dreamy, indecisive almost ex-child of a certain inexperienced and non-tough temperament, were about to do O levels, and could entertain the possibility of being a nature poet, a Donovan record was a shoo-in. It seems to me, though no-one can now verify it, that I spent a lot of time in those weeks around the time of Donovan's first two singles and first album walking along the canal with the sound of the words and tune of Colours in my head, looking at the fields, the green-ish water and purple edging bricks, thinking about who knows what now, possibly how to do something, or avoid doing something, or writing.

The canal is an important part of my growing up and one of the features that identify both that area and the time. That time of growing up and that area merge, so that each becomes a representative of the other. That's where when I was a teenager I thought about the Beatles and Bob Dylan as I knew them then, and also where I thought about their childhoods, and then wondered how my childhood compared with theirs, in those receding infinities that continue throughout a life. We all have a Hibbing that raised us. That area – Bloxwich, Blakenall, Walsall – is recorded as settlements further back than Bob's North Country town. Bloxwich has origins before the Domesday Book that lists it too. Coal and iron were mined from early times, not on the scale of Minnesota's vast open cast pit, but an intermittent scattering of smaller enterprises. Coal lay near the surface, and beds of ironstone were associated with it, and the area was one of coal mines, iron mines, limestone working, brickworks and furnaces, and the making of all kinds of metal goods, often to do with the bits and pieces horses required. Walsall itself was also noted for its saddles and harnesses, as well as other leather goods. All of which meant that when canals began to be constructed in the 1790s it was the kind of transport system these heavy enterprises needed. The Essington and Wyrley (rhymes with curly) canal was part of a system connecting Birmingham, Wolverhampton and Lichfield. Our little local bit was probably not important even in its heyday, but it was important when I was a child because of the pleasure ground aspect. You could watch the barges going past, sometimes seeming to have a work purpose but often suggesting water gypsies or Mr Toad, a regular chug chug and blue smoke, with the bright designs and the tiller making the water shape smooth and green against the liquid grain of a flow, the consistency suggesting a very, very thin treacle. A dog might run along the edge of the boat and show you what it was like to be daring and unaware. My dad and his friends had swum in the canal in the summers of the 1920s, – those 1920s where I imagined he had had a life like that glimpsed in the James Cagney films we used to slump in front of the tv and watch together, the time of Fitzgerald and bootlegs, both of which wove into my life and stayed there. It wasn't just the past though, kids still jumped in and swam when I was little. I didn't learn how to swim until later, but I don't think I would have jumped into that dirty water, no matter how invitingly it gleamed in sunlight. People often called it the cut. Throwing bricks in to make a splash was throwing half end duckers in the cut. It's not just Black Country dialect at work there, that warm and rounded, often slow and kind, gentle resonance that may be how Chaucer and Shakespeare would have sounded to everyone, and not at all like the RSC. The sound of the Black Country was typified for me in a story my Dad told about people in the betting shop, in the time when bookmaker Knock was able to leave the street corner and everyone could study form and pick winners in the smoke and minimal decoration. There was a Damon Runyon feel to the names people had or were given. One of Knock's successors was always called Jesus because of long hair. A regular there was always reported to me as being called Bumperomer, in the way that email names are all run together now. He may have been Bumper Homer, or Bumper Omer, or 'omer, and actually his first name could have been Benjamin. He was quietly reading the runners and riders, my dad said, and not seeming to pay attention when one of the women regulars was listing for my dad her husband's various failings. "And," my dad said, "Bumper looked up over his glasses, holding the paper, and said very slow and kindly, 'Now Mary, yo' won't be saying that when 'e's bollock deep and the gravy's running.' And that tickled me." One of the few times dad used a rude word when telling me anything, but that's not why I remember the story. It's not a phrase I knew, or have heard since, but it seems so of the place that I come from, that's part of me, I see the shop and the scene in my mind as if I was present. I see the expression I never saw. Something about the jokiness and the tolerance in that accent and its cadence sounds in my inner ear as much as words I did hear, like half end duckers in the cut. The cut, in fact, is also the technical term used for the making of the spurs and side shoots of the canals route, right there in the 1792 Act. The canal became a reality and a symbol that would stay with me.

The Black Country may be called that because of the earlier industrial smoke and air pollution from the widespread smelting and metal working industries, or, as others think and seems quite plausible to me, because coal seams lying on and near the surface meant that the ground actually was black. Because of its name people elsewhere think it must be ugly, and there are harsh aspects to it, and in the years since I left it has been subject, as many towns have, to all kinds of social blight and loss, sink estates of vandalism and violence, followed by schemes of regeneration and renewal. But when I was growing up what I associated it with was the country that the 49 bus route made me think of, the real, which is to say imaginary, country that you saw in children's books farms, partly because of trees, there were always lots of trees it seemed to me, but chiefly because of the canal. The bridges lent a more rural air than concrete street lights. Where the canal followed the contour, trying to keep level and away from inclines, there were fields and hawthorn visible, cow parsley thronging green and white along the towpath. Horses and carts too were familiar to us growing up. Because my father was the youngest of a large family, and he was born in 1911, his brothers and sisters went back a long way. Aunt Nance, a little gnome with a long, friendly face and the mild sound of an entirely unself-conscious Walsall accent, always referred to "the horse road", thee oss road, when worrying about grand-children straying into it, because that's what it used to be when she was a girl, and that would have been before the First World War. Steptoe and Son wasn't fanciful in having rag and bone men as its characters. They clopped down Thames Road, someone often sitting on the side of the cart, waggling a Wellington-booted leg, while the driver up front shouted "Any ol' ragbow", in a loosely musical, rough and careless rise and fall. Another cart was a regular and its driver was known to everyone as Ay Aitch, which was more or less what he used to call out to encourage the horse as he snapped the reins. He wasn't a rag and bone man but had a more agricultural, if not now quite locatable, character. There was always a sense that not far from the streets there were little growing patches and small hold-ings, down tracts between houses, tucked away in the vicinity of the canal and the Barley Mow, or even by Blakenall Heath, where Ingram Road and the bus turn-around were, a presence still discernible of the land where council estates had grown in the 1930s and then again at the end of the 1940s, the bits of land where eggs and vegetables were still produced.

None of the industrial past impinged on me. I knew nothing about it and never knowingly saw a mine, though I did see cool-ing towers alongside a canal with submerged barges where we played dangerously, a bike ride away from home. The cooling towers were our open cast mine equivalents of Bob Dylan's childhood. I was a post-war child and so we lived in an estate outside of the town, near to openness and aware of the skies overhead. When I heard Penny Lane, and Paul McCartney's heartfelt blue suburban skies, I knew what he meant precisely. I was looking at them while I heard the record, and I was remembering them too, as he was, from when you could watch them and not have any real cares, only the tiniest amount of time before, and the suburbs themselves were a sign that things had been ordered for you to do your best in an education system and a society so arranged that your life would work if you did your part. The near-est we came to industry was a copper refiner called Elkington which occupied a road at the far end of the chunk of land where all our houses were, on the road to Goscote, another area where there was a kind of rural overlap, but close enough so that sometimes people addressed post to us with that as our district. We were slightly huffy. We were Blakenall, not Goscote, and not Blakenhall either, with an h, and which was miles away the other side of Wolverhampton and thus another world. I grew up with Elkington's. Their parent com-pany acquired the site in 1949, which was when my parents acquired me, so it had always been in the background. From my bedroom window you could see the lights and the thin metal towers with their fumes, all rising like those in Smokestack Lightning. Later, after reading a recommendation from Donovan, I started Lord of The Rings (this was another big dividing line indicating the major differences between Donovan and Bob Dylan) and subliminally superimposed the Elkington scene whenever Mordor was mentioned. The canal worked the same way, a background illustration to words.

My dad told me a story of when he and my mother were walking out together, courting, and they had no money and nowhere really to go, so they spent hours walking, and along the canal was where they walked. I supposed it wouldn't have been the stretch of canal I knew because this was when they lived in the town, but perhaps it was, they walked for hours after all. My mother had a new hat and my father said something jokey about it. He said it wasn't really disparaging, but she took the hat off and sailed it out over a field. That's how annoyed she was. But they couldn't go home without her hat because it was new and her mother would be angry. So he had to cross a fence and go into a field and retrieve it and the situation, and then they had to make up and walk all the way home. And it became a story, and he told me the story, and as long as I'm alive that moment is alive, a moment I couldn't witness, so I don't know where it took place. But when I see a canal now with fields alongside, or when I think back to the canal that was where I used to go, I can see it happening, see something I never saw but I'm seeing it in the memory I'd like to remember, the dream film that not only one's own past, but other people's pasts causes to exist. This links to songs. My dad said that whenever he heard the song Walking My Baby Back Home he thought about those times when all they had to do, all they could do, was walk out together if it was evening and summer. He liked the lines "arm in arm over meadow and farm," because it reminded him. As it reminds me and always will. I have it by James Taylor who sings it in just the right careful fond way. It makes me sad because it lets me know what has gone, but also it's a source of happiness, showing how much people can mean to each other, just everyday, unextravagant love that makes things work. That's what songs are for, allowing different kinds of reality and illusion to co-exist. I remember the canal, my canal, symbol and reality, and the times I walked along thinking of Donovan and his green sparkling corn, wondering if life would go on being as easy, or if these exams would be the end of something.

CHAPTER TEN
I SHALL BE FREE

1965 going on all around and within me, the sound of the records that meant what it was like to be alive now, breathing the air along the canal, walking or cycling to school. From Thames Road you walked down to Smithfield Road and saw the different houses. They were private houses and the feel of that street was also always different to me. One could imagine some kind of adult life where living in houses like that might be possible, but not what it was that one would be doing to pay for such a life. From Smithfield a quick turn in and out of the end of Green Rock Lane, (a name I loved) at the other end of which was the Green Rock public house, in whose off licence my mother would get bottles of Bruno or Jumbo, or sometimes Mackeson, stout at the weekend.

My father didn't drink at all, having lost a brother to alcohol, and that was a common pattern in big families of his time: temperance and boozers under the same roof. Ansells was a local brewery and its pubs, he told me, in his day of the 20s and 30s were known as "blood tubs," because they were rough places. It was a regular practice, he said, for men to drink 5 or 6 pints, go out the back to be sick and make room for the 5 or 6 more they intended to drink afterwards. The only other regular alcohol in our house, wine being unknown, was each Christmas when our next door neighbour brought round as an offering of friendship, though he was more or less invisible the rest of the year, a little cardboard pack of Babycham, with its leaping, cheerful fawn, and, proving how successful advertising was, this seemed like the summit of luxury. Even I was allowed a sip or two.

After the Green Rock wiggle, out onto Ingram Road, a long, slight hill with the kind of red 1930s council houses my Uncle Lou lived in. It was in Ingram Road that I can remember going through the words of To Ramona in my head, looking at grass verges and leaves on trees near to where the trolley bus turn around was. On that street on my way to and from school I'd be hearing in my mind about the flowers of the city, breath like and death like. I hadn't really been in a city then, only outskirts. Then Field Road and out onto Lichfield Road, with its bus route traffic and its tall trees and the school which gave everyday life its context. The school was glass and blue-grey brick modernity, hundreds of children and really a surprisingly small number that one actually knew in any detail.

It was a modern school for modern times, just two years old when I first went there in 1960, and I went as part of the last intake of 11 Plus entrants. The next year it became Comprehensive but retained the trappings and ethos of a grammar school, with its Latin motto (Semper Altiora Speramus) its uniforms and ties, and its Combined Cadet Force. This was a Friday afternoon taste of service life for the older years, to encourage team spirit doing something you might not choose but would learn to like, then getting the chance to go away to camp or barracks to knock about, muck in and fire rifles. Young people had been called up for real right up until the year we began at school, Johnny Green a few doors down from us had gone into the RAF and we all wondered what it would be like. It was a big school, widespread, with blocks for the individual Houses, (four of them, named after English admirals, that pupils and teachers were organised into,) and teaching blocks around a large campus setting, separate premises for woodwork and metal work, a school hall and library, its own swimming pool, whose hard wall in a swirling blue-white, short-sighted haze I once head-butted, thus chipping a front tooth, with permanent dental consequences. Behind all these buildings were seemingly vast sports fields which backed onto Stoney Lane, a rural look-alike in contrast to glass and blue brick modernity, with the pond at one end, and the big houses in Stafford Road that ran alongside. There's a slight air of unreality when I think that 20 years before that time everything about the country was different. Compared to wartime England the low and high level glass novelty might have been dropped from outer space, and yet Dunkirk was closer in time to my going there than Margaret Thatcher's sway, so important and influential in shaping the society we now live in, is to us now. Mostly we don't notice being part of social and demographic forces: we immerse ourselves in days and their minutiae.

There's a difference between primary and secondary school and everyone feels it immediately. By the time you leave primary you're in the top year, one of the big boys or girls. An adult might not be able to tell the difference when faced with a playground full of darting similar shapes. A parent might notice that in the very same year group the variation in size between individual pupils is enormous, but may not appreciate what a difference it can make to the way someone carries themselves or thinks of themselves. If they tried though a parent might remember how small they felt when first going to the big school, and what a jolt to perception it is, that change, knowing you were previously significant, and now you can see all of what is above you and how far you have to go, and you don't feel significant at all. Even in your own body you can feel the pendulum swing between one state and another. Alongside some friend who was on the short side I could feel expansive with big shoulders. Next to someone else made to bigger specifications I could become small and cheeky, actually hearing the tone of my voice altering, my arms move differently. Or so it seemed. Later when I read reports of people who had knocked about with Bob Dylan in the very early days, when he was in London, they described how despite wearing the same clothes sometimes he seemed like a gnome, sometimes like husky working guy. I knew how that might feel from the inside.

For a while, being unduly influenced by the Billy Bunter books I had munched through, (and who these days would say that?), and the more modern and funny Jennings and Darbishire by Anthony Buckeridge, a better writer than Frank Richards though that wasn't a concern at the time, I had a vague feeling that secondary schools were like boarding schools, although I hadn't quite worked out where the going home part came into it. The other myth that spread like a virus was that all new pupils would be grabbed by older kids and be ritually humiliated in some way, perhaps involving heads and toilets. That didn't happen any more than staying overnight did. During that first autumn term, autumn always being just as much a beginning as spring for anyone involved in education, we were all finding out what it was like to be part of this big layout, which was quite like a campus, and did remind me of what I'd seen or read of American high schools. In the block where the assembly took place there was a wide stone staircase leading up to the balcony and library, the library where in the morning Catholics could have their own assembly. In the first weeks of being there I could walk under those stone steps and my hair just whisked against the underside of the step. It was odd but satisfying to feel such a close fit, but also to know that there was no more exacting measure that could be devised. Soon I wouldn't fit underneath, and standing alongside in times to come my height would show by how far my head had moved up the steps.

Other things that happened, or at least tiny fragments remembered, are connected with pop, the way most people of whatever generation seem to connect the dots of their lives. There was lunchtime playing of records in the assembly hall that autumn and I remember the strangeness and perfection of two in particular: Only The Lonely by Roy Orbison, and His Latest Flame by Elvis, although even the Shadows and Apache could sound transporting. The sound of records was more exciting then, being not simply the perception of something existing in the normal world, but more akin to lifting a veil to reveal another world adjoining this one, or contained within it in some way. If I hear them now, in totally different, innocuous and bland circumstances, there is still a resonance and a flavour, a texture, of just how odd and moving both of those records seemed to be. Elvis with his controlled, not wild, voice singing, "The uh way she war awks, the uh way she taw awks", and Orbison with his grand move up the register, "know why eye eye, I cry, only the lonely." But wait. There's something wrong with this memory. The records were released a year apart. I could have heard Roy Orbison in the autumn of 1960, but Elvis didn't appear until the August of 1961. And yet in my mind I have this unclear, distant but definite scene of them both being played. Perhaps I heard them both in the autumn of 1961, that would be possible from a chronological point of view, but then doesn't accord with the other element of my memory, which is that I think of it being heard, and taking extra meaning from, the context of it being in the first term, when it all seemed like a new world, and those records were part of the newness and strangeness, were in fact a proof of it. It feels like it happened. Most of my life I believed that it happened. What is the greater component of history: feeling or chronology? But hold on, wait again. Those words aren't from (Marie's The Name of) His Latest Flame at all. The way she walks, the way she talk, surely that's The Girl of My Best Friend, and if that is checked in the ubiquitous chronologies it was the right time, so my memory is correct, except it scrambles up the names of the songs. Calling things by their right name turns out to be the thing we must learn to do most, out in the adult world; although in that case I think the mix-up is forgivable, the tunes and his voice seeming to slide in and out of each other so readily, especially in the personal juke box that is situated inside everyone's head.

The other pleasing aspect of it now is that in those times when the Beatles were loutish lads in leather learning a trade in Hamburg and suburban cellars, these were the records that were at the poles of what they liked and wanted to sound like. As they were for Bob Dylan, and later he was actually in a band with Roy Orbison, long after Elvis had gone and a stricken Bob took to his room for a week, and by then an ex-Beatle was a band mate too. For us in the first couple of years, changing from little kids to less little kids, before Bob Dylan, before The Beatles, it was going to school and finding out what it was like to get along with people and want to be them, or be liked by them; to wear ridiculous green tweed jackets to dances and not know how terrible you looked until you saw someone else wearing the same, and the awful truth became apparent, and you realised how friends had lied to be kind; the alternation between school and home, with the interior privacy of reading and TV; on Thursdays knowing that the du duddle du doo dooo du music signalled Roger Moore as the Saint, long before he was judged to be inadequate, though popular and right for the times, as James Bond. In these ITC world-wide, revenue-gaining, episodes he could raise an eyebrow, smile, look devil-may-care, speak in his surprising deep posh voice lines like "One way or another Maurice, you're going to talk", and generally encourage the library tracking down of Saint books with their titles like a children's series, and colourful dust jacket illustrations, which encouraged the drawing of his little stick man figure on exercise books. He was part of the fabric of those days as much as pop music.

School was the place where people became what they were. At least if you were anything like the people that I knew. Later one could read about others who had made their mark in the world, the celebrity world, describing how school had done nothing for them, been nothing for them, and how they couldn't wait to get out and be in the real world, where life and work existed. I never knew that feeling and was never made unhappy or rebellious at school. It wasn't that I was a star pupil, it was everything to do with it being part of something that seemed like the right reality. Then of course there was the presence of girls at a time when everyone, boys and girls, but girls always earlier than boys, is being warped and transfused by hormonal infusions. The blend of sexual awareness and idealised fantasy image is experienced everyday, a pattern and prediction of perceptions for years to come. The crudity of one aspect of thinking about and referring to girls was in direct contrast to the effect their faces, or simply their existence in a room, could have. It was possible sometimes, trying perhaps to beam telepathic communication from the back of the classroom to the front, to believe that, though related, girls weren't necessarily part of the same species as males at all. Or it was easy to believe if you were a moony innocent who didn't have to share a house with a sister. One of Jim's friends, with a sister, was trying to explain this to someone once. He had the exasperated, incredulous look of someone who knows best. "People think you like each other like a girlfriend, like you're going out because you're in the same house. It's not like that. It's nothing like that" No doubt there were tougher nuts than me, but whatever their confidence or base desires they would have fallen in love with faces. Girls' faces, or, let's be honest, some girls' faces, seemed to signify something more than the normality all around, in the way pop music did. There was a gateway, or a signpost at least, to an order of existence which had nothing to do with knickers and fingers, was something other than furtive, squishy and sticky sexual objectivity, but like music too would always be connected to it. And at school all of it opens out and comes to you, letting you know that this is how it will be from now on: always the conjunction between physical, erotic desires and their expressions, (which seem to come from a part of you beyond conscious intention or control often); and the knowledge that the qualities of a person's face and character, the wider relationship between girls and boys, men and women, have to do with an inner identity that it may be pretentious to name, and which is not solely represented by the body but can't live anywhere else. We want there to be good girls and bad girls, and then find that we want them to be in one person. And then we find that these proportions and ratios work best if they can arrange themselves to match the shifting balances within us All of adult life is concerned with what you start to see at secondary school: how everything you can consider as real life, to do with work and intellect, the ordinary, has to find a way of co-existing with the other reality, the sexual imperative and a spiritual dimension, whose quality often seems to be to require a life outside of the one people must lead, with the daily obligations and the layered complication that each person is

That first autumn, Roy Orbison singing Only The Lonely, and the Lady Chatterley trial going on, and me finding my way from classroom to classroom across open spaces, and studying The Wind In The Willows in English lesson and having it pointed out why "and so declared itself to be a face" was good writing, and then back to Nelson House and across the quadrangle and round to the gate for home. All of it was around the same time Bob Dylan would have been familiarising himself with Dinkytown, Minneapolis and planning his escape to Madison and points east. I was part of an atmosphere, a culture, a social movement that built good houses for people who'd come through a war to rent from councils in suburbs outside of towns, and built good schools for their children to go to. All we had to do was use the advantages which had been placed in front of us. You don't know you're born, my dad used to remark when some new evidence of unappreciated fortune passed before me. He didn't sound too annoyed about it. I think it pleased him in some way to be superior about the real state of the world. The school and rock music and eventually Bob Dylan all became part of the same thing. In higher years I'd sit in our school library not working, reading Punch, which seemed the height of sophistication with its context thick with signs of a society that seemed to wait for us in the life we were preparing for, a world that apparently resembled Surrey between the Wars, and think about what I'd read about Paul McCartney teaching Gerry Marsden how to play a chord in their school library, and it made us connect.

So we thought about the life to come, and got on with the life we had. On afternoons when cross-country runs were on the sports activity list we would go out of the gate beyond the sports fields, down Stoney Lane and settle into a punishing shuffle a little faster than an amble, pounding and incompetently pounding, and then, because he lived so close Jim and I would cut away to his house, and spend a plausible amount of time there listening to records, drinking tea, eating toast, before setting off again to school and the end of the lesson. We had no interest in cheating to complete the course more quickly and arrived well down the numbers who had started out and already returned. This lack of intent and training did for us at the annual event when all of the boys had to take part in a more monitored race. We always came in the last 50 or so out of hundreds. But before that there was nothing nicer than being in Jim's living room, with its radiogram, dining table, shelves and mantelpiece with ornaments and photographs, listening to the Byrds single All I Really Want To Do, with its orange label and orange emblazoned paper bag sleeve. It was in Jim's living room that I got the sense of how different rooms can seem, can be, at different times, how much the time of day affects your perception of, as Bob put it around the same time, what's real and what is not.

I'd been there at night, with his family and sometimes with neighbours. The liveliness of it was not something I was used to.

There might be With The Beatles playing and a neighbour, a grown up, an adult, a working man, saying, "You've got to admit they've got something." This didn't happen in my house. Even having a gramophone made it seem almost American in its suburban plenty. And then there we were in the day time, everyone else at work or school, the daytime world and the whole atmosphere would be something else: the quiet and the furniture in the room occupying it as if glad of the solitude. This sounds unimpressive perhaps, or obvious, but it seemed to me then, and seems so now, that it's the centrality of what the past and history mean. How the places we know aren't always the same place. How they change because their circumstances do, and how our reactions and feelings about these things arranges the world for us, makes us believe what we think it is. If I think about me and Jim listening to the Byrds, or looking at his brother's collection of Shadows LPs, (a couple of years difference in age being all that was needed for micro-generational shifts in taste, and by then the Shads, despite flourishing, seemed of an earlier time) the gap between the fact of when it happened and now, when I'm looking back to something that exists only in my mind, is no further away really, no matter how much time has elapsed, than me being there at the time and remembering just the previous week when the room was thronging and people came in and out with drinks and there was music and conversation. LPs too, with their glossy photographs and the glowing black grooves with a hint of rainbow shine, always mysterious and appealing, are themselves, like the songs they transmitted, treasure trove evidence of history unearthed and carried down to us. It's all gone, vanished, and the only proof is the evidence of consciousness.

And when I hear the Byrds playing All I Really Want To Do these days, because I choose to, or through the happy fluke of someone's radio playlist, it can have many associations, some to do with Bob Dylan, and some to do with the group, but mostly to do with that year when Jim and I took a little time off from being good boys, and cut through to his street near the canal and a couple of bridges we knew, near the big green playing area where a couple of years previously I had heard one of the boys who lived near him singing the B side of She Loves You called I'll Get You (the one that starts, Imagine I'm in love with you, years before Imagine, or Yoko Ono) and believed because of it, with no other proof, such seeking out of almost-hidden gems was endemic in that neighbourhood, unlike mine. From that green we could look out to more trees and fields and Pelsall in the distance, and over to the right the canal bent to the bridge by the tree I fell out of in the Barley Mow field where Aunt May and my mother bought me Vimto and Smith's crisps. And I recall, as I do now, when Jim and I had tea and toast as the sun shone, then made our way back to school, pounding and pounding with a goal and home time in mind.

Still 1965 in all around I see, something that in various ways will remain the case. I rode a bike and ate Fry's Chocolate Cream, the dark chocolate such a contrast to the white, aromatic, soft but stiffened filling. I could eat just one piece a day, snapping it off along the indentation, and make the bar last, discovering the pleasure of conserving happiness. An album appeared. A tour happened. And then, weeks later, another album appeared. Things seemed to happen faster then, presumably because of the age we were; the way we perceived and experienced the world made it a different world. Except in this case the facts tell the same story. Bringing It All Back Home: recorded in January 1965 released in March. The tour took place in May. He returned to America and wrote, amongst others, Like A Rolling Stone, writing and recording songs from June through July into the beginning of August, and still finding time to play the Newport Folk Festival and preview what was to become the signature song for him and the time, along with an electric band sound. Then at the end of August the album Highway 61 Revisited is released, whose cover picture with its gaudy purple shirt and motorbike emblazoned T-shirt was as contemporary as tomorrow's newspaper, and had been taken on some palatial steps in the Newport environs.

Two albums in less than six months – four months, faster than the Beatles could manage and they were no slouches in the work rate department, and it wasn't the days of two hits and forgettable makeweight filler albums either. Hardly had your bedroom got used to you poring over the minutiae of one album sleeve while listening over and over to what it contained, when a fresh candidate appeared. Highway 61 Revisited is a step up from its immediate predecessor in its sound and coherence. Bringing It All Back Home divides deliberately into its two sides: long, long acoustic songs on one, and the first side with its band that has a flimsy, almost amateur quality. Nothing on Highway 61 Revisited sounds like that. All is focused and defined in the way the words and the music connect. It's a real sound and one not heard before. What we didn't appreciate then is how what he was doing fitted into and also disrupted an historical process, both in actuality and symbolically. But then we were alive and lost in details and moments.

Even though we'd come into the Bob Dylan fold via Freewheelin' and had heard his next album, his most overt and intentionally political collection, the position he occupied in the American folk scene couldn't have the same meaning for us, where folk had different shades of meaning. What you might call his symbolic meaning had more layers, and was intense with more resonances, than an innocent like me was going to get. For us he was part of a scene that had as its context music, and that music was part of youth. Naturally this meant there were intrinsic oppositional sympathies against what might be thought of as the status quo, or the adult world, but in broad, rather than programmatic, party political action terms (though many went that route too). It was more in the way any school child knows that the world they experience at school is never the world parents are going to know about, no matter how much they may be told about homework, prizes or detentions. Home is one world and school is more like a secret society in some of its aspects. So the music, and all it represented, and what we understood by it, bent and shaped itself around us as an atmosphere does about a planet. I didn't realise it then but this related to the way I had seen that writing created a parallel world. Life required you to do various things, but left you space for enjoyment, and experiencing music was one of the things you made space for. Music offered access to another world too, but one that suggested, unlike writing, it was also actuality because you heard it in this world. Later you see that, silly or overblown and mystical though it may sound, being transported by music and songs also takes place in a different world. There's an interior dimension that exists, overlapping and alongside the one that need you to attend school or work. It allies to the romantic and idealistic, and so includes a wider sense of politics. This imaginative world is probably felt most intensely as a teenager, and why we believe in it so strongly then, and why it persists. The song world is always closer to a dream, and in those years Bob Dylan was part of a dream and a biosphere among whose elements were pop and rock and folk.

In America he was seen, and apparently not long before had seen himself too, as part of folk music, and that music was allied to, broadly, causes on the Left. It drew from collections gathered by social anthropologists, or ethnomusicologists, or simply collectors of old blues records, but it connected to the past and was on the side of the People. The People were folk, and they included the poor, the oppressed, the disadvantaged and the dispossessed, and folk music, so-called, didn't have to be necessarily cowboy songs, or English murder ballads transplanted to the Appalachians, but it did have to give a voice to a communal spirit. It did have to offer a chance for people to come together and express their humanity in song, and through the act of singing together. The point about folk music, and all the collectors who found and transcribed tunes and words as if they were an intangible, somewhat ghostly archaeological object that had survived to be with us, – like fossils or coins, but their burnishing and restoring would take place when they came alive again in the mouths of people, – was that the songs allowed us an insight into an earlier society, and yet one that wouldn't differ in essentials from our own. The songs demonstrate the strange relationship between memory and the past and what is happening right now. Pete Seeger and his confreres in the Almanac Singers and the Weavers took it for granted that a song from 300 years ago could still apply to any appropriate human situation as if it were as fresh as the day's headlines. And they believed too that the singing of these songs by a mass of people reinforced and made clear how a song could help in understanding emotion or a specific situation. Further, the joining together of people in song – the act of singing with a lot of other people – in itself helped them better to see the stratification of society, all the us and thems that there are, and the kinds of conflict that arise between interest groups, an introduction to what kinds of interest groups exist, and thus what sides there might be, and which of them you could be on. Actually what Pete Seeger believed then, and just as much now, is that singing, especially when a big crowd of people sings together, assists you to become a better human being. Part of this is in not believing performers to be worth more than the audience, but anyone who has been in an audience knows that the act of witnessing a performer creates the desire to prize them slightly more than oneself, even if in other circumstances the performer is part of your normal life. Just as at children's performances you will look at the ones who can sing or play well a little differently, and be impressed. You look at performers and you look at the audience, and you see a distinction, and in the audience you feel the multiplication of a dressing table's facing mirrors. All the people like you stare back. I is another, except it's hard to keep that in mind in Wembley Arena or IKEA check outs. We want performers to be better than us in various ways, something that people wanted from Bob Dylan early on.

Young as he was Bob Dylan seemed so thoroughly grounded in English and American folk sources, in blues, and then most specifically in Woody Guthrie, both as a maker of songs and a model for behaviour, that of course he was seen as a new embodiment of a type and a spirit that had existed 20 years or so before he hit NYC, as Guthrie had before him. And coming to the big city out of the American heartland, making your way in the arts and representing something deemed more real, in a way non-logical but very power-fully felt, was also part of a tradition in various cultural genres. 1965 was the year that narrative changed into something else for him. Murray Lerner's film, The Other Side of The Mirror neatly encloses this period of time when I was first aware of Bob Dylan, though more or less unaware of the Newport Folk Festival, like a story of my life with me left out of it. It reveals, as a rapid motion film of a flower bud coming into blossom, flourishing and then falling, a process at work, more slowly, in real time, but, given the short span involved, fast enough. Processes are always coming to an end. Lerner's film ends with the 1965 Newport Festival and Bob's brief, but inadvertently cataclysmic, performance with members of Paul Butterfield's Blues Band; and then his encore on an acoustic guitar, singing (was it to make a point or gathered by coincidence?) It's All Over Now Baby Blue. During these end days I played Highway 61 Revisited and read the sleeve notes and knew that this was an order of hipness not hav-ing much connection with the world I'd assumed was represented by The Times They Are A-Changin'. My friend Jim listening to the actual track Highway 61 Revisited, to the sound that could conceiv-ably be a slide guitar or a whistle, and on some individualistic sleeve credits is billed as Police Car, said, "This isn't folk music." Of course it is, I replied. Why would I do that? The only explanation is that I believed, or wanted, folk music to be the good thing and Bob Dylan to be part of it. Jim was just listening and noticing what it sounded like. It didn't sound like any other Bob Dylan album so far, that much was clear, not even its immediate predecessor.

There was a mixture of styles and moods. All the songs were written by him, but what was most notable was the band. How could it be folk, even if that had a definition become so elastic as to mean anyone who played an acoustic guitar and sang songs they had written, rather than ancient songs that everyone had written, and then performing this self-written material with varying degrees of earnest or wet sincerity. What Bob Dylan seemed to be engaged in was a genre called Bob Dylan albums. He was, as he'd written in his previous sleeve notes, sketching us a picture of what went on around here. The songs were not political in the way that Only A Pawn In Their Game was, or Times They Are A-Changin' itself, but they demonstrated someone with an eye for society's absurdities. Another difference was that instead of being rooted in the perception of someone who wished they had been a hobo, they had the tone and deadpan skewering of the scene's elements to be found in Andy Warhol. The hobo had gone up in the world. The songs were full of characters with strange cartoon names, – Mack The Finger, Louie The King, Dr. Filth, Saint Annie, – and so was the back of the album, the prose in its twisted syntax and ampersand addiction now nothing like the Hootenanny poems, and also, we discovered later, existing in two versions with very slight word changes. In both of them he seemed to be saying that his autobiographical impulse wasn't enough, that weirdness and illogic had to be shown by letting his audience see the kind of people who were out there.

It was as if the carnival world that Bob Dylan claimed to have been part of when he was first giving interviews in New York, the distorted mirror world that seemed so attractive to the imagination of someone enclosed in the experiences of suburban safeness, a small town resident always a ride away from big city excitement, now existed at large. His work, his profession that he'd plotted and stumbled into, this acclaim and celebrity and travel let him see it, confirming what he knew inside already. This surreal and absurd take wasn't a folksinger's one, and neither was the music. His voice was the same, but the context seemed to alter it, and in any case gave it a chance to express greater variation of tone. How fantastic that in a few months he could have on the charts The Times They Are A-Changin', entirely within a folk mode of guitar, voice, harmonica and anthem tune, whose delivery, while wholly personal, also obviously wanted to be the representation of a crowd it was assuming would feel the same; and then Subterranean Homesick Blues, pinning down aspects of surrounding society in a rapid-fire rock rhyme which has its impressive points but is finally unsatisfactory as a rock sound because it is rushed and ramshackle, inadequate to the task; then reaching Like A Rolling Stone, a breakthrough to something new for him and all of us, where an imperfect perfection is reached not by design but because of elements collaborated upon and improvised, not arranged but arrived at, and not sounding the same kind of ramshackle at all, encoding and blazoning forth all the strength and powers and changes he now stood for. But what was that? To reviewers of all capacities it still seemed to be connected to a character who had essentially a political purpose summed up in the more or less meaningless word, protest. To those of us who experienced Like A Rolling Stone it was more difficult to say what we were getting from it, except the concrete immediacy of the sound of it and his voice, and wanting to be connected to it, wanting perhaps to have some of the fearlessness that was plain in that old and young voice that had had the nerve to import into pop and rock the rough-edged tones of the amateurs who did sing folk and traditional songs. We heard the beat of the drum, the tumbling and interweaving of the piano and organ lines, the shrill interjections of the harmonica which sound so out balanced by the rest of the band, and then sound like a symbol of Dylan's stubbornness in standing there and being exactly himself. Could we do that, be brave enough to be exactly who we were and wanted to be?

The quiet of the concert halls around Bob Dylan experienced by me in the May of the year was banished by Like A Rolling Stone. So much has been written about it since, whole books on what it meant, what it signified, how it is both mysteriously and paradoxically a two-way mirror and a rune stone that foretells the past as well as the future. It acts as a prism to refract theories that people raise and cherish. At the time it was also a record that took its place amongst all the other everyday riches that happenstance allowed us to hear in the radio world in the summer of August and the late summer of September 1965. The times sounded like what was in the air: See My Friends, Help, Satisfaction, Make It Easy On Yourself, but also Tears by Ken Dodd. Guitars and fragments of melody and a 1920s song sung completely straight by a comedian, without a wink or irony, and it stayed at number one for weeks, all in the same time and place. Tears let the past inhabit the present. Had it been given a more grandiose arrangement, and treatment from a deeper, more idiosyncratic singer, then it would be a slightly distorted version of the Walker Brothers emotional terrain. As it was it acted like a reminder that an older England poked through the pop colour of 1965, the way a horse and cart still made their way down the street. What did shift was the sense that Bob Dylan came from one world but was now in another. Young people were still concerned about civil rights, politics, peace, but somehow it seemed that this could be now be as well expressed through clothes, pleasure and listening to music. Enjoying yourself was enough to start putting the world to rights. Folk seemed to have a root in an educative process. Rock grew up into the hedonistic skies.

CHAPTER ELEVEN
YOU BETTER MOVE ON

What we took from all of this was the paradox that had been there from the beginning: we wanted him to be a better, more perceptive analyst of what was happening all around us, and to put it down in words more effective than we could manage. But we also wanted him to be saying something personal too and of himself. Like the best writing it was to be of its most universal import when detailing a specific personal experience. He understood that too. The next year in an interview he spoke contemptuously of all his concert goers waiting for him to turn them on like lamps. I listened in my bedroom, and sometimes Jim and I listened in my bedroom, and we didn't realise that his teenage experience would have been similar to ours, that he too had listened to music in his bedroom with his friends, and been moved to see another world. Of course we also entirely lacked his ambition and drive and desire to succeed and make it in music. But we did share, without necessarily knowing it, the experience of politics filtered, mediated and constructed by the kind of life we led, and the place where we led it. Bob Dylan had moved from writing songs with political concerns in a specific sense, to songs that dealt with the carnival of the senses, while recognising that carnivals as much as any other aspect of everyday life are the result of political considerations.

What we knew about politics could probably have been written on one page of a school exercise book. There was Labour and there was Conservative, and despite my Dad taking the Daily Express we were Labour. This didn't mean in any detailed, doctrinal way, or that we joined anything or went to meetings. It was simply assumed that the kind of people we were would be best represented by Labour because they were about the working man, the people, the poor, there to speak up for our little, particular and easily ignored interests. In this we were taking the same vague but heartfelt attitude, religious in impulse really, that people took to folk music, and had since the 1930s in America. What complicates matters is that given that this was our view, and with the kind of area and businesses that Walsall consisted of, one would assume that all of it was a solid Labour constituency. This was so after the war when the changed mood of the country gave Labour its momentum everywhere, and the National Liberal was ousted. But Walsall was big enough to be divided up into two Parliamentary constituencies in 1955, and though Walsall North, into which area we came, did return the same post-War Labour MP, Walsall South elected the most marvellously Conservative-sounding MP one could invent: Sir Henry D'Avigdor Goldsmith, and he was there for the next 19 years representing Walsall proper with his bullion and gold market expertise, while out there on the leafy outskirts we wondered how that could be so, yet never really knowing what either of them did, or even in my case, that they had to represent you whether you agreed with their politics or not.

The other thing we knew was that in 1964 there was a chance to witness a big change in British politics because of the General Election. At school we got caught up and excited by this possibility, believing in the phrases and publicity so derided and ridiculed by columnists and satirists. That was all part of what we thought politics was too. Having been banned from Maverick I later, not much later really, graduated to being allowed to see That Was The Week That Was, whose theme song words I'd been reminded of by John Lennon's flower monocle, and its successor, Not So Much A Programme, and it felt like a privilege. The late nightness and spontaneous, rough-edged nature of them; the combination of mockery with knowing what was *really* going on, was tremendously appealing. It did seem to be part of some bigger atmosphere, connected to pop too, and youth, so while you made fun you also wanted things to be right and fair and just. Obviously what we thought was right had to be so. I recall too when the Sun, which was not the paper now called the Sun, was first published, that same year, I half-believed and wanted to believe its launch slogan: A Paper Born Of The Age We Live In, and dutifully bought a copy in order to take part in my own life. I can't say that this connected at that stage to Bob Dylan, but it did connect to the Beatles, and not long afterwards it all began to merge. The white heat of technology, another tag line ad-copy phrase, didn't sound so silly if you thought that the world could be like that, and that you could be part of it, because after all you were growing into it. You would automatically be part of change. Coming after the scandals and exposes of the previous year it seemed that it was only right and inevitable that the Conservatives would go and that Harold Wilson would take over.

On the night of the election Jim came to watch the results special at our house. Both his Mom and Dad went to work so they didn't want to stay up late, or have him stay up late because it would disturb the household. My parents didn't have to go to work and were quite happy for him to come around. My dad always called Jim Jimmy, even after he was, in our terms, grown up. There's something about a name making you who you are that this demonstrated to me, the identities inherent in the change. There's a sound and a swing to Jimmy, something young, something cheeky, whereas Jim already sounds dependable and approaching middle-age. So Jimmy came to us and we watched it and saw that the requisite swing was taking place, but it was going to be a close run thing. As it turned out it was as close a run thing as an election could be and still be workable, the kind of a victory that isn't really but yielded the tiny majority that allowed a new Government to form. And because there was only my bed to sleep in, when we had come to the point when it was late enough, which I'm sure wouldn't have been really late at all, we went to my bed as innocent and friendly as Laurel and Hardy, excited still by feeling that we were not only witnesses but participants in a national event that was going to have significance for us and everybody else. Then we went to sleep as if we were in a tent, camping out for democratic change. It didn't occur to us, we didn't really know, that the whole shape and momentum of our lives was because of the 1944 Education Act, by Conservative politician R. A. Butler, and that aside from the great post-War Labour gift of the National Health Service, we had inhabited a Conservative world. We weren't grateful. We thought we had taken part in vanquishing it by watching the results and wishing for it to come about. It's not possible to have that belief ever again, because even when a huge change that you want does actually take place you know that it will end in tears and let downs of various kinds. 1997 comes to mind, and never leaves it. One residual element from then though is that I always do vote. To do otherwise would be to insult in some obscure, but genuine, way what I loved about my father, and whatever values I absorbed from him. I never think voting doesn't matter, though I have wondered, more than ever of late, whether it makes any difference which party gets elected, given the hermetic, confrontational world of party politics and its apparently detached position from the intricate, detailed capability government requires. But then hope needs things to be simple and dramatic, and we were young and hopeful. Disillusion and discouragement are the old folks diet.

One political event where we were definitely witnesses and not participants – along with most of the world, including politicians, statesmen, and world leaders – was the Cuban missile crisis in those October weeks of 1962. That has been so much written about and dramatised, and has such large importance, that trying to recall what a schoolboy, a child, felt, experienced or perceived then might seem beside the point. Nevertheless, it happened while I was alive and paying a kind of attention. I read about it in, of course, the Daily

Express, with its photographs and diagrams, and I saw it on television news, with its footage of ships on blockading seas, and President Kennedy managing to still look boyish and determined. Kennedy was an emblematic figure. He had become President in the autumn we had all gone to high school and I felt as I did later with our 1964 General Election that something about him connected to us, and that we were part of whatever might be good about him, and he did seem an symbol and a promise of good things about to begin just as we were beginning the big school. There were three things that happened around that week in my first November there: Kennedy was elected; Lady Chatterley's Lover was published; and in some kind of break-time messing around I was thrown or pulled completely over the shoulder of a class mate who was at least six inches shorter than me, perhaps more. I was shocked, surprised at how this had suddenly happened, wondering how I had got from there to here, a re-run of the tree sensation, feeling too that mixture of unfairness and implacable "this is where you are" quality. It was an emotion and a sensation I came across more frequently later in life, most especially when an argument, or a row, seems to be underway, and you are part of it, and you have no real idea why it's happening, having no appetite or righteous anger for it, and no logical reason to offer as to why you said the thing that seemed to precipitate the whole mess, but knowing, indisputably, that you did. I concede too that not all of these ancient pictures have equal importance politically or otherwise, but when I remember them they do, and somehow I think they offer me a clue as to the way things work.

I can't remember if I really believed the world was going to end. I don't think I did, though I could have been drawn up into the excitement of speculating if it might be so. The world and our lives can always be changed at any moment, for ever and for the worse. Accidents of every predictable and unpredictable kind can rob us of parents, children, limbs or the ability to move. There is any number of malign, impersonal forces out there to render merciless, personal effect. We all know this is so, but few of us truly believe it will happen this moment, or tomorrow, not to us, to someone we know perhaps, but no closer. So although I was as aware as anyone else of why this was a major crisis I probably didn't think we would all be involved in retaliatory and counter-retaliatory attack leaving the globe a radioactive cinder. Who knows for sure? We can try to remember, but we can't actually recreate, the person we used to be. That too has become one of the lessons Bob Dylan seems, involuntarily, to have been teaching us. In a sense it doesn't matter whether I did or didn't: that was the atmosphere of the time that surrounded me. It's also true that the scale of our own lives, at that age or perhaps any age, is bigger than a global perspective. So the prospect of double maths the next day, or a lost homework book, can hang over one more than the fear that a rocket that will precipitate a nuclear knockabout is about to be unleashed. Of course memoirs and history always run the risk of bathos with their combination of events of high importance existing in tandem with the domestic and the banal, but we all live in daily life. Great banks collapse and take thousands of jobs with them. We shake our heads and then go to do the weekly shop. We have to experience life in the order it happens, but we remember it in accordance with a logic we don't necessarily identify, and assign importance to events we hardly knew we remembered. Some things don't feel as if you are remembering them; it's more meaningful to say they've always been at rest in your head. You remind yourself that you never forgot them.

So for some people the missile crisis confirmed all their worst predictions about what a balance of peace dependent on mutually assured destruction meant. But even for those people the question they had to face was the same as all of us who might have regarded ourselves as mere witnesses, the same onlookers who watch economies fall. What could we do about it? One felt the same powerlessness and the need to believe in charmed lives when news of Chernobyl was broadcast. We looked up at the April skies and wondered if, as we looked up to the clouds that seemed the same as ever, invisible poison, whose effects wouldn't be realised for years, was already seeping into us. The people who seemed to have the power in 1962 were the various political cadres and factions in the respective West and East empires headed by Kennedy and Khrushchev. And the way they faced each other was like an enactment of scenes from all the Westerns that had entertained us from John Wayne films down through the TV shows of the 1950s. Kennedy was being a James Stewart figure standing up to the saloon bully in the black hat, and he wasn't going to back down even if he was softly spoken. But would he take us all down with him or would it work out?

The past folds into the present. You have to start from where you are, but where you are is shaped by what persists. This crisis was exactly what the peace movement from 1958 onwards had feared. The social mix and milieu that seemed to provide the impetus for that movement called beatnik, which seemed to mean young and scruffy, though of course CND always had a high proportion of older and respectable people from the Church and Academia. The bearded duffle-coat wearers and their long-haired girlfriends marching in sensible or suede shoes on their way out of London, through the outer suburbs on their way to Berkshire's Aldermaston, the Mordor representing Britain's nuclear capability, existed in real and cartoon versions, and didn't have much to do with Ferlinghetti or San Francisco, and certainly not with Kookie Byrnes. And though it seemed unlikely at the time, given that a lot of marching took place to trad jazz, an earlier music for outraging parents and older people, there was a cross-pollination with the idealism of American folk music, as represented by Pete Seeger. Hence the emergence eventually of Donovan and his heroes, the acoustic scene where folk and jazz intermingled, and everyone was on the side of the desolation angels that graced terrible flats and cliquey coffee bars. Were people really living their lives as if annihilation was imminent? That kind of pleasure-grabbing hedonism I associate more with real war than Cold

War, and even so I doubt that my parents had ever behaved like characters in Elizabeth Bowen or Julian Maclaren-Ross. Still, young and
old people had really cared and were prepared to put themselves out,
trying to make a difference. Simultaneously, whatever good-hearted
people think, politics operates at a complicated remove and with its
own impervious, imperious power.

In any event a change occurred because of the hard-nosed realpo-
litik practised by Kennedy and Khrushchev. Russia was faced down.
We didn't all go up in smoke. Sincere good-hearted people were side-
lined, and whatever their feelings and actions had found they had to
be dependent on John Wayne, someone tough enough to show the
bad guy that he couldn't get away with it this time. Everything was
goin to be all right. As is the way with political events, sequences of
facts and chronologies of the attitudes of participants don't become
known until much later, sometimes decades later, and despite the
public world-wide nature of the crisis we didn't know how near it was
to everything being all wrong. The discharge of nuclear warheads
on both sides depended on the individual reactions of military com-
manders some way from the Kremlin or the White House. The leaders were involved in horse-trading, saving face, and trying to reconcile
opposing views within the various offices of state and armed forces
that were all involved. Nevertheless what seemed to come out of it
was a sense that they did want to avoid nuclear strike, and therefore
that was possible, as indeed had proved to be the case, and so we were
all safer than we had been. Involvement and fatalism, the tincture of
youth. We all breathed a sigh of relief and that was our part in the
crisis of the age complete. Meanwhile, deploying all the resources of
folk, politics and literature, Bob Dylan had encapsulated the whole
terrifying scenario by writing A Hard Rain's A Gonna Fall.

Or at least that's the version everyone accepts now, and it's one
promulgated by Dylan himself, who has described it at different
times as being written during the October blockade crisis, banged
out on a typewriter in the basement of the Village Gate club where

his friend Chip Monck lived. Every line in it could be the start of a whole song, he has said, and he was trying to capture the feeling of terror and nothingness. This version of events is summarised too on the sleeve of Freewheelin', the album that includes the song, and the album where his character as the Village savant was established, politics and protest and youth and folk fused into his person and persona. As such it's a demonstration of the way versions of Dylan circulate and accumulate, some he too wants to believe, and some he must resent. The facts gathered by easily derided, (often by me) but valuable, set list writers and their assiduous doggedness, show however that he sang Hard Rain twice in the second half of *September*: once at a Sing Out organised concert, and once at The Gaslight Café. September was a month before the crisis developed, before even the US spy plane had noticed what proved to be Russian missile sites being built in Cuba. So what did he write it about given that it couldn't have been written as a real-time reaction to the October crisis? Impossible to say for sure, but what seems likely is there was a combination of feelings, some of which were to do with that constant background to everyday life summarised in the words "The Bomb". He had written Let Me Die In My Footsteps earlier in the year in response to the underground bomb shelter fad, seeming genuinely to find it repugnant and immoral. And he'd written, also earlier that year, the more comic and juvenile poem Go Away You Bomb in Izzy Young's notebook in the Folklore Center. So the subject was pervasive in his circle, and everyone else's, before the specifics of the Cuban aspect. But what seems possible as the source of facing nothingness is the loneliness of the separation from Suze Rotolo, who had gone to Italy in the June of the year, and therefore the end and the ending he experienced was closer to home than the fear of a nuclear strike. He's been obsessed with endings ever since. Despite saying that he had written the song because of the blockade he was also firm in saying that the hard rain was not atomic rain, "It isn't that at all." When you say a hard rain what do you mean, he was asked by Studs

Terkel in a radio broadcast. "I mean just some sort of end, that's just gotta to happen y'know." The kind, perhaps, when couples break up and a consciousness faces the empty day stretching ahead. After he'd performed the song though, and during the initial crisis caused by the President's announcement, he did write to Suze, still in Italy, to tell her that he'd stayed up all night in the Figaro Café with everyone, all thinking that this might be the end of the world.

When the legend become facts, print the legend, is the tag of the Western The Man Who Shot Liberty Valance, released the previous year to Hard Rain's A Gonna Fall, and that has operated around Bob Dylan in one way or another since the beginning. The past folds into the present and helps obscure it. The importance of Hard Rain was not that its subject matter could have been the threat of nuclear annihilation, but that in writing it Bob Dylan had distanced himself from anyone else who seemed to be in the same game of topical or protest songs, by the nature of the language that he used, and the way he sang it. Despite adapting the refrain of the traditional song Lord Randall, the character of the words is more closely allied with the poetry then modern, a vast litany of images to evoke a state of mind. Answering the questions asked in the traditional ballad, they recount where someone has been, what they saw, heard, and what they intend to do, all of it worked symbolically and by association in words that are rich as language and as pictures, pictures whose meaning can't be pinned down precisely, but all of which summon a shifting response to a situation that is emotionally real, but fantastical, one that more closely resembles a dream in fact.

There's a sense in which all songs occupy us as dreams do, but here the comparison is closer. The images aren't explained, merely presented, as the events in dreams are. The song ends and we are left, as we are when we wake up, to try to work out what it means, how it relates to everyday life. In writing it Dylan had moved beyond the simplicities of his mentor Woody Guthrie, and used more of the method of Beat poets, while still linking to folk music with the refrain. Even here however he had adapted the Lord Randall line from "Lord Randall my son", and the chorus's "handsome young man," or "bonny young man" and blended them into blue-eyed son, evoking the fondness of the favoured blue-eyed boy. Dylan has blue eyes. This careful and detailed re-working was something that became a stock in trade, and his characteristic way of approaching writing, no matter how original he seemed to be. With this song too he seemed to expand what songwriting meant. This had little to do with hit parade manufacturers, or Broadway tunesmiths. It didn't exist as a song to be sung by anyone else, which hasn't stopped it being sung by others, but not then. At the same time it was light years away from what was understood by protest songs, the banalities and one-dimensional obviousness that decried one view and championed another. More importantly it floated free of its immediate circumstance, and what people hailed as its subject. When I listened to it, albeit on that brief timeshare basis, a couple of years later, what struck me was the sound of his voice, and an imagination that could conjure ten thousand talkers whose tongues were all broken, the rhythm of the words and the texture of his voice. The Cuban missile crisis didn't enter my mind.

CHAPTER TWELVE
NOT A SECOND TIME

And what happened next, and what happened next, is the question narrative wants to prompt, is required to engender. And because of biographies we can easily believe that lives can have the same structure and chapter endings, not appreciating how much work is required to make it appear so. Often though, in life, while we may plan for a future, and have an idea what we would like to happen next, the space where we are looks very much like what was there before us. The past continues, barely in disguise. Aside from the lucky accident and eternal blessing of experiencing the Sixties in the order they happened, much of those 1960s could as easily have still been the 1950s of my childhood, or skipping out the war there were elements too of the 1930s, or earlier. Remnants of folk customs survived. Each New Year I went out the back door and in through the front with a piece of coal and a sixpence. We were strangers to carpets, the floors being layered with lino, scratchily softened in places with squares of coconut matting. The kitchen drawer where tools were kept only had about 5 items, including the mashed-down, boiler chipping chisel. For a long time we had the kind of irons actually made of iron, their smooth triangle sides placed directly on a gas jet to heat up, and then the hot handle held with a rag. You would test how hot it was in the traditional way, holding the triangle up towards your face, dropping a tiny amount of spittle onto it, and watching the ball fizz and roll off the dark glossy surface. This is never quite as satisfying with electric irons, although everything else is. We also had the black cast-iron cobbler's last that looks like a conceptual sculptor's 3-D attempt at the Isle of Man symbol. These differently sized shoe shapes were sometimes clothed with a shoe upside down, and then a hammer and a nail were brought into play, or glue and a stick-on sole. That too lived in the tools drawer. Both of these hardcore manufacturing items, though not admittedly the exact same ones, are still in daily use as door stops, ideal unless one is careless in bare feet.

Washing machines, that staple indicator of the consumer, convenience, modern society didn't enter our life until quite late on, and even then it was a machine that would look like an inadequate workshop prototype for today's technological marvels. Twin tubs were still to come in and be supplanted as the acme of washing desirability. For all of the Fifties and on into the Sixties we had a tub into which hot water and soap powder were poured, (the hot water having to be heated elsewhere) the kind of grey metal washtub that looks like a grooved barrel. The clothes were agitated and pummelled with a posher, a broom handle with a bell-shaped metal end, copper, punctuated with holes around its rim and elsewhere to let the water through. This also made a convenient pretend steering wheel on non-washing days, which, also in the old style, were usually not Monday. And when the tub of clothes had been sufficiently poshed and rinsed and re-poshed, they were fed through the mangle, which was a proper metal heavy mangle, its hard rubber cylinders set far enough apart to let the right amount of folded clothes through, and close enough to squeeze the water out, although usually the operation was done at least twice for each lot. That could be surprisingly hard work. So the past, the Thirties and the War, was alive and well and my mother and father handed it on to me. Not so surprising, that's when they, older than my contemporaries' parents, had been young adults after all, where they had learned to act as people, to bring up and love a child. As they did.

Two doors down from us there was the Lawton family with two children, both older than me by enough to make it seem that I was a child and they weren't for quite a while. Jean went to the best girls' grammar school in town, the one Meera Syal later attended. Jean became a bus conductress. It's hard to say if this was what hindsight might label Sixties rebellion or Fifties conformity. When I saw her sometimes in her uniform that seemed too tight she appeared happy and defiant, knowing that people thought it a tremendous waste. "Buses," my Dad said, "they're right pairing pens," referring to the way relationships blossomed between drivers and conductresses, although in fact it seems true of any workplace. It would have been appropriate symbolism for the Lawtons because they kept pigeons and chickens in home-made wire runs and an odd-looking loft that our huge back gardens gave them plenty of space for. No-one did much gardening in those big spaces, and other people kept chickens and pigeons, but not I think at the same time, and only two doors down from us. A sound I associate with their pigeons is their feed, the dry, crowded rattle of corn in the tin it was kept in. This was the tall, white tin of National Dried Milk with its dark blue label, the one that had begun in the war, and then nourished babies like me in the austere times of the decade following the war, the same kind of tin we too had on a kitchen shelf above the tool drawer, doing something useful with storage long after its original use. So there was the sound of the shaking granules, and the comforting sound too of Mr Lawton clucking and saying, "Come on then, come on," trying to attract the tiny swirl of birds back to the coop. The same tin I think was used to scatter the feed for the chickens.

I've no idea why they had these birds. It's possible the hens laid and the eggs were useful. They never sold or gave any to us. Some people raced pigeons but I don't recall that being the case with the Lawton's birds. I know from seeing them, and what I must have been told, that there were two types of pigeons, at least. Some flew around, not excessively high, fluttering in circuits and then being coaxed back by the rain rattle of the corn tin, and the soothing mouth noises. Others flew almost out of sight, and then fell as if shot, only to recover, fly again and fall once more, rolling in a flurry of wings. There were tipplers and tumblers apparently, and the tumblers were the most exciting to watch, soaring and mock dying over the gardens and the bit of sky I thought of as ours as much as the garden segments all joined together that I could see from my bedroom window. I learned later that tipplers were ones that were bred for endurance and long distance flight. As this didn't seem to be a Lawton hobby it's most likely that all of his pigeons were tumblers and some were less keen on tumbling than others. Whatever the reason for keeping them it would have kept people occupied at the very least, given them a work load to get through. There's an awful lot of feeding and cleaning out to be done when there are chickens and pigeons in the vicinity.

The decades are named and then history books assign them characteristics, and soon whole tracts of time can be summarised by a roster of familiar images or a roll call of slogans. PowerPoint history. And in the years that weren't then called the early 1960s there were wartime and post-war tins in the gardens with pigeons and chickens, gardens that might, were it not for their size, still be in the 1930s. And Vernon Lawton, Jean's brother, older than Jean and so seniority layers above me, whose schooling is a mystery but didn't involve the best grammar school in town, whose whole persona and impact is entirely 1950s in the pictures of him that remain in my mind. Vernon, Vernie, not too tall, with the back of his collar turned up against his neck, but the points down as normal, his not-plentiful-enough hair greased up to a quiff, and the nape hair in what Americans called a ducktail or Tony Curtis; and his notice-me walk. Examples of it, or, more accurately, distant descendants of it, can be seen still, but then there are so many funny walks these days. His was more associated with Teddy Boys, though not exclusive to them, and involved a bantam cock holding of the head, an implied but not necessarily overt swagger, and the knees seeming to flick out sideways. His walking was always a saunter with a mechanistic aspect to it. All of these elements were in the service of saying, "Get a load of me", and must have been exhausting to remember to do.

I don't know what Vernie ever did for a living, and it's melancholy to acknowledge that there's no-one now to ask. I wonder who is alive that he might cross the mind of as he does mine. I do know that later when I read about the Deep South, or the extended family that formed Elvis's entourage, it was Vernie's face, – a slight but definite suggestion of an unidentified rodent, if one is being harsh, or clear-eyed, – that subliminally and involuntarily I associated with those good ol' boys and trailer trash, the way one always transfers and substitutes bits of one's own life into other people's lives, or other people's art. The decades overlay each other. The past wears the face of the present. Bob Dylan and I grew up in the 1950s and met in the 1960s. All of us to whom that happened can't help but feel this gives us more in common than Johnny-come-latelys. But everyone, anyone, also feels at different times that they were born too early or too late to fully apprehend the golden moment that someone else enjoyed. There was a party that you missed even if you think you're not a party-going animal. And what come next, and what comes next, asks the iron rule of narrative.

There is a context of what seems to be so and what is the case, and sometimes no matter how powerful the evidence of your senses, what you think is happening is something else. On a plane you look out of a window and seem to be inching past the snowy, rumpled, marshmallow attractiveness of cloud fields and plains, buttes and mesas, not particularly quickly. People are walking up and down the aisles, queueing for toilets, burrowing into a luggage locker. No-one is being jolted off their feet and rolling about like tumbleweeds in a stiff breeze. No-one is sitting back in their seat with the G force face of a racing driver. And yet the plane is travelling at between 5 and 6 hundred miles an hour, and inching is not what we're doing. The reason why these disparities seem to exist is because of perception. History appears to work in a similar way. An authoritative historical narrative goes through the range of known facts, analyses and under-stands a variety of motives, assesses a selection of personalities. It seems to be dealing with the unfolding of change in a particular direction, often with a confident explanation of why one direction was more successful than another. Whereas one's own life for long periods doesn't seem to be about change, and great or important external events don't seem to have much effect on it. Things stay the same and we try to notice details and remember them. Even here we fail. Memory has fuzziness and holes. You return to a town where you enjoyed a holiday, was it 2, perhaps 4, years ago. You walked its streets. You enjoyed evening meals at a restaurant in the square, so appealing, so impressive, so unforgettable. Now none of the streets look familiar enough. You find the square and then can't exactly place the restaurant that you have in photographs still. We read histories of times we lived through to find out what we didn't know, to confirm what we do, hoping that a teenage imprint has some value beyond an evening restaurant, and that we may compare indelibilities.

The triumphs of Highway 61 Revisited and Like a Rolling Stone started to recede, though as instances of paradox and history they have been there ever since. They demonstrated that what Bob Dylan was involved in, was engaged by, had almost nothing to do now with the earnest, committed, topical, political persona that all articles or pieces or reviews about him referred to. He started the process by which he stopped being part of that identity, and that disengagement has continued ever since. Cuttings files though have a life like radioactive carbon, more specifically regurgitated radioactive carbon, and they never go away, and, like this moment of reading or writing, are ever-present. In sociological terms he was a construct called Bob Dylan, and what he seemed to be, and what he represented, would always be connected to the fact that he wrote and sang Blowing In The Wind, that he performed before thousands and thousands at the Washington March of 1963 prior to Martin Luther King's I Have A Dream speech. The civil rights battles were still being fought, the Vietnam War was a focus for dissent, and was going to remain one into the unimaginable 1970s, but with the ubiquity of pop and youth and groups, their culture and scene, the Folk years were behind him and moving further away with the playing of each single. He was in the charts and was going to have to work like the Beatles and the Stones if he wanted to stay there. His productivity in the first part of the year matched them, but then tailed away. The requirements that had grown up so rapidly to become the norm seemed to be two albums a year, and 3 or 4 singles, and they had to be hits. What came next was Positively 4th St, a record I came to love later for the sound of its interlocking elements and his voice, which only sounded as it did then for that record and never quite again. At the time however, undeniably, it lacked the new to the world grandeur and surprise of Like A Rolling Stone, seeming slighter by comparison, as well as too much of a similar type.

Pop and rock wasn't the only thing that was happening that 1965 year, though there were times that it seemed so, and times now looking back when one forgets that so much else happened that really formed the texture of life, moment by moment and day by day. As an adult, work seems the most important structure and former of identity and value, but school must have a deeper psychological impact. Why else do our dreams reconstruct examination rooms decades after the fact? Why else do those characters we developed then stay so close to the surface no matter how we disguise that surface with years?

One of the shaping events that happened because of school was an English Literature class visit to Stratford Upon Avon by coach, to see Hamlet. Not any old Hamlet, but the one that seemed to be part of the spirit that was in the air: David Warner playing a Hamlet for our times, a student prince indeed, and also widely reviewed as a sort of beatnik or redbrick Prince, very far from being royal. If only I could remember more specifics about when it was seen, the month, the date, what it was like to go into the theatre and where we sat. It was a Thursday. I can be sure of that because it was the night of Top Of The Pops and even Hamlet couldn't prevent a slight pang at missing Top Of The Pops. Was it summer, or Spring? Was it even the next year, because it played again in 1966 as it had in 1965 What difference does it make? The fact remains that I saw it, and that will always be so. I can't remember which Ophelia I would have seen, the actress having changed for different runs of the play. We may have seen Glenda Jackson, not having a clue who she was of course. What a brilliant serendipity and example of state school education that we should see a production so talked-about at the time, such a rouser of antipathy and excitement, and something that has stayed with me ever since. Did I read about the play before we went, did I have any idea of why it was controversial for traditional critics, did I know who David Warner was any more than I knew Glenda Jackson, Janet Suzman or Estelle Kohler, the other Ophelias? Lots of questions and no-one around now to provide answers. There's always much to be uncertain about, but one certainty is that inside the theatre, wherever we sat, I was captivated. What I was looking at was David Warner, as most young people were, with his long, leggy droopiness, and his long droopy woollen scarf, and his antic, gangling disposition. Everything about being in the presence of the play appealed to me as if it were separate from the procedures one had to do to be there. It's not as if one always knew what was happening on a word by word basis. Hamlet wasn't a play we were studying, Richard II and Anthony and Cleopatra were our texts, but tones of voice and the way people moved carried you through a lot of meaning in addition to words. This in itself was a minor revelation. The whole heightened reality aspect of it, with the sound of the music, the swirl of clothes and the ornate and archaic grandiosity of gestures made it more involving than film or TV even though one couldn't see as much of faces and expressions as was possible on the little box in the corner of the room.

Of course I have no idea how good, objectively, this Hamlet was. I don't think these days, when there has been a further queue of actors who have tried to embody the life that only exists in pages, that David Warner ranks very high among the many definitions of definitive that are available now. But he ranked high then, seeming to be both bringing to the part and finding something in it that was entirely of the time, that moment. There was something appealing and fascinating for me, and the next year (or the year after) when he became a cinema star, briefly, in Morgan – A Suitable Case For Treatment, I travelled to a suburb of Wolverhampton I'd never been to especially to see it, taking a couple of buses, feeling bold and arty, and I loved it whole-heartedly, and therefore, as previously noted, without cavil. It probably would have added to my pleasure had I known then what became commonplace for Bob fans later, that Warner had been in the TV play mentioned earlier that most of us never saw, and will never see, Madhouse On Castle Street, as another inhabitant of the boarding house setting, so prevalent in early 60s drama, in which the Bob character was a fleeting presence. Any dialogue that the producer had briefly imagined might be handled by Bob had to be given to a real actor, and so was funnelled David Warner's way. They were almost the same age and they got on, and now here it was, 1965 and 1966, and Bob Dylan has stopped being a hobo and David Warner has become Hamlet.

For a long time I had the programme from that production and still regret that I don't any more, having at different times managed to hang onto, without trying, various other reminders and souvenirs of outings. It used to be around the house, often under the stairs in the hallway on top of the cupboard where a meter was, the cupboard providing a convenient flat space, not highly noticeable, that let things lie. And then it wasn't, and one wants to blame a tidying mother, but in reality I've no idea where it went or why. The stylised chiaroscuro image on the front, with Warner's Hamlet in full face and profile simultaneously, and all of the details about the music and the organised unit of crafts and trades that made the production possible, were a reminder for me, as I flicked through it, of some of what I experienced. There was something about the sound of the play, the way the music suggested the ancient time the play came from, the voices carrying the words and the way those words mixed in with the movement of bodies. There have been so many Hamlets, and so many ways of judging what each means or represents. The emotional fascination of it was beyond logic really, in the way that should I now see an episode of Wagon Train or 77 Sunset Strip I would be incapable of feeling what I felt. But with Hamlet the text can live outside individual time no matter how an individual epoch will shape and refract a meaning for it. What was true then was that something in a particular cultural world, capable of being reviewed or critiqued in a certain orthodox way, had escaped from that. There was something else that connected to people, young people, something transcending orthodoxy that you got or didn't, and the theatre seemed to be wired up the way rock, pop, folk and blues were.

Sometimes you hear a couple of bars of a song played in the background of a scene in a play, or even these days a gardening programme, part of a tune, (one wants to say fragment but that suggests sharp edges, and the way these abstracts of melody work is much less defined than that.) You hear the music and it moves through you the way thistle-down does through air. And for a moment, perhaps longer, you get a sense of inhabiting a previous time and place, which of course means a previous you, when the time and place were as indissoluble as heads and tails. It's a fleeting, dissolving sensation, and you are aware as it happens of the vast separation that exists – all the things that have happened in the time since, not just to you but everywhere and to everyone – between the consciousness now perceiving these musical promptings, and the person who experienced what is being remembered. And yet part of that memory doesn't seem far away, is not tarnished or diminished by the years that have somehow contrived to elapse, to be used up. In your head, at least if it's like my head, memory seems to occupy an area which, as in aspects of modern physics, has time and space capable of being separate and the same, depending on perception, like waves and particles, there being no way at that point to measure reliably how far away the past is, or if it is still here.

One way to feel that disparity is to look at the Friends Reunited website, reading the entries of people who left school in the same year as you. They don't have to have been close friends, simply faces you can still put a name to in a photograph taken out now and then from a tiny suitcase that has travelled with you around the years and locations to where you now are. And on the site you may be able to read a one or two sentence summary of a lifetime. Grown up children. Married nearly 40 years. Grandmother 3 times over. Co-existing with this information, an overload despite its brevity, is a reputation hazy and possibly mis-remembered of a girl forward and knowing, along with the odd, indefinite image of a teenage face, like looking at something in the dark, not seen if glanced at too directly. There was a time when some of us used to walk after school towards Bloxwich along Lichfield Road, and in one of those spaces that exists between rows of houses, where some have been bombed or knocked down, there was a little brick remnant of part of a house, about as big as a shed set back from the road among overgrown grass, brambles, nettles, the usual bombsite nature reserve. Someone had named it the Snuff Box, because people went there to smoke and some went to smooch. I don't know who called it that but I wish I'd thought of it. It seemed brilliant to me, acknowledging the purpose of the visit, making fun of it, but also having real affection. It also fitted the size of the place. There wasn't that much smoking there, and I didn't anyway, though I remember being impressed by the sophistication of boys who bought packets of 25 cigarettes, which seemed for inexplicable reasons of a different order to the normal 20. Sometimes this seems so odd I think I dreamt it. Have I made it up? Perhaps, but surely Sobranie Black Russian and Peter Stuyvesant are true.

As for smooching nothing happened that was as rude as the boy and girl I saw once on a street corner nearby, in Bloxwich itself, in broad mid-afternoon light. He was standing behind her with his arms through her armpits, cupping her breasts. I knew him by sight only, and was impressed and amazed. She looked not only as if she didn't mind but perfectly at ease. It was one of those revelations that later you get from dirty photos. It had never even crossed your mind that such a configuration was possible, and then, for better or worse, it's hard to stop thinking about it. So now here we are, looking to the left or right of a star, trying to perceive a shape that used to be by the light of what reaches us now. It's not like looking at a file or a photograph, but it does have some sort of existence and it's not exactly like the past. It feels as if it's always going to be there whenever it happens to be brought to your attention. Decades have gone by, and yet someone you knew, or at least saw, for such a small fraction, five or six years, of that overall time span is stored away. You know perfectly well that in real life, real time, coming across that granny would be an unsettling experience that would only confirm the destructive power of years on flesh and blood. But after that, a day, a week, whenever it needed to be, something would prompt the reappearance of that girl as she was, as you knew her, with her combed forward, modified beehive, her navy blue skirt and jumper, her dark, innuendo-comprehending eye, and she would be unchanged still. It occurs to one that having come across Bob Dylan in the 1960s is also like this.

CHAPTER THIRTEEN
ILL KEEP IT WITH MINE

1965 becomes 1966. Everything mixes and complements something else when you are at a certain mid teenage time, everything becomes pop, or at least it did then. There was the range of groups, American and English, and they formed a constant background with points of reference. At the same time one loved Hamlet and that way of speaking, having a sense that Elizabethan times weren't so far away even if they might be hard to understand, while knowing too that it was acting, play acting, it wasn't real. What it did though was let you see that language was real, and gesture and appearance. And besides, there was the Man From UNCLE. This was the kind of TV smash that soared to unpredictable heights of popularity, rising on some thermal of demographic or zeitgeist that none of the squadrons involved in its production could have known in advance. It was like 77 Sunset Strip for the post-Bond era, and as obsessed with hairstyles and surface. In the teen magazines that percolated over from America it was ubiquitous. An amazing success for David McCallum, formerly a little known actor who now had very blonde hair cut in a way that caused comment and requests for similar please. Mr Tambourine Man, Illya Kuryakin, David Warner, the Lovin' Spoonful, all mix and match into a quilt of interest and knowledge.

How to convey now the attraction of the Lovin' Spoonful? As they sang in John Sebastian's words, "It's like trying to tell a stranger about rock 'n' roll." They looked like cartoons with their funny, odd colourful clothes, joke cowboy hats and hooped T shirts and jumpers, and, despite boots, looked nothing like the West Coast affected cool of the Byrds who one would expect to be similar, both being rock groups of a similar age, and presumably to a Martian they did. But they didn't. The Byrds, you could see, were about looking impassive and remote, whereas the Spoonful were about being fun and silly. Thrift sale fancy dress and beatnik garb was the aura that surrounded them, in the days before hippies, when all was a variant of pop. John Sebastian had been brought up in Greenwich Village, the arty scene, as we know, for a century or more in New York, and more specifically since the 1940s where jazz, folk and comedy clubs came in waves, residing in the same streets, succeeding and one-upping each other in serial overlappings. So the area that attracted wannabes from all over the country was already his home. His mother was a comedy scriptwriter, his father a classical musician, he grew up knowing the clubs and was able to see the folk and blues guys first hand, learning mouth organ and guitar and sitting in on sessions barely out of his teens. I didn't know this immediately at the time, but you looked at the photographs and something in them carried that old New York as well as the fun pop aspect. The Cagney films I had watched on the settee with my father had a presence here too.

Then there were Sebastian's glasses. People in rock tried not to wear glasses, aside from Buddy Holly and his almost immediate clone Hank B Marvin. The famously short-sighted John Lennon needed glasses in practically every area of his life but wouldn't wear them onstage, contributing massively to his expression, looking down his long nose, that grew longer with the years and the thinning of his cheeks, allowing him and Michael Caine to share the same hooded cobra look that seemed to indicate they would always know much more than any of their audience could. Later he moved to contact lenses, and later to the NHS style he had hated as a boy, and couldn't have been unaware of Sebastian's innovation, here in

1965, little metal round-framed glasses and suddenly they seemed not ridiculous or geeky, but hip and knowing. Sebastian selflessly acknowledged that the idea for them had come from Fritz Richmond, a fellow musician and stylistic innovator on the folky blues and old time music scene, but as far as we were concerned John Sebastian was the man. And as a glasses wearer myself this couldn't be ignored. Not long afterwards, I was informed by a tolerant optician that the much despised NHS frames could look like that by the simple measure of stripping the brown plastic covering away. Voila: golden, round, old-fashioned, suddenly desirable frames.

Connections and connections. John Sebastian was brought up on Bank Street, the same street where John Lennon, after the demise of the Beatles, moved to New York City and rented an apartment, before moving to the gothic and doomed grandeur of the Dakota. The same deep-in-the-Village street where much later a friend of mine married his American love and moved to an apartment on there, a place that had been his fantasy and vision for years, and was now everyday reality, the place where he walked to meetings or shops, or waited for the mailman, took his deliveries from Fed-Ex, but all still with a heightened edge, the difference between flatness and 3D. Which is one way of thinking about what music meant to us, and can still mean though now it is filtered and refracted through words and memory. He had looked at Spoonful albums and read their sleeve notes too, feeling the world that those covers and funny words called up. Sebastian in a fur coat, (fur coat?) putting his head fondly on the shoulder of a band mate. And them reminiscing about the basement cellar they had been forced to rehearse in before fame struck – all of a few months before the EP sleeve note that gave me this information had been released – speculating about sightless fish moving in the waters down there. And a line that could have come straight from Top Cat's compadre Choo Choo, "And all of a sudden no more things for free, and like that," which is what they all reminded us of, the Top Cat crew, our other insider view of New York

What Top Cat reminded us of was Sgt. Bilko, the show starring Phil Silvers and whose specific name would be a dilemma for librarians, or whoever else needed to pin it down on cards. It was Sgt Bilko or Sergeant Bilko or The Phil Silvers Show. It began as You'll Never Get Rich, but no-one here knew. What we did know was how sharp it was in all ways, its beautiful black and white sparkling clear as water no matter how many years had passed since it was made. It was a picture of America in the 1950s, picking up and using the fads, like Elvis, but working through the kind of fast dialogue perfected in screwball movies from the 30s and 40s, and Silvers work in vaudeville, ensemble playing with character actors, a situation comedy where a world was concertinaed into less than half an hour. Bilko also turned up as a Christmas annual, though of course there was no possibility of capturing what happened onscreen in cartoons. But when did that ever stop us buying comics? Decades later the show would turn up tucked away at odd times, late at night, or early morning in school holidays, – the past, always with us. – and it never failed. One was always drawn in like the suckers Ernie Bilko needed to make his life worthwhile, watching the credits roll, entrancing as Bewitched, and hearing an announcer's voice reading out some of the individual names in a way that symbolised and parodied 50s broadcasting in America.

In a couple of years John Sebastian wrote four albums, created soundtracks, and had a string of hit singles, came up with one good post-Spoonful album, and then the magic moved on. You could say that it was to do with drug busts and fallings out between people, but it seems more mysterious than that. The longevity of the records, and of some of the bands from that time, obscures how transient being the recipient of a gift and good fortune is. John Sebastian is still a talented musician, and he plays songs from a musical past far older than his, but the ability that he had to write those songs out of all his influences and musical companions at that point, as far as we can judge from what he has done since, disappeared like yesterday or the previous moment. Their first hit, their first release, and, he said, his first song, asked Do You Believe In Magic, and everyone did. We experienced it everyday. One time after seeing the Summer In The City film clip on Top Of The Pops, (one didn't say pop video then), I cycled down to Jim's house, down towards Green Rock and over the canal bridge there, his estate of houses different to ours on the left, and on the right the trees and greenery of Shelfield and Pelsall and the places I didn't normally go, and I felt that my belt and jeans were just right, reminding me, no matter what they really looked like, of that Spoonful vibe, still in my head as they clowned around in 1966 New York and their brilliant single played behind and around them. And on my bike, with the evening warm and the wind moving around me I felt everything was right, just right. It was an illusion and it was real. What else would it feel like being a teenager in the Sixties? Hearing a record on the radio one tends not dwell on the manufacturing process that shapes and imprints a vinyl blob with a continuous wavy line intaglio encoding sound waves. You're entering the realm of the spirits and allowing something to inhabit your heart. Once that has happened it never leaves, you never forget it, and the success of future digital radio stations calibrated to satisfy golden oldie generations in their chronological and demographic demarcations is assured.

So much time has passed, decades, so long ago, and everything takes such a long time to pass, except when you consider all the bits that matter, and they were so short. So were the bits that didn't seem to matter, but somehow that never notices in quite the same way. It all takes such a long time, and no time at all. And how come it took decades more before one found that Sebastian had been one of Dylan's Woodstock pals in 1964, when he was a stranger to little round metal glasses, had a greasy Fifties hair do, and on the whole looked a good deal more straight or square, not to mention chunky, than his Spoonful incarnation; and, further, that he had hung around and, surprisingly, played bass while Bringing It All Back Home was brought into being? Everything connects eventually but all you know is what you know at the time. At the time one knew hardly anything but felt as if the world had been vouchsafed in the sound of a voice, a guitar, theme music passing by, and the light switch clicking off at bedtime, 1965 moving into 1966.

1965 had seemed the best year for pop and rock music there had ever been. It began with the melancholy, impassioned, piano-clonking erupting choruses of Go Now by the first incarnation of the Moody Blues, Birmingham blues and soul band, and nothing to do with the ponderous pomposities of the later line up, that seemed to take its songwriting very seriously indeed. From there the year had encompassed the growth and changes that allowed the Beatles to put out Help and Rubber Soul, the very essence of fabness; and the Stones to find the template of Satisfaction; the Walker Brothers to bring the richness of Bacharach, a deep voice, and an orchestra to us all; the Kinks to move from r&b standards to the insinuating, quirky strangeness of Ray Davies. I'd seen the Walker Brothers as a poster on the door of tiny record shop just along from a fish and chip shop where a couple of years previously, after the heady excitement of school dances, we would hang around the night counter waiting for six pennorth with our heads resting on our hands like a David Hockney drawing. The Walker faces surmounted by hair so styled and large it looked like an extravagantly arranged wig, looked out of place on the almost-residential door of the small shop, next to an equally poky flower shop, and both of them in a slip road behind the public toilet in Bloxwich. That's one way to think about the Sixties and what they mean. Every year was a different Sixties and the music was always the clue wherever it took place.

The success of the Walker Brothers pointed up one of the main aspects of the scene then, and how the charts reflected it. It wasn't only about lads in groups, the big beat and guitars. Burt Bacharach was one of the major elements in the Sixties sound, those singable, memorable tunes set in arrangements that were both grand and minutely detailed, unusual in their instrumentation, with English horns, tympani, and glockenspiels amongst others, as well as saxophones and the string section. His songs were covered by all kinds of singers, and his arrangements were templates, so it didn't have to be one of the records he worked on for you to hear what he had invented. The cover versions were as faithful as talents allowed. Bacharach songs succeeded not just because of the melodies but because of the way the melodies were wedded to Hal David's words, the way it was impossible to say which of them grew the other. We'd heard this partnership before of course, in another lifetime, when instead of the adult sophistication now presented they had filled the airwaves with Magic Moments and The Story of My Life, when singers from both sides of the Atlantic would have cover versions of the same song in the charts simultaneously, The Story of My Life being a hit here for the man who sang like Bing, which is to say perfectly. It was the late 1950s, when rock'n'roll had been unleashed and was well into its stride, but smooth crooning and family entertainment were loved by all the families I knew, allowing children like me to glimpse an idealised suburban existence in the songs, – as it was in the ads – and years later to remember when we first heard them and sang them, wanting to believe that the time being remembered was as ideal as the life in the songs, all those base metal moments that also existed being transmuted by the alchemy of song. In fact even now if I hear Magic Moments it evokes the same sensations, its chirruping, jaunty tune, the easy unfolding rhymes, and the almost belief that my 1950s was like the one in the song, though we never had a hayride or a sleigh ride, scored a touchdown or have the car floor collapse when we put the clutch down. What we did have, what I had, was a time filled with love.

Cilla Black, with her voice that alternated between a klaxon and the heartfelt, managed to represent both the Liverpool of the Beatles – quite specifically with her time as a Cavern Club cloakroom girl – and also the orchestral, showbiz end of things with Anyone

Who Had A Heart, and then later with Burt himself at the torturous helm of a definitive Alfie. The earlier song, though disparaged as mere copycat by Bacharach and David's in-house muse Dionne Warwick, succeeded here because of its mystery, melancholy and sudden sweeping outbursts that make their songs so engrossing to listen to, and impossible not to irrupt into sing along with. Bob Dylan seemed to be altering what songs were by importing vast swathes of modern poetry, along with a traditional root in ancient ballads, but the sense of it being an authentic testimony from his own consciousness was what appeared to give him such importance. Bacharach and David were a reminder that songs were more than that, wonderfully wide, and depended on the alchemy of words and melodies wherever they originated, Broadway, the Brill Building, or the folk revival. A further British representative of the Bacharach franchise was Sandie Shaw, who became a beneficiary by singing Always Something There To Remind Me, and became too an example of the kind of girl who, though you only knew her from the other side of a TV screen, could as easily have come walking out from one of the Sixth Form blocks. This wasn't true of Marianne Faithfull, who belonged in a different class of school with her above-it-all downcast eyes, and almost pout precisely held. No-one would have imagined her crossing our quadrangle, ensuring her hair moved just so to make a point, shining as she smiled at her girl friends, and acknowledging, by ignoring, the boys on the periphery thinking their simple, predictable, carnal thoughts. Sandie Shaw, avoiding her factory or secretary fate to take up singing, looked like she'd just left our world, while clearly Marianne had never been in it.

Whatever their individual qualities, Sandie and Cilla were always in the shadow of Dionne, who was extraordinary from the beginning, and she was very young at the beginning. Even now a radio can deliver you an early hit while you are thinking of maybe pouring a cup of tea, or dropping a plate into a washing up bowl, and catch you up completely. Don't Make Me Over makes itself known and you are thrilled, uplifted, surprised by the open emotion, the simple clarity, the swift uprush into yearning and power when she sings the words that on the page seem unassuming:

> Accept me for what I am,
> Accept me for the things that I do

but in the air, in her upper register, they soar and shimmer with pain. They also link the subject not only with a romantic dilemma but a racial one. It's fantastic grown-up songwriting and arranging, and was part of the Sixties like the Beatles, The Stones and Bob Dylan. What it made clear though was that by calling both Bacharach and Dylan songwriters a lot of subsequent work would need to be done to make a useful definition, to see what they shared. There were songs and songs, and the context and where people started from seemed to require attention. Aside from all this however was the important part. You could like them both. You could love them both. Certainly the cheering thing was you could turn on a wireless and hear them both.

All of it was coming at us every day, all of those groups, bands, singers on a treadmill to put out records. And we were there to hear them as they happened. This is one of the main factors in the teenage identification of a music as its own. It doesn't come from a time before you were around. It didn't exist in the background for you to suddenly notice. It comes into existence and into your life while you're paying attention, and it makes a difference, and you feel it belongs to you because it says something about you. 1965 and the Byrds making Bob Dylan into rock, or was it pop; and Bob Dylan making his break from old people's expectation with Like A Rolling Stone, plus his follow up and most poppy rock record yet, and ever, with Positively 4th St: the sound of his voice where youth and age intertwine like strips around a barber's pole; the touch and go coherence of the ensemble, with the instruments almost not fitting together while the tune stays endlessly beguiling; then the final put down with its blend of street language and fairy tale, lives and shoes swapped, a familiar unexamined phrase becoming an image from a film. All of this greatness on the radio and in the air and in your dreams, no, not your dreams, the atmosphere in your everyday waking thoughts, the place where thoughts are the land where daydreams exist. Yet the biggest selling records of the year were by the most definitely non-teenage Ken Dodd and the Seekers. How could that be so and yet all still seemed perfect in a perfect world? Could 1966 keep up these exalted standards?

We're always travelling between two opposing states of mind. One is that all this, everything, everything we know, can go away, will go away. The other is that things will go on like this forever. What we seem to experience most, until a change occurs, is the sense that things are everlasting, even if they mutate slowly. It's like the differences between days. One week succeeds another, but Mondays still feel different not only from such landmarks as Fridays, but any other day. This sense of the texture and promise of days being different is felt most strongly at school, when whatever lessons are due, and what TV programmes will be on later that evening, give a flavour to the air passing before you. 1965 passed on into 1966. Could it be more of the same, but even better? It turned out that it could, and that through some accidental collision and collusion involving birth rates, education and cultural developments thousands of young people formed groups, spawning songs and sounds, and millions of other young people who couldn't or didn't found their self-expression by taking the songs and the sounds and the groups to their hearts, and their souls. What one remembers always feels true even when it can't be so. Check the weather reports for 1966, come to a consensus, it will be normal, as expected, the days doling out their weather and contributing to the average that constitutes climate. In the mind's eye though it seems bright, always bright, with the sun that shines when you are sixteen going on seventeen. There are always later, and often better, fair days ahead, but there is something about an ignorance which doesn't recognise its limitations or its nature that makes the sun sweeter in those days. There's no-one who won't think that the music scene that is around during the teenage years is the best there ever was, and won't imprint it inside them forever. But even given this partiality there is something to be said for the gold rush of 1966 for those of us who experienced it day by different day. It gave us something to always look back on and measure things by.

Bob Dylan travelled into 1966 by building on what he'd created, or stumbled upon, in the Newport Festival performance that was destined ever after to be invoked as the point at which everything changed, and, as far as Dylan history was concerned, the modern world began. It really was as if he'd come through Murray Lerner's mirror and into a world beyond its confines, one where he was freed to be what he always wanted to be, one where his possibilities and vague wishes were going to become absolute concrete reality, not only for him but crowds of people he had never known or imagined. In the late summer and on into the autumn he played concerts with a band consisting of some musicians who had played on Highway 61 Revisited, but with Robbie Robertson as a constant element, until the people who with Robertson had formed the band for old time rocker and full time character Ronnie Hawkins, stopped being Ronnie's Hawks, rejoined forces with Robbie, and morphed into Bob's touring band. A format had been devised which inadvertently echoed the two sides of Bringing It All Back Home: a solo Bob first half, and then a band-based second half, though the topical, committed, civil-rights conscious, political creature he had once appeared to be, was absent even from the acoustic guitar set. And the electric songs that took shape and developed, gradually moved from the demo, still-working-it-out aspect of the Newport rock band, to the force, the almost deranged character, that the 1966 Bob Dylan tour will now always have. Needless to say we had no idea of this progress then, no rock weeklies keeping us up to date with a continuing Bob tour. We listened to the albums we had, and not realising how embarrassing it might have been, tried to explain the imagery of Gates Of Eden to a girl who had blue school jumpers in soft, bobbley wool; smooth, swing-forward shining hair, like smaller Cilla or Sandie Shaw scythes, but in light auburn; an impish face, reminiscent of a Teddy Bear if a Teddy Bear could smile; and an unfortunate favoured friend who delivered messages about the imminent demise of a going out status, though if we went out at all it would have been just kissing or not, and talking. A small girl in a blue jumper and strawberry-blonde hair, busy kissing or not kissing, busy conveying the inconceivability of ever being a pensioner or a granny, working on the sweet counter in Woolworth's each Saturday and seeing a hanging around, would-be beau expelled by the management, an experience that prompted, inevitably, a poem in the style of Bob Dylan sleeve notes.

Everything passes, everything changes, Bob Dylan wrote, one of his most acute lines and voicings. And here it was, history about to repeat itself, except that's just a phrase and it never does. For what history is, and is like, you have to consider great and unexpected snowfall. White layers, surprising inches deep, cover and balance on gateposts, cars, roofs. It's amazing. Everything is the same but clearly not. Now it's been singled out, made exceptional, revealed to be something different even as it is hidden, revealed by being hidden. We slump and slosh and slide, ankle deep, knee deep, and take photographs. It lasts as long as it's fated to, hours, days. And then it's gone, and the world is returned to its disappointing familiarity, as it was, and all that's left are the pictures on our cameras and computers (increasingly rarely in our hand or packets from chemists), and those other less definable pictures in our head. These are the pictures that will create the narratives, the stories people will tell about that day, the first day the snow fell, and we woke to the whirl of flakes and wild weather. Perhaps it was a child's birthday, what a chance, and they will never forget it. And all the other people's stories will make sense because everyone is comparing what they know of the real event. Eventually though enough time will pass for the stories and pictures to spread out and about and be for the benefit of people who didn't experience the snow, who just missed it. And these versions will give them a good idea certainly, but not quite the reality. There is no other reality now except the world left as it is. Every day can be an unremarkable succession of repetitions, and yet history we will find to be full of momentous events and revolutionary changes of mind, appearance and personnel.

We look at bound volumes of newspaper or magazines trying to reconstruct in imagination the time we want to believe they are an objective record of, while reading our own daily paper and taking for granted its partiality and bias. Instead of being an impartial record old newspaper and magazines have an appeal and attraction because of what we have learned and experienced subsequently. Something one would have no interest in at the time assumes a piquant or serendipity aspect because of connections only possible through a later development. People who were unknown are revealed to be the known in waiting, in disguise. Literary journals one could hardly bear to limp through on publication day, years later teem with nuggets of entertainment. Did they change? Everyone knows that thinking made it so.

CHAPTER FOURTEEN
THE LAST TIME

There's no piece of commonplace, disposable material, equipment or printed ephemera created to make commerce and domesticity work – stamps, coins, phone cards, bus tickets, bills, receipts, invoices, inscribed coat hangers – that won't be obsessively collected, catalogued, differentiated and filed away, holy relics of something vanished, proof that though you can keep objects, where they came from always disappears. The collections and their descriptive entries persist, but that's all. We believe it when we read a definitive history of a country or a war, while knowing that creating a prose version of a week from our own lives would be a task of slippery trickiness. Nevertheless, one month of May was succeeding another. The history that Bob Dylan seemed about to repeat was to tour again in May. He'd been in England in May 1964, May 1965, and now he was to be here again in May 1966. But then to look at him and hear him was to know that this was not the same Bob Dylan.

He looked different. He didn't look exactly well with his dark-ringed eyes and odd tight suits. The integrity set in granite expression, the proletarian probity of only 3 years before, have dissolved in pop strangeness. His hair had grown out into a wilder tangle and immediately became the subject of a squiggle portrait that has been sketched with varying degrees of repeated fidelity ever since, the Everlasting Dylan Doodle.

Of course the way he looks and the way we look here in the heart of the Sixties blazing cadenza will always give us something to use later as a corrective to any idea that our appearance matched the myth everyone can access and believe in.

...

It's 1966. He's about to release an album and perform shows that will always give us something to look back on and measure things by. The interviews were as tricky and as packed with protracted loggerheads of purpose and intention as ever. There were witnesses aplenty to the tour but this time I was not one of them. For reasons to do with dopiness and not having my head on straight I blew what money I had (still from those same mysterious, gone to ground sources) and bought an LP instead. That tells you something about relative economics. One modern value test is comparing what things cost in Mars bars. My failure to show in 1966 tells you that an album and a concert ticket had some kind of equivalence then. Given that CDs still go anywhere between £8 and £15, while a concert can be £50 to £150 it's clear that property isn't the only indicator of a society gone mad. We can misremember and forget the past, but not alter it, and impressed for a moment by Birmingham band – which made them almost local – the Spencer Davis Group, featuring boy wonder Stevie Winwood, I bought their second album, somewhat lazily called The Second Album. It didn't even have as smart a cover as their first, a blend of sepia and dark blue, but it did have lots of 17 year old Stevie sounding unnervingly like Ray Charles. Good enough, but not one of life's survivors and it left my collection and its passing went unmarked. But it meant I never did get to see Bob Dylan at Birmingham New St Odeon on May 12 1966, because the price of a ticket was absent. And in one of those little coincidences that seem to have meaning but may have none, the afternoon of the day of the concert Bob Dylan was diverted by being shown a house that was supposed to be haunted in the nearby West Midlands countryside by, amongst others, the very same Stevie. So I contrived to miss the tour that would be an indelible cultural event forever, at least for anyone who gave a damn, which it's hard to remember if you are one who does and did, is, realistically speaking, quite a tiny proportion of the population. You only see the truth of this of course if you should happen to be trapped in a living room with a relative who is working his way through a DVD of a concert of someone *you* don't care for, and feel what it's like to be behind the glass wall of other people's adoration, the songs and the emotion and the noise of instruments, and the yearning, wracked faces of the crowd, the singer wrenching out the words, and all of it entirely without meaning as far you are concerned, like a play in a foreign language. But then one of the reasons for liking albums is that in concerts you have to be in the presence of people being someone else en masse.

It's possible to rationalise even this away, as it is possible to rationalise a position that makes us feel better from any event we care to. I was present in 1965 and I have some scrumpled mental scraps of it I smooth out and review from time to time, and other internal memos that fuse those images with all the film versions I've seen since to create new files. I wasn't present in 1966 but my total imperfect recall suggests I was. And then there's the testimony of witnesses that one absorbs in to the nervous system until it can seem like it was born there. At school there was a boy called John Hedges, in the upper 6th as we were in the lower, and he went to the show. He described Bob Dylan at one stage bending down to draw attention to something on stage. "A piece of dirt," John reported him saying, "on the same stage as me." And he described too the seats banging up as people left when the loud second half started, "Excuse me, excuse me." He liked the music.

There are other witnesses real and fictional, though of course novelists always like to claim that only fiction allows the truth to be displayed. More rationalisation we all recognise. Here's someone who wants to testify, someone in the relatively unusual position, like the dermatologist Dr Cream, of bearing a name similar to his occupation, that aptonym Ron Bobfan.

"The best thing about Bob Dylan in 1966 was that after 4 fast years, from the blues and blowing and Village basements, after stealing from everyone in order to make his own way, he went on, he went way beyond that. He didn't know where he was going and he was desperate to get there. In 1966 he didn't sound like anybody else. The Hawks and him didn't sound like anybody else. It definitely wasn't folk. It wasn't really r&b. It wasn't exactly rock. It was ... them, unique. They went out there and sounded wilder, more case-hardened, better than the Stones. But who knew that then? It could be my memory, my story, it could be everyone's. I remember everything in the second half was loud and weird. I didn't know what was happening but I recognised that I'd never heard singing like it. All I knew, or think I knew, is that in the acoustic half he was so primitive it was like he'd forgotten how to play the guitar. He was in stoned time. And after the interval he switched to electric, amphetamine tempo. Out of his loyalties and loves, his weaknesses and spite; out of Woody Guthrie and Robert Johnson; out of his rage and humour; out of Mickey Mouse, James Dean, Little Richard, and Buddy Holly; out of the Beats and Jimmie Rodgers and Hank Williams; out of his hatred and self-hatred; out of celebrity and drugs, the blues and country, guitars and voices; out of rock and out of roll came Blonde On Blonde, the tour, and the end of the tour."

And another witness to tumultuous times:

When 'Like A Rolling Stone' came out I was hugely disappointed, I thought he had gone commercial and generally I turned back – in some disillusion – to rock music, eventually. The strange thing is I did like Rolling Stone as a record and had it been by the Stones or the Animals or someone, I would have loved it. But I thought Bob Dylan was *better* than that – that he did serious stuff not just rock. I expected so much more from him. That was the problem.

Then in April '66 my mate said Dylan's coming to Leicester. We've hired a bus and got 40 tickets do you want one? It was that easy – no mad scramble the day the tickets go on sale like now. So I went – out of curiosity really. And I was dumbfounded by this little scrawny stick insect – I had always assumed Dylan must be big. And the music was weird in the first half and deafening in the second and there were all these people slow handclapping and shouting and rows of them got up and walked out. The weirdest theatre experience ever. And when I watch the film of 1966 now I think it is so wonderful and think how lucky I was to be there, but that isn't what I thought at the time. What you heard in the theatre was nothing like what I now hear on CD or on the video. I swear it was virtually impossible to hear the words above the noise, the sheer LOUDness overwhelmed your senses so that you couldn't know what you were hearing. My memory of those who walked out is not of short-haired speccies but of people looking like Peter, Paul & Mary. For me, I neither booed nor cheered – I just sat on my hands. But you had to have lived through Dylan in 1964 to understand why so many of us felt so betrayed. He had seemed to be way above just a rock'n'roll singer or any sort of mere musician. 'Freewheelin' in Jan 1964 was a transcendent experience. I had heard nothing as powerful as this. It was nigh on religious in the way it took me over. This was bigger than music or art – it seemed to be telling me how I should live my life. Most of the people who went on the bus to see Dylan had never been into Dylan in '64. They had come to him purely because of 'Like A Rolling Stone'. And maybe because of The Byrds. And they loved the second half. So there were certainly two factions even before the show began; it never was a homogeneous audience in '66

And this is how indelible cultural events coalesce and form, their life persisting like radium or starlight. The text of the Sixties is stolen, modified, edited, changed, arranged and adapted by anyone who took part. The times are changing and things have changed. You rouse and fall asleep on the way to getting up for real in the morning, and at intervals you see the little illuminated figures on the bedside clock become anagrams of themselves. The past is always with us and never there. He came in 1965 then went away and a little later played with a band and was booed. Then he went on a tour and played with a slightly different band and was booed further, and people walked out. And here he was again coming to tour in 1966 and now we'd read about people booing and walking out. And some people went along expecting to boo and walk out, and others went along not knowing what to expect, and afterwards what remained was the chat and the articles and the general documentation of the event. Or as this was a tour, the series of events. It was as if it had happened like a snow storm and these stories and pictures were all that could remain of it, because, like snow, everything must disappear, and at heart all fans are a species of archivist or librarian, or weatherman trying to explain both how something that disappeared came to be, and what its subsequent documentation means. The meaning of meaning. Everything happens in its own time. Everything can be a link in a chain, but actually there wouldn't be a chain if it weren't for the perception of all those meteorologists. They, we, are what give the links meaning. Until then they are simply things that happen. Bob Dylan was who he was because of the time he came along in, all the times, those changing times. Murray Lerner's film shows the change over three years, from topical song writer to proto-rocker. He had seemed to be a figurehead of a movement where songs were socially and politically aware, and the singing of them united the people who sang and heard them, engendering a consciousness of right, wrong, oppression and the relationship of workers to owners and governments, and black people to white people, and black people to brutality and injustice. Dylan's earlier songs had been to do with what was happening in America, not elsewhere, and concerned his perception of civil rights. Then he distanced himself from being a representative and looked for ways to be himself, cut loose from committed obligations, knowing that all of those political forms and forces didn't fit what he experienced as a rock 'n' roll teenager, and all the feelings loose in the air chain-linking to that. The times that the Beatles and the Rolling Stones were making were his times. So now here he was in 1966 no tentative rocker anymore, but heading up a tough, experienced rock band who could play anything and didn't sound like anyone else. It's hard to recognise something new. No-one has enough to compare it with and they don't know how to assess it. So people tried to see it in terms what he had been, or what they had heard he was, and press conferences asked about protest songs, the word itself a joke, or Vietnam, a subject on which he'd never sung any kind of word. He was confused and lumped in with Phil Ochs, Buffy Sainte-Marie, Donovan, and even that laughable cartoon exaggeration of protest, Barry McGuire. None of which was his fault.

What was happening was a miniature version of what has been happening ever since. Whatever version of Bob Dylan is current tends to be viewed through overlays of previous editions. Transparencies, or possibly opacities, are one atop another, perhaps wildly out of true, perhaps only a degree or two overlap to show the difference. The year before he played to quiet, respectful, adoring audiences, where the silence was like a sponge that absorbed him until the clatter of applause broke it. That year Times They Are A-Changin' and

Subterranean Homesick Blues were on the chart at the same time, a perfect summary of the quick change nature in what Bob Dylan meant and thought he meant. I'm not sure that, unlike for others, he ever showed me the way to live, or that folk music did, or that any of it seriously increased my social consciousness or conscience. If you're a teenager rebellion doesn't need to have a polemical dimension: being careless of responsibility or wanting to be selfish is a base point. What Bob Dylan was part of was that wider music scene, and the intermittent consciousness it allowed that you were young and, sometimes, not all the time, exciting things seemed to be happening all around, and could happen to you. But would it change your life?

CHAPTER FIFTEEN
THIS BOY

It is possible to feel that a record changes your life, but usually because it opens you up to pleasure, and the pleasure of perceiving how good someone else's prowess is. It doesn't necessarily make you want to *do* anything, or change the world. And yet the received wisdom is that the Sixties can be characterised by the radicalising of youth, the encouragement of a can-do, we're here to change things for the better attitude. That must have been true but perhaps not in our street. What I saw at school wasn't so epochal. Some would go to apprenticeships. Most hoped to get O levels then A levels, go on to college, be a teacher perhaps, or to university and then be, what, who knew? What we would do with our lives in the long term was a largely unexamined area. What kind of job would we get, where would we live, would we change the world or would the world change us? I don't remember any of these being conscious thoughts, except perhaps what would I do in exams, nor did I recognise any potential revolutionaries. We lived in the moment that accumulated into days, absorbing music into the tissues like oxygen.

We're always travelling between two opposing states of mind. One is that all this, everything, everything we know, can go away, will go away. The other is that things will go on like this forever.
What we did know was that music was important to how you felt, and was a sign of something bigger happening, because even 4 years

previously singles hadn't sounded like this. What you felt, what gave you pleasure, what you wanted, being connected to individuals who felt as you did, was as political as many people got. The interface would be the one it always had been for teenagers or anybody: work and pleasure. There are no secrets, only basics. Hard work, discipline, indefatigability, intelligence, and patience would be as necessary now as in previous decades. That was clear even to someone who seemed the perfect Sixties mirrored figurehead, the apparently null and vacant Andy Warhol, but he evangelised work endlessly to his circle, asking Lou Reed how many songs he'd written that day, then telling him to write more. It's arguable that the importance of pleasure, and selfishness, at that time led to the later consumer culture that we still have, people feeling that they are entitled to goods and luxuries, some of which is fuelled by repackaged Sixties records, box set art objects made of what used to be maltreated singles. But all of the performers around then, however they spent their leisure time, had to work to provide our pleasure and they turned the stuff out, with their annual production figures of two albums, four singles and a couple of tours. As Bob Dylan was now proving.

The tour would leave its memories, and decades later beautiful colour film would be released to show what it was really like, even for people who were there. But what was left behind of that time for people to find over and over, and to make it new in their own minds was the record Blonde On Blonde. Hundreds of people may have seen the tour, but thousands were going to buy the record and know it forever, although it's unlikely that any of us suspected that it would continue to be sold in various incarnations for 40 years, or that anniversaries and decades would have to be marked by thinking about it and assessing it again and again, and that those original thousands were going to be added to continuously. All we did know, or care about, was seeing it as something special and something that would be used to identify and characterise what Bob Dylan was right now, here, as contemporary as the next moment. We knew too that it was as if there was another Bob Dylan who had recorded Freewheelin', or, having backtracked to investigate beginnings, his first album. This didn't prey on my mind. I didn't think if that was a short or long time ago. After all, every version was there to hear as required. I remember seeing in the Smiths branch where I had first chanced upon Western Film and TV Annual 7 years previously, a big poster for the album which reproduced the photograph you saw if the double album was opened out. As you walked down from the top floor of the shop it was on the wall of the stairs for everyone to see, and it looked odd. Not many album covers were in blurred focus then, and folded out to give you a photograph of a man in a short brown coat with a fuzzy puffball of hair and no expression, a man who 3 years before, or was it 2, had appeared in tight head focus, beautiful graduated black and white, short wayward hair and denim shirt, his sensitive, intense features in a carved face, downcast eyes seeming to understand and encompass various kinds of suffering humanity from behind invisible bars, on the cover of another album that seemed to typify the times that created it. Looking at Blonde On Blonde confirmed that they were a-changing.

In the cold and clutter, watching the last of the microgroove
endlessly swirl and spiral out to where it ceases to move,
saturating the cassette with love and heartache, the past's taste, a preference that
can be stored and replayed and erased at the drop of a small hat.
Because of the accidents of birth rates, and the incidence of mortality and morbidity, people who were teenagers in 1966 carried on travelling through the years, in the way a small antelope might make its way through a python, the peristalsis of time. Which means that all the albums they ever loved then turn up in the list of all time best ever albums, (in magazines edited by people whose age and readership we are.) Predictable, but if you like pop and rock music at all 1966 genuinely was a rich year. Looking back 3 decades later Ron Bobfan was rhetorical:

What did you have that year? What didn't you have? The Beatles with Revolver. The Stones with Aftermath. The Beach Boys with Pet Sounds and Good Vibrations. Not even mentioning Love, the Byrds, the Loving Spoonful, the Mamas and Papas. So many, and that's only the American contingent. Over here there was the Kinks, the Who, the Small Faces, the Troggs, yes even the Troggs. Plus a group who managed to be both American and English, weirdly middle-of-the road and a genuine teenscream hormonal uproar, the Walker Brothers. People who liked folk could enjoy hearing jazz. People who favoured blues would drift across to r&b and rock. Marvellous Motown, fantastic Stax. In the Sixties everything connected, or seemed to. Soul, pop, rock, folk, r&b, jazz. It was all part of the same thing, like music being part of youth.

But obviously we weren't looking back. We were looking around and trying to catch it on the fly. An album then was an artistic package, an object with a concrete existence; it embodied and symbolised and stood for a variety of meanings. It came into your life, into your bedroom. It opened up into your life. It opened up your life, a gatefold and gateway. There the face takes up almost the entirety of one side of the sleeve, a foot square. He looks out at you, a slightly blurred, inscrutable expression in washed-out colour above that odd little check scarf, and then the delight of opening it out and seeing that you got the rest of his jacket and this was a big picture. The black and white shots inside also put Bob in a different context. This smoky, hazy, unclear world of restaurants and hangers-on was a tiny insight of the touring go-round; looking like some elderly witch onstage behind, what, an electric guitar?; and Bob at the mercy of others in hotel rooms and public places, was all referred to and replicated in his voice, variously muzzy, hazy, unclear, mysterious, so that his naming of Peter Lorre as his favourite folk singer seems not only a great joke but a true reference. If Joel Cairo were to sing this is what he would sound like. There was a synaesthetic blending of the atmosphere evoked by those photographs, and the cover, with the sound of the songs. Now, we surmised, he was in the society world that musicians experienced on the New York night scene, the cosmopolitan riches of the mind. Now, trying to penetrate and see through hindsight I remember sitting in that familiar bedroom, with that equally familiar buzzing Dansette-style player, and listening especially to Visions of Johanna and Sad Eyed Lady Of The Lowlands, getting something from the sound of his voice and the interplay of the instruments, flexible, interlocking arrangements, mostly taking their cue from the precise, often almost pattering, drum sound, that judicious and restrained drumming being the organising principle around which the songs seemed to grow organically. I knew that this was very different to all of the feelings evoked not only by socially concerned songs on Freewheelin' but also Highway 61 Revisited of the previous summer, (Highway 61 having a particularity and a diamond-hard clarity about it, unlike Blonde on Blonde's haziness, that its sound demonstrated too)

With this album the qualities that had seemed most associated with Bob Dylan blended in with the aspects of pop singles and culture, so that what one heard was these words in a network and context, an acoustic space created by the musicians, and the grain and texture of a voice singing words whose meaning is and isn't in the words themselves. Blonde On Blonde made the relationship of his voice to the words, and the sound of the words to the fibres of the instrumental effects, crucial to any meaning one might want to take from the album. The meaning of the album and the songs, aside from any other consideration, is in the totality of what it sounds like for Bob Dylan to sing and play with these people. Songs are always about that interplay of a voice singing words to a tune; that's the only place meaning can come from, and you have to be open to it. Of course being open to it can also mean for some enthusiasts finding things where they might not exist. What Bob Dylan is giving is not a steady state view where there is cause and effect, where the working of the world might be regarded as political in a wider sense, but a kaleidoscope derived from his own emotions and what he knows and has observed. You can hear the words as they pass by, and seem to know what they mean, or find particular images and formulations striking, but at the end of any song you'd be hard put to summarise it. It's not the world that's the subject, it's *his* world, and all of it in the sounds his voice can carry, that extraordinary range of vocal attitudes pushed to parody and caricature, only Elvis operating so close to that limit, the context his fans are aware of while remaining capable of hearing why it is a great singing voice too. Civilians hear only the mannerism and excess.

"You think he can sing," he asked, "You like his singing? You like his voice?"
It wasn't the only album I played then or the only music I listened to. The droll, five minute children's TV programme The Magic Roundabout that everyone, including me and my friends, made more of than was strictly necessary, had an occasional theme that played under the stop-go animation. It reminded me of Hang On To A Dream, the sad little piano tune that the cracked-voice Tim Hardin sang, asking how could we hang onto a dream, a question that was going to preoccupy us more than it did right then. That summer I listened to the Beatles with Revolver, where not just the songs but the whole sound of it is so different to their 1964 Fabs existence. They had undergone changes too, as Bob Dylan had, and were now part of the pop aristocracy, would never be the Moptops again, all of which could be heard in the bass-prominent production of the album, and more specifically in the single Paperback Writer and its wonderful B side Rain. The way they sang, and the words they sang, and the way the record sounded now, all was changed, not utterly perhaps, but enough for it to be very different from I Want To Hold Your Hand, which was still and always would be a most fantastic gift to the world. All of the groups seemed to be engaged in an automatic, involuntary process of self-improvement, each album a step forward from what had gone before. The Beach Boys, formerly of Fun, Fun, Fun, now gave us Pet Sounds, which was also

on the turntable at least as much as Bob and The Beatles. What's hard to quantify though is what meant the most and what that meaning might be, which of them was more important. Such different styles of music and songs coming out of America in 1966, both masterminded by singular individuals with a personal vision that needed other people to bring it into the world. The Beach Boys were by miles the most commercially successful, selling tons of records, and, which is more, putting beautiful songs and sounds into people's perceptions and memories, as well as inspiring other bands to see what might be achieved by thinking at the level of an album's achievement. Van Dyke Parks described Brian Wilson as wanting to saturate the tape with music, and hearing God Only Knows, Good Vibrations or the more simple and painful Caroline No, which seems to offer a true glimpse into the child always operating just below the surface of Brian Wilson, you believe it to be precisely so. His next album, it was reported, was going to be called Dumb Angel, and again this was an evocative juxtaposition. (Angel is never not evocative actually, and in this case created an instinctive connection with Kerouac's Desolation Angels of the previous year, links and chains, though on the surface nothing could seem to be further from Kerouac's dream of the good life well lived than the one the Beach Boys symbolised. Of course their vision of a California teen life would probably suggest an opposition to Kerouac's ideal, but neither version was quite what it seemed, though they cast a spell of equivalent power and in many cases enchanted exactly the same market share.) It was further reported, aeons before Bob went evangelical, that the album in preparation was to be a teenage symphony to God, another connection given that, amid his disappointments, travels and come-downs what Kerouac was concerned with was the Catholic God of his childhood, and what he took to be Buddhist God consciousness and the forms it took for poor, suffering, beat humanity. It was possible to think, if you were the right age, that everything we heard coming over the airwaves that summer and late summer was a teenage symphony to God in one way or another.

You could like or love the music of Brian Wilson and Bob Dylan, but the main difference was that Bob Dylan was the one that you would choose to be like if it could be arranged. From the start he had the thing that some boys have from earliest school days. You look at them and envy them, you want to be like them, you want to be them, or what you imagine, dream, them to be. Most people would want to have Brian Wilson's musical gift, or singing voice, but few, I imagine, would want to be like Brian Wilson, because outside of music it was difficult to say what he was except troubled and then unwell. Still, what remains the case is that even though I may have spent time reading, thinking about and listening to Brian Wilson's music ever since, I didn't write about it at increasing length, as I did with Bob Dylan.

Blonde On Blonde. One says it like a charm or mantra as if to conjure up something, and it's used as much against him as for him when wanting to mark out where he now is, where he figures on some scale of excellence we keep fashioning. Unhappiness is caused by wanting things to be other than they are. An old record by remaining the same has the power to make you happy or unhappy by bringing to life that different, earlier state of affairs, and by reminding you that those circumstances no longer obtain. The point about the past in general or our own specific past is that like art or recorded music, it doesn't go away, though one's own history often seems to have the ungraspable quality of a dream, just beyond recall, compared with the specifics of public events. It waits to be rediscovered and to inform the present. In 1966 in interviews Bob Dylan wouldn't willingly give the time of day; now he can't help but remind you of it with every record you add to the growing queue patiently waiting on the CD racks; the queue that might one day exceed the dusty yards of vinyl refugees, those entities, those statements, – with their accumulated Dylan inches – always trying to secure a permanent resting place somewhere about the house. As the means of music production and distribution inexorably changes, everything drifts to the landing, to the loft or the attic. The music centre with its overlarge deck doesn't suit the living room any longer in its new, open minimal guise, you can see that darling, surely. All the sleeves that have journeyed in cardboard box after cardboard box from domicile to domicile just don't fit. So off they go, up under the roof, to take their place alongside those old stereo players and their huge speakers – how do they make these micro systems so small and efficient these days sweetie? – and a box of distressed 45s, the shoebox of C90s one never plays but can't quite throw out, the teetering piles of books and magazines; and the mementos of that real child who becomes your inner one forever: all of the Thomas The Tank Engine slightly scratched and battered fleet, the discarded cuddly toys that must be kept in perpetuity, and that tiny lovable hat with flaps that once seemed so big and lasted all of one winter and always reminded everyone of a Chechen guerrilla cap. Not thrown away, stored to be revisited, always above your head and in your head, waiting for you to come and copy what you need to know again. These visions of Johanna are all that remain, and the place they will always remain is on Blonde On Blonde.

Now Blonde On Blonde is used as a symbol, a quintessence of those times, that Bob touchstone, that yardstick, that altar, that shrine, that holy relic. Then it was part of the parade passing by in one of the tiny connecting eras that are labelled the Sixties. An album, like an argument, is always about what it is about, and also something more. An album represents itself, and something more than itself. It was a sign, a confirmation of the way everything was going to be in a constant state of improvement. You liked the last album? Wait until you hear the next one. You liked black and white? Now it's in colour. You heard it in mono? We have it in stereo. We believed that we had lucked into a set of circumstances where everything was possible. If it could be imagined it could be made to be so. In fact that's really the corny 1950s credo that we hadn't bothered to recognise: Every day in every way we are getting better and better. Dylan gave us a magnificent unexpected album with Highway

61 Revisited. What could he possibly do to improve on it? What? A double album? And one song takes up a complete side? My God, what's he trying to do to us? Continuous flux and amelioration, and everything for the best in the best of all possible worlds. I can hardly bear to think what he will come up with next time. In fact there was no next time. What appeared to be a glorious indication of a new road ahead was a terminus. He never made an album that sounded like Blonde On Blonde again and after the tour he was back in America where he had a motorbike accident, much disputed as to cause and severity. After that he took time out and the world heard the kind of silence that had been palpable in the concert halls during the acoustic set. He recuperated. He recovered. Eventually he came back but when he did it was, inevitably, to changed times, and on a different set of tracks.

Jimmy Gatz from North Dakota by way of southern Minnesota, willow fields, snowy woods and sky blue lakes, made his way to the Lake Superior shore where he came to the attention of his eventual benefactor Dan Cody, a cowboy resonance for those who notice these things. Kitted out for sailing life in Duluth, Bob Dylan's birthplace, he eventually finds his way east, all the way to New York, under a new name that he believes is more impressive, more indicative of who he really is. Who does this remind us of? There are other ground bass themes in common. Jay Gatsby watches the green light flashing at the end of the dock belonging to the house where the girl who used to be his fiancée now lives, a mother and married to someone else. He watches and dreams how to change things so that they will be together once more, but with everything just as it was. The green light tells him about the future that will consist of the past restored.

Since its release, and probably because of the circumstances of the motorbike accident and its career consequences, Blonde On Blonde has seemed to function as a green light, winking at us, representing in this case not the future but the past that delivered us to the contemporaneity of its release. What a fluke and lucky break that rock'n'roll happened to us in the order that it did, knowing what we knew, which wasn't much but perhaps just enough, out there in the decade after the war on the new estates under suburban clouds. Stretching away behind that record is all of the lives its buyers and listeners led up to that point, selfish and innocent, solemn, compla-cent – its canals, cooling towers, markets, and streets of trees, its bus rides to town, its libraries, its schools with their secret away-from-home life, its visions of girls and television, its succession of records and songs listened to in bedrooms, its modest enfolding homes of love, undramatic, unsensational, familiar as Weetabix suppers, its society of aunts and cousins, neighbours, and the parents we loved and sometimes suspected couldn't really be ours because we were so different, only to discover as the years added up that we were on the way to becoming versions of them. And more immediately standing behind the record, and what it has since come to symbolise, is the 5 short years that led up to it, so short and still a lifetime, during which all of the versions and embodiments of Bob Dylan to that point, some of which were seen in Murray Lerner's record of Newport Festivals, moved and had their being. I feel as Nick Carraway did when he looked back on the train rides of his youth. That's my Sixties, not the revolution or the politics but the thrilling, and for that moment, endless parade of songs, and the place where I experienced them. Not a Mid West winter reverie, but a summer evocation. Of course there were dreary gloomy days, but recalling those years what one brings forth are magic moments and golden days, like the festival fields in Murray Lerner's film, the false and true memories of being young in the sunshine, where all is shining, faces alive in the air that surrounds us, kindly and warm, carrying our songs to us, serial and overlapping, a fountainhead. Out of rock and roll and blues and old-fashioned pop, but as if from nowhere, so different and enticing were the guitars and voices. It was not only Bob Dylan, but him foremost amongst them, shaping what other musicians wanted to do by revealing what was possible. That succession of days and nights, that essentially short time, stretching back like America into infinity, rolling under clouded or cloudless skies, is the legacy Bob Dylan laid down and why whatever he now does is accorded such scrutiny. We dreamed a dream. Whatever excellence he was able to create later, why he is considered important, a genius even, is because of what he did during this time, now gone, long gone, this time everyone keeps thinking about still. It's because of who he was then, and who we were and how he entered our dreams. We all have a Hibbing that raised us, with us wherever we go.

DREAM HOME

At times, when consciousness begins to fade,
when beam ends of light start absolving me,
my first bedroom is there, as it was then,
in the house where if not born I was made,
(raised up toward the person I would be.)
And though it's true you can't go home again,

not that home, still, there are times I awake
expecting to see again the old space,
those surroundings, ceilings and walls I keep
from a childhood ago. The morning light,
its eyelid glow ancient and new, will break
on curtains and windows I turn to face,
trying to distinguish waking from sleep,
surfacing and sinking each day and night

into years, the years come and gone.
The serial rooms dissolve and I find
that room I dreamt in until 21,
the room for improvement I bear in mind.

PART TWO

RAMBLIN' DOWN THROUGH
THE WORLD

"And beyond the Wild Wood again? Where it's all blue and dim,
and one sees what may be hills or perhaps they mayn't,
and something like the smoke of towns, or is it only cloud-drift?"
Kenneth Grahame **The Wind In The Willows**

If they asked me, I could write a book About the way you walk,
and whisper, and look. I could write a preface On how we met
I Could Write A Book Rodgers&Hart
1940

CHAPTER SIXTEEN
TUNE OF THE TIMES

You look in the mirror and see where you are. But what if the mirror can only show you what used to be? 1966. Is that a mirror, the mirror that shows all the years that approached its looking glass, the years like a trail, a yellow brick road leading to this time where happiness and colour seem to be in the air like sound waves? 1966 and the motorcycle accident, then absence and silence, and the sound of music already created travelling like the waves we imagine leaving this planet and moving out across the emptiness between one world and the next, becoming more and more attenuated until it's difficult to say whether they exist or not. Absence and silence behind the blossom world, like the dark backing that makes reflection possible. 1966, the mirror that everyone came through to find the world in waiting on the other side, and Bob Dylan out in the woods and dirt roads beyond the city, needing to see what kind of person he appears to be.

We read about the motorcycle accident as we read about everything else, in Disc, which also travelled under the names Disc and Music Echo, and Disc Weekly, or in the Melody Maker, or both in those weeks when they seemed essential and money allowed. It was difficult to know then how serious it was. There were rumours and gloomy predictions, nothing substantiated. What it seemed to mean was that all bets were off for immediate Bob Dylan plans, and we would have to get by without him. Which is what happened. After all it was the summer of 1966 with the finest flowering of pop and rock music underway, the finest since the previous summer anyway, and I Want You was still in the charts, Manfred Mann was scoring with their version of Just Like A Woman. Bob Dylan wasn't forgotten, and still seemed to be there. People do and don't exist in the recorded world, and besides, our heads were also full of the Beatles and the Beach Boys with their latest album masterworks, and the singles that came from them, Eleanor Rigby and God Only Knows, both full of beauty and sadness. Sunny Afternoon, Summer In The City, Good Day Sunshine, all of them on the radio and in your life, the summer made sound. The 1966 Sixties, so different from the Freddie and The Dreamers Sixties of only 3 years before; although it was also true that someone so resolutely of an even earlier era, Jim Reeves, would have a hit with Distant Drums in September and that it would go on to become, as charts prove but memory doesn't, the best-selling single of the year. Still, the world was full of music, our kind of music, and also the idea that it would never cease and would only, could only, get better and better. It was as if everything had been arranged so that this was how it could be now. Our futures were bound up in it too. After the summer was over we would start the next year at school, the final one, the one that culminated in A levels, and after that we would be launched upon the world, the wide world, and into whatever we had thought that we might be and do, which probably involved college or university and thus leaving home. No doubt some people already had not only an idea but an ambition, a vision, as Bob Dylan had had, though his was always at a tangent to college conformity. Having a clear idea of what you want to be, then bending all your energies to making it happen will shape your life. Unfortunately so will the opposite, when not only do you not have an idea of what could occupy your life, a lot of the time you're not even sure what kind of person you are. This too will get you to a destination, even if it's not one you ever had in mind. Decisions and choices will be taken and you will find yourself along the highway, looking forward and looking back, pondering what's to come.

What was to come in the short term was the entwining of more songs on the radio with school life, and checking on that other world that existed chiefly in the columns of the papers. Disc didn't seem to be the heavyweight authority that Melody Maker was, but it did have two writers who you wanted to read every week. Penny Valentine reviewed and did interviews. She had long blonde hair, bright sparkling eyes, and an elongated, rather questing nose. She looked Sixties to her fingertips. Derek Taylor wrote about the exotic world of the West Coast from his insider position as Beach Boys press agent and ex-Beatles confidante and ghost. He had a judicious common-sense tone, a thick, dark, hip moustache and an air of having seen it all before while telling you how brand new it was. He was the one who had written the sleeve notes to Byrds albums, as he had done Beatles For Sale, and the result was stylishly over-the-top, but knowingly so, and thus undercutting itself. He called the Byrds raffish and rakish, gliding out of the canyons of the Hollywood Hills on their motor-cycles at night. Naturally this was tremendously appealing in the Walsall area. The previous year he had pointed out how strange it was that a song like Tears could be such a massive English hit, under-standing its appeal, and he would know coming from Liverpool, but underlining how it could never happen in America. And now here he was in wintertime talking about the Beach Boys Good Vibrations. What better summer song, but their own God Only Knows, yanked from Pet Sounds, had been the hit of August and September, and so November was the time we heard about the blossom world, with its perfumed air, colourful clothes and sunlight playing on girls' hair. It was Derek Taylor who reported that the next album, the one that would take even Good Vibrations and make it look like the aural equivalent of a cocked hat, was to be called Dumb Angel, that pebble dropped in the pool of associations, resonances spreading out in wave form. And it was Derek Taylor who further gave us the later instalment that this great title was now off, and the record, confidently expected to be the finest achievement in modern pop, was to be named Smile. Frustratingly the release date of this wonder was postponed on a regular basis and the original never did appear. One clue to the dashing of hopes might have been that, lovely though God Only Know had been, its sales had been outpaced by the other single taken from Pet Sounds, the much more orthodox reworking of the folk song Sloop John B, earlier made collegiate by the Kingston Trio. It was skilfully done but entirely lacking in the transcendent awareness of things passing, the heartbreaking, Shakespearean sense of children becoming adults, that seemed to be Brian Wilson's characteristic trait. He felt more deeply and melodically what Bob Dylan had said a couple of years before, Everything passes, everything changes. What Brian Wilson asked was, Where did your long hair go? And he made it seem the saddest and most important question there could be. The record was to be called Smile because of a pre-hippie phrase: The Smile You Send Out Returns To You, but it could as easily have been because of a phrase from an older song, Smile though your heart is breaking.

Meanwhile in the same wintry month the other fantastic record to rush the charts and pirouette on the sales summit was Reach Out I'll Be There. Penny Valentine's review began with a sentence something like, "This is the record that you'll see on the shelves of your record shop with light shining from it." I loved this because of its unguarded but smart enthusiasm. You felt, as she did, that we were in a time when brilliant record after brilliant record would emerge, and it was only right and proper, and we were there to see it all happen. And for the moment Bob Dylan had nothing to do with it.

What did you have that year? What didn't you have? Marvellous Motown, fantastic Stax.
Except that he did have something to do with even the faultlessly professional production line of Motown roughening up, getting

hoarse and churning. And though he was absent, having heard him, having had him give permission by example to sound like that, to breathe like that, to break up or recklessly extend the lines like that, to change the possibilities simply by having the ignorance, naiveté, courage or calculation to do what he wanted to do, and then do something else, well it opened things up for everyone. Some people just took the chance to try and sing like him, others saw that his example could be less obvious, more indirect. On the Beatles it seemed that his effect was to show John Lennon that he could do songs that came out of what mattered to him, and not the character-free pop zone of what his Beatle songs had been to that point; though as previously mentioned the interviewer Kenneth Allsop had indicated that the taste for the wordplay proven by his books was going to waste if it couldn't appear in the songs as well. What mattered to John Lennon was his childhood and that's what he was drawn to write about. While the charts of November and December were dominated by summer songs, and country and western style prison laments from Tom Jones about grass and home, quite a stylistic shift from What's New Pussycat, the Beatles were engaged in an album version of a nuclear arms race to see whether they or the Beach Boys could come up with the album that would change the face of rock music forever. They read the pop weeklies too. After that all the answers would be in and worries would be over.

In the winter months when the Beatles began the album that didn't exist yet with two new songs, one of which was Strawberry Fields Forever, John Lennon created something that came to flower in the summertime. It was Strawberry Fields Forever that, appropriately, really changed things forever. I can't say on first hearing it that I thought Bob Dylan had contributed to what it was, to how it sounded. It's impossible to believe that Dylan would have had any interest in making those kinds of sounds at all. But now, knowing how all kinds of words, sounds and attitudes permeate our thoughts involuntarily, how other events and emotions from childhood stay within you, at once permanent, arbitrary and hidden, and how what is written or created draws on all of this whatever the conscious intent, I understand it differently. I believe the example of Bob Dylan had allowed John Lennon to move beyond the imitation and homage of I'm A Loser and You've Got To Hide Your Love Away. Now he could use what he felt was true and deep in his character. If he did this then the artist genius he had suspected he was from childhood could exist in songs. Not the songs that had brought such worldly success. For the most part they had been impersonal, the words used to fit to tunes that made songs and sounds whose purpose was not to fuel analysis or introspection. Even Help!, which came from a real place inside him, was a jolly chart topper that no-one believed to be a genuine cry from a desperate heart.

In the heat of Spain the previous summer, in the enforced inactivity between filming takes, and the fear of the inactivity to come, knowing, as we did not, that the Beatles would never tour again, he went back in his thoughts to memories of the summer fete he had loved as a child, around the corner from his home in Aunt Mimi's house, the fete held in the Salvation Army children's home called Strawberry Field, which he changed because it sounds and sings better. Bob Dylan's role in enlarging not only the Beatles idea of what they could do with songs, but everyone's, is an area for debate that can never *prove* anything but may indicate how interwoven influences were then. Would John Lennon have changed the kinds of songs he wrote without the example of Bob Dylan? It sounds like a reasonable question, but the influences and exposures were so multifarious. They influenced him; he influenced them; all the groups were writing songs and watching each other. Think of it like a deck of cards in two halves, and they flicker and shuffle back into a whole again. And what he took from Bob Dylan I believe was the possibility of writing a song that would be open, personal and yet work like something from the tradition. Let me take you down it begins, as inviting and matter of fact as, Come gather round friends. And in writing it and then submitting it to musical treatment and adaptation under the guidance of George Martin – who against type, one would have thought, adored the song and John Lennon's voice, – the Beatles, but chiefly John Lennon, invented English psychedelia as it took over the country and then the world in the coming months.

The album Revolver had shown how interested the Beatles were in sounds, in altering volumes and balances and textures of what had been conventional rock guitars and drums. Tomorrow Never Knows on that record had been more experimental, avant-garde, than anyone could have expected from a group that only the year before had put out something so of the 50s as Dizzy Miss Lizzy, and the year before that a dreamily reverential version of a Buddy Holly song. But it wasn't the experimental aspect of Strawberry Fields alone that caught the imagination; it was the way it sounded almost classical, not really like a rock record, and this from the most famous rock group there was. It was the way John Lennon's voice and words blended with the sounds of the Mellotron, which could seem to be so many instruments, especially swooning cellos, that proved so touching and heartfelt. Anyone could hear that this was something other than a pop or rock record as we had known it. There was pain, regret and the process of someone thinking aloud melodically, all of which demonstrated and revealed a mystery and a grace. Something had shifted. This was new and different from even Revolver. It seemed to require another way of responding to it. Now pop had to be significant in a way it hadn't quite before, even if it had always been a matter of life and death.

So Strawberry Fields Forever and Penny Lane came out as a double A side, and their publicising film clips (not called videos then) were shown on Tops of The Pops. There were the Beatles in the frock coats and bits of beards and moustaches, the vague but definite associations with the past, Victoriana, which seemed to stand for their past too, because both of the songs were about the Liverpool they had known as children and teenagers. And with its night filming, and colours that we could only see in the still of the record sleeve, all telly being black and white, its strings coming out of a tree, moody looks and mysterious goings on offered as art rather than pop, some of the elements of what was to come with things psychedelic were already in place. Other people could claim to have had a hand in coming up with the factors that psychedelic music became identified with, which in a broad and not well-defined way was an aural aspect or equivalence, or at least reference to, the LSD experience. Since most of us had only read about this and were never likely to know it for real it was all to do with what you could hear. In practice this meant a mixing of styles, and bringing something more to the words than had usually been the case. Donovan had been as speedy a changer of identity as Bob Dylan. He too moved from denim authenticity and protest polemic though not, in his case, to fronting a seasoned band of bar veterans and reinventing a rock style, but being a dandy of sorts, one who would shortly adorn recently acquired satins and velvet with beads and flowers. His second album, Fairy Tale, still 1965, pre-satin and velvet attire, although they were mentioned in a representative lyric right there on the front of the record cover, had the beginning of a shift into extra instrumentation, and a sound that suggested both jazz and a kind of chamber folk ensemble, with cellos and harpsichord. His voice too became much more ornate and emphatic in the way it pronounced words and rolled r's, to create the effect of his Celtic heritage either genuine or wished for. Atmosphere and ambience were of the essence. Mostly this worked very well, occasionally it sounded overdone and silly, but it distinguished him from Bob Dylan immediately. One of the reasons this was so was the brilliant record production he had, where everything was very clear and located in the sound, particularly his voice. And although there were difficulties with contracts that prevented records being released here, he produced two records for U.S. release, Sunshine Superman and Mellow Yellow, where his subject matter of young people in a specific London location, and the carefully arranged instrumentation with flavours of jazz, folk and blues was absolutely of the moment.

Where this differed from what John Lennon had done was in the importance of childhood to Strawberry Fields Forever. By the time the Beatles had completed the album of which the double-sided-single songs had been a starting point, psychedelia was one word but two distinct styles. English psychedelia was distinguished from what was called psychedelia in America by the nuances of subject matter. America's version was to do with the sounds and the words of minds reaching for some other dimension. England went in another direction, not examining the edges of perception but poring over what had already happened. John Lennon and Syd Barrett had complicated relationships with their childhoods, seeming to yearn for its rituals and safety, while acknowledging, in a quasi-Victorian way, as the fancy dress indicated, the pain and loss that also centres on the child state. American bands used the psychedelic to imagine the future; English ones looked to the past. Strawberry Fields Forever, even the title has a double edge, as a kind of hooray for them slogan, but also an acknowledgement that some parts of childhood last forever and have to keep being dealt with.

What begins as a real expression of one person's individual view on the world, one that takes its form in their style, soon becomes a series of techniques or tricks that other people feel they should master in order to produce something that they don't see as slavish imitation, but as a genuine expression of their own individuality. So the Beatles big extravaganza masterwork album, Sgt Pepper's Lonely Hearts Club Band, (always Sgt and never Sergeant) trumpeted and blazoned forth with more publicity than had formerly been the case, they saw as being inspired by the American West Coast bands who, influenced by Old West typography, graphic design and various recreational drugs, had loosened up and grown more colourful. This starting point allowed the Beatles to evolve their specifically English album from what they knew and what they'd been. Then it became

a template and indicator to all the other groups of what they should
be playing next, as well as making them think that maybe groups
was not the right term anymore. Perhaps they should start referring
to themselves as bands instead. What had been hard-drinking blues
or r&b combos were exposed to LSD, softened up and began thinking about madmen running through the fields. Former provincial hit
makers who came from a background of narrow ties, shiny mohair
suits and winkle-pickers, shifted to brocade, Indian shirt collars and
mouth-framing beards and moustaches. Almost immediately too
what had been personal and dark became caricatured, hackneyed and
trivialised. Boy wonder Stevie Winwood left Ray Charles behind to
join Traffic, adopting an envied, copied, and no doubt misunderstood
communal living and rehearsing in the countryside ethos. This eventually came up with the totally sincere, yet apparent self parody, Hole
In My Shoe, and other bands imitated that. All of which began to be
called Enid Blyton Rock, where the twee, the childish and the distorting application of phasing were never far away, and mystery and
grace absent. It's what many people still think of when they use the
term Sixties, and itemise afghans, kaftans, bell bottoms, beads, flowers, and fluorescent colours, in a children's text book précised digest
of that fabulous, hallucinatory decade, whose falsifications endure,
like Strawberry Fields, forever. And this was the era of flower power,
symbolised, typified and broadcast at large by the blessed Beatles
showing that they too had misunderstood what they had created
with Lennon's channelling of childhood anguish. Even the Monkees
were part of it, the Monkees who had been created in a business-like,
if not actively cynical, spirit to recreate the pop group, filmic hi-jinks
of A Hard Day's Night two years after the fact, but not in arty black
and white, in colourful 1966 West Coast sunshine, and who with
the assistance of crack teams of writers and players had made records
that not only typified the era but would last as long as the genuine
article. In fact what they demonstrated was with great records, no
matter how they came into being, if the public response is genuine

and emotional and long-lasting they are always the real thing. And all of it was to do with 1967, not a decade, a year; and 1967 with its rapidly applied brand name Summer of Love was the year when Bob Dylan released no new records and played no part in the culture and counter-culture, and, in every way you can think of, had *nothing* to do with 1967's hippy heaven at all. Which has made no difference to his being claimed as its figurehead and exemplar ever since.

The summer of Sgt. Pepper was also the summer of A levels. I remember some of us walking along in school time but out of school, early afternoon in sunlight, laughing, holding buttercup chains, and the glasses wearers had little buttercup sprigs pinioned in their folding hinges. We were enacting, it seems, flower power. We looked silly and young, as we were supposed to. Given that we were so light-hearted no doubt this was after the exams but before the results. The results were one of those things that, as is claimed for Sgt. Pepper, changed the world, my world at least, and that was the only one I had to live in. The exact details might be capable of being found now in the little suitcases and packets of papers that move from property to property, decade to decade but somehow I doubt it, and it's not something I can imagine trying. To say one reasonable, one not good, and one fail is the ballad version I've carried down the years, almost but not quite forgotten. They weren't good enough was the point. The offer I had been made, and where was it from I wonder now, was dependent on something I hadn't achieved. The immediate result of which was that times changed. Or to be precise, the future changed.

I wasn't hurt but was completely astounded about the sudden jump in time, and couldn't work out what had happened to the moments between one thing and the next. Why was I sitting on the ground looking bemused with no memory of getting there?

What had been a proposed and supposed future wouldn't now take place. Something would, but what would it be? That time of not long before, the choices and form filling and offers, the possibilities dependent on 3 slightly more than reasonable grades, didn't exist now, any more than yesterday. There were no re-sits, no clearing house which might take up not so hot candidates, no advice on how to move beyond this. Or at least there might be, but not for me. What's the point of staying on and doing them again, Dad asked. Why should you do better then than you have now? You need to think about a job. That vague mirage of a college or a university that I hadn't thought about too closely, but had expected to come true, was over and it was an empty, scary feeling. I looked ahead, emerging from the comfort and safety and the not having to think about anything but school and me, and realised how unsuited I was to having to want something badly enough to get it. How unlike Bob Dylan I was. He had pursued his dream east, thousands of miles, hitching a ride, knowing hardly anyone, and making people notice him in New York, always packed to the penthouses with people who came from America's small towns and wanted to make it in something or other. Whereas I wasn't good enough to even start what I had thought was my track. It was like looking up from the sofa, covered with my Dad's blue overcoat, and seeing the moustached doctor appear at the door. I hadn't known I was born, but now I was getting an idea. The future I might have had, what was going to happen to it? Would it dissolve entirely, because after all it had never existed; or would it go to another? Elsewhere, I was going to have to make a different way, and eventually I would come to know what happened next, and what happened next.

Bob Dylan came through the mirror of the motorcycle accident and found that the world he had been part of had disappeared, could be made to disappear. The tour that had taken him to the top and bottom of the world to be booed and cheered had been planned to continue, and now it wouldn't. The sickness, the ups and the downs, the medicines he said kept the machine going, could dissolve. He was off a conveyor and could find out now what else he wanted to do and who he preferred to be. I looked around and wondered what I could do. Somehow a suggestion emerged. What had I spent a lot of time doing? What place had I spent a reasonable amount of time visiting? If you like to be around books a library is a venue of choice surely? Then why not try to work in one? This reasoning seemed to operate well enough not only on me. A variety of people, suited and ill-suited in all kinds of meanings, found their way into library employment. These days, as with most jobs, anyone should ask themselves are they clued up and happy enough to be a blend of auditor, IT consultant and MBA aspirant. We didn't, it has to be admitted, subject ourselves to such an interrogation, and neither did Bob Dylan in the continuation of his, at that point, interrupted career. Bob played for fun with the Band in different houses, sometime his, sometimes theirs: no boos, no cheers, no audience, putting down songs and tracks that they remembered or wrote or amended, in sequences no-one itemised. All of it was something at the time we knew nothing about. Its emergence in stages, and what the revealed and then revealed again and again collection of songs means and meant has become, in an odd way, like Blonde On Blonde, a permanent marker and memorial of that time, issued in different versions, covertly then overtly, discussed and analysed, becoming, as it all does, historical studies. Right then 1967 Sixties was going on somewhere else and he was ignoring it. And I joined Walsall Library Service and was sent to work in Willenhall Library, dark and old-fashioned and about as far from flower-power as one could get, even though it was supposed to be everywhere. One of the reasons for this was around the time I began so did Radio One, and almost-local band The Move had the first song played on it, the carefully of the moment Flowers In The Rain, to be mentioned forever afterwards in rock annals and pub quizzes. 1967 was going on nearby and I was trying to take notice.

So I woke up one morning half asleep with all my prospects in a heap and dimly realised the child I was still, thinking that life would arrange itself the way I wanted it to be, that it was only fair. A couple of years earlier Bob Dylan had sung about people who thought they were nothing more than something to invest in. Now I began to see I was ill-equipped to think that way. Some people recognised what their qualities were and decided how to use or develop them. Others saw what they thought was an area that made money and went with that. I'd had only the vaguest notion of what to do, and ambition seemed to be a quality as evident as an eiderdown's colour. It's a joke of sorts that people applying for library work say they like books and people. It's true the work can accommodate being able to memorise various things, some of which include book titles and writers' names, but like any office job it really requires management skills and a taste for logistics and seeing how things can be changed. As for people, well anyone working at a public counter finds out that they can like individuals, but you're always going to find "the public" an awkward bunch, incapable of saying what they really want, reacting unpredictably to innocuous remarks and generally being slow to grasp the obvious. But here I was, working for the library service I had used so often, though not in the branch I'd most visited, and finding it fairly congenial. After the Willenhall outpost I moved to the Central Library and found out how to do what was required and get along with colleagues and the readers, and listened as the rest of the pop world went by and Bob Dylan was only an irregular mention in the music press. There was still great music around. The Kinks had issued one of their most touching songs, Autumn Almanac, which I have a ghost memory of as hearing while I was at school, thinking about it while in lessons, at a desk. I look away, or close my eyes, and the pictures that I get away from the influence of the eyes, in the darkness inside my head, seem to indicate this. At those times the desk seems very real. But I must be thinking of another song of theirs, an earlier desk, because Autumn Almanac was released after I left school, the same month Radio One began, which is surely where I heard it, despite its not being the first record played. One of its lines says, This is my street, and I'm never going to leave it. As he sings it in his moving, underrated, always well-recorded voice, he is celebrating working class tradition and longevity, but also raising the question of how that could be an unambiguously good thing. Tea and toasted buttered currant bun can't compensate for lack of sun. Autumns keep coming back. Autumns, for those who had spent years at school, or had hoped for college, were the true beginnings of the year, with their familiar sights: coloured leaves falling, the leaf-coloured sun going down, and the change in the scent of the evening air. People had to change and grow and improve and move on, not stay in their own street forever. What else had the years we were living through been about so far?

CHAPTER SEVENTEEN
OUR LOCAL HEAVENS

1967 disappeared with its fancy clothes and flowers, whose photographs have persisted ever since, that true and accurate and false record of folk costume believed to be common to all then alive and young, and the Summer of Love proved to have no more power of longevity than any other summer. And then it was 1968. Who knew what 1968 would bring? Bob Dylan perhaps? And yes, Bob Dylan started to come back to music papers after a year when his activities had been private rather than public. There were reports of new songs offered to various groups; then following the death of his first idol in October he was invited to appear at a Woody Guthrie tribute concert; and, more excitingly, not long after there was a new album called John Wesley Harding. There were high hopes for this. During the more than a year he'd been absent, the way he looked in 1966, and the Blonde on Blonde outpouring of hair, the triangular jaw line, had become design staples in what we had learned was to be called the counter-culture. He became a graphic design poster and a thousand photographic posters. His 1966 face had become an emblem seeming to stand for a whole network of connections, associations and inchoate causes. That last music he had produced, the long songs with their city poetry that made sense even while it wasn't making sense, had been what other groups aspired to. It had given a lead and an example and was a template either hidden or obvious for much of what had developed inside those record sleeves adorned with curlicue typography and colours more vivid, startling, intense and various than the washed-out haze that rainbows normally offer.

As so often when comparing memory and written facts, accounts differ. Discographies and biographies tell us that John Wesley Harding was issued in December 1967. Perhaps this was so in America. I have a memory of walking past someone in the street, under the grand trees on that attractive street the Central Library was in. I saw that the record was under his arm. There's no reason why I should remember the date but it's as if there's a label attached to the picture of this memory, and the label reads, February 1968. I rushed back and said, "Is it out then?", because I didn't think it was. He nodded and said he'd just bought it from Taylor's the record shop whose familiar back room, home of the Lou Christie joke, was a few yards further down. As with all albums, especially his albums, the whole entity was something to ponder. And that's exactly what I promptly did with the cover photograph, the little fable on the back, trying to relate the feeling that these things evoked with the actual sound of the album, back in the bedroom with the record player's red light and staticky buzz for accompaniment. John Wesley Harding marks the beginning of the public change in what we thought Bob Dylan was. His appearance for instance. Because the Woody Guthrie tribute concert was so close to the album's release there were two lots of new visual information to co-ordinate. At the concert he wore a fringe of black beard, a grey suit and his hair looked longish, but flattened, brushed back, almost centre parted. Not at all the Medusa model that became the starting point for the look that Jimi Hendrix could do even more naturally, the impetus for the frizzy perms that started to mutate through bands, skipping from head to head. The album cover, though he wore a hat, showed a shorter, more orthodox trim, and the dusting of whiskers at an earlier stage. So as had become traditional I looked at the pictures and listened to the album. What was it one heard then, and can hear still each time it is played via whatever system happens to be contemporary, (which won't, assuredly, be a staticky lid-opening box with a deck). Well, the truth is that no matter how improved or remastered, any record and its songs will be either exactly as it was, or more or less as it was. What will have changed is the person listening.

What it was when first heard in February 1968, is one of Bob's strongest albums ever in the sense of it having an encompassing identity. Nothing as vulgar as a concept album, or a rock opera, but a definite collection of songs that belong together, and sound like they belong together, recorded in a short time with specific intent. Everyone refers to its austerity, restraint to the point of inhibition. It's the work of someone walking a careful line. The actual recording quality is as good as he ever achieved, crisp, clear, with the drums crucial to the dynamics of every song, and some of the best harmonica he ever contributed, sparing and ever-present, high and exact, nagging like a memory. The subject matter, along with the folk based tunes, has returned to a mythic land, rather than a city, somewhere sharing characteristics with the Old West that drifters knew long before there were Beats. He's singing about man's relationship with God, the Devil, desire, sin, temptation, peace, ease, love, security, and mortality, and hardly a song going beyond three minutes. The long songs he had become renowned for seemed to be over. All that remained of Blonde on Blonde was a nucleus, its drummer and bassist and, reassuringly somehow, that suede, double-breasted jacket, removed from the accompanying checked scarf and cosmopolitan riches, to the stark, wooded hinterland. The sound and the style are light years from Blonde On Blonde with its poison headaches and substance abuse, tinctures and syrups of wild quicksilver. What it doesn't sound like, as a consequence, is exciting in what come to be the conventional manner, turning away from not only its predecessor but the whole world of rock and pop around it. He's not concerned with the contemporary scene, but the eternal one. It has the peculiar characteristic of being a considerable piece of work, groundbreaking

and one that will stand the test of time, and, strangely, a disappointment from the man who – was it only a couple of years ago or a
lifetime? – had brought the electric carnival of Highway 61 to town,
and whose last mad whirled tour had earned this wonderfully on-
the-nose quoted tribute from Marlon Brando, not normally noted as
a rock aficionado: "The two loudest things I've ever heard are a freight
train going by, and Bob Dylan and The Band." Well, you heard John
Wesley Harding and you knew times had changed.

The way he had changed seemed to be connected with the way
time and things had changed for me. There was more music but the
feeling in the air was not that of 1966. In Birmingham Town Hall,
where I had seen Bob, I saw the Incredible String Band and aside
from being charmed by Robin Williamson saying, "Are the crocuses
out yet", I loved what I'd heard on the albums done right here before
us. There was a sense of their connection with some older Britain, a
Celtic past that had national reverberations, particularly on songs
like Witch's Hat, but also of their coming of age in the times we
knew. They had too all the flavourings of exotic countries far form us
because of the range of instruments they played. What I also noticed,
when they called audience members up on stage to help them out,
was the difference between their hair and post-psychedelic, gypsy
finery, and the resolutely non-descript ordinary scruffiness of the willing assistants. That's us, I thought, that's me, that's the gulf between
being the band and the fans. 1968 unreeling and I went down the
town on the bus as ever, did my best at work, carefully carried home a
Marks strawberry yoghurt in a little bag, (yoghurt, which my parents
didn't understand in any way) and thought I was doing something
pretty special, read the Beatles Monthly magazine as before, along
with Hunter Davies's biography, entranced by all the details of their
lives when they lived in places like I did, before they were the Beatles
and were only people. Hunter Davies had also produced Here We Go
Round The Mulberry Bush, a comic novel in a long tradition which
was a true picture of a slightly earlier time. It could be our story, my

story: of boys in school, the difficulties with girls, the separation education reveals and causes between where you are and where you might be, and the way you regard your parents. Because of the way success strikes the film made from the novel came out two years later, not very long after the time it was published but far enough for the film treatment to be in an entirely different idiom. It was now a film to flaunt cinema's current Pop conventions in style, subject matter and camera angles, with a title song by the of the moment group Traffic, and the soundtrack divided between them and Stevie Winwood's band of the moment before last, The Spencer Davis Group.

In the record racks of Boots, Smiths and Taylor's we assessed the sleeves we riffled slowly through, always assigning subliminal marks, studying form in a sense as my dad had done in the pages of the Daily Express. Record companies had an identity and evoked an ethos. CBS had a presence in our lives because so many of the people who were important to us could be found there. That's where Bob Dylan was, and the Byrds, Simon and Garfunkel and latterly Leonard Cohen, in addition to a range of stars that came from the wider showbusiness and Broadway community. CBS was also the company that put out the influential, budget-priced, sampler album, The Rock Machine Turns You On, where we could hear English and American acts and get a sense of what was out there, even if we didn't buy their complete albums. On this record you could find the quirkiness of a group with the temerity to call itself The United States of America, with their deceptively innocent-sounding song called I Won't Leave My Wooden Wife For You, Sugar, and another odd sounding ensemble, Spirit, with that paradoxical title meant to be an emblem of the times, Fresh Garbage. The quality English group the Zombies, there since the early days of 1964, had an example of their latest incarnation with Time Of The Season, a song that also seemed to sound like these times we were experiencing. There was a lot of music and much of it was good, but none of it felt like 1966 anymore even though the music scene, as it seemed normal to think of it, seemed to be bigger than ever.

Elektra was certainly bigger than ever, a company with a distinct identity that other companies would envy, gathering credibility since the middle of the decade. All of Elektra's artists were special in their substantial, colourful, cardboard sleeves that we would stand in the shops and gaze at, looking and looking, absorbed in their careful artwork, the quality design and typography, the immediately recognisable Elektra initial icon. It seemed to be the label that stood for quality and the days we were living in, these days right now. It encapsulated the spread and story of what had happened to us over the last few years. Judy Collins had begun on Elektra back in 1962 or 63, and then along came other folk notables like Phil Ochs, Tom Paxton and, some time later, the Incredible String Band. But there too were the blues of Paul Butterfield's Band, and Koerner, Ray and Glover. More than this was music representing what this time, this year, consisted of, seeming to blend all kinds of aspects of everything that might go under the broad church label of alternative, counter cultural, underground: Tim Buckley was on the label, The Doors, as well as the groups we didn't necessarily buy but approved of conceptually and in an impartial, non-purchasing sort of way were glad existed: Clear Light, the Holy Modal Rounders, Eclection, Earth Opera; and, more importantly, Love, who obviously we did buy and were of a higher, and more popular, order of achievement.

Away from the record rack I further studied the air that we breathed by ingesting any relevant magazine article within reach, as well as reading Tom Wolfe and Norman Mailer. Mailer, though you can't imagine him liking Bob Dylan much, connected in various ways. He was one of the first to anatomise what being hip meant, and how it came out of blackness in actuality and music. He had been in the group that began the Village Voice newspaper in 1950s Greenwich Village. His Advertisements For Myself, borrowed from Bloxwich library, had been a starting point for me, and I continued with his non-fiction paperbacks: Cannibals and Christians, The Presidential Papers, and on to the contemporaneous The Armies Of The Night. His alive, autodidact mind and exploratory, encompassing prose were the best teaching aids in trying to see and understand what was going on around us, though he would have been disappointed that I never really got on with, or made much effort to complete, his novels. There was also the New Writing In The USA, a Penguin book edited by a couple of American poets that had poetry and prose excerpts from a variety of people, and was where I first came across Richard Brautigan, who couldn't have been more Sixties, having started out in the 1950s, wide-eyed and deadpan with a troubled background and a lyrical, odd way of putting things down. The section here from a book I'd never heard of, but appreciated the title of immediately, Trout Fishing In America, was about buying lengths of used trout streams from the Cleveland Wrecking Yard, treated as if it were perfectly possible, waterfalls and flowers included, and made you want to find out more about him and read more of him. The poetry in the collection didn't appeal quite so much. I had more of a conservative core than I realised, although I should have given that, as well as S. J. Perelman, another of my passions, both in writing and in TV versions of his work, in the middle Sixties, just the same time I was ingesting Top Of the Pops, was consummate stylist P G. Wodehouse. (Although it wasn't essential for writers to have only initials for me to adore them.) After the false trail of the Liverpool Poets, the triumvirate of Roger McGough, Brian Patten and Adrian Henri, all whimsical lyrical notions and ampersands, who had appeared in 1965 in a red and black blaze of hardback glory, and then more widespread with the Penguin New Poets 10, The Mersey Sound, conspicuously championed by Allen Ginsberg who famously declared that Liverpool was the centre of human consciousness, I came across other poetry of course. Leonard Cohen was a beguiling but wrong route for awhile, at least as a poet to imitate. He did however sound a lot like a poet when he sang, and I thought there were two or three songs on that first album that couldn't be improved upon. I couldn't see how anyone could not appreciate Suzanne or The Stranger Song with his sepia voice and the incisive, picked strings of his guitar in small insinuating melody, but then I was always someone who tended to think that people thought as I did, and then gradually realised that what you are taught as you meet more people is that this is a misunderstanding most of us share.

What was shared too was the feeling that poetry was worth looking at and hearing. It wasn't necessarily old-hat, or Eng Lit or elitist. It could be part of rock, an adjunct, although I'd realised that Leonard notwithstanding there were usually going to be differences between words conceived as a lyric, and those written to be a poem. There were always other written poets to try. I happened upon Ted Walker in the Central Library where I was working and without any blinding revelation realised that this was something that appealed to me more; this seemed to be something I might try: English poetry that was careful and exact, rhymed, was based in unflashy observation of the natural world as much as towns. It made a connection with a book I had read around then too, The Peregrine by J. A. Baker, a distillation of a decade of peregrine stalking and observation in precisely detailed but extravagant prose. Kenneth Allsop, always a bird watcher and lover of the country, in contrast to what his TV persona suggested, gave it high praise. Ted Walker had some of that book's quality. Even if I never thought of being a nature poet I liked that the poems were sentences unreeling in a formal design of sense and sound. I liked, it seemed, their orthodoxy. It was more related to music than the effects the Liverpool guys and their imitators, or the school of Ginsberg were interested in, notwithstanding their apparent closeness to rock. This poetry made a different kind of music. It was nothing to do with rock or hip or cool, but concerned with language, care and form grounded in the traditional. Philip Larkin could have imparted similar information, but for some reason he escaped me then, and perhaps I wasn't ready for his underlying gloom and misanthropy. Ted Walker, as it turned out, was a good role model, as well as, which I didn't particularly notice then, being a published New Yorker poet and must have made a great deal more from his poetry than Philip Larkin, or even Roger McGough ever did.

So we all went along from day to day without, it seemed to me, the certainties, the colour and the splendour, of 1966 and 1967. Whether someone, say, a crucial year younger than me, not facing life decisions about what to do next, would have felt that there had been some kind of change for the worse in music and what pop music symbolised since the summer, and certainly since the previous year, is a matter for speculation rather than certainty. To such a person it might have appeared as the best of all possible worlds. It seemed to me though that there had been a shift. When there's a change we always seek the certainty of what we knew before, wanting to stop time, to reverse it to the point before the arm was jolted and the tiny needle dug irrevocably into the record's shiny, spinning, rainbowed black surface. What was going to happen to us all? There were two things to reconcile. One was that the way events were unfolding meant that I was a witness rather than a participant. The other was that a short time before I had thought I was taking part rather only observing. A reasonable judge might say that in fact there was no change at all between the two states. I was no more of a participant then than I was now. I was simply a witness who had thought he was involved. Objectively I can't deny the truth of it, but I can say it didn't *feel* like that, and feeling is the context in which perception must always occur.

Everything seemed more messy now, less focused. Half-baked notions abounded. Being young with long hair seemed enough, was political in itself apparently. At least young Americans had the justification that they faced the possibility of being drafted to a foreign war and dying, or coming home paralysed and disfigured. Elsewhere, even if it wasn't America, the stakes seemed real and high. Here there was the working up to righteous anger and wondering where to go out. Following the events that became codified and entered the realm of legend in May, to be a student was to be the very quintessence of being young, alive and important in 1968. And come September, by a roundabout, unconsidered route, that is what I would be too. So I wouldn't go to university, wouldn't make the friends or join the clubs or plan the flight path that would carry me through to whatever enviable life and career lay in waiting, but my A levels and general aptitude were good enough for the library school that a couple of us young workers were encouraged to apply for. I was, after all, to be a student of sorts, vocationally based and in a way becoming current again in difficult economic times, not living away from home. Travelling to and from home to Birmingham to go to the nearest library school was the plan arrived at. I've no idea why now. It wasn't because there was a formal arrangement with the library service. There certainly was no promise of a job at the end of the two year course. Clearly I should have paid more attention instead of being distracted by books and poems and issues of The Beatles Monthly magazine. Perhaps I thought, like other dreamy individuals, that someone else was in charge of my life.

What John Wesley Harding signalled was the beginning of the Sixties comparisons. Before, there had been an endless, inevitable flow that carried us with it. Now we assessed what he had produced and tried to see whether it was better or worse than what had been done before, before and after the crash that is, and the absence that followed. What does that mean, given that there were differences between each album that had been produced in that run from 1962 to 1966, was there no comparison made then? I suppose it's because the changes between seemed to be unified by the continuous nature, and the fact that we came across them all together in a short time. They were all still happening. Now there was such a disjunction between how he looked, and what he had produced, at the time of the previous album that comparing now and then was impossible to avoid. And not only did he differ in style and content from that last double album he stood out from what was happening all around in rock and pop. That's why there was something symbolic, if silly, about seeing the Blonde On Blonde jacket on the front of John Wesley Harding. From now on we would want those mementoes and artefacts from the time before, when we thought things made sense, or were more satisfactory. Everything about the album was designed to demonstrate that these weren't his times. He had no allegiance to the prevailing fads and enthusiasms. And this had its parallel, its mirror, with his fans who had to make sense of their own progressions, while hankering after what had been. It was here, one could say, that the other universe that has become Bob Dylan's career, the doppelganger world of bootlegs, outtakes and former glories, had its genesis.

So John Wesley Harding came out and there was a deal of excitement, but after that people were looking for signs of Bob activity and there weren't many. By default a new album from the group that had played with him through the electric tour, with the re-addition of one who hadn't, became the focus of attention. The album was called Music From Big Pink, which couldn't have sounded more psychedelic, and of course was totally at odds with what they represented. It was. we learned, a reference to the house where they had created the songs. Now calling themselves, rather reductively, The Band, they were inextricably associated with Bob Dylan because of them all living, working and hanging out in Woodstock, recording songs he'd written and co-written with them; and also because it was his childish but colourful painting on the cover. There were reports too of the so-called Acetate, the songs that had been created by him and the Band as, we were told, a kind of demo for other artists. Given the titles listed (The Mighty Quinn, This Wheel's On Fire) and the fact that some of them did become records by people like Manfred Mann, the Byrds and Julie Driscoll this was true in its way, but not the whole story. Like all whole stories that only emerged over years. Later its name became the Basement Tapes. Meanwhile the pop paper adverts showed what seemed to be a bunch of moustachioed and bearded chaps up in the mountains, something at variance with the normal rock group look. What the album sounded like was also a surprise. There was a willed, formal, stately element and an expertise with various styles of playing and singing that didn't sound much like a bar band who'd drifted into being loud behind Bob Dylan for months. At that stage, to be accurate, few of us had really heard what that 1966 electric half sounded like, and wouldn't until a couple of years later when coloured vinyl bootleg records began to exist bringing various time zones into the present. In any event this record sounded chiefly like itself, even though it was undeniable that the association with Bob Dylan was a major factor in shifting the public gaze their way. Later in the year, still starved for concrete Bob news or achievement, those of us who scoured the back page of the Melody Maker saw that an issue of Sing Out, the venerable folk artefact magazine from when the American Folk Revival was in its glory days, was running an interview with Bob conducted by Happy Traum and John Cohen, long term Village practitioners who had known Bob forever (which is to say about 7 years, and at the rate of exchange then current it was a lifetime.) This was the same John Cohen whose name had come up in the Highway 61 sleeve notes. And on the cover of the magazine was another painting by Bob, somewhat more accomplished than the one that had decorated Music From Big Pink, but still suggesting a weekend artist enrolled in the Grandma Moses art by correspondence school. Links and chains, but not much connection it seemed between the person who emerged from these words and the spiky interviewee of the cataclysmic world tour. How do you know I am not, as you say, for the War, he asked, and there could have been no more dramatic indication of his estrangement from the surrounding youth scene and perceived consensus, no matter how mildly it was phrased.

I was not that much in the surrounding youth scene myself, a commuting student who went to Birmingham by train from Walsall, and went to Walsall and back by bus. I was so dopey, so preoccupied, that it took me a while before I realised there were different routes that one took to Birmingham: one stopping more than another, a loop line no doubt. There are always loop lines. I'd noticed different scenery and never formulated what it meant, the same kind of self-absorbed dreamer who not heard a coal lorry drop the heavy bags of shiny black geometric chunks, thump, thump. Or at least that's what it seemed like for a time. And when we reached New Street Station, the same New Street containing the very Odeon where I had failed to see Bob Dylan in 1966 and the seats also went thump, thump, I had to walk all through the main street, Corporation Street, out to Gosta Green where one found the College of Commerce that contained the Library School. This allowed me to come across a city sight I'd not really seen before, and which impressed itself on me being both strange and ordinary, everyday. It was birds flocking and making noise when I walked back to the train, in the evening with the light changing and the sense that always imparts of another world about to come into existence. The unexpected numbers of pigeons and starlings blurring the edges of buildings, the unsettlement and activity as night approaches, has power because of the context. If there were trees it wouldn't hold your imagination in the same way though it would still be a sight to see. It's the wild wood in another incarnation come to your world, the silhouettes that make the hardness of brick and stone insubstantial, the knowledge that there are such a lot of creatures who don't share any of the things that move in your head, and are making their life where you are. There are so many swirling and moving, a scattered mass but always with an orientation and a purpose. Night comes as it did in the Sixteenth Century, or any century, and the birds move, making the sky a little darker, and despite all the lights you feel some of the fear that is always on call when the day ends.

CHAPTER EIGHTEEN
SHADOW OF A DREAM

Past the time that was the heart of the decade, the heart of the Sixties, but in the years that for some people characterise it more, recall becomes even more elusive than those of childhood. On television there was a series called Take Three Girls which traded too on that Sixties sense of young people finding themselves in London, still swinging London, using the familiar device of flat-sharing to gather together disparate characters from different backgrounds. The music for the theme was from Pentangle and was called Light Flight, a resonant, bouncing, jazzy double bass, a rattle of drums moving along, and a girl singing in a straight folk English voice. All of it was a reminder of the blend of influences at work in music only a few years before, proving by its existence how much had already changed and been lost. This life that the girls were living, would mine be anything like it? Flat sharing, finding a circuit of friends and places when working in a place that wouldn't be home, a home that I would make away from the home I'd grown up in, what kind of a success could I make of it? What lay beyond this learning time, this library school and its easy requirements? You live through the days one at a time, like words in a sentence, and the months become paragraphs. You live in prose, but you remember in poems, with editing and highlights and a syntax modulated for a different purpose. Vietnam still in the background, a political brand like Paris and Czechoslovakia. Oh yes, politics and young people, the world changing as youth rose to the challenge; but not in my personal experience at Gosta Green. One day in the College of Art next door to us, whose library we tended to prefer to not do work in, there was a sit-in, at least we had to pick our way through crowds sitting on a main staircase, the way annoying people always did at parties or outside Town Halls, mistaking a flight of steps for chairs. It all seemed good-natured and confused and not really capable of making the walls of the city shake. Mostly that life was trains to come and trains to go and waiting on stations, lectures and essays, unoccupied hours in the Student Union talking about Monty Python, the Jackson Five, and Carlos Castaneda's Yaqui sorcerer. Wasting time, someone once described it, drinking coffee and trying to look up girls' skirts, wondering how people moved beyond easy chairs and aimless chat.

There were gigs attended and shouting inaudibly in someone's ear an inch away, then turning to offer one of your own when they wanted to impart something, while a band heard of, but not famous enough, flogged through something loud and unknown, and the thin glue of spilled beer stuck dancers and wallflowers to the wooden floor. Coming out of one like this I once saw John Peel, then in his very long straight hair, slightly tilted mouth and beard incarnation, standing on the pavement outside, surrounded by students brought alive by his presence, asking him things inaudible but intense as I went past. It provoked a small epiphany on how easily we assign a star category, superiority, to people who do a job but happen to do it in entertainment, the industry of human happiness. Of course Peel had a great community connection. Most people around us seemed to listen to his radio programmes, and assembled cultural action lists from what he played, recommended or read out; as well being exposed to the underground poets, so billed, who all had one or two poems included in the Children Of Albion anthology, the bare minimum for literary credentials, though mostly they tended to confirm my view that the kind of poetry I liked and thought I wanted to write, the kind worth writing, lay elsewhere. Peel of course was the great champion of Captain Beefheart who seemed to typify something that had happened to rock and pop. First heard by us as a super-charged blues singer in the Howlin' Wolf style but with a great rock band, he had shifted into the wilfully weird. He was always in character, which must have been exhausting, unless he genuinely was mentally disturbed. This was possible given the way he drilled his band, and the way his latest album, a double called Trout Mask Replica, had moved from turbo-warped blues to a kind of free-form dyslexic pun poetry set against a type of atonal equally free-form jazz. Sometimes it had a mad, bracing quality to it that was energising, but it was something that you knew inside you were cranking yourself up to be enthusiastic for on an intellectual basis and wouldn't want to play over and over. If you wanted electric jazz for real, as one of my friend's did, there were the 4 sides of Bitches Brew to go at. Earlier Beefheart albums, Safe As Milk for example, where the band wore suits rather than dresses or vacuum cleaner parts, required no such theorising to make you fall for them immediately and repetitively. Everything had become more self-consciously serious and art-based and was some distance from 1964 pop.

Aside from such sporadic gigs there was a party or two, none of them as exciting as ones in my last years at school, in dark and loud front rooms with parents banished to the kitchen, when the kind of close dancing where a girl's adventurous knee finds a busy purpose in your groin, became a surprising reality, and you find it's possible to kiss with open mouths, (what a revelation it is when first it happens) and tongues are surprisingly slippery, strong, agile, independent, arousing creatures, and then soon enough the lights come on, the music ends and parents emerge from their careful ignorance to bid everyone, "Safe home, safe home."

At library school a friend and I were asked around to a girl's house, a friend of ours on the course, and were told we could stay over. Stay over? A sleepover, like 1950s America, that fantasy parallel world, or in movies we never saw. Our friend had a friend, a girl, who was coming along too. A pyjama party? There was a lot of uneasiness about the form, about what was expected. Were we friends, or the going to bed friends we hadn't been up to that point certainly. If we were, were we up to it? The fears proved unnecessary, inevitably. Sex, whatever their previous experience, and there was no doubt of it outranking ours, was not, they had obviously decided, in the cards for the kind of friends we clearly were. Friends in night attire we passed the time in some innocent, dispiriting way, was it crossword puzzles – the detail has dissolved – as if we were slightly older versions of characters in The Secret Seven or Swallows and Amazons. Still, I did get as a result of that meeting, all unexpectedly, some 78 records as a gift, and one of them was Frankie Lymon and The Teenagers, I'm Not A Juvenile Delinquent. That was a record of a bit more than a decade previously and it could have been a memento of a parallel world, so unlike current music was it. But playing that clear, high, ecstatic voice with its repetition of No around 19 times in succession, denying that he was a juvenile delinquent, was a longer lasting joy than the sleep-over sex might have been, though I can't say it wasn't a deep sorrow that the sex never happened. So the 1950s was coming forward to visit the next decade, and everyday life was the kind of slow-motion confusion it often was. And yet here it was 1968, assassinations and student uprising, the intensification of the war in Vietnam, the violence and chaos of American political conventions, the year fated to be written about, eulogized and analysed ever after. And here I was, not sitting-in or having an uprising in an unfamiliar bedroom. I was reading. I read Penguin's Thomas Berger cowboy cornucopia and fantasia on Western themes, Little Big Man, – which obviously I loved for enfolded reasons, and Hunter Thompson on the Hell's Angels, both of which suited the times from different ends of the century. The next year my reading matter was Kurt Vonnegut's Slaughterhouse Five, a surprise success for someone who had been writing for quite a while, with its prescient narrative device of a protagonist who moved back and forth in time. You could also pick up in Hudson's Bookshop, a Gosta Green mecca, the Pocket Poets series, those little Studio Vista paperbacks whose titles included selections from Laurie Lee and Beat Poets and Famous American Poems, all bought by me. That was where I picked up as well the title that united poetry and rock in the slightly obvious, The Poetry Of Rock, but that with its gold cover sporting a psychedelic drawing, its bright yellow-edged pages and the fact that it was an American import Bantam Book gave it tremendous desirability. It reprinted various song lyrics, each with its own quirky introductory piece, not over-adulatory, and some, most importantly, went right back to the Fifties, demonstrating that all this latter-day largesse was part of a continuum. Much as I loved this book it was, like the status of Captain Beefheart, a sign of the intellectual self-consciousness that now surrounded the rock and pop world. We looked about us, surveying the view from previously unknown heights. Moreover, this belief didn't lead to the conclusion that things could only go down-hill from here. The book, and the state of mind that produced it and surrounded us, proceeded from the position that everything was brilliant and could only continue to get better. Progression, improvement, and things getting better all the time, wasn't that what right now was all about, this time about to be labelled the Sixties? The sky was the limit. There was no limit.

One of the treats of the book was that it made you want to investigate acts or songs you'd not been that aware of, as well as in the case of Leonard Cohen including a song, Dress Rehearsal Rag, he hadn't even recorded yet, and of whose existence we were all unaware, but according it masterpiece status. I looked at that book a lot and it's moved down the years with me from location to location. I look at it now, on the inside cover at the handwriting that used to be mine and now isn't, and get a sense of how songs change and never change. That wasn't the only prize I got there that I retained for decades. The gentleman bookseller who seemed to be in charge, who with his smart suit, white hair, white moustache, gold glasses and upper class voice was like an actor playing the part of a gentleman bookseller, also sold me, cheap, his own hardback copy, inscribed to him, of Kenneth Allsop's Hard Travelling, a history of the America hobo. His own, he stressed, but one he was prepared to sell now, if second-hand was all right with me, and I didn't mind an autograph for someone else. I grabbed the chance of course. This united a hero of mine and a background to Bob Dylan, and gave me an autograph I would otherwise never have sought out or received, but valued and kept until now. It was in Hudson's too while flipping the shelves I read on the back of a novel whose author and title I never retained, "Is he the only 19 year old virgin in the world", and had to reply, Well, actually, no,

Aside from the rock and folk world I still liked and listened to, and was in a way entranced by, someone like Scott Walker. He was a connection to that other song world, the songs that derived from musicals or what might be loosely called the American Songbook. Even in the fantasia of their teen success the Walker Brothers albums had contained oddities like Once Upon a Summertime, which I did think of as poetry as much as anything in Leonard Cohen: "Now another wintertime has come and gone, the pigeons feeding in the square have flown, but I remember when the vespers chime you loved me once upon a summertime." The autumn following the Summer of Love, presided over by the Beatles and practically everyone, Scott had released his first solo album, still working the "loneliness is a cloak I wear" seam. That had the first popular versions of Jacques Brel songs, as well as great orchestrated schlock like The Big Hurt. I had no difficulty in loving this along with folk, blues and Bob. And now, with the Walker Brothers long in demise, and his solo career looking less certain, an ill-fated attempt for Scott to have a TV success brought an accompanying album of standards that contained one that had a particular appeal called Lost In The Stars. It was a song about as old as I was, from a musical I'd never heard of, and ended with the image of us all blowing through the night among the stars, little stars, big stars. Here we all were, out here, lost in the stars.

I could see that, travelling at night from districts I didn't know, looking at my face in the dark inadequate mirror of a bus window, the strange shadow world you always pass through then, always following, noticing how unlike my idea of myself I was, how unsatisfactory my hair after an unwise, much too severe cut. Waking in a strange house after sleeping on the floor, trying to smooth out a body that seemed to be unfolding like a scrumpled-up crisp packet, and thinking this is what you are supposed to do being the age you are. Then making your bright and grey way home on a bus and a bus, the Auntie May route by other means, to spend most of the day in bed under childhood's yellow embossed bedspread that means something else now. Outside the windows of the steel house the gardens are still all gathered together, the grasses still unkempt, shivering and rippling in the disappointed wind. And you lie there as if recovering from a cold, trying to reconcile how you feel with how you think you should feel, like the repeated reflections in a dressing room mirror, the ones with the unflattering light. Parents come in to shake their heads. All the people you don't know, and all the ones you have to meet, pass by and you think they're doing what you're doing, more or less, and think the same way as you do, sharing your inchoate but genuine beliefs, only to spend time finding it ain't necessarily so.

Folk that was not American permeated the airwaves. Donovan's Celtic singing mannerisms became more marked, and the songs more ambitious, his embracing of castles, cloaks and flowers feverish. No one would ever believe that once he had seemed such a Dylan or Guthrie disciple with Jennifer Juniper vibrating in your direction, or Atlantis, with its long, portentous, spoken piece, so redolent of Tolkien's manner. Shirley and Dolly Collins, with their English songs, pipe organ and Sussex accents, in the racks on the newly existing and immediately superior Harvest record label, now joining the list of logo identities that seemed to make the weather, were unlikely but admired names to drop and purchases to make. The past seemed to be a major component of the present for English and American bands. Shirley and Dolly recorded with a consort of musicians from the classical end of the spectrum who played mediaeval instruments to add exactly the right touch to their ancient songs. And The Band had moved further into an imagined Americana past with their second album, also called, a touch dourly after the sprightly, intriguing Music From Big Pink, The Band. The dwelling on the past and Americana, as if they were constantly providing a soundtrack to either the real Civil War or a mythical John Ford movie that was never made, became the main focus for all the articles and reviews about them. For a while they were viewed as the saviours of the scene, and a vindication of all the hopes that champions of the alternative and counter culture had desired. Other musicians, admiring the way that like-minded guys could just get together and play what they wanted to, may have been more influenced by them than fans were. It was like Traffic's "getting their heads together in the country, man" with none of the psychedelic fripperies.

It was communal music making, and on the record sleeves we could see The Incredible String Band too had the equivalent of a school photograph, a rustic gathering of communal followers, not in their recent Town Hall gypsy best but what might have been costume shop, tatterdemalion motley, looking out at browsers from some distant rural location. This is how we live, the photograph said, how do you? Remembering the night clouds of birds about to roost, darkness incoming, right there in the second city, bus routes busy and trains nearby, even so it was easy to feel the imagined, ancient England that folkies and psychedelic folkies like the Watersons, the Incredible String Band, and Pentangle, amongst others, tried to conjure again with the old songs, or their own in that style. It seemed connected to the media clichés of hippiedom that we believed, and quite distinct from the West Coast version also flourishing. English and Americans however did share a look. On the album-flippers in the subterranean record shop down the subway on the Corporation Street route, peering down into the looking-glass of sleeve-shuffled bins, there was hair that was long but could never be mistaken for stylish; there were inadequate beards, duffle coats, Army coats, RAF coats, long scarves, woolly hats, granddad vests, plimsolls, jeans and jeans and jeans, the whole, apparently mandatory, student folk costume, except perhaps on library school students. A blurred slovenliness spread out, an exponential shabbiness, economising on washing, reducing ironing, emphasising that the expensive colour and dandy finery of 1966 were long gone.

Staring back from racks and bins, as well as the Incredibles family, were various purveyors of mutant folk and warped blues. The Edgar Broughton Band, with their madly ambitious acres of beards and curving moustaches, and, oddly, signed to the roster of that authentically zeitgeist Harvest label, odd given their reduction of both politics and mysticism into sloganeering. That was also authentically zeitgeist it's true, but somehow Harvest seemed to promise more quality than the Edgars suggested. Perhaps it was thought they would be similar to label mates the Third Ear Band, who evoked other countries and earlier times with their blend of styles and range of instruments, classical and electronic, rather than the thick ear, broad brush of the Broughtons. To show they were absolutely of the moment the Third Ear album was called Alchemy. To a stranger all the bands looked similar, but most had little to do with politics directly. Music and putting it out there was why they existed: Blodwyn Pig and Jethro Tull for example. They were on Island which had a longer musical history than Harvest and, for reasons hard to specify, but might have been to do both with its pleasing pink label and the essential people they already represented, was considered a cut above its neophyte rack companion. The people on all the record sleeves and the gaggle crowding the store tended to look like the cover shot of the Island sampler album You Can All Join In, a crew in a park that seemed to symbolise so much more. In duffle coats and

woolly hats, performers and audience appeared to be wearing a mirrored disguise, wanting to pass for each other.

It took the recent past to remind you of a different world. In
front of some vanished shop on a forgotten street I saw a second hand
copy of David Blue's 1966 album. Dylan's pseudonymous friend from
Gaslight Café days, Blue was from the same scene but cursed by
being a singer and songwriter always to remind people of his Dylan
associations while not being him. The sleeve notes talked about
wearing cowboy boots in case someone decided to make a cowboy
movie on the street. That sounded very like 1966 to me. Even so, I
resisted buying it, though the same place yielded a Lovin' Spoonful
album called Everything Playing. It featured a child-like cover painting, a reminder now, though it preceded it, of the same enthusiastic
primitive colourfulness fronting the Band's Big Pink, courtesy of
their erstwhile employer, and Basement pal Bob. The Spoonful I did
buy, but though they had the same name and it had some good John
Sebastian songs, it was a reminder that something more than Zal
Yanovsky had moved on. What do we look for in record racks and
bins, something new or something old? Bob Dylan, who by then had
less to do with Student Uprisings than I did, released something new
called Nashville Skyline.

Nashville Skyline. If John Wesley Harding was a jump cut from
Blonde On Blonde, then this album was a further movement, away
not only from the pre-accident sound but John Wesley Harding too.
That album with its stripped-down group sound, reduced to the
instruments Bob could play alongside a bassist and drummer, suggested in sound the character of the black and white photograph on
the cover. That snapshot simplicity had a relationship to the songs,
morality tales, mostly brief, seeming to take from both old folk
songs, with their mysterious characters and impacted narratives, and
the Old Testament. By contrast Nashville Skyline concerned itself
with love and domestic arrangements. No black and white allegories
and, if you had a fanciful temperament the songs sounded red-brown,

glowing, polished, like Bob's guitar in that wonderfully emblematic, posed, but totally successful Elliott Landy photograph. There were a couple of aspects of Nashville Skyline that caught the attention. The most obvious was the sound of his voice. Although John Wesley Harding had an austere, restrained character informing what one took to be the album's overall identity, the last two songs had established a different, more relaxed mood. Down Along The Cove and I'll Be Your Baby Tonight were country style, and at times one suspected they were even country pastiche, and in those his voice is not as it is elsewhere on the album, where although under tight control we hear some of the grit and abrasion of earlier times. On these songs he sounds smooth but as if he's deliberately having to hold his throat a certain way in order to get that effect. This is intensified on Nashville Skyline where the sense of a country pastiche, but sincerely delivered, is all there is, and the absence of the voice we know is crucial to what exists. What it made us ask was which of those voices was the genuine Bob voice, if either could be assumed at will. Bob's voice had either completely changed due to lack of cigarettes, or it was an act of will that he could turn on and off to suit his purpose. Whichever it was, a real change had occurred. He croons here, and crooning is a sound associated with pleasure rather than moral parables no matter how fashioned with artistry they might be. The album associated him firmly with country music at a time when, although the Byrds in the previous year had more or less invented country-rock with the Sweetheart Of The Rodeo album, country wasn't exactly hip, cool or fashionable. Bob Dylan was some vocal distance from druggy or droogy or Peter Lorre as a speech therapist, but after all it was 3 years since the double album, the tour and the motorcycle album. 3 years. Could it be true? A lifetime moving fast and slow, like all lifetimes, the space between Freewheelin' and Blonde On Blonde. And about this time too, as if to emphasise and drive home just how the present differed from the past a showing of Don't Look Back became available.

*And what of film, the indelible record, which with the elapse of time becomes
a supplemented and amended indelibility, aside from any changes that a
changed consciousness will bring. What if everything you had ever done in
your life were recorded and you could bring it back, any time?*

It was an event organised by some kind of arty film club and it was to
be shown at Birmingham Town Hall, the same place where I'd seen
him during the tour that was the subject of the documentary, the
kind of coincidence you couldn't arrange but might perhaps invent.
The film was shown on the kind of little screen most often used in
classrooms or, these days, management training courses. The sound,
when it began, was terrible, muffled and clearly a case of unclear
fraud perpetrated on us paying mugs, who cheered up when a couple
of tougher souls stormed the stage and said how disgraceful it was,
and that if this was the best on offer we wanted our money back.
Cheers and general relief greeted this, paying mug to baying mug,
and then, by coincidence I'm sure, the loudspeakers began to work
and the film was started again. After that we all settled down to
watch this black and white tininess, to revisit a past that wasn't so far
away but even then seemed like a news bulletin from a distant planet,
the distance between 1969 and 1965. When you look at the numbers
it doesn't seem like much time at all, a gap between albums for modern bands. Then it felt like a few lifetimes. It was difficult to define
precisely but, as Thunderclap Newman put it, neatly encapsulating
by their very existence how different and wrongly things had turned
out, there was something in the air.

And if I try to remember what it was that I felt when I saw
Don't Look Back for the first time, on that little screen, in that odd
circumstance, it's like trying to recall a dream. I know it happened.
And I know I remember talking and thinking about it at various
times; but it seems that what I mainly remember now is that telling
of the tale rather than the experience itself. I'm remembering memories. What I think is true is that it seemed very small and black and
white and a strange kind of life for the people onscreen to undergo.

When I saw it I'm sure I would also have been remembering those two half hour BBC shows from 1965, the same repertoire from the same tour. They too were emblematic of that particular Bob moment: his almost androgynous face, the leather jacket, his skinny legs and jeans, his pointy boots and the way they moved; and his hair, not the tumbling perm-a-like of 1966 thousands of us learned to cartoon as a Dylan doodle on exercise books, but the cloudy brush that suggested a wilder James Dean, an almost 50s reference so at variance with the flop, hang and dangle of the Stones and grown-out Beatle cuts he was sharing the charts with.

What emerged from the film was how the two elements of it, the packed, bitty, harried life offstage, the spotlit solitary intensely observed one onstage, seemed almost to be dreaming each other. The two areas of his life as sharply delineated as sleeping and waking. Dreams can feel as if they have the logic of a story but when you try to say what happened it can sound like, "I was in this room, well it seemed like a room but when I looked around it was more like a field, although not exactly a field either. It felt like a room. And my dad was there. Not like now. When he was young, when he was alive, except later we seemed to be here, in the house we live in now, and he's never been here." James Stewart said that when people stopped him to talk about a favourite film of his they'd say, "You were in this room" and proceed from there. The compelling narrative drive in dreams has nothing to do with the *connections* between scenes though. It comes from the overwhelming emotion and distorted presence of what's happening in the moment. When dreams unfold from scene to scene there's no reason for the changes and they are never questioned. The reason why they are so vivid is because they're the only reality in the consciousness of the dreamer. In the dark, surrounded by other people, films can work like that.

Life is like dreams in this: the present moment is all you have. In dreams you wonder how did you get to this place? Sometimes you know, sometimes you don't, but it becomes irrelevant. All you know is the emotion, intensity and information of right now. What's going to happen next? You don't know. Scenes move into other scenes and you pay attention when you're there. Much of the meaning of looking back at a film so old is because we know what happened next, we know some of the splendours waiting in his future. Bob Dylan's Dream and his World War III Dream, and his 115th Dream, and his 1,965th Dream. But right now all we know is what we know in dreams. Which is nothing. How did you get from there to here? What will happen after this? The paradox about films is that if left alone, free from Special Editions, Director's Cuts, and Never Seen Before Extras, they don't change, but neither do they stay the same. What changes is everything around them, particularly us watching them. And when we change so does their meaning. We bring to films all of our prejudice and enthusiasm; and later we bring new prejudices and memories. In looking at a film again we look at a screen and see both what's there and sometimes the people we used to be, and are surprised when the film lets us know how we've changed. Change, the subject Bob Dylan took to himself and then gave to everyone, personally customised. What a film can't do, even a film of a concert that you were present at, is bring back the actuality of being in a room, even if the room is the size of an arena, being surrounded by people, all of the unreliable witnesses, and experiencing that event which will never happen again. You can watch a version of it again but it won't happen again, even if you view the film over and over and you feel the sound waves travelling and dying.

Library school was over, and the Sixties were over, and a TV documentary that cannot be verified, narrated perhaps by Paul Newman, at least that's what I seem to remember, itemised the glory in a list of events that modulated into a last rites litany that has been read more or less continuously ever since. The Sixties, alive and not alive and always with us. After that was finding a job and moving away. Now the chance that had been lost before, of moving away from home to college or university to find the kind of person

I was, or could be, had come again, though college and university weren't involved. There were a couple of interviews for jobs in libraries. I went by train to Shrewsbury and passing dry, heat-exhausted fields I thought about a recent feature in Rolling Stone all about the Beach Boys and the album that never happened. The words to some of the songs we hadn't heard were there. The train went along past the fields and I was thinking, Who ran the iron horse, and The crow cries uncover the corn field. Was this on the way to or from the interview? Was it indicative of a lack of seriousness or focus on my part? Perhaps. At any rate I didn't get that job. But when there seemed to be a mass taking on of people in Richmond, Surrey, which was actually the London Borough of Richmond, I was taken on, and it was there that I would be moving to. My friends thought of this as going down to the Smoke, London was always the Smoke, which is pots and kettles in the Black Country. Jim thought I was probably the least-suited person to make his way in the world, basing this analysis on the fact that years before I hadn't known how to use an electric kettle in his house. (It was true. Our house had gas and we made tea differently.) But here I was and I'd got a job elsewhere, and that's where I was going to be. You could put it grandiosely and say all of us have to be the core of who we are while learning to be who we might be. Or even more grandiosely, but not falsely for a certain kind of fan, and think, All of us have to try to be the Bob Dylan we're capable of. My mother sat at the kitchen table and cried and I tried to reassure her, saying I would be back in a fortnight, knowing that was when my first Saturday off would be. It didn't help. She carried on crying and I felt separate and not capable of giving any real comfort no matter what I said. Feeling too the callousness that comes with that realisation. She knew, as I didn't, that once you leave it doesn't matter how many times you come back, you never actually return.

And so in a new suit and new short hair, (though it hadn't been that long to start with, the fabled long hair supposed to be the badge of the Sixties didn't really blossom as I saw it, and on me specifically, until the subsequent years of the 1970s, not much later in geological time it's true, but an important distinction right then) I reported in for my first day. That first day was in the month when, although we are in the last quarter of the year, so many things begin. So on the first day of the autumn that is promised, and the last real day of the summer that has passed, at the beginning of another September, in its sad and gentle sunshine, which might grow fierce around noon but melancholy is never far away, I started, as if it was a new term at school, a new life in Richmond, a place least like the Smoke that one could conjure. In fact I was so dim, innocent might be a kinder word and an accurate one, I actually travelled a hundred miles or so and started work with a suitcase and no fixed long term place to stay. I've no idea why this didn't concern me or anyone else more. In the first week or two senior staff with misgivings about my commonsense tried to help and I found myself in a couple of bed and breakfast rooms, one above a small run-down garage, one in a house run by an Indian couple, and was told by the man that the lack of cooking facilities wouldn't matter because I didn't look like much of a cook to him. I felt that oddness of being adrift and cut loose from what the world had been, the shape of my life that made sense. It's chastening when your own cluelessness becomes clear to you. Then one fine day in that first few I walked into an accommodation agency at the bottom of Richmond Hill and the lady told me there was nothing on the books, nothing at all; but, she said, like a magician with the prospect of a rabbit and an apparently empty hat, there was a tiny room right here, above the office, at the back of her house. If it would help? Would I like to see it? It wasn't, she emphasised, big. No, but then it was available, and even someone innocent and dim can know desperation. It was a bit longer than me doing a couple of forward rolls, slightly wider than a tall person with their arms outstretched, and mostly occupied by a little single bed. I lived in it for about six months.

You reached it by a twisty staircase with a dusty red carpet, and stretched across the wall going up was a bookshelf with the traditional, mostly Penguin, arrangement of paperbacks, where The Ballad Of Peckham Rye took my eye. At different times I opened it and flicked the pages, reading the beginning but never bothering to go further. I didn't need to. It had done its work with the title, making me think, or rather not even think, but alerting me to an atmosphere of belief that this was what I too was involved in. I was acting out, performing, giving voice to a narrative, the ballad of everyday life I was on stage for. It was as if my life was already a blend of paperback, film and song. Here I was in a miniature bedsit at the bottom of Richmond Hill, buoyed up and inadequate. What would happen next?

Down the twisty stairs and round the corner behind the ground floor agency office was a palely bleak, almost empty kitchen, of whose stove or pots and pans and implements I can remember nothing. There was a Baby Belling I believe and nothing more substantial. This was well before microwaves. What did I eat, what did I live on? It had to be more than words and dreams. The space was dominated by an object which looked like a steamer trunk sarcophagus. That contained the bath and when it was in use no-one could go in the kitchen. There was no other place to fit a bath in that narrow tall house of 3 floors. That was the place where that season, those first months, the radio let me hear Band Of Gold by Freda Payne, which was like Motown old style, War by Edwin Starr, Motown new style, and Woodstock by Matthew's Southern Comfort, with its plaintive pedal steel glissade, a celebration of something quintessentially Sixties and also a lament. All of them repeated in my head at various other times, and were always linked together because of the accident of release dates. I understood that I was being provided with my own soundtrack for that time, forever in fact. If you're clueless, being lucky sometimes can be a great help. This was obviously the place to begin the song of the boy who had known the Sixties and moved away from the West Midlands: a diminutive room above a bath-containing kitchen, and a girl in the other room off the landing near the bookcase to say hello to when we passed on the stairs or in the kitchen, all in a house in Richmond. In those first weeks Leslie Thomas typed in a room across the street, and I saw him walking, though never typing; Richmond Park was waiting for me to visit on Sundays, a mile or so uphill and past the great sweeping bend of the Thames painted by everyone; I bought Blessed McGill by Edwin Shrake in the newsagent right next door because it mentioned Little Big Man on the cover as a point of reference to the kind of book contained within, and in the Terrace Gardens all neat and green, thought about Apaches in the wild American Southwest and never forgot it and have the book still; and some friends came from home and brought the police-staticky record player and the few LPs I requested to help make the miniature space my own. And though this all coincided with Bob Dylan releasing New Morning what I played a lot then was Neil Young's After The Goldrush, where the inner shot of his palimpsest-patched jeans, stitching on stitching, is as much a quintessence of the time as his high, affecting voice and odd tunes; and a cheap reissue of 1940s Frank Sinatra, resplendent and arms outstretched in a wide pinstripe 1940s suit, singing Where Or When, which seemed right, as well as the great Autumn In New York, whose line "lovers who bless the dark on benches in Central Park" I thought Leonard Cohen would wish he had written. I wasn't a lover, certainly not a fighter, but I had moved away from home, had come somewhere near a big city but, enviably, to what everyone agreed was a lovely location. All the films I had taken in from the atmosphere down the years, where people went to New York to try and make it, no matter how inaccurate in comparable detail they might be to my situation, seemed to speak to me through this song. After all that was the season I was immersed in, saturating the streets and trees, the landscape wild and tamed that was a mile or so up the hill, and then a few miles beyond that, with its trees, its deer and the two ponds separated by the sandy walkway, ponds big as lakes, the wind-harassed water glittering in the pensive, gentle sun, all surrounded by the couples and families, babies and toddlers, in their scarfed and warm-coated, hooped and woolly Sunday walking best.

CHAPTER NINETEEN
THE COLOUR OF AN AUTUMN LEAF

Autumn, when seasons begin and end and new mornings chill the face. It's the end of the summer, which means it brings back the end of all summers, but also when new school and college terms begin. It's an odd time, currents of emotion and the most obtuse people can feel the changes in the air as the planet turns at morning and evening, and feel the air inside them move too. At school I once won a prize for English work and was allowed to choose a book. I picked Ray Bradbury's Something Wicked This Way Comes. He was a powerful presence Ray Bradbury, and for awhile I felt as he did about the sinister magic of carnivals, even though the actuality was always a good deal less literary. But autumn was definitely Ray Bradbury's time. He wrote a book of stories called The October Country and because I had always responded to autumn even before I had read him he only cemented my reactions. The changing air is full of things that fall. The light is golden but sad. In those first few weeks after I left home, Jimi Hendrix and Janis Joplin went to their careless and avoidable deaths. Hendrix was the more important and moving of course because he was an alchemical blending of so many elements that formed the actual nature of the Sixties, and also a most powerful symbol of them. Not least was the speed with which everything took place for him. Brought over to England in 1966 he'd impressed fans and inspired musicians to fear, envy and admiration through his act in little clubs, then on those cinema venue package shows – where on one tour he was in the company of other American expats the Walker Brothers, and, as evidence of how broad a church the Sixties was, Englebert Humperdinck, – and also by 1968 in only two years had released the three albums that remade the boundaries of what guitar groups could do. He mattered in so many ways: his hairstyle alone had spread like a pandemic; whenever Hey Joe was heard it would always encapsulate that rhythmic mystery of what the group did, so simple and so deep; and then there was his connection to Bob Dylan. He'd come out of various black music backgrounds but it was hearing Bob Dylan that made him think he could sing and write personal songs, songs where poetry and dreams would be expressed in his words and the sound he and his group made, and no-one sounded quite like him, or would. He acknowledged Bob Dylan quite directly though with his versions of Like A Rolling Stone and All Along The Watchtower. People who wouldn't get Dylan would certainly get him, but after the third album, the double one of Electric Ladyland, The Jimi Hendrix Experience had broken up and various subsequent projects and alliances were half-started or half-finished, and now were all finished, except for the afterlife, immortal as radioactivity, of post-humous releases and reworkings, the infighting of contesting claims to ownership and the right to curate golden eggs. Four years was all he'd had, but all he'd needed, after coming to England to change things forever, and then he was gone, sad and wasteful, and you felt the loss because it signified, as Brian Jones's death did, that more than an individual had come to an end.

I read about these deaths in the staff room's silence and tea cup clinks, one anorexic girl so doused in perfume that her cup retained the distinctive musky scent on the draining board for some time after the perfunctory rinsing out. I read about them in issues of Rolling Stone magazine, its old-style size, A4 opening up to A3, the same size and tea room location where I first made my way through John Lennon's candid looking back marathon interview, pictured in his dungarees and close beard, his hair grown back somewhat from the shocking crop he'd had the year before, a contribution to peace apparently, and we learned in a madly frank conversation that expanded on the litany list from the song God on his first album following the collapse of the Beatles, detailing all the things he didn't believe in anymore, that the dream was over, and whatever the Beatles had been no longer signified. The Sixties had never seemed further away, and where were we now? What could New Morning tell us, released only a few months after the double album Self Portrait, whose title had seemed to be a puzzling joke, and whose inner fold-out sleeve photographs were all the proof you needed of the existence of time. They were a continuing demonstration that the 1966 weirdness had most definitely left the building and would not be found under the big sky or down among the chicken coops, a little reminder of my Thames Road upbringing. Who could look at that neat little, chubby little, white-suited Isle of Wight fellow, with his odd short hair and short odd beard (as make-do and mend as any Corporation St student) and not wonder how only three years could make such a difference? That Bob Dylan was still in residence and seemed to be saying that if we thought we knew him then we would recognise him through other people's work. The songs were by other people, and the general air was him still trying to inhabit his country gentleman persona and vocal styling, trying things out. What people resented was that even more than Nashville Skyline, whose voice it used, the person going by the name Bob Dylan here didn't seem to be the one we thought we valued. It seemed to have nothing to do either with the young kid once hailed as the voice and prophet of his generation in terms of politics, civil rights and idealism, or the drug-inspired electric rock seer from not much later. If one could put that aside, as few could, there was some great singing and playing throughout, performances to come back to again and again, but that would be a project for decades, a future that most of us couldn't manage to imagine or believe in.

On the new record, on sale in a mini-supermart across the road and down the Hill from my perch, catering for people buying things on their evening way home from work and who might find themselves in need of vinyl displayed on a wire carousel, his voice was rougher-edged once more. He was working with a smaller more orthodox band, he had written the songs and seemed to be trying to say something outside of standards or country sounds. Or at least that's what critics lined up to say, and what we all were keen to believe. The cover photograph showed the fullest Dylan beard yet, so that was an achievement. But the back cover was from 1961 and showed the young wide-eyed Bob Dylan, the apprentice folksinger, complete with corduroy cap and sheepherder's jacket, in the company of a black woman blues singer, who, we learned later, and certainly not from the album sleeve, was Victoria Spivey, for whom Bob had played harmonica on sessions not released at the time, and in any case not known by the lads who fell for Freewheelin'. This was also an indication of the way Bob Dylan's progress would be viewed now. He would make records for whatever reason and his public would always make connections with the past, connections he would sometimes encourage or collude in. More than this, things we hadn't known about the past would surface intermittently and make us reconsider where we were or what we thought we knew. Any new morning was always about to be compared to the previous year, or as he made clear in this instance, the previous decade.

"You were in this room", people said to James Stewart, and that was the traditional way to begin life on your own. In bedsits or flat-sharing is how young people began, putting up with whatever was wrong because it was understood this was only a phase, strictly temporary, and we were all headed for better things. Light Flight bounced though our heads too, or through mine anyway, a subliminal theme tune as I became a character in a drama that had less plot, incident or girls. We were all starting out, in a new morning. Those first few months though I did feel lonely and what I thought of as homesick.

Most Saturdays off, and they only came every 3 weeks, I would go back by train to visit home, this being well before learning to drive or buying a car. So some Friday night I would be making my way to Euston by train and tube, toting a bag, and then on by Inter City to Birmingham, then to Walsall, so buses would also be involved. What a complication to travel such a short distance in Kerouac currency. And on the train coming back on a Sunday, the segmented curve of carriages bending about tracks like a dragon's tail, in the darkness that was bright with dark shapes, lights and yellow windows, the darkness I knew outside the Reference Library, working late on winter nights, that made you remember all the dark there had ever been. I would think on the train about all the rooms there were out there: all those houses scaffolded with pipes and gutters, blocks and rectangles of rooms stuck together, decorated bedrooms, and bathrooms and living rooms and kitchens, all in functional comfort. And the people who led their lives in little rooms like mine, tucked away in houses full of separate rooms and their occupants, accidental contingencies of people in bedsits and shared bathrooms, not surrounded by their families. And I thought about all that moving through the dark, and connections and transfers from vehicle to vehicle, so that that I could end up ensconced in this space, my living quarters at the back of a house at the end of a night-time hill where I had a place in the world; and I wondered if all the people I saw jammed and moving in and out of conveyances ever felt quite the same. It was a little unnerving to think of it that way but that's how everyone started out in fiction, and films, and Bob Dylan's story of coming east a thousand miles to make his way in the crowds and walk-ups of New York, also with no place to stay, digging it all, as he said, the way he dug iron ore mines and snow. This is how I was starting out too. In the back of my mind was the idea that I could always go back. I didn't have to stay here, but I did feel that I had to stay at least six months to give it a fair chance. And then, on one of my regular return visits well before the six months was up, I had the revelation that I couldn't come back, of course not, obviously not. I heard a girl passing by say to her friend, "I looked like a pace o' bacon. Me face only went pair-pull", and heard how I must sound to others elsewhere, and I saw the look of the streets. I think of it now as something that symbolised the change rather than causing it, but suddenly there it was. It's like a switch between black and white: as if you are seeing something that's always been clearly in front of you and can't understand why you missed seeing it before.

It has to do with an idea of home, with who you are and where you come from always indissoluble, an idea of home as something you have to journey to find. Where you are from and the way it shapes you helps you recognise what your new place is.

What would I be returning to? Did I think I would just get a job as I had done before? What if I didn't, as seemed most likely. Would I fit into my parent's house once again? What would I do here? And I looked around and tried comparing the streets and the people in them with what surrounded me in my miniature billet at the foot of Richmond Hill, at the edge of the possibility of grandeur, and saw in the area I had known a kind of mean, run-down quality that may have been an illusion, but would have made me more of a dissatisfied snob than I was already, and certainly than was good for me if I came back. I realised that back here I was as out of place, and it was as strange to me, as the place I had found when I went off to start working over a hundred miles away. Dim and naïve as I was, and not wanting to be disloyal to anything, and loving my parents but wondering how I would relate to their lives now, it came to me that perhaps I hadn't been homesick for the place that was there after all, but longing for something I knew and felt at home in. But that was childhood really, and hadn't been an option for quite a while now.

A couple of things happened to emphasise that it was up to me what happened to me. Once, I managed to leave without my key and it was awhile before anyone else was going to be there. I had nothing to do and nowhere to go and felt very keenly that sense of being on the outside where no-one cares, how the world can flip, until I had my chance to get back in again. Another time the opposite occurred and walking back up the Hill, past the Odeon, thinking about whatever was important to me at the time, a young chap half swayed towards me and was obviously going to beg. I didn't say anything but I looked up and must have conveyed such irritation that he made a placatory gesture with his hands and swayed away again. And one Saturday or Sunday night when I was alone in the agency, the owner and my fellow tenant both being at large elsewhere, and me with nothing to do, I rang a couple of people I knew from work trying to fix up a meeting of some kind, and it proved impossible because of their arrangements. "Right, yes. Okay. No, I understand, I see. See you at work." I put the phone down and realised that it was only me that was involved this night and, in fact, any night. I was the one who had to make the best of it. I was in this room and dependent on what I could bring to it. My homesick revelation brought me to the same conclusion. It wasn't like Bob going to New York and knocking everyone's eye out with his promise and force of personality, and then quite soon actually writing Blowin' In The Wind. It was, however, as close as I was likely to come. Everyone leaving home to work or study was finding out what they were capable of, making their way in whatever version of Greenwich Village they found themselves, the way I was, remembering where I came from and seeing what happened next.

The present is all we have, and when you're a child that works perfectly. When you're a child the present is all you know or want. Later the present gets tugs of dissatisfaction from memories of a different state of affairs, or an imagining of how things might change, might improve. Towards the end of 1970, when New Morning was there to demonstrate what Bob Dylan was, and where he was artistically at this moment, as well as how far he had come from what we recalled of that 4 year eternity ago, I was learning how you always join something when a golden age has recently departed. Giants used to walk the earth, giants of hipness, smartness or sexual availability.

You feel this quite distinctly when you are told about the parties or
gatherings there had been, or the way work used to be, and simultaneously your logical mind tells you that these days where the stories
are being told will be the golden age for someone, perhaps even for
you, these days right now that you experience, waking by waking,
sleep by sleep. You missed those parties where people got drunk and
did silly or terrible things, waking with a stranger, or two strangers,
one of each gender and found, with surprise, that they liked both
equally; or met their future spouses, thus creating the possibility of
later divorce and generational calamity: the present, always generating the future. Chance and luck reporting in, or absent without leave.
But there would be other parties and people to meet and fears to be
overcome, finding out what sort of person you were and what your
present day might be. You had just missed the best of it, and the best
was yet to be, exactly the way it always is for everyone.

I walked out of the agency premises containing my little eyrie
up at the rear of the house from the front door that was alongside
and wasn't the office door, down the Hill towards the town and
passed Potter's Music Shop. In the time when the interest following
the release of New Morning receded and tended to show that what
we experiencing was actually a false dawn, other music occupied our
senses. Potter's was the place to look for it. The owner was a man
called Gerry, who was a burly, bearded Jerry Garcia look alike, and his
surname wasn't Potter, but everyone assumed it was. He had all kinds
of jazz LPs as well as instruments and song books, and his recurrent
technique was to ask what you wanted and suggest something else.
He did in person what Amazon later made endemic: if you looked
at that, then we think you'll be interested in, and might buy, this.
He'd bring out albums and proffer them like a conjurer inviting you
to choose a card. He had lots of second hand albums too, and an
hour could be spent there, sometimes buying specific rock records,
the Stones Sticky Fingers for example, but often buying a record that
looked as if it might be worth hearing, or just because it had an aura

or association that made it seem worth owning for reasons indefinable. You felt that you were supporting the shop and being part of
something wider and more important than buying and selling, quite
a trick for a shopkeeper to accomplish. You may not have been a tremendous or committed jazz fan, but handling the substantial, almost
cardboard thickness of the sleeve of, say, a second-hand Riverside label
Thelonius Monk LP, and examining the odd cover photograph, made
you feel it was worth buying because, quite aside from music, it was
a genuine piece of history that had come down through time, even if
it was only the 1950s. I remembered how in the time after school and
before library school people said those jazz names that began with
M – Monk, Miles, Mingus – as if they were magic particles of sound.
It wasn't that we were keen jazz aficionados, more that we recognised
by such people that there was an attractive and dramatic other world
alongside this one, and the music was the sign that it existed. Even
Donovan on only his second album had tried to create some of the
atmosphere by singing of the Mingus, mellow, fantastic, feeling of
those times. Holding one of Potter's albums you felt for a moment
as Pete Seeger must about songs that travelled the centuries, proving by their existence that a previous way of life still had value, that
somehow the life and the value were eternal. Later I found out that
many people had felt this way over the years about Potter's and what
they found there. It always stood for more than the exchange of goods
and money. It was what the records represented, and, one understood,
was another way of perceiving how everything, everything we know,
can go away, will go away no matter how one feels that they will go
on like this forever. The shop had been there since the late Fifties and
had seen the cultural and musical waves roll in and recede. It was a
few yards from another landmark in Richmond's social history, a café
called L'Auberge, the kind of establishment that existed in Greenwich
Village or Soho, a meeting place for the young and hip, or those who
thought themselves hip, which amounted to the same thing, though
hip would have been beatnik then and meant people who went to art

school. The Stones had played in this very town, in a pub near the station, where the Beatles had come to see them, and also at Eel Pie Island along the river in Twickenham where jazz, rhythm and blues, and young people enjoying themselves had all flourished. That wasn't so long ago but might as well have been last century rather than last decade by the changes made. There was a lot of recent history here and I walked down to work and passed the sites where it had happened, and when I was at work I talked to someone who knew it first hand.

On that first day at work, when I was so ill-prepared to live in the town, I met John Platt, one of the first people I spoke to, who was also beginning that very day. We went out to lunch in the kind of café that could have been in an Ealing film, the waitress toothy in an overall, like a skinnier version of Aunt Dossie, older, though admittedly I hadn't seen Dorothy in awhile, her pale glasses reflecting the light as she asked, "What would you like dear?" from the few dishes chalked on the board. The room was all Formica tables and steam, boiled vegetables, steak and kidney pies, fish and chips, bread and butter, and two cups of tea, "And do you want jam roly poly and custard to follow dear?" Old people went there, young lads with tremendously bushy long hair, let loose from offices, and all of us came out smelling of grease, food and smoke.

> Characteristic café smells, so tenacious
> every clothing fibre will retain them
>
> for more than a day. Rain will not wash
> them out, sad hot fat no longer hot,
>
> as the bus queue stares at puddles,
> furious, circled surfaces, miniature spouts.

Over this fabulous repast, day after day, in premises having since undergone many karmic reincarnations, here and elsewhere John educated me. He knew all about rock and pop, had seen many of the bands and groups that had made the area so rich for club and gig goers in the middle and end Sixties, but he was also irradiated by the psychedelic culture of America's West Coast, steeped in minutiae of famous and unknown bands who rose and fell there. He loved the Grateful Dead but was also encyclopaedic on the little-known, and not known at all by me, Charlatans, who hardly released anything in their Sixties heyday, and none of it was the original band recorded at their peak, and therefore it was incapable of showing how innovative they were, what they had meant, in the mid-1960s when dressing like characters from the Old West, but also being able to produce psychedelic posters and write songs like We're Not On The Same Trip, were such zeitgeist accomplishments. Later John began a magazine he called Comstock Lode, a symbolic summation of the treasure and the location where it was to be found, whether in precious metal or precious sounds. He collected the colourful, ambitious posters that had been used to advertise gigs at the legendary Fillmore ballrooms, East and West coast versions, and was fluent about the artists who made them, as well as the cartoonists whose comics had proliferated then, Robert Crumb obviously, but also Gilbert Shelton, Rick Griffin, Victor Moscoso; people whose names alone sounded impressive. He wrote about what had been, – long chatty articles in the style of Zig Zag, a magazine he loved, another enthusiast's venture that grew into a proper magazine and had wide circulation, some of whose editorial mainstays John knew – but he wrote too of what was happening now, the records and acts that seemed to be a continuation of that 1960s line. Simultaneously he adored English eccentrics like the Bonzo Dog Band, or a group I hardly knew, the Idle Race, who though Birmingham rather than London, were part of the English sub-branch of psychedelia and also had the distinction, shared by many English bands, of being influenced by music hall. The vocal influence of Flanagan and Allen on Jeff Lynne would be apparent to anyone, and until the Electric Light Orchestra for some of us Flanagan and Allen were more familiar than Jeff. John knew this, and the Pre-Raphaelites, and Arthur Rackham, and while checking what albums the Grateful Dead were putting out, now that what had seemed to be the high water mark of their double Live/Dead was slipping further away behind us, he also looked for signs that the West Coast torch was passed on and held by groups here. There was a Welsh band called Man who seemed promising to him for a time. I could play one specific side of the 4 available on Live/Dead (which I would probably never have bothered with had it not been for John) and marvel at it, be carried away by the soaring guitars and the apparent telepathy between the players, but see too that the times that had made them and sustained them were over. They would carry on releasing albums and performing, everyone who loved them would still do so, that world would seem to be still continuing, but simply walking down the street told you it wasn't really the case. The truth was that something else was going to happen, was developing under the surface of the present, and it couldn't be seen using hindsight. Like many others however, John felt that though the numbers on the calendar had changed, the Sixties would carry on if everyone wanted it to be so. Credulity, naivety and wishful thinking were woven into those years after all.

The autogyro, inner-directed momentum of the 1960s seemed to have foundered, particularly in relation to Bob Dylan, whose sure touch had become a stranger to him. What arose to fill the vacuum one was experiencing, as might be expected, was the past. The book Tarantula, that Bob Dylan had written around 1965 and 1966, although publicised at the time, never made it to hard covers then, but now became something that one could send off for as a pirated A4 paper-covered copy. An example of that overlap between hippie lifestyle and private enterprise, you could hold the stapled, home-made collection and try to make sense of these oddly titled sections with their relentless fusillade of names, invented and proper, implausible and surreal, along with a hail of ampersands, all interspersed by jokey fake letters signed with jokey fake names. You understood why it hadn't been published. It was like a collection of Highway 61 Revisited sleeve notes, something that didn't really lend itself to sustained repetition. You could, more importantly, prize it as an object to possess, because that was really its point, a record of a sensibility that didn't exist now. And around the same time bootleg records began to emerge, (Tarantula being that neologism a bookleg), evidence that Bob Dylan had a more varied recording career than civilian fans like me knew about. There were songs that had been recorded for albums and left out; there were different versions of songs that had stayed in; there were, even more interestingly, strings of songs he had played for friends in living rooms and bedrooms captured on reel to reel tape recorders. These records came out on coloured vinyl with label names like Trade Mark Of Quality and were already owned by fans who were more serious and knowledgeable than me. The first time I saw them was in the home of a temporary library worker who had the longest hair I'd ever seen up to that point on a male person I actually knew. He pulled it back in a pony tail that hung between his shoulder blades, looking with his long features and sincere eyes not unlike a plain-faced Brown Owl, though with a shadier past than most youth leaders I imagine. He'd left university over some drug thing and was now trying to straighten up and fly right. He had a friendly, over-emphatic way of speaking, and after some mix up when our coats hung on the same coat rack swapped identities and some money from my pocket went into his hand, to his great embarrassment it has to be said, I visited his house in posh Hinchley Wood one afternoon, and met his mother who I could see wanted me to be in the office of Good Influence, and beheld all these examples of a cottage industry and an unknown dimension. They were much more fun and exciting, it had to be admitted, than New Morning or the man who made it now appeared to be. The past is always a competitor when Bob Dylan seems to be merely stranded in the present.

Bob Dylan was adrift, guesting on the albums of friends, contributing harmonica or odd songs, and generally demonstrating that he had come unplugged from the force that had previously sustained his singular drive, the one that carried him from the snowy north to snowy New York, then from the folk coterie of cafés and basements to the Washington Monument where thousands and thousands had stretched out before him, had believed that he sang their thoughts and convictions specifically about their country's treatment of black people, and more generally about the way things were and what should be done. Then he had retreated from that generational approbation, from being a representative of other people's thoughts, into the making of personal songs about what he experienced, and from there, with the inevitability of a dream, into working with a band, not so much writing songs as creating sounds, and no matter how many words were in the songs it was the sound the words and the music made together that possessed him. What had driven him? What had driven all of those groups to turn out albums and tours, making songs, sounds, seem to be a constituent element in all the forces at work in a society that was changing. Whatever it was, a sense of aftermath and a failure of sorts seemed to permeate the days now. Everyone was still working on their own unknown tomorrow, but the assumption that we were sharing a bright inevitability had evaporated. Perhaps it was to do with the feeling, previously present like oxygen, that being young was enough, and it took a few years, only a little time really, to underline the Shakespearean realisation that such a sensation was inherently ephemeral.

While Dylan was coasting and working out what to do next so was I, not because I had come unmoored from an exceptional driving ambition but because I had always been a stranger to it. I had work; I had my room; I had visits to home, by which I meant where I came from; I had Creative Writing classes at the Adult College where we wrote various little pieces and read them out and were careful not to hurt other people's feeling if we could help it; and where too I had a crush on a girl who actually came out for a drink with me, in the course of which she said yes, she lived with someone, which put the evening into a downspin from which it never recovered. I had record shops other than Potter's to painstakingly riffle through the wooden bins. One Stop Records was the kind of independent place where by some covert arrangement a record would be in stock so in advance of normal release date that it would only be available without a sleeve. Vouchers were issued to claim them when they were supplied a week or so later. It was in their window that I saw the cover of Umma Gumma on display, Pink Floyd's double album statement after Syd Barrett's departure, and thought how Dave Gilmour's hair, dress, posture, situation, and the life they suggested, were so of the moment and yet so far from the people who would see it there.

And aside from all this I had the cinema. At that time there were three cinemas in town and another a short distance away in Twickenham. Two of these were examples of the 1930s Odeon splendour which gave you a glimpse of what an event cinema going had once been, with the richness of decoration, the balconies apparently inspired by Spanish haciendas, the curving inner roof and the red, swagged, pleated, gold curlicue-embossed sweep and furl of curtain hectares. Even the two that weren't the full size Odeon grandeur, a Gaumont and an ABC, were still cinemas of the old style, with the one big screen, not chopped and channelled into the individual viewing chambers that were soon to be familiar. Not all of them showed latest release films. The sound of film music, and the experience of watching a film in a cinema and having it envelop you with its world was, I realised, as much a signature sensation of the Sixties as music. It was in the ABC where I saw Camelot, a film of a few years before, and resonant with echoes and connections. Nothing to do with rock music at all, and yet starring Richard Harris who had stumbled into higher grade pop in the company of Jimmy Webb two years ago, the time of Hey Jude, with his grandiose single MacArthur Park, that I bought. He was working the Beach Boys symphonic patch with the kind of singing voice actors have, the projection of confidence and illusion. The Kennedy era had been dubbed Camelot too by hacks and flacks, an imagined nobility associated with the President in the time when Bob Dylan was regarded chiefly as the writer of Blowin' In The Wind and represented the idealism of the young. The days seemed of a piece, before details of the President's moral failings were widely known, all of it now seeming to be confidence, illusion and myths receding into a mirrored infinity.

And around the time the film of Camelot was being put round the paddock again Harris was to be seen in the saga of the early west A Man Called Horse, bringing back memories of what Westerns used to be, and making one realise that Westerns are always made from the temper of the times that creates them. What did these times mean when a Western contained initiation ceremonies that required being strung up by your pectorals to become a man and part of the tribe? Well, they meant a way of thinking about what the Vietnam War represented, it seemed, arranged in symbolic form. Soldier Blue showed the cavalry butchering the innocent Indians and invited you to draw your own comparisons. To emphasise the authenticity of the protest the title song was delivered by Buffy Sainte-Marie in her strong, vibrating warble, a little reminder of her 1960s concern. Most unexpectedly of all there was actually a film of the book I'd loved, Little Big Man, capturing as much as it could of its big set pieces and clever shifts between guying clichés of the form and being a straight Western. Its music was also a Sixties reminder: John Hammond playing anachronistic bluesy guitar, but a reminder to those who cared of the father who gave Bob Dylan a break and the son who put him onto the Band.

More echoes and connections occurred with The Owl and The Pussycat, a film I saw more than once, with the great, funny and skilful George Segal and Barbra Streisand, a romantic comedy about a man trying to make it in New York, a would-be writer and lover of a girl much more street-wise than him. Obviously I was looking for parallels and so far lacked only a manuscript and a girl. I was probably more detained by the cinema then since the time about a decade before, when, as a child, I didn't go so much but regularly read the little monthly picture magazine ABC Film Review, put out by ABC Cinemas. Once on a whim I walked all the way to Walsall and back, miles, passing the second-hand shop where Hootenanny would be chanced upon, and the newsagents where the cash-in exploitation souvenir colour magazine Meet The Beatles was available for 2/6, a route march simply in order to allow me to look at photographs and read about, for instance, Billy Budd and Terence Stamp, laying down a memory as one would add a snap to an album. With free time, and surrounded by cinemas, you immersed yourself in darkness and the light of imaginary lives, leaving the foyer still yourself, but steeped a little in the story's shapes, sound and words. It seemed to help, to be of assistance, when a little oddly shaped space in the air, modelled from bricks and planks and walls and plaster and decorating materials, containing a bed and a record player, was afterwards going to be the resting place for a head now busy with images and notions.

Watching films, luckily, was only part of it. Friendship and being shown the various, metaphorical ropes, was happening too. *You were in this room,* and then you were in another room, and sometimes the people around you changed and sometimes they didn't. After the first six months or so on the lower reaches of Richmond Hill and my cinema apprenticeship, using an internal version of Morning Morgantown as a soundtrack to my stroll to work and After The Goldrush as evening mood instigator, a chance came to share a house with a friend made at work and his girlfriend, all the way from Italy, Italy. He could cook. The miniature room at the bottom of Richmond Hill gave way to a shared house in East Sheen that was only for a season. Shared houses or flats should always make people how aware how precarious democracy is, and how not to take it for granted. But we always take it for granted, forgetting that a government and the population getting along and being sensible is no more easy than people taking their turn washing up or cleaning the bath. I don't remember the bad bits and mostly I don't remember the good bits either, except as a general mood and not in specifics. The shape of the rooms and what was in them, whether we had the downstairs of the house only or ventured further, the texture of the days, it's all evaporated the way morning steam rises in white-grey lines and curls from damp wooden slat fences along the attractive sunlit streets, behind 1890s or 1910 rather grand houses, more impressive than anything in Smithfield Road. This was now. The Sixties had stopped being a reality but would always be there, like the bedsit one used to live in, or what the inhabited portion of this rented house actually looked like, detail by detail, when, living in whatever came next, it was time to compare. The Sixties had expired but one acted as if that weren't so, without trying necessarily, without thinking about it. Hence the listening to Neil Young and/or Sticky Fingers, bought suitably a stone's throw from the micro bed sit. What had to occupy your mind was this daily round, these pleasures and duties and obligations, working out what was happening and what needed to happen, day by day.

I remember going to a small shop nearby and asking for elbow macaroni because that was what a recipe specified, and the shopkeeper being surprised because he said he'd just had to tell someone else that he'd never heard of it. This was my friend the house sharer, not the information sharer. In the end macaroni cheese must have been made with the non-elbow quick boil variety bought in cardboard boxes from corner shops and bemused shopkeepers. I remember going to work, catching the bus and sweeping down the main road to Richmond on bright and blue mornings and Morning Morgantown still crossed my mind. Actually by then Joni's album Blue had been released and was one we played a lot and knew by heart and thought clearly superior to anything she had previously done in words and the sounds she achieved. She was someone thinking about then and now. That was my problem right there. My inner life revolved around revolving records. I was preoccupied with comparing internalised songs. I had ingrained in me something that was fatal to ambition or getting on. This was something that may or may not have been a working class belief, but must have derived from my family circumstance where no-one went out to work. Your life and what you thought, your interests, these were separate from your work, what you did. Successful people, it seemed later, though probably not perceptible to me at the time, subordinated what I thought of as normal life, concentrating on the area where they wanted to succeed. Whether they really succeeded or not they tended to find things easier simply by having an idea where success might lie for them, then pursuing it at maximum force.

CHAPTER TWENTY
KING OF INFINITE SPACE

Bob Dylan's maximum force, though still no doubt many foot pounds per square inch higher than mine, seemed to have subsided too. Whatever Bob Dylan had meant had sunk into the sand, the way streams carried on working away from sight. And then he percolated back into public consciousness and you could feel people trying to make it mean something. A single was released called Watching The River Flow, a lively, bluesy performance of a new song by him which seemed to be about the state he was in, not doing much and wanting to be able to do more. The B side however was the one to prize if you had ever been any kind of Bob enthusiast. It was called Spanish Is The Loving Tongue. It wasn't his song though you couldn't have asked for a more poetic, Dylanesque phrase. He made it his own. It was an old song, though we didn't know how old then, and was a cowboy song the way El Paso was. He sang it with real feeling and a slight cold, but what made it a Bob Dylan song was his characteristic piano playing, as heard intermittently throughout his recorded career. It was, as it had always been, the musical equivalent of a child's painting: primitive, charming, effective. There was more Bob activity on the way. One evening, in the August summertime, I walked back from the shop around the corner from the house, no doubt bringing more macaroni cheese ingredients, reading the London Evening Standard. What could make one feel more a resident, or did then, of that place London which is both actual and an act of imagination, even out on the outer south west area of its circle, and reading there the report of the Concert For Bangla Desh, where a triumph of luck and George Harrison's persuasion convinced Bob Dylan to perform. We looked at his newsprint all-denim outfit, his scratch of beard, the busker disguise, and registered the shift in time and the impress the years put on everybody.

Some of the songs he sang to help George's cause were old favourites not heard in concert for a long time, even performing again Blowin' In The Wind. People were happy to hear them all, and glad to see him there, but it was inescapable that it was all a harking back to something, a situation, that didn't seem to be around anymore. His presence was to act as a seal of approval and a proof that the idealism of a decade ago could still be summoned when a political situation seemed to demand it. Towards the end of the year, he released a single about George Jackson., someone convicted of armed robbery as a teenager then forced to spend the rest of his life in prison, where undeterred by intermittent solitary confinement he educated himself, becoming a Marxist, a writer and a revolutionary focus because of his views on the inherent structural racism of America, and the brutality of the prison system to all inmates, but black ones in particular. He was almost exactly the same age as Bob Dylan, and was shot dead in an alleged escape attempt the same month as the Bangla Desh concert. The single, like the concert, seemed designed to remind people of what Bob Dylan used to do. The song, deliberately simple, summarised Jackson's life and death and affirmed his power and his love. One side was done in old-style straight guitar and harmonica as it might have been before the blitzkrieg of 1966; the flip side was the same song performed with a group and was referred to as the big band version. The problem was two fold. People in England, even old-style Dylan fans, didn't know or care much about George Jackson;

and there was a problem with song itself. There was a straining for an effect evident that left it unconvincing. Unfair though it may have been it didn't seem like a genuine response so much as an opportunity to put out a record. The excitement aroused by its release faded. Dylan's appearances became sporadic guest shots in clubs or on other people's records. Proper albums by him weren't around anymore. There had always been more people in music to think about than Bob Dylan, and now though in plain sight he seemed to be retired in some way.

He wasn't the only symptom of absence. As well as the entrancing, extrasensory guitar interplay of St Stephen and The Eleven by the Dead, John Platt schooled me in other examples of what had been happening just prior to where we now found ourselves. He'd known L'Auberge and Eel Pie Island, the school kids and the college kids, the weekend beatniks, the innocence that wanted experience of hanging out and staying out and music. The Island had begun in a kind of Utopian, very English, social work attempt to give young people a place to go to enjoy themselves, keep out of trouble, liberating and harnessing energy with beer and jazz, not rock, which only came in afterwards via blues and rhythm & blues. That scene, and the scene, after had dissolved, and more recently it was variations on a squat, a commune, tense with drifters or dopers, people who were thinking of getting their heads together in India or Ireland or Goa but meantime were loitering there. Not long afterwards the hotel where all the music and people had gathered burnt down. It was derelict by then anyway. The end of the Sixties was so close, but already over the horizon. So John talked about and played me music, and delved into all matters pertaining. He liked tall, quite posh, educated English types, people somewhat like himself, and was knowledgeable about favourites like, amongst others, Kevin Ayers and Soft Machine, the first two Nick Drake albums, Van Morrison's Astral Weeks and Moondance, as well as Syd Barrett, his time in Pink Floyd and after. John probably valued Syd's solo, post-Floyd, albums more highly, obvious though it was that while he retained his wonderfully appealing, very English voice – and the oddity of hearing that shouldn't be underestimated when most native rock and pop guys, with the exception of Nick Drake, wanted to sound authentically transatlantic, – something irrevocable had happened to him. You could hear a mind emptying. Not only was what he could do now of a very different order to what he had done previously, it seemed likely that he would never do anything musically again. Still, he was a symbol of the constellation, that empire of consciousness consisting of sensitivity, string arrangements, and poetic words. The English Underground and its accents was never far away from John. To investigate some of its material manifestations he took me to Compendium Bookshop in Camden, then unrivalled for its music, alternative, and political stock, though its right-on leftness – a natural home for George Jackson's books – had no appeal for me.

This aspect of Camden was also evident in the general vibe one felt walking from the Tube station up the street to the bookshop ... What became of the Sixties could be found there if you went by sense impressions. The Eel Pie drift into the kind of life that had nothing to do with the way I thought about mine seemed to be alive behind the shopfronts. The alternative lifestyle so trumpeted not that long ago appeared to be a parasitical make-do-and-mend attachment on the despised straight life led by most people, wage slaves like me. Compendium's shelves of isms and ideologies symbolised what I saw walking by, interleaved layers of scruffiness of clothes and thought. Music and dance were adjacent to life, but couldn't be your life. Politics couldn't be fashion, or deciding to share a derelict house and thinking that's what the world could or should do. George Harrison's reaction to the reality of Haight Ashbury, seeing that the "peace and love" and colourful silks and feathers fashions of 1967 inevitably led to horrible spotty teenagers strung out on drugs made sense to me. I thought too of Syd Barrett who had seemed such a bright colourful presence and now had become unmoored from himself. The ancient songs that Pentangle, Fairport Convention and Steeleye Span brought to life again were a long way from Camden High Street, except in this: mediaeval times would have been just as grim, though they would have had ways other than dirty bricks and exhaust fumes to express it.

So George Jackson and similar fare didn't attract me in those Compendium levels. What was of more appeal was the presence of books that were also records of an earlier time, one that like 1966 was beguiling now. Richard Brautigan's work, whose Trout Fishing excerpt had puzzled and amused me a couple of years before, when I was still at home and reading the New Writing In America anthology, was here. I'd come across him again after that initial introduction in the copies of Rolling Stone that I took to the staff room, educating myself in the tea silences. He had a little piece in each issue headed with a characteristic photograph: long hair, moustache, big hat. One couldn't call this offering a story exactly, some were barely a paragraph, though all had the exact flavour of the kind of thing he did at greater length in his books. In Compendium I bought the American edition of what I came to believe was his best, most characteristic, book, A Confederate General At Big Sur, a version smaller than the Picador editions but more desirable simply by being American. This attitude of mine was a left over from where I first used to buy and swap comics, ah Aquaman and The Atom of long ago, and sometimes used to dwell on how odd it was that some editorial and publishing building, so random in time and space, faraway Connecticut perhaps, could produce something that would find its way to me in my little world, crossing oceans to do it, stacked in little rooms in buildings, then vans, then the newsagent I walked into not far from my house. In this case not only was it more desirable simply because it was American, the cover really was more impressive.

Publisher imprints had their cachet and appeal just as record labels did and in the early 1970s Picador was quite the Elektra of book outfits, and was on everyone's shelves with one fashionable author or another. They didn't lose out here because of Compendium's import. Eventually I bought not only this same title again, with a different cover featuring Brautigan's famous long hair, moustache and glasses, (though not in this case his large hat), but also his other later titles too. It's sad in one way that though it was one of his earliest books, published later here, he never really did better work. He did things as well but not with this freshness again. The title made one recall Kerouac's novel named Big Sur, but the book only made plain how very different they were, how gloomy really Kerouac's connection with the world was. All of Brautigan's characteristics, virtues and faults, are present and correct from the start. The rhythm of the words seems to take something from Hemingway, a parodic younger brother perhaps, less earnest one might say. The book concerns the things – killing time, looking at the ocean, meeting and making girls, being in love, living with little money in a cabin on the cliffs of Big Sur – that happen to Jesse, the narrator, and Lee Mellon, whose ancestor may have been a Civil War confederate general. Their other base is San Francisco, and Brautigan had scuffled there years before when that was the town most associated with the Beats, and when he was very much a struggling writer who wasn't part of the scene. This book demonstrates in its style, in Brautigan's odd take on the world and sentences, the transformation that took place when the Beats were slowly becoming, or being replaced by, hippies. Early as it was, already written and offered to publishers in 1963, published the next year, Brautigan's book seemed to offer an aspect of the playfulness, or childishness, which was a feature of the later Summer of Love. Confusingly, he's also been written about by literary critics as a writer of the Seventies. Like many creators, Elvis for instance, all of his good points are aspects of his bad ones. Later, his life became as gloomy, alcoholic, disappointed and confused as Kerouac's had. Success, mis-understood success, and then failure follow a pattern whether Beats, hippies or yuppies are in the ascendant, but all I had in front of me then was the book. What it's really about, like all of his work, is writing: how one may describe, understand, or refer to people and things in the world so that it's funny and interesting for someone else. Because of that I paid attention in the way I had with Bob Dylan and S.J. Perelman, but, like them, because he was such an individual styl-ist he was no model to follow in specifics, only in trying to find your own way to do what you can do.

Every singer or band we had ever liked was facing the same prob-lem although as fans we had somehow assumed they were immune to doubt and were following a course that was both planned and clear to them. Later I saw that an enthusiasm for a band or a singer can carry you through several albums, but often there comes a point when you find that somehow you haven't acquired the latest offering by Van Morrison or Ry Cooder, and you realise your interest seems to have fallen away without you quite noticing. Before you know it a few albums have come and gone and now you are hopelessly adrift and will never catch up. Why not make the connection that they too could feel the same drift from the thing that made it all happen for them in the first place. Meanwhile there you are with your small collection that stays as it is while the stars continue to produce albums that you have only the sketchiest knowledge of, the albums that will be marked as great or patchy or not required when the verdicts are handed out in the rock press retrospectives. What did you think? Would they stop working because you weren't buying? And somehow that becomes a symbol and a metaphor for people and enthusiasms and aspects of yourself. They come and go, whether you pay attention or not. And the days that these things occur in accumulate and disappear, putting changes on every surface, animate and inanimate alike. Around this time I noticed on the roads green trucks, the kind used in the building industry, wide and open-backed, the tipper trucks Van Morrison sang about on Astral Weeks, and on the side it had the local company name: Day Aggregates. That seemed to be just right. Each day arrives and you walk down the street knowing that every car, every item of clothing, each hairstyle, moustache, newspaper hoarding, if included in a photograph and then examined five years, ten years, decades later, will be itself and something more than itself. It will reveal what the nature and flavour of the time was when this record was taken and held fast. It will become an account in which resonances and emotions will be available to be withdrawn as soon as anyone casually takes it and glances. And sometimes within the day it's possible to imagine that the photograph has already been taken, that you are in the future and trying to see what life was like, back then, walking in this moment, aware of the way people look and move, the air on your skin, or the general and particular inadequacies that exist, preventing you being what you thought you were, or might be, and life a slight disappointment that had the possibility of becoming a triumph, and more importantly, an *unexpected* triumph. The days went by, fated to become precious or notable later, but as lived through they were simply common coin.

My friend Nigel was going to study for a postgraduate degree in librarianship and information technology, moving up and away to Sheffield. I visited, and among many hilly streets we listened to the raucous and compelling 1966 concert, on coloured vinyl of course, and later fell through a living room doorway while drunkenly and enthusiastically singing a selection from Ziggy Stardust. His girlfriend was going to go back to her hometown of Venice. I was going to the western edges of Twickenham where once the land shone with glass houses, and was fruitful with market gardens and orchards. It was a shabby house that must have been rather grand once, at the end of a cul de sac of similar houses, most of them still grand, different styles of architecture but almost all detached, the kind of houses that come into their own at Christmas with tree lights visible in the living room and a wreath on the front door. This was a major difference between where I came from and where I was. The houses here might be 1860s or 1890s or 1930s, but, they weren't, as the streets I came from were, late 1940s or 1950s council estates. The house I was going to live in, and I have no idea now how I found it, was white and sprawling, with an upstairs corridor reminiscent of small hotels, with bedsit rooms off it, and a bathroom that everyone shared and locked. First I had a bedsit downstairs at the back of the house, facing the concrete garden and its plastic wash line where I once left a pink towel in the sun, the rain, and the grey breeze for days, and forgot about it and when I remembered it had disappeared. It was a little and inadequate towel. That narrow, cool room had a French window metal door, its own tiny little kitchen area, from which a door led upstairs, so that one didn't have to go out of the side of the house and in through the front door to go up to the bathroom. A little later I was asked to move to another room to accommodate a fire exit that the authorities were insisting on, due to come down those stairs and right through that kitchen.

The alternative room was also downstairs, but at the front and was more your standard bedsit with everything in one room: an elderly wardrobe that wore a hat of suitcases; a kitchen table in the centre facing the window; and to the right a sink, a stove and a fridge all in a row, the fridge also acting as a kind of tall night table next to the single bed, which was against the wall that the door was in.. It was on that fridge top, with its nightly collection of decanted coins, a clock and my watch, I somehow lost the little gold cross I wore in my ear after falling under a Keith Richards spell and deciding to have my ear pierced. This was extremely uncharacteristic and I couldn't explain the appeal, but I decided to have it done. It didn't hurt, and wasn't sleazily romantic like tales of pirates, corks and needles, but carried out under the neat safety of a small High Street jeweller. I remember the soft crunch of the lobe, and the pressure as it was punctured by the machine very like a stapler. I hadn't thought that an earring would cause trouble at home, but then I hadn't thought at all, and there was shock and some horror. It was proof that I had, eventually, succumbed and gone, or started to go, to the bad. Bob Dylan went a thousand miles east, rang his parents every week and to the press said he was an orphan, but even so small a thing as a gold sleeper had consequences. There was something funny about the gap between what it represented to my parents and the real innocuous state of my life, but on return visits, whatever Bob might have done, the earring was removed. My life was as I described it in my weekly letter to them, making pages out of ordinary everyday details, the same as my dad did for me. He assumed the role of amanuensis with his blue biro and letterpad, and his gift for being able to write his thoughts exactly as he spoke.

So the room was small, and everything had to be in it, but even here the ceilings were high, the height reached by Edwardian builders who weren't thinking in terms of Housing Department geometry. The contrast only came home to me, you might say, when I once took back to Walsall the kind of large Chinese globe lamp shade wildly popular then with so many people in circumstances like mine, all white concertina paper and wire frame. In my front-of-house, slightly slipshod premises it was up there like the moon beaming down on Vesta meals, or the more ambitious proper apple crumble. Back in the steel house it hung huge and low, not far above head height and was laughably inappropriate. I felt ashamed not because their ceiling was low but because I'd not realised the difference, not even when I'd had to stand on a chair and stretch to attach it to the Twickenham light cord. It seemed to symbolise more general lacunae and failings in my character and perceptions.

The young couple we all handed over rent to, representatives of whoever owned the place, had the grace to charge me a little less for the changed situation. All prices from former times sound ridiculous later. The sums mentioned have floated away from specific circumstance and become as meaningless as a groat or farthing, though they seem to have a mirage of actuality because the same denominations still exist. In modern terms each week cost me a few pounds less than the price now of a new paperback. Or to put it another way and to get a perspective: you might have bought between 8 or 10 paperbacks then for the price of the weekly rent. What would 8 or 10 of today's paperback prices fetch in the rented sector now? I handed my money over with my little blue, bought in a shop, rent book to the wife of the owner's agents. They had a little girl of about three or four, and lived downstairs too, in, I assumed, not many more rooms than mine, fitted between my new and old locations. The house was a sad looking place, the way houses are when there is a shifting population in little rooms where mugs are bleached to convincingly remove stains; and, surmounted by ill-advised houseplants drooping over the screen, you will find big old second hand TVs because it's thought, wrongly, that the lack of a licence is less easy to detect that way. On such a TV it became apparent that the soundtrack theme for life in rooms in London was no longer Light Flight but the music for Man About The House, although that didn't have much correspondence with life as we knew it. There all was blithe, larky house-sharing with two attractive girls and the constant possibility of sex. Rising Damp, with its desperation and seedy making-do would have been a more accurate comparison. Once, a girl in one of the upstairs rooms won on the football pools. She didn't say how much but it excited her enough to knock on doors and offer whoever answered a glass of sparkling wine. Presumably she was funded now to leave behind the desolate, unclean look of the entrance hall, where leaves blew in the usually left-open front door, and collected around the table under the pay phone bolted to the wall. This was where the post was piled and where I had at least one mail order record in its chunky cardboard container stolen. Somewhat more worryingly, the husband of the young couple committed suicide not that long after my move to the front premises, though I don't remember being told how he had done so. I do remember I was told his age, 27. It wasn't much of a difference in years, but 27 and married with a wife and child, didn't seem close to my situation at all. When I'd seen him he didn't seem troubled especially. I couldn't work out why someone so mature, as it seemed to me, would get into a position where he felt that was his only choice. He was an adult, where he wanted to be, I'd thought, whereas I was now enacting the kind of life I'd imagined in some general way, but not really in this detail, when I set off from Walsall with a little leather bag and a suitcase. This was the life people had when they were starting out. Characters in novels and films began like this. Bob Dylan started out this way, for God's sake. Toughen up. It's the phase of your life that you don't necessarily enjoy much. It's there to look back on at a later, more luxurious stage of the life cycle, trying to make a funny or a touching story about it. How did I live like that, you ask or think. While you're living it you ignore it by accepting it, and intermittently wonder how you might contrive to change it for another. It hadn't occurred to me that the less than perfect circumstances of the bedsit house might have seemed more permanent to a person who collected the rent, and he couldn't envisage where he might possibly move onto next.

The perception of time passing is our commonest experience, and yet the one hardest to identify to oneself. It's because it seems to have several different rates of movement and all are true, like light and matter, sometimes a particle and sometimes a wave and the way you call it seems to depend on the methods of observation. The days zip by. You pick up a breakfast mug on Monday and the act of replacing it on the table takes you to Friday tea. The weeks become seasons. People who were young in the Sixties accept they took place a long time ago, but find it more difficult to accept the same about the Seventies. For those people the time with that label may also have a more amorphous, less summarisable quality than Sixties signposts. For other people however the Seventies has the same intense quality of any time passed through as a teenager. Slightly older people have a different story to tell. I started out in 1970 and before I knew it there were 1971 and 1972, and calling it the Seventies wasn't uppermost in my mind. What was I doing and what was Bob Dylan up to?

One of the attractions of biography or history is that patterns can be discerned, people's characters are revealed, there is some kind of sense being made. Scanning the business pages or reading about actors, clearly there are people who do operate according to a plan devised by ambition, or some other inner demon, and where they are going is more important than where they are. While Bob Dylan was disconnected from whatever had propelled him to the status he commanded in the middle 1960s, rock and pop too had frayed and become more messy. In England Dylan's voice could be heard unmistakeably in Bryan Ferry's singing for Roxy Music, for those who cared or remembered. Elsewhere what Dylan had done or seemed to represent was very far away. Music was more fragmented than ever and several distinct styles and scenes existed without much connection.

Roxy appealed to the dandy strain in pop. Arty references were expected. Being clever wasn't frowned upon. This was very different from the metal mutation that had developed, seemingly, out of the Corporation Street familiars Blodwyn Pig, Free and the subliminal template that Led Zeppelin offered. The sound was loud, repetitive and unsubtle and the clothes of the bands fitted in. They could have been motor mechanics on a break. Long hair that formerly might have been accused of being girly because it was actually cut that way, one thinks of course of Brian Jones, was now long hair in a race to be longer, and the styling or washing of such centre-parted curtains was apparently irrelevant. It may have been an illusion but there had been a feeling half a decade before that folk, blues, jazz could all share elements, and that someone who saw himself as an adaptable rock and pop fan would be aware of those other adjacent territories and like aspects of them at least. In my own person I knew that no longer held.

I had no interest in the wider and wilder fringes of metal even while recognising that there were boys no doubt who plotted every move and personnel change and album song just as my friend John Platt had done, and did, with his West Coast familiars, with copies of Pete Frame Family Trees to hand. Rock kept splitting off like an amoeba into distinct identities. Now we were delivered from the Whistle Test Sixties continuations of the likes of Lindisfarne, with their cardy-wearing, long hair, bearded student shabbiness, by the trans-sexual, cross-dressing fey space creature David Bowie, a Sixties veteran but young, who had mutated through time to be here with songs and sounds that had nothing to do with his Laughing Gnome incarnation. I saw him, through some odd collection of coincidence and chance, from a front and centre seat at a cinema in Worcester at the peak of his Ziggy phase. I was writing in a notebook and a girl next to me said, "Write down that he started late." "I'm not a journalist," I said, "this is just for me." "Write it down," she insisted. He did his trapped behind a glass wall mime, and his hits, and wore his skimpy costume to show off his overall slenderness and bare legs, and was altogether entrancing. Then there was the arty cleverness of Roxy Music, who allied themselves to the futuristic clothes and ornaments associated with, but actually greater than, the character-istics named glam rock. Spangles, shiny clothes, platform boots and make-up for men became the norm. Even I dabbed on patchouli, wore ridiculous tank tops and for a while a pair of shoes with soles high enough to raise blisters as large as damsons on both feet. The mechanics who formed heavy metal bands were supplemented now by the attractions of what seemed to be bricklayers raiding wives or girlfriends wardrobes and cosmetic bags. Glam itself became broader and coarser almost immediately, so that not only glitter or stars on faces were relevant, but almost any kind of novelty or clownish attire. Only two seconds were all it took to see that none of the members of Sweet, no matter how feather cut their hair, had the genuine and slightly alarming androgyny of David Bowie. To my surprise I found that Slade, formerly a skinhead-styled band called Ambrose Slade, were now big on hair and clownish attire. They came from my part of the world quite precisely, and had in Noddy Holder a singer whose every interview claimed him to be a year younger than me. This was a surprise because when I had seen him walking across the quad-rangle in our shared alma mater, T. P. Riley, he was Neville, and 2, probably 3, years above me. The hippy mainstay from John Peel's initial Radio 1 days, Tyrannosaurus Rex, altered their odd, wailing, folk-based warblings, and became a surprise teen sensation, a strange blend of glam and metal. Simultaneously, demonstrating just how much of a shuffled pack this present was, and obviously more allied to what people thought Bob Dylan represented, came the continuing success of Sixties types Neil Young, James Taylor and the rich post-hippie Laurel Canyon crowd symbolised by the Eagles..

Neil Young had something that Bob Dylan didn't have, which was his desire and ability to create electric guitar storms and then disappear into them. But anyone hearing Heart of Gold, the big hit of

1972 knew what occupied the other side of his musical consciousness. Bob Dylan loomed large but not in the foreground. He could still be found in some of the newer monthly magazines that appeared, Let It Rock and Cream, where music was the point but the atmosphere and vibe still carried reverberations of the Underground, that late Sixties blend of politics, sex, dope, self-righteousness and cheek found in magazines of the era, Oz, Ink and that English offshoot of Rolling Stone, Friends, which rapidly warped into Frendz. It was in magazines like this that one could read Clive James contributing essays on, for instance, the vocal art of Sandy Denny, the essays one would look for in vain when he published The Metropolitan Critic a couple of years later. That was for his more serious bids at renown. Of course the only connection some of us had with the famed Underground was reading those magazines. There was one time also when I visited the Oz office. One of the sleep-over girls, not the one who gave me Frankie Lymon, had a subscription and was missing an issue. We were still in touch and she asked me if I could get it. The office had exactly the air of laid back no-hassle you hoped for, long-haired blokes sitting at desks, not furiously typing, not surprised that someone would turn up to claim a missing issue. "Yeah, man, there you go." My brush with luminaries of the English underground. On that same London visit I bought, around 5 years late, the Velvet Underground and Nico album and never tired of Waitin' For The Man.

It was in those newer music monthlies too that coverage could be found of the bootleg records that kept us so up to date with the past. The advocates of official release of the recordings of Dylan's 1966 tour also set out their stall here. The most famous bootleg was called The Royal Albert Hall concert and was available in actual record shops, if you chose the right shop. But there was a feeling that if it were to be released properly, by CBS, by The Man, then scales would fall from eyes and Dylan would be revealed for the true rock prophet he was, in all his sonic grandeur. The level of intensity would do its work and this nondescript present wouldn't matter. No-one realised that particular periods from the past need to meet the right kind of present to succeed. The planets have to be in alignment for the magic to work. Like Smile, the Beach Boys eternal lost masterpiece, the 1966 Dylan concert was something perpetually invoked and wished for.

In the absence of records what kept Dylan in mind for those who cared was printed material. A year or so before, the same year as the Bangla Desh concert, Tarantula had made it to hardback status from a proper publisher. Scholars would have set to comparing the earlier opportunistic stapled version with this official book, just to see what textual differences there were. I couldn't do this, my bookleg now absent, not having travelled down with me, and no longer visible in the spare bedroom at home. The most notable thing about the real book was the cover, a Jerrold Schatzberg photograph from the dandy 1965/66 era, his stern, coolly regarding face bisected into light and shade. The text itself was as remembered. Sometimes you could look through it and a phrase or a tone of voice would raise a smile. Mostly though everything about it, especially the cover photograph, was a proof, like archaeological remains, of historical times now lost to us.

There were other books that helped Bob fans get through a lean period, and better reads than Tarantula. The first examination of Dylan's work from an English Literature angle came from Michael Gray. He had a background in the study of poetry, as well as the rock monthly magazines, and knew his historical examples, able to point out the startling similarities of parts of Subterranean Homesick Blues to Robert Browning, or bits of William Blake to the sleeve notes of Highway 61 Revisited. This was all nourishment in those times after New Morning when a new album seemed increasingly unlikely. And around the same time was a really absorbing and essential read for anyone who thought of themselves as a Bob follower. The first hardback, properly researched, biography appeared. Anthony Scaduto, its author, had been a reporter and knew about getting information and interviewing sources. Surprisingly, Dylan himself contributed but that wasn't the best part. The best part was reading about what he had been when he was someone who wanted to make it and set about trying to make that happen. All of those rooms and basements in New York, the people who were much better than him, and better known, and yet within months he became someone to watch, and then someone to envy. He camped out with Dave Van Ronk and pretended he didn't know Rimbaud, and then wrote Blowin' In The Wind. We read a novel wanting to know what comes next, while understanding that it already exists because someone wrote it all down and we hold it in our hands. It's the past and the future. It's waiting for us to discover what has happened. Whereas we read a biography already knowing what came next up to a certain point, but wanting to know instead what came before, the detail we didn't know when the famous person was merely someone in the world, possibly a little like you or me. And of course we also want to know more about what happened behind the public façade, which may involve scandal, bad behaviour, or perhaps to the contrary, our undefined hope that the apparent goodness of someone we don't really know will be confirmed. In both cases what is encouraged is a view that life can be understood as a series of actions and incidents, motives and attainment, and they happen in chapters that end at the right time and make sense with what comes next. There's a pattern and a structure and often something from childhood will provide a clue to understanding why similar scenes recur and are played out again and again. It's more difficult at the endlessly unfolding moment of one's own life to discern a pattern and a structure, when a night will come and a day will follow, and unlike someone driven by ambition for money or power or women, – such people always being clear if they are ahead of or behind the game, – we seem to be mere movers through the seasons.

CHAPTER TWENTY-ONE

JUST PERSONAL

I loved Scaduto's book and could get lost in it, reading and re-reading and imagining the life it detailed. It was the way I had felt when consuming Hunter Davies's Beatles biography. What's in the book takes you over like a dream. Perhaps Bob had dreamed his life too before he made it come true. Certainly he seemed to have invented parts of it. Perhaps he too had read Ray Bradbury, they both came from the Mid West after all, to have given himself a background in carnivals that emphasised the travelling and the camaraderie of the freak show, a former life entirely fictitious. My other source on his past was treasure trove from another Compendium visit with John. There were a couple of publications there, Commemoration and Praxis One, both were large format paperback equivalents, available as far as we knew nowhere else, assembled by some Dylan fan, an American zealot. They had home-made collages, put together like a butterfly collection, of old Bob Dylan interviews and badly printed photographs, as well as reproductions of writing he'd done for magazines or concert programmes, almost anything not widely known, and all in all each was a jewel box for a fan like me, familiar with the official releases and history but not this historic collecting and reproduction. There were a couple of quotes that struck me. Of his fans he said "All of these people, waiting for me to turn them on like lamps." And of giving autographs, "Why do they value my name on a piece of paper more than their own." Naturally if you think of yourself as an admirer or follower of some artist these are points of view that are going to give you pause. Why did I value that Kenneth Allsop book with the accidental inscription more than I would one without it? I'd never collected autographs, but coming across a book or a record that had one did cause a frisson. It's a feeling most fans recognise, and is something to do with connections being made, but also with some residual primitive religious impulse. The same desire that generates a trade in holy relics. Another quote also had an impact. Speaking of where he came from and why he left it, Dylan said how leaving home wasn't unusual or particular to him. Everyone a certain age did it. There was just nothing there in his hometown for people his age. But then he spoke affectionately about Hibbing, "My brains and feelings have come from there. I wouldn't amputate on a drowning man, nobody from up there would." Obviously I connected that with Bloxwich, where my brains and feelings had been formed. Where you are from and the way you are brought up stays with you in ways you don't necessarily recognise; or that you stray from but then notice how they have reclaimed you. It wasn't that I could forget about it. I had a Saturday off once in 3 weeks, and if I didn't go up on every one of those I did go on many. In a sense I was enacting where I was with Bob Dylan, visiting the past and trying to make sense of the present.

The scrapbook gatherings of Commemoration made cause with the coloured vinyl bootlegs that mixed and rearranged the different styles Bob Dylan had previously tried out, the different times he had lived in. It was an odd juxtaposition that now this hidden historic Bob Dylan was so real and present to me, and had been so unknown when I had first fallen for him. At the time I was listening to and loving something like To Ramona this recorded presence, only a couple of years before, was as unknown to me as if it had never happened. The earliest songs were home tapings of performances for friends, in living rooms or at parties. They were a reminder of how young he was when he began doing all this, and also of how his voice was entirely his more or less from the start, the grain, the texture and what he could do with it. When I say "his" I don't mean that he hadn't heard Woody Guthrie and tried to absorb what he most prized about him. Nevertheless while one might pay lip service to Guthrie I found it impossible to take to him and his sound, his voice and his guitar, in the way it seemed Bob Dylan had. Woody may have rambled clear across the country and slept in hobo jungles, bedded down in boxcars and played in Okie migrant camps, but he hadn't been a teenager who loved rock'n'roll in the 1950s and Bob Dylan indisputably had. Some of that was concurrent in Bob's voice too. To be honest, analysing why his voice held such an elemental appeal didn't occupy me too much. What one heard on the Trade Mark of Quality albums was that early voice, where he seemed limited in what he could do, working the same harmonica riff over and over, and yet making himself known in a way that carried you through doubt. One also heard the other element that was surprising, the fact that released albums could have been other than they were. Outtakes, where things had gone wrong, or earlier versions of songs that were later seen to be in need of some improvement either lyrically or in the playing and so were left out, meant that now the version of a song that was indelible within the strange textures that are, and are not, physical inside one's skull, could now have a rival demonstrating variations. None of this would have been new to jazz fans, but then aside from a peripheral knowledge of some names we weren't fledged jazz fans, or I wasn't, though I liked the idea of it and some sounds. Earlier I had assumed, without really considering that it was an assumption, that albums were somehow inevitable once the people involved had decided to make them, in the same way that from the outside careers seemed to have an arc and a momentum that worked by itself.

Here we were in the present, time-travelling with the aid of coloured vinyl, biographies and old programme notes, experiencing the sense of those times and the life he led, the different music he made, and how much of a focus he had seemed for energies and spirits. And here I was going back to the street and the house that were the same but weren't, and finding I didn't fit there anymore. Perhaps that's how he felt too. Wanting to make things happen the way he had decided they should be was what Bob Dylan had set himself to, and he had succeeded. What would have happened to him if that hadn't been the case? What became of the people who played better guitar than him back in Minneapolis or Madison or New York but lacked his voice or his capacity to put words together? What became of the people who saw him in cellars and rooms, the people who fell for him or the ones who couldn't see the point? The fountain of the present, always itself and another, a symbol for the social history of fountains. What was happening to Bob Dylan now, now that a whole scene and its world had become history that kept receding, as it has for all of us who thought we came from some aspect of it. And now here it was in the early 1970s, and what did music mean, along with that double A side single release, work and life?

The Seventies shares at least one characteristic with the Sixties. People refer to it by that name as if it is one thing when in fact it is lots of different time zones serving a consecutive sentence. Like everyone who has ended one thing and begun another, what I was mainly doing in those early days was simply trying to find my way. The friends I visited most were young married couples who had small children, which made me see how far I had to go; or John Platt and his wife who didn't have children but demonstrated a different life and another distance, where the Pre-Raphaelites and the West Coast, Arthur Rackham and Pink Floyd, were all part of the same thing and everything was worth thinking about. One couple lived in the downstairs part of a small terraced house where things were cramped, shabby and smelt a lot of the time of nappies. They'd been students about five minutes ago, and now because of the toddler were parents who still lived quite like students. It was one version of an alternative lifestyle. I didn't mind that. I needed all the friends I could get. The music I associate most clearly with them and that time is

Joni Mitchell. The younger sister of the wife, also a frequent visitor, admired Joni very much, would have liked to have absorbed all of her talents if it were possible. I had Ladies Of The Canyon that I'd played in the little room on Richmond Hill, and then Blue in the shared house, but not the one we mostly played there. Clouds, with its odd tunes and tunings, twinkling guitar lines – Tin Angel and Fiddle And The Drum – evokes that front room with its cushions on the floor, a mattress too as might be expected, candles and the scent of curry, gloomy, friendly winter time. Joni never stopped trying to change and improve musically, and so inevitably she moved away from this sound and these kinds of song; but no matter how successful she might think she was later, she would never be so much of her time, distilling it to come alive on each repeated play, as she was here. She captured the young ache and hope of the last years of the Sixties, and then the complication of 1971, simply with the sound of instruments and her voice singing her words, the magic of spheres and harmony even there on a narrow Twickenham back street with bakery smells nearby. It was already a report from a lost world even when I heard it here. And so there was darkness and reporting-in carrying the plastic shopping bag in which I toted the LPs and bottles I thought a visitor should bring, and talking about who knows what now. Except once it was Bob Dylan; me enthusiastically declaiming and acclaiming the surreal quality of his much earlier line, "If he needs a third eye he just grows one", (possibly because I'd just read Michael Gray praising it,) and receiving a deadpan response that didn't even try to look convinced.

My other young married parent friends had a brighter flat, more children, no nappy smells and different music. In addition to the wine and records I often took a tiny portable record player there, the kind where the speakers clipped over the deck to form a travelling case. I'd bought it cheaply at Boots having shown my little blue rent book as odd proof that the cheque wouldn't bounce in those days before guarantee cards were widespread. My old police-radio reception one

I gave to the other friends who rapidly realised what its problem was. The Sixties also continued its Seventies existence in the brighter, more fragrant accommodation. A sampler of the Transatlantic label featuring guitar wizards like Bert Jansch was always to hand, and the Velvet Underground's first, because I took it, with its clonking, insistent and catchy in its way, Waiting For The Man. Its unlikely playmate was Déjà Vu by Crosby, Stills, Nash and Young – that most unwieldy pop group name – whose South of The Border cover showed that they too, like us, had spent a childhood under the 1950s cowboy spell. The previous year their debut album, sans Neil Young, had a cover was equally enticing. It persuaded me, in a repeat of the Keith Richard cloth cap error, to wear a pair of boots I thought were a reproduction of Stills's style but only made me look like a clunky rambler who had lost his way.

The record that makes me think of those friends more is Paul Simon's first solo album, often in the ubiquitous plastic bag. Superficially similar to Bob Dylan in his folk club background, there were distinct differences between Paul Simon and Dylan. No matter how self-manufactured or illusory there was always something of the wild and untamed about Bob Dylan, an aura of hoboes and carnivals and blues singers. He may never have experienced the stories he retailed in his early interviews, but something was there in his voice that told you he connected with these things. And in the 1966 tour with the Hawks he was at the eye of an electrical storm that was perfectly genuine. Paul Simon was much more like the neat, Jewish middle-class suburban boy that Dylan tried to disguise and escape from. Simon is reined in, careful, confiding, compared to Dylan's scattergun, heaping quality. Because of this he is probably less regarded than he should be, but he was part of the times, and he did come over to England to find himself in tiny clubs alongside guitar maestros like Bert Jansch and Davy Graham. Bridge Over Troubled Water, the final Simon and Garfunkel album, in addition to staying in the album charts for years, had been a soundtrack at our sad and laughable library school sleepover. I didn't hold it against him. I always associated it too with a Walsall party that same year. Not knowing it was soft drinks only, a rule enforced by the mother of the girl whose party it was, my Bitches Brew friend, who had a moustache David Crosby would envy, memorably, and secretly, tried to drink the half bottle of sherry he'd presumed it was okay to bring, not wanting it, of course, to go to waste. We had to force a way into the toilet where he'd smuggled the bottle, help him to be sick and then, because we were all asked to leave, semi-carry him home, while he laughed, kicked out at shop windows and failed to walk properly. The background music for the party scenes was Cecilia, whose bedroom words gave the prim parent another reason to disapprove, and the memory of that song's bouncing, jerky rhythm was subliminally perfect for a teenage sherry drunkard and his eruptive progress.

Fittingly, Simon continued his move away from his pretty and poeticised words, the striving for the poetic, of the mid 60s songs, many written in England, and began to develop his own interest in more laconic, every day American speech. His new album showed that this was an area he was going to colonise. When placed against the careful, and sometimes exotic, and well-recorded music tracks he devised, this juxtaposition, conversational, closely observed, produced its own poetry. On the new album he had "Couple in the next room bound to win a prize, they been going at it all night long"; and "Sweep up, I been sweepin' up the tips I made, I been living on Gatorade", something I didn't know but liked the way it fitted in there. Neither of which, in their knowing tone and hinted humour, could you imagine him writing at the time of Parsley, Sage, Rosemary and Thyme. His solo album was notable for the way he demonstrated that there was no point in harking back to Simon and Garfunkel, and in showing how his soft, tuneful voice suited the circumspect words. I liked everything about it, from his giant, fur-trimmed anorak hood, from beneath which he peeked out as if wishing he had that kind of rock hairdo, to the words on the inner silver cover, to the actual sound of it all, and never thought it had anything to do with Bob Dylan, and never made any detrimental comparisons. He was from the Sixties trying to make his way in the Seventies. Who did he remind me of? Everybody. There was a lot of music around, and good music, but there wasn't a scene that made it all make sense, the kind of scene that needed to exist as much in our heads as out there in the world. Perhaps we were already disqualified from it, and if we had checked with people about 6 years younger they would have had a different perception.

A book I bought for my Paul Simon friends was by a writer mysteriously called L. Woiwode, who later revealed himself to be Larry. Its title was, What I'm Going To Do, I Think, and seemed to sum up everything. I lived in a bedsit and thought about as much as I could, but actually, thinking about it now, it was as if I couldn't think much beyond my nose. I was delighted by things as small as finding, in what was for a short time the treasure cave of Twickenham Woolworth's book sale bins, Peter Beagle's I See By My Outfit, a writer's slim volume about a cross-America trip by motor scooter. Older than Bob Dylan, the same age as Phil Everly, he was a guitar player too but would, I suspected, have scoffed at rock and roll, being more of a French chanson guy. He had reverberations of the Greenwich Village world Scaduto evoked, while being at a tangent to it. I loved his book and the chance that brought me to it, and kept it like a lucky charm, a charm whose lovely coloured jacket is raggedy and frayed now. Woolworth's trove also supplied a dinky hardback screenplay whose idea fascinated me. Two For The Road by Frederic Raphael, was a screenplay for a film I'd not seen but was intriguing enough to buy. It was about trips up and down roads in France at different times in a couple's life, cross-cutting to show what the years do and how people become strangers to each other, how they might see their future or past selves going by and not recognise them. It could only work as a film although I read it many times. Decades went by before I did see the film, on DVD inevitably, and unlike my readings of the book, and though it preserved Sixties sunshine and Sixties Audrey Hepburn, it was, equally inevitably, a disappointment. Which wasn't the case with my other great find there, an American album by the band Kaleidoscope, their third, Incredible Kaleidoscope, the summation of the Middle Eastern and deeply American forms they pioneered and only released in the USA. The American copy, never released in England. How did it end up here? Even John Platt didn't have it. That kind of success meant something to me. About work I had no ambition and only occasionally did I realise that this was not a good thing. I bought a tiny, slim, grey-white Olympia typewriter because it seemed to me that, whatever the external evidence suggested to the world at large, my thinking was that of a writer, and obviously if stuff was to be sent out typing aced handwriting. I was aware of the resemblance this suggested to George Segal's character in The Owl and The Pussycat, but then I'd seen Bob tip-tapping away in Don't Look Back. The only way to be a writer was not to feel like one but to produce writing. My dad, an older generation than most of my contemporaries enjoyed, had said years before he thought everyone should be taught typing and how to drive when they were still at school. I was quite impressed by the modernity of this, and still am. Given the way there's hardly a house now without a couple of keyboards in action he was more prescient than he could know. So I typed up parental letters, the beginnings of stories, what I thought of as radio plays, and the poems I wrote and re-wrote in a notebook, trying as everyone does who begins writing, to find the note that is personal to them, the one you come to recognise and then pursue. I'd written "poems" since school and so knew it's always a hit and miss affair no matter how much the one you are currently writing seems for a little time to be the best yet. That absorption and belief when writing seems to be the constant; it's only retrospect that causes doubt to set in. Both apparently are essential parts of the process. At that point it was a kind of record of what was before me, and what occupied my mind, wanting to make something that stayed outside of the flow and preserved an individual's voice, which in this case happened to be mine.

> Because of the position
> of the window
> and the position
> of the wall plug,
> I iron with my left hand.
> I am right-handed.
> I could burn myself easily
> though I am careful.
> This, the inevitable
> germs in the rug:
> I like to live dangerously

> Or:

> The table holds chaos
> fixedly. A letter waits to be sent.
> A milk bottle with an inch of milk
> waits to be consumed.
> Papers lie in geological layers.
> I sit calmly drinking unsweetened tea.

These were under the influence of Hugo Williams, who was himself under the influence of Ian Hamilton, and what they liked was something plain and somewhat prosey, but with depth and delicacy, a sound of lines on a page with the breaks just so, to intensify emotion. I had both of Hugo's books at that stage. Sugar Daddy, he'd titled one, and later another was called Some Sweet Day, showing he was an Everlys fan. He also liked Roxy Music and the Sugar Daddy photograph indicated he might have passed as a background member of the band. I liked to attempt rhyme more than him or Ian Hamilton but we try on influences without logic necessarily being involved. Clearly my oeuvre wasn't necessarily at the sending out stage, perhaps not quite yet, but I believed, or not even believed in the sense of consciously repeating it to myself, but automatically behaved as if the dogged act of thinking and hearing an internal tone of voice, then writing it down, the act of regularly writing these things down, was worth doing, was its own reward and would lead me somewhere.

It wasn't only writing or trying to write. Reading played as much a part as it had from the time of Bloxwich library. A Dance To The Music Of Time is something I should have been aware of but wasn't, or hadn't regarded it until that point. Like all things of which you have only recently become aware that have been going on for some time, there are mixed emotions. In this case one was that there's a lot of material now that can occupy you in the months to come, no need to worry about reading matter. The other the vague shame that in the house you lived in there was a party going on in another room of which you were so self-enclosed that you were wholly ignorant. People had been reading him and talking about it for years, and here you were coming across it for, as far as you were concerned, the first time. Well, everyone has to start somewhere. Powell thought of it as one long novel that happens to appear in instalments, but it was hard to believe that he had genuinely imagined the whole sequence back in 1950, knowing it was going to occupy him for another 25 years, and cover even more fictional time; as well of course as including social types and events that didn't exist or hadn't happened at the point he began.

The people he wrote about inhabited a London world of pubs and restaurants though they had been to the old school and the older universities. There was also the other world they were familiar with, country houses and debutante parties and interlocking relatives. Because of this there were echoes of P. G. Wodehouse, a suggestion of a connection. Still, though hailed by reviewers as a comic achievement Powell's work obviously had nothing to do with Wodehouse's comic intent, the lightness of his farce and misunderstandings. A friend of mine was baffled by this description of Powell in any case and told me that he couldn't see that there was a laugh in it. I knew what he meant but tried to persuade him that it was more a technical distinction, a work that wasn't a tragedy. The comedy, for people who had a taste for it, was all to do with tones of voice, the mis-match between attitudes and behaviour, and how that might be described, revealing a character's pomposity or purblindness while he or she might be quite unaware. What it did share with Wodehouse was a world created from language, the sound and style of sentences that might, at a stretch, be thought of as a darker, adult version of that sunnier, child-like world. I was always struck by the long, cool, fastidious sentences, clauses linked together by commas or semi-colons, the confident way judgement was passed on what people did, or how an analysis of deeper motive that lay beneath appearances was thoroughly interpreted and authoritatively offered. His people worked in publishing, or were writers, or artists, or industrialists, moved in political groups or had an interest in magic and the arcane. The narrator shared Powell's interest in genealogy and the hierarchy of military ranks and regiments, useful when it came to the sequence of books that took the characters into the Second World War. Not much direct comparison with my circle then, but the relevance was more to do with how they moved through time and demonstrated how connections were made and recurred, how coincidence brought past and present together. It was also to do with the way things changed. What appeared to be the way life was didn't have to be permanent. Arrangements shifted and a new pattern emerged. This was a useful model to internalise when contemplating the changes that had taken most us from the 1960s, already assuming the malleable character of a myth, and the places where we grew up, mutating and modulating, always there and not there.

Given that Powell's world is that of English upper middle classes, and their higher and lower gradations, it might be thought that the

continuing Dance wouldn't make too many connections with a council house child of the 1950s. But there it was. It might have been the
subject matter, or, more likely, something in the sentences and their
sound that spoke to me in a way that writers from a similar background to mine no longer did, people we had tried at school, Stan
Barstow and Alan Sillitoe say. I didn't investigate them anymore and
had no idea what they were up to now. What I liked about Powell
was also obviously at odds with Americana I was drawn to, the Beats,
Brautigan, Bellow, (and other people who didn't begin with B, Ken
Kesey and the New Journalists); but there had always been a pull
towards English qualities in the way I thought. The sentences generated there, and this formality didn't feel unnatural to me when I came
to write. Once, on one of my weekend visits, my dad, surprised by my
trying to downplay my teenage love of The World Of Wooster TV
series (ridiculous how we will deny, almost involuntarily, something
that is obviously true but for that moment is an embarrassment),
reminded me that he clearly remembered I'd adored both it and the
books. He was right of course, as well as slightly exasperated. I'd
bought those Wodehouse Penguins. I'd imbibed those programmes
week after week, no matter that the actors were too old really for the
characters. Even now the words of the theme song are safely filed
away, invisible and silent and almost as if they don't exist, until they
are required and then reappear, magically intact.

A Powell element not shared by Wodehouse, although his plot
necessities always call for engagements or their breakings off, was
Powell's preoccupation with love and desire, the somewhat hidden
world of the erotic generally in fact. Wodehouse's immortals never
know, or want to know, what actual sex is. Anthony Powell showed
how relationships are always subject to dissatisfactions and demurs.
People wanted someone other than the one they were with; desires and
predilections weren't reciprocal or reciprocated. Besides, some of his
characters just have strange tastes all round. This too made him have
more in common with the recent Sixties though first acquaintance

with his prose style didn't suggest this. The back of the book I'd seen in Hudson's Bookshop still applied to me, though now the only virgin title was being held by an older person. This didn't bother me too much, although it was rather like being on the other side of a glass wall trying to break through. How could this be when publicity said everyone was at it and had been for years? When you live by yourself being alone can seem sufficient. I can remember lying on top of the bed fully clothed, just thinking and lying there, feeling as I did when I was about 15, – how strange to be a person, something inside something, you inside a body living out its life n a collection of rooms – seeming to be who I was and somebody else, aware of who I was and not having to define it, at moments not feeling male or female, believing this was as natural as I could be, that any kind of meeting with other people was always going to involve some falsification. Later, when your reality derives precisely from your interaction with people you live with, it's impossible to understand what it meant when you were alone and why it didn't seem lonely. Then it didn't seem odd. I hung in and didn't feel panicked even though bedroom activity consisted of events like this:

I slept on the arm for some time
before its deadness woke me.
A yard or so of butcher's material
hung there, useless. A hank
of bone and meat angled the sheets
with a hook of fingers for bait.

I feel it swell with the minutes
until it becomes light-headed,
dizzy. It is pulsing gigantically,
singing in the soft darkness. Hot
blood flushes out the veins and burns
the absent arm back into my possession.

These were credulous times. Friends lived in shared flats in terraces not quite as grand as once they had been, all rumoured to be ready for development, which is to say removal or gutting. Some fasted one day a week, (for health reasons? assisting the planet? karmic discipline) but the fasting included going out to a café for egg on toast at least. Oh, that kind of fasting. I wonder if these are the exception, or if it's me that is the oddity. It was from them I learned that depending on the time of the day you would weigh more or less. Even weight was inconstant on a diurnal basis it seemed, something that had never occurred to me, and which I was foolish enough to deny for awhile. I was at the time a stranger to bathroom scales, in or out of a bathroom. It was the 1970s but some of the rhetoric and mores from the 1960s seemed to survive in a shabbier run-down way. The books and albums acquired ended up in cardboard boxes, there being no shelves. For a time I even had on the window sill of the bedsit, by the terrible curtains, next to the mounting, sliding egg box peaks I seemed to accumulate centuries before recycling, an ill-made, do-it-yourself cardboard pyramid which various authorities assured us would sharpen razor blades. I never found this to be the case but was sufficiently of my time to suspect, even believe, that it might work if only I were capable of making a better, proper pyramid. I was surprised once when an older lady I got talking to in the street pointed to my window and said, "That always makes me laugh. Someone piles up all those egg boxes. I wonder why." Knowing that odd sensation when your reality is present in someone else's thoughts, and for a moment you see yourself afresh, I admitted they were mine, but had no real answer as to why I did it. I threw them out shortly afterwards and felt better for it.

The pyramid was a leftover from the kind of child's wish for magic that I shared, probably the only thing, with the politically intense Yippies of 1968, who tried to levitate the Pentagon by encircling it with enough righteous souls and chanting Out Demons Out. Characteristically, and inevitably, this chant became a song performed only slightly later by those Corporation St irregulars, The Edgar Broughton Band, almost as their theme tune. So much so that they were credited with its invention by some English students when it was invoked at provincial levitation attempts on their own less militant bastions of repression, such as the Vice Chancellor's building of Keele University. All around was scruffiness and wishful thinking and a background hope that even without ambition this was a stage that one was going through towards better things. But I could walk through the streets in Twickenham and see people ageing before my eyes. The marionette youth with the puffball Afro, skinny shanks and child-size jeans walks by as he'd done for a couple of years and for the first time you notice something has been blowing time on his hair. The past folds into the present to help form an origami that makes sense. The past folds into the present and the future doesn't exist.

The past's appeal is that we think we know it. The present and the immediate future can be harder to get a handle on. If you weren't extraordinary what could you do to demonstrate otherwise? But perhaps you were. At least there were times when it seemed clear you didn't see things as others did, or react in quite the same way. Often incandescently self-conscious, nervous, easily scared, and yet part of me always was capable of assuming I was brighter than anyone else in the room, or would want to be funnier perhaps. Bob Dylan sang once scornfully about someone being nothing more than something they invest in. Perhaps I took this too much to heart, or perhaps some genetic flaw left me without ambition. I did my library jobs happily enough and had no real impetus to move on or up or out. I ticked and poodled away at various bits of writing, including poetry, and overall if I'd looked hard and cold-eyed, didn't produce an awful lot. That seemed to make no difference. I still regarded myself as someone who wrote, and a persistence that was the backing of the ambition-lacking mirror kept me doing it. One day I looked beyond the egg boxes and the window panes crawling with white and clear drops, out to the green leaves of some shrub I couldn't name, uncared for and doing the best it could against the wall fronting the street. It was a grey Monday morning, my day off in the week, a wet, dreary start to the week, and I wrote a poem about it, not quite aware then of how much of the little Studio Vista Laurie Lee paperback I was channelling.

The rains came today. The world dissolved
into thick slow spikes drizzling slowly.
Yesterday's savage glitter is gone.
The melted air, full of soft teeth,
prickles and grazes us beneath
a close sky, grey with muffling clouds.
The roses, drenched and tattered, droop.
Black umbrellas sail past the wall.
I watch the watery minutes fall,
the dripping green leaves dripping.
Now birds are melodious fish fluting
their tunes in submarine light.
June drowns. Glumly we sympathise with its plight.

It was accepted in a respectable tiny poetry magazine, my first. There I was, on a page with my name and my words, and people who knew the magazine would get to read them. I was realistic enough to know that this wouldn't be many, and besides some of those would be flipping past anyone who wasn't themselves. In addition to this minuscule gloire (which nevertheless was crucial) there was also money. In fact the postal order was never cashed, at first accidentally, and then allowing inertia to make some kind of point. I remained always 50p poorer, but with a better internal credibility. Or so I could persuade myself sometimes. That magazine never took another even though my submissions were of more or less the same quality, or it seemed to me, and though, naturally, encouraged by initial acceptance a regular persistence had ensued. This brought me up against the central and continuing conundrum about the reception of any writing. How can what is judged to be good by someone else be separated from their taste? Would anyone ever find something to be of quality if it didn't match their personal taste? Could they publish something they didn't actually like, or is liking something a basic indicator that a work is good? Is what you do worthwhile if you can find no-one who happens to like the kind of thing you do? I wrote as before and sent things elsewhere. But where would the future be and how would it get there

CHAPTER TWENTY-TWO
SECRET PART OF FORTUNE

Perennials of course, that Bob Dylan didn't have to worry about, made concrete by the regular appearance of sad, self-addressed, stamped envelopes in the forlorn hallway bringing back the unwanted poems that were "not quite" what was required. The inner flame wavered somewhat when subjected to these draughts of doubt. Still, there it was, a poem in a little magazine, exactly as it should be. It was as if Hamlet, oh David Warner of long ago, gave me a clue in this grubby, windowed cube that was my home. I could live in a nutshell and count myself king of infinite space were it not for wet dreams. But there was a launderette where everyone had to learn the routines of coins and powder cups and slots and the queue for tumble dryers, and I went there each week so that was all right for the sheets; and there were friends at work, and then a party being thrown by someone one knows at work, which means you get asked along. And so it becomes possible to meet different people, and in finding out about them you find something out about yourself. I could feel my body change and my voice, or at least my tone of voice, when I found that one person seemed to be like this, while another one was like that, and different shading and nuancing were required. Perhaps they felt the same way and none of us were really being ourselves, just allowing sectioned wheels to turn slowly in front of each other, occasionally finding that matching segments were facing. It was possible to be brash and slightly rude, or understanding and receptive almost on an involuntary basis, or at least to be surprised as you heard these notes sound. That was the falsification I'd meant although it seemed that being yourself meant being other aspects as required. This was similar to the sensation I'd had at school where with a friend who was smaller than me I felt tall and clunky, (like Bobby Wesley, over whose shoulder I had tumbled so unexpectedly), and with someone bigger I became this subliminal neat and diminutive figure, an involuntary Paul Simon. And at one party one Friday night I found I was leaving with a younger, smaller, livelier and quite keen girl, which was, it seemed, all that had been necessary. After we found ourselves outside walking we made the obligatory reference to your place or mine (me thinking of George Segal and Barbra Streisand) and went to hers because it was closer, two streets from the party in fact. It was also, obviously, much nicer being a proper flat and not a bedsit, although there were other unseen flatmates on the premises. She put me, as John Platt used to say, on the team. Not only on her team of course but allowed me through that door or curtain or glass wall that marks the non-participant from the active soul. I was now in the squad and available for future selection.

That first time was not, as it is for many people, an awkwardness, a rush, a fumble, an embarrassment, a disappointment. It was more in the nature of a revelation and a delight. So I'd missed out before, nothing to be done about that, maybe I'd needed to be this old to feel like this about it. As with death, so with little death: if it be not now, yet it will come. And so it did. I remembered that joke about an aristocratic or royal female who asked after her first time, "Is this what the poor people do... Well, it's too good for them." In that free and slippy, warm and bodied luxury, I understood her patrician attitude completely, knowing the rude pleasure, so imagined and now so there, of a vagina slick with what seemed like thinned syrup: fleshy; substantial; softened; a receptive host welcoming guests. The imagery of the East invoking the texture of dates and figs made more sense now, though no-one I knew had made mention of the subliminal feeling of woods, forest glades, clearings, that rose up in me, not clear like a picture, more like a sensation, that came into and receded from my consciousness in an imprecise but noticeable way. After the first couple of times I lay back and started to laugh, almost fell off the bed, saying, "I can't tell you what I'm laughing about." I'm sure she knew perfectly well, but being kind and polite and familiar with the penile imperative said nothing and waited until it was seconds out again. In fact I later thought I did mean something else too. It was to do with feeling fully human and finding it was a very good thing to be, and also the relief because all had gone well and here I was, newly normal. Next morning I went to work, maybe as many did all over the country, not from home, in yesterday's clothes and without shaving or showering but with some kind of wash having taken place, possibly still fragrant, as Richard Brautigan put it, from Cupid's gym.

When you haven't had sex it tends to preoccupy your mind and you focus on possibilities that might bring it your way, no matter how unsuccessful or how accidental eventual success is later. On the other side of whatever symbol seems most potent, – door, glass wall, mirror, – nothing seemed more pleasing, or less likely, than having access, as a children's book title put it, to a strong willing girl happy to show you the ropes. Once achieved though you realise that you're still likely to want things to be other than they are. Odd and ridiculous how easily dissatisfaction and pickiness set in. Before sex happens it seems so crucial that one should be experiencing it. But what do you do the rest of the time? Afterwards it becomes clear that though it remains base-level crucial nothing else changes, and dealing with all the other things and personality quirks that happen between people is what constitutes and develops a relationship. There are times when that doesn't seem as obvious as we'd like to believe. How easy it is to be selfish and how easy not to recognise it. Once through the inauguration, surprised and grateful, the subconscious strains of It Ain't Me Babe began to sound under the action with self-centred speed. Still, the advantage is that once you are on the team you seem to become more of a safe bet for others. Not that those nutshell confines became exceedingly busy, but where I had lain so quiet and so self-sufficient and so true to a conception of myself, a couple of visitors did grace that bijou slovenly setting to investigate affection and nakedness. Things that you hadn't known about before become possible. Did you know about this nook, or that cranny? You've never done this? Now you can. Oh, but, no, that you can't. Discover the simple, ancient pleasures: how a hand may move so pleasurably the length, no matter how short, of smooth legs to reach a moist and recessed destination; how an area and declivity so enclosed can feel so lusciously, slippery smooth to a finger that can then be made to disappear; and how a kiss can do the same to time.

Sex is everything and then it's not enough. You try to examine it and it seems as much of an alternative world as the past or dreams. You can't imagine, so disparate are they, how sexual activity seems to be connected to the ordinary world which for much of the time exists reasonably enough without it. People have to take part in, and take seriously, endless duties and responsibilities, all the things that constitute work and money, and what have they to do with the constant background of love and its gymnastics? No wonder we need help from popular culture in reconciling these dimensions. Most people, because of songs and films, think, at least some of the time, that in all the world full of people there is a special one meant for them, and who knows where that one may be. This may be more or less serially true, but it takes a while before the realisation sets in, mathematically obvious though it is, that no matter how many people there are, and how large the world, the special one will only become apparent when a meeting takes place, and the number of people one tends to meet is a more limited affair controlled by predictable, for the most part, circumstances. You could have missed the one person who was definitely meant for you, you speculate, because you never met. The truth is the one meant for you has to be someone you meet. No other person is eligible. Everyone else is to that extent fictitious. Where you go to school, where you go to college, where you go to work, social gatherings where people who know people you know but are outside of your hinterland and thus alter the mix, these are the most likely places where stars will be crossed and the heart will be pierced.

I may have felt that other people were having a better time than me. Maybe they felt the same about me. Everyone can feel that they know how other people work a little better than themselves, Bob Dylan for instance, perhaps because they seem to have a more objective existence than one's own imprecise qualities. It's probably true that during the early 1970s I was more familiar with what I thought Bob Dylan was like than knowing my own strengths or weaknesses. The days went by and I was immersed in them. To understand one's own motives, that can be the tricky task. Tectonic plates were shifting. Even I, less adventurous than many, moved around. The Lake District in late October, exactly the wrong time, the air damp, the grass wet, the mountains shrouded, the season over and us calling out the AA at motorway service stations and hearing All Around My Hat everywhere.

Or in Sheffield dissecting Van Morrison albums, extolling David Bowie's virtues, listening to Dylan's bootleg Live 1966 album on green, amazingly, vinyl, and appreciating its mad, noisy splendour, or falling backwards through party doorways to the accompaniment of the Spiders from Mars. Nigel's Venetian girlfriend inspired a trip there for a week, travelling by train, hitting the platform at Basle and running with bags to catch some connection. It was an odd image, hoofing and puffing across a Swiss station but seemed to be exactly the kind of thing young people should be doing. Venice was a wonder and a puzzle, how the buildings, palaces and warehouses, grew right out of the water. Everything was dazzling and we did our best to dazzle right back, noticing the city's other world aspect, the hint of the East even in girls' clothes.

There was sitting at a bar to watch the sunshine in St Mark's Square, then registering the shift in consciousness that two glasses of beer caused, the receptivity to the world and the sensation of well-being towards it. What, we wondered, would everything be like if one could stay permanently at this stage of consciousness and never spoil it by even one glass more? And what if it could be achieved without the aid of beer at all? Was the world simply as it was, or did the act of perceiving it impose a shape that was only personal? Were these Sixties or Seventies questions?

One way I imposed myself upon the world was in learning to drive, as my dad years ago had said everyone should. Eventually I even managed to use the clutch pedal while keeping my heel on the floor at the same time, quite an accomplishment from someone whose first tendency was a flying buttress, free-floating foot approach. The foot steadiness helped me to not panic when driving in traffic. Everyone gets annoyed behind a learner driver dithering or being unpredictable, having forgotten that moment of fear felt the first time ever a car starts and suddenly the only thing controlling this big lump of moving dangerous machinery is the collection of limbs and understanding that constitutes you. You have to know what you're doing and you're not sure that you do. I had however many lessons it took to be judged ready for the test, at the kind of prices that would now sound as mediaevally insignificant as the rent I paid then, and I passed first time. I felt almost as good as I had on that Friday night initiation and grinned ecstatically at the examiner. "What's your name?" I asked him, because it somehow seemed important, and he pointed with his biro and economical understatement to where he had signed the form he had just given me confirming that I had passed. No doubt he had seen this kind of reaction before. Some of the best drivers I have known since didn't pass first time so it's no indication of quality one way or another, but at the time I felt it was. I'd wanted to do it and was thrilled that I had. I still am. Then, not long after, with the help of another library person who was bound to know more about it than me, I bought a Ford Cortina Mark 2 for around £300 from a small-time garage that sold a few cars as well. That garage is long gone and so is the car. Every time I see the small block of almost-luxury apartments where the oily forecourt was, I remember that big blue motor, old-fashioned and of its time; although unlike many people who can reel off the registration of every car they ever had, I don't remember the number, and usually have the same trouble with whatever vehicle I currently drive. It seemed as big as a boat and handled about as well, a fairground boy's car as one friend laughed at it.

I could drive; I had a car; and yet that feeling of luxury and comfort, the newness of being transported at speed on a sofa-like seat in a moving vehicle that somehow seemed to have something to do with 77 Sunset Strip, and which had enveloped me so strongly when I first had a ride in my friend Raymond's car in those far-off Fifties, would never be summoned up again no matter how exciting or convenient it was to be in the situation I was now. Raymond Ferguson, who lived over the road in the houses whose front lawn sloped down, whose dad had always had a car, and told people we were the best of friends and never argued, something I found puzzling because I knew we did. Raymond, who once amazed some of us by going in and out of his kitchen while we were talking on his back door step and eating 5 or 6 pieces of bread and brown sauce, and every one was a crust. When we pointed out that his mother might be annoyed by him removing the crusts from each end of three loaves he shrugged. Somebody had to eat them. Impossible, as with the car sensations, to make those emotions exist again, or to refer automatically to any snack involving bread as "a piece", as we had always done, except the car prompted memories. I could go back home, but I couldn't return to *that* home. To go back now I didn't need trains and buses, but I was required to pay attention to motorway exits, road signs and the numbers of A and B cross-country jigsaw pieces in that time before all the motorways joined together..

So fair one Friday setting out like a ballad,
grabbing a tuna sandwich and summer-dressed salad,
heading north for the past 3 hours from here..

A parent shrunken, a garden overgrown,
a dark viewpoint looking down on a space once known..

Cabined in sickly light an icy someone
streams into a seamless world where the boy is gone.

I had a little glimpse of what bands and Bob Dylan meant when they were on the road, the way other people's towns and High Streets, their everyday reality, took on some of the aspects of a stage set. You sensed too how thinking the whole world was a stage set might encourage a belief that everything was play-acting. What would happen then to responsibilities and consequences? No wonder rock stars went off their heads. Being Bob Dylan was probably a lot harder than it looked.

Life went on in the foreground and, as in mass-produced cartoons, the background of music and popular culture rolled by behind us. In the previous decade for long spells the background became the foreground, and for all intents and purposes was the personal life. 1965 and 1966 of course, where in a sense the music and its world occupied more of my imagination, and thus had more reality, than civilian life. Now civvy street rose up and reasserted itself and made the charts recede. This was a time when I went to see Randy Newman and Roxy Music concerts, (Bryan as a gaucho, Bryan as a G.I., and the audiences at Finsbury park or Wembley dressed likewise, except people like me); when I went to see Al Pacino in David Mamet's American Buffalo, bowled over by the swearing, spitting and manic arm-scratching, but later realised that this wasn't my internal voice; and so was drawn back to attend the plays of Tom Stoppard and Michael Frayn and bought them to read aloud to myself, looking for clues.

CHAPTER TWENTY-THREE
HALF IN LOVE & TREMENDOUSLY SORRY

In my foreground life however was the business of paying, as I came to see it later, for the casual small cruelty of distancing and passive rejection of my initiator. My heart hadn't been pierced and now it was, or something was. I was confused and miserable enough at least. From that same circle of workmates and their friends I became involved with someone already absolutely involved with someone else, about to be uninvolved but for indefinite reasons, and fell into obsessive currents of possession and infatuation. It was the kind of situation where someone finds themselves coming out of relationship, and not sure why, and someone else is trying to begin one, and there's a lot of compensatory emotion and confusion. This is particularly so when a girl has moved back with her parents and you're in the teenage situation of them having gone to bed, leaving you in the living room. One symptom of the intensity that percolates a collusion of such mixed motives is the kissing, stroking and caressing that generates enough sexual pressure for some clothes to be partly removed or shrugged aside, allowing rude and risky insertion kneeling on the carpet, braced against the family sofa. Madness. The parents left only 15 minutes before. They might come back in at any time, but of course that was part of the reason for doing it. The rudeness is all.

You can call it lots of things, and love might be one of them, before finding out by experiencing what works and what doesn't work that love may be, more than anything else, that fluke where two temperaments match, including physically, but every other kind of matching bears equal weight.. When that's the case something has a chance to develop. Before that things work or don't work, and don't work more frequently. Songs can come into their own then. Almost any, not only Bob Dylan ones, can seem to take on specific personal revelatory meaning, where before their status had been that of neutral text. Now they activate within you like DNA code simply by the mood state you inhabit. That's it, you think, that's exactly how I feel. All things in that sphere are heightened, including misery. And so in addition to Venice and Sheffield I, we at that point, managed to visit Paris and had the kind of tortured time that you write down in a cheap notebook and can still, decades afterwards, only look at while wincing. I was quite capable of writing that I was a visitor in Paris and a tourist in her emotions. It was here I understood the simple act of someone saying "What?" often enough after your attempt to begin a conversation eventually makes all communication break down. Some kind of good heart is needed to let social wheels run smooth. Banalities grease them. When it's absent you find yourself in a strange city in a room or a street, approaching mealtime or retreating from it, with someone who doesn't want to be here or with you, and all you know is silence pulsing with recrimination.

There are various kinds of shame and embarrassment. Those from the past, layered and remote, forgotten or *almost* forgotten. The night, that one night, supplanted by hundreds and hundreds since, on a street carved from aloof buildings, when trying to be slightly adventurous and find a restaurant that wasn't the one already visited twice. There is the walking, looking for something that seems possible, the kind of area that supports restaurants, then realising that you've wandered away from that part of town, and here you are, where?, and the time is going by with the footsteps, irritation and frustration are increasing on a slow simmer; and both of you are wondering how you came to be in this situation, in a foreign country with someone who makes life so difficult, the dark tall streets hospitable as slate, the prospect of even a meal, let alone a relaxed enjoyable one, now around zero, and all this time still to get through until we go home. Then there is the related shame, embarrassment and curiosity of looking at words written at the time to capture it all. Obvious observations layered with intense, impractical, self-justifying analysis, notes to self and to-do lists for the soul, can only be taken in tiny doses, especially when many of the actual events and all their sense-memories have long since evaporated.

"Walked about in warm rain and got damp. Later, the kind of sex that seems hallucinatory. Vivid at the time but later it merges into the realm of not knowing whether it actually occurred. Chartres cathedral I found gloomy. Too much detail overwhelms me & I see no outlines or pattern. We shall split."
Not retained either is the last conversation, the details of how things ended, although it would have been in England later, a limping, awkward production of words entirely inadequate for the task. It happened and disappeared. The slate canyon walk happened and will never disappear. These thoughts and events happened, but to someone you used to know, not in the way you know that you are now in a room watching a ginger cat relax on a blue rug as if that's what he was born to do. This person who used to be, who is and isn't you, wrote these things down, probably while the other person was in the room, felt tip words on lined paper, and here they are. A cheap wire bound note book, offering Superb Value in ruled feint form, still in existence but whose reality, whatever the authenticity and provenance of the holograph, is tenuous. The words describe things that happened once upon a time while being thin and insubstantial, less real, one realises, than the fiction of a favourite novel, than the world created by Anthony Powell that lives in thousands of heads. And then like a chink of light through the crack of a door you have a slant on

what it might be like for Bob Dylan to sing, try to bring alive, words he wrote in notebooks 45 years before.

Certain sensitive boys, the kind with a history of dwelling on Donovan lyrics, are likely to think that girls, females in general, in addition to having the physical existence and necessary dimension that gifts suitability and opportunity for sexual activity, are somehow intrinsically superior to boys, or males in general. What can be experienced as the spiritual aspect of physical release and ecstasy transmutes and broadens, informing a view that somehow girls can be a better class of human being. Of course beauty has something to do with this. In general girls provide more examples of beauty than boys do, but in either case beauty can make us believe that someone has a character or qualities they simply don't. It doesn't need beauty as such however. A girl's face in itself, – admittedly a young teenage girl's face seems to work best, – can mislead an impressionable lad into believing that girls are on a different plane, even though forced to be more practical on a physical biological level. Boys from different backgrounds and temperaments, who, for example, never came across Donovan, don't share this attitude. Actually there seem to be some who think that any kind of dealing with women, no matter how dominant you are, in some ways taints and weakens you. Any exposure to female qualities, even in desired acts, could be undermining. Sensitive boys of course are riding for a fall at some point because they are going to find out that there are girls who will be just as selfish, weak or vengeful as boys, as generally disappointing; but it's more probable they will still have a happier time of it than young men who start from a point where women are believed inherently inferior and, at root, to be feared. After all, the naïve, trusting boys will, when they are lucky, find that some women *are* naturally better than men, and may end up with such a one, capable, sensible and sexy. We all want different aspects of people at different times of our lives, but come up against the kind of person we seem to be designed to be; and that person may work best in a situation you currently find hard to create or inhabit. An internal setting may mean you, nervous though arrogant, poetry writing boy, will flourish best in a settled relationship where safety and predictability are prized. Unfortunately you find yourself at an age where lots of girls are more alive to harder, unreliable bastards who know their way around and take control, often by two-timing or otherwise letting a girl down, but in any event making life interesting. There are stages in life where being interesting gets awarded more points than safety.

The kind of thing one says to oneself when practising a certain kind of philosophical approach sounds something like: *You have to come from where you come from, and you have to be who you are.* The difficulty is when circumstances make you lose sight of who that might be; or when your notion of yourself is at odds with your background and its perception. Norman Mailer was a much-loved Jewish boy from Brooklyn who became an engineering, not literature, student, joined the army, but then transformed into an autodidact writer with a wild eye for detail, a mystical bent, a taste for skewed existential philosophy, a prodigious work rate and a liking for confrontations of all kinds, social, marital, political, literary. He looked, and behaved, like some lost offspring of Victor McLaglen in a John Ford bar-room. Except he wrote and wrote. Bob Dylan had been a privileged Jewish boy too, always nursing his own private agenda of dreams, then changing from a schoolboy so shy he wouldn't read out loud in class, to the singer and guitar player who needed to practise in public, moving from rock to folk&blues and back to rock, taking in an elevation to a symbolic status along the way, before retreating back into something that had to do with lack of definition and a private existence. Most people don't have a chance for these dramatic altera-tions, but all of us have times when our inner idea of ourselves seems to blur, we lose heart and sight of what we are, feel that we're on a path that's not right but can't see how to change it, and in any case have no knowledge that a different route would be closer to what was required. You look at the constant rolling background of the culture of the day and it can appear that the way other people's lives proceed is pre-ordained. You can't decide whether you want to believe that or not, or, even if it were possible, how could it be a good thing. But even being a fan, a bit player, a spear carrier in the bigger production will push you back to the question of how you will try to shape what happens to you, this day and the next.

My character flaw was in believing that the future would take care of itself. What kind of business plan is that? Well it was one that for awhile Bob Dylan seemed to have had too, a background to my own exploration and investigations. He surfaced to catch media lightning at the Bangla Desh concert, drifted around in gig assistant mode at other people's shows and recording sessions, but then he perked up. He decided to make a film in the company of Sam Peckinpah chiefly because it was about Billy The Kid. He was looking to the past, the imagined past that all 1950s children shared, and it seemed to revitalise him. In Pat Garrett and Billy The Kid he is an onlooker, a witness to the playing out of social and political forces in a landscape of rivers and plains. It was a distorting mirror of the real life role he had seemed to enact, a decade before the film was made, when he was widely regarded as an embodiment, symbol and spokesman for just such social and political changes even though he believed later, or even at the time, that this was a mistaken assumption. All of which was nudgingly compacted into one dialogue exchange in the film, referring back to the actual Bob Dylan as well as the characters in the made up Old West: "How does it feel? " "It feels like times have changed"

A soundtrack album came out and, surprisingly, one song from it released as a single became a genuine hit, and has rarely left the repertoire of buskers since. The album was an oddity, not really a soundtrack, and of course the idea of Dylan as a real arranger and writer of music that could be fitted to the rhythm of edited scenes, in the manner of master like Bernard Herrmann or Henry Mancini, was always hyperbole. What he was there for was to add some frisson of Dylanity to the proceedings, and suggest there were aspects of that Sixties life buried in both the Old West, and representations of the Old West, re-imaginings that made us think about different Americas. In this he was quite successful. One friend of a friend somehow contrived to make Pat Garrett and Billy The Kid the first Bob album he owned. Even at the time this was eccentric. It may have been coincidental but even if the film and its soundtrack creation was not what he had expected, or as enjoyable, something seemed to enliven him. He made an album of new songs called Planet Waves with the band of musicians who had so galvanised his 1966 performances, and who in those last Sixties years had become so influential for a swathe of English musicians, including his pal George Harrison. The album was big news on two counts. First because he hadn't released an original album since New Morning, and second because to do so he had left CBS in favour of Asylum Records in the States, released through Island here. He did seem to believe in business plans after all. Then he undertook a big North American tour with the Band, their sets alternating with his, once more letting people see what he could do in the company of the people who had made the tour of 8 years before something closer to myth or legend than reality. And not long afterwards a double album recorded on some of the tour dates was also released. Both albums were capable of interpretation in various ways, although Bob watchers could agree that it was not the kind of thing he used to do, in writing or singing. The live album in particular was marked down for being shouty and not up to previous grandeur. It was nothing like their last outing, only familiar from bootlegs. But then what was? We were placed in the position unnecessary for us in 1965 and 1966 of trying to decide what it was he did do now, and how it might be valued. It was the kind of theoretical activity that could as easily be applied to oneself.

There were other kinds of moving on. I had vague ideas about getting educated and using the education to drift into some other activity. The Open University seemed to be one way of getting a degree while still receiving a salary, but first I thought, having read about the preparations of jazz musicians, I should get my studying chops up. I enrolled for an A level at evening classes to take me up to the start time, and chose Politics because it was outside of my usual interests, and perhaps after being a non-combatant in the epochal upheavals a little knowledge of orthodox British politics might not be a bad thing. We'd lived through power cuts, on a rota basis with the measures that required for business, and the rhetoric from both sides of government and unions, where it seemed that almost any company or management could be deemed a proto-representative of government forced into ideological combat. We appeared to be at the beginning of something, or the end, and in either case unless you were a committed combatant on either side the times were dispiriting. The main image I had retained from the Three Day Week, the meaning it seemed to have, was how close to reality dystopian novels and films were. When the rota blackouts began and people stocked up on and used candles, it was true one could experience a sense of something one might call romance, a little glimpse of how the past would have differed from the world we knew, how it would have existed in a flickering, precarious light. In earlier times the change from day to night would have atavistic meaning we usually only received in a much attenuated form. The absence of street lamps meant the perpetual patterns of the stars could be seen clearly, which normally wasn't possible because of the glare we push out around us continually. The Sixteenth Century again, or any century, as it had been when I saw the squawk and swirl of starlings in Corporation Street, and the reason why the switch from light to dark, day to night, means so much as imagery. It didn't begin as images but frightening reality. When I looked at houses, or blocks of flat where rooms could be seen gloomy and wavering, what I thought of was not romance but how like caves rooms were, little cave cubes in the side of many a cliff, and how difficult it was to live in caves without the ability to cook or heat them or to get hot water easily. This was the other side, the reality, of that pastoralism we'd thought was as easy as fancy dress on pretty album covers, the fancy dress that could be seen now in Laura Ashley products. The way we lived depended on so much, so many systems working and interconnecting, and when they didn't then everything we thought life was, everything that seemed of such importance, whether it be Bob Dylan or the making of lots of money, would dissolve.

As Bob had helpfully pointed out a decade before, the times were a-changin'. You could feel it in different ways. Starting an A level would at least require more than existing in the current of days, taking little directional activity. Besides it was an opportunity to meet other people and that is always promising, chiefly because other people give you a chance not only to see a different point of view but also to become more familiar with what you think too, perhaps surprising yourself. The work itself was not difficult. Reading the texts and then producing the essays was the kind of writing practice I found congenial, construction work that I'd had in mind. What we were required to do, as in any exam of course, was write answers that demonstrated we had a mastery of the learned facts and understood the implications of question. Heartfelt personal opinions weren't really needed because really we were acting out the part of people who knew answers for people who also knew the answers. The subject was British Political History but as the old hand teacher emphasised, in a joke one knew he re-used year after year, "For god's sake keep politics out of it." I became friendly with one younger guy and we talked about the course and various things. Once he was talking about hunger, saying when he had been really hungry. The direction of the conversation was that I'd offer some examples of my own. I hesitated, not sure how to respond. I may have skipped a meal or two in my time, but, you know, real hunger? Mmm. My pause exasperated him a little. "Don't tell me you've never been hungry." He was laughing and incredulous but I think we were talking about different things. In the context of the Jarrow March or hunger strikes I probably hadn't. But I also saw that this had a wider application. How hungry had Bob Dylan been when he set off for New York, arriving in a hitch-hike car, a snowstorm and toting a guitar. Had I ever been that hungry for success in anything? Did he really think he was going to make it in music even to the practical extent of getting regular gigs and being respected by other musicians? How good did he think he was then? Did he ever imagine that he would be lifted out of the snow scuffle and be known all over the world? What drove him? Was it hunger or dreams, or were they the same thing with a different name. It was a fruitless exercise but one couldn't help comparing oneself to him, or other people who made it in some way. The real question was how could you be a success in life using what you had, a success that didn't involve fame or acclaim. Trying to do well in an A level at that point seemed to be a start for me. I said before the exam itself to my hunger expert that I was quietly confident. I wasn't ruling out an A grade. This was a joke and not a joke. What I thought was we were all people in our 20s. A levels were for people at school, no matter how hip, knowing or mature they might be. If we couldn't do better than them, knowing what we did and having elected to do it, I thought you would have to put under the heading of poor show.

Things were changing on the surface and under the surface. Bob Dylan was also interested in not putting on a poor show. After revisiting scenes of his childhood in the songs on Planet Waves, and undergoing the gratefully received but somehow not quite right tour with the Band, as the next year began he released a new album that was a different order of achievement. Blood On The Tracks marked a return to Bob Dylan being of the moment and involved again, for those who cared about him at all. There was a connection with the childhood of Planet Waves subject matter because he'd recorded it back in Minneapolis with local musicians, contacts of the brother everyone had difficulty in believing Bob Dylan could have. The NME reported in passing that there was a different, earlier version of the album, and it was true that the sleeve notes, by New York journalist

Pete Hamill, quoted words to a verse of If You See Her Say Hello that weren't ones that Bob sang here. We had to hear what was in front of us however, and that, it was true, was not quite like anything Bob had done before, even though his easily imitable, but inimitable, voice was absolutely characteristic throughout. What made it different was the way the songs were written and the unguarded subject matter. What he returned to was love and its troubles, relationships breaking down while life and seasons carried on unreeling. The music had flavours and residues of everything that had ever had a hold on him, but relating back more to the folk and blues he'd inhabited prior to the mid 60s successes that had so seemed to define him. It was 10 years since those triumphs and now, after various kinds of doldrums, he had re-established himself. The song words and titles were direct and evocative – If You See Her Say Hello, Shelter From The Storm – and had no need of the flashier name-dropping and phrase making so evident in the Highway 61 album.

The year of that album, and on into the following one, he had been the focus of all the synonyms for hip, cool, modern, contemporary; everything to do with New York, Pop and a certain quality of city sharpness that shaded into the vicious. It was nothing at all to do with the earlier earnestness of causes and politics. In the songs were characters like Dr Filth; in the sleeve notes the Cream Judge and Savage Rose, all language cartoons skewering a certain scene that had meaning because he was observing it. With Blood On The Tracks he was trying to describe and enact something real and true for himself, a heartbreak, an ending, and perhaps another beginning. He had a subject that was absolutely personal but inevitably universal, and so the potential for anyone else to connect with it was that much greater. Those songs and that album marked a resurgence, a renaissance one might say. He acknowledged it by beginning a different kind of tour from the one that started with Planet Waves. Now he seemed to be looking back again, doing what we all did, remembering aspects of the Sixties, but bringing them to a changed life. He assembled a travelling troupe of musicians, some new, some from the previous decade. He was going out there once more, playing smaller venues but not like the almost-suburban guy that he'd resembled (aside from his scratchy beard) on the tour that produced Before The Flood. Now he was skinny, wired, whiteface, be-scarfed and wearing a cowboy hat, except unlike the cowboys of that Fifties childhood which never goes away, there were flowers on it. He was going out with the Rolling Thunder Revue, a phrase that invoked both Indians and the Vietnam War. Perhaps he was remembering his tall-tale carnival stories as if they were true, those Ray Bradbury Midwest travelling shows; or trying to re-enact his 1963 song Dusty Old Fairgrounds, the hardwork hobo downbeat romance of trucks and trailers moving on, moving on, surrounded by characters in costume, bringing a thrill to the crowd. He'd had an album where the subject was the failure of a relationship and now he had one where he was casting a wider net with subject matter and instruments; but the inclusion of the song Sara, seemingly as naked an autobiographical piece as Ballad In Plain D eleven years previously, appeared to indicate that a rapprochement had occurred. He was demonstrating how far he had travelled and moved on from that 1964 character. No longer the solo troubadour, he was interested in ensemble work, as he had been with the Hawks, but was clearly trying a wider variety of styles. The songs in the shows were drawn too from all over. His Voice Of A Generation heyday was represented of course, but also his most recent albums. There were versions of other people's work and traditional songs, all of it showing that what he was to himself was based in a conception of music and performance that went beyond our limited and probably prescriptive assumptions. Flux was his natural state. In love, out of love, married, almost not married, trying to be in the moment and singing about the past, being alive to all of it and trying to capture it by letting it fly.

The record company marked the events by releasing Desire, where he wore his Rolling Thunder hat and a violin was prominent;

and also The Basement Tapes, where an unsatisfactory selection of songs that people knew from their earliest bootlegs, sometimes in takes that were different, was added to Band songs from studios rather than the Basement. There was a general feeling of disappointment and sources being messed about. There was too a sense that if they wanted to release something unofficial and worthwhile why not go with the 1966 shows. So we grumbled and read the Melody Maker reports of the tour, and wondered what it would be like to see one of those shows, not knowing a film and a couple of writers were also trying to capture it, and eventually what we had missed would appear. The reality was that what you'd missed could stick around and maybe you could miss it again some other time. Meanwhile we could shadow his life and have our own problems with love and non-love and working out how to be with someone. The aftermath of the break-up with the Paris girl went on for a long time. It's possible to know that there was nothing else to be done, and also to be in a mind loop that goes over and over it, wanting things to be as they were. It's as if there are parallel tracks and the logical, intelligent part of the brain can't simply make one set disappear. Haven't you got over it yet, people ask, as you ask yourself, but an effort of will doesn't seem to do it. Except, no doubt, squads of counsellors and therapists would say it does when done properly. Nothing either good or bad but thinking makes it so. It's also true that nothing makes you forget a bad experience like a good experience.

There was a pub garden in late summer, not autumn, though occasionally leaves fell and bounced off a couple sharing one of the tables, surprisingly noticeable a sound for something so slight. They were sitting under a tree so they couldn't count this as a surprise exactly. Friends who had met through working together, then one of them moved on to work somewhere else, and now they met up sometimes for a lunchtime drink, and one being male and one female there was, as there often is, a slight undercurrent of flirtation. But then nothing would happen because she was a married woman, that strange sounding characterisation for someone in their early 20s who was like a girl still. All of us seemed boys and girls really, not adults in training, but there it was, a married woman. Married, with Celtic hair and eyes that made you see why it was normal to write about eyes lighting up or sparkling. Something amused her and everything about her was alight and it started with her eyes, though her face could have been a lantern. I always found it remarkable that being with someone in this way made me more aware of their reality as people, if you can put it that way; every moment and current of affection or dismay is transmitted through movement and position of a body, or the smallest movement of a face, – eyes and mouth and brow –, all contributing to the force-field a person generates, which is lacking at less charged times. Every moment one is intensely aware; every moment each word forming behind the eyes is judged and held in the balance. Can it be uttered, allowed out into the world? It's in this time that the full intensity of a person, so close to embarrassment, becomes clear, in fact even more so than when people make love, all of those physical details, in a flurry of succession, a blur of activity disappearing almost as soon as it is created.

So at a pub table in late summer, with the ticking sounds of leaves falling, then, as Scott Fitzgerald wrote and the Beach Boys reiterated, I kissed her. What would have happened if I hadn't? There would have been a friendship, with always a slight undercurrent of flirtation, between two people who liked and knew each other. And what happened when I did? It could have been a miscalculation that ended such meetings altogether. Instead it offered another example of the way a girl will take you on even when you least expect it. In the pub by Twickenham Green that some of us used to go to on Fridays, one guy said that he routinely asked most girls he came across if they would sleep with him. He didn't make a big deal of it. He accepted all slaps and rebuffs. But out of 10 perhaps you might get one who said, Why not? His view was that even a small profit margin made it all worthwhile. This was something I'd never contemplated as a course of action, let alone attempted, so any considerations were entirely theoretical. Yet, here I was kissing a married woman who, as it turned out, was quite surprised but not actually averse.

So it was that something began. Calling it an affair seemed as odd and silly as thinking of her as a married woman. What name remained? A dalliance, a romance, a dangerous liaison? Call things what you will, their name should match their real identity. Her real identity included a husband and it was quite likely that he wouldn't be sanguine if he found out, though the consequences could have been bloody. Still, it didn't feel like an affair, the kind grown-ups had. It felt like a voyage of discovery. I wondered at the time and wondered since what prompted her to carry on after that first kiss to further meetings and afternoons in the Nutshell, enjoying dates and figs in a bower. She couldn't see a way to change her status quo, and had so much to lose. I had that familiar sensation of rehearsing something that didn't yet exist, trying to see what the future might be like. I think I was trying to see, and of course feeling the excitement of, what it would be like to be with someone who liked me, who found me sexually attractive; and trying too to look into a crystal ball and see the shapes and shadows of married life. Which sounds ridiculous now and wasn't quite consciously formulated thus at the time, but I don't think that's too far out. It was play acting, as children do, and some afternoons she came along to look at flats I was ostensibly thinking about, trying to escape the gravitational pull of life in one room.. It was as if we were pretending that we might live in them, walking around those empty spaces suspended within a building, within the air, trying to imagine what possessions and what lives could occupy them later. If I had met her first would we have been such a good apparent match? After all if things had been different, well that's what they would have been, different. It was possible that we might have been different to each other had we not been in this time zone and arrangement that took us away from real life.

There was too other music and other ways of thinking about who you were and where you came from. Around this time I listened to the Chieftains a lot, for reasons I can't quite now locate. Was it because I had heard them in Barry Lyndon, or did I know them before that, from my friend Brendan maybe, whose family really were Irish and had come over this generation, unlike me where someone had arrived two or three grandfathers ago. Brendan, whose family also lived in a steel house like mine and had gone to the same school, same year, but who I had not known so well until we both met up on the changeable trains that went to and from Walsall and Birmingham, where he too pursued a college education and then moved to another part of the country, a different part to me. He was an unorthodox intellectual who liked Bob Dylan and Samuel Beckett and, in the Irish way, a drink. He used X rays on conversations he said, and once on the train pronounced of Highway 61, "Let's not sully it with words." In any event I acquired a couple of Chieftain albums and listened a lot, trying to feel something essential inside me that was Irish, though at removes now, that might respond to the absolute Irishness they created and were made from. Their music was all kinds of things, as virtuosic and technically demanding as any classical repertoire and falling broadly into two main types. The jigs, reel and slides with their mad intricate clockwork sound, where all the instrument sounds interlocked and seemed to have been slightly retuned through Chinese radio, were one kind. Then there were the airs, where slow heartbreaking, yearning tunes, as if rain and mist had found a way to become sound, tore at you.

There were a lot of young people around me, some of whom, like the recent or long gone Irish, had moved a long way to be not living with their parents, and some of whom had moved not very far at all, but the life was that of flats and bedsits and scruffiness, inadequate kitchen bins, laundrettes, and sheets that should really have been thrown away and immediately replaced. It was the life you had to have until the real one came along, pro tem, though some were making it and most weren't, but at a certain point thoughts of the future entered and I began to wonder was I meant to live like this, or would I have the kind of life my mother and father would recognise as a proper one. Domesticity and a real house hovered in the background and seemed impossibly far away. There was a culture of articles and TV that told us how feminism was a rising force, how the relationships between men and women were being created anew under the heat and pressure of new political and personal forces, and little evidence of it near me, aside from the familiarity with some of its rote vocabulary and the importance of contraception. There was a sense of people ready to settle down. Couples split up and relationships reconfigured. People were looking for the one, or at least the one who would do. Ones who weren't married were thinking about it, or something quite like it. My original initiator into mysteries and delight was with someone and it looked as if permanence was on the cards

The days go by in succession, endless succession, and in the right order. Remembering them is a trickier proposition, and scenes become shuffled together, producing an arrangement where what happened first and the order of precedence is almost as tricky to assign as the chronology of Shakespeare's sonnets. What is more or less definite is that I was studying for an A level. I was seeing at irregular intervals a married girl and wondering what it would have been like if things had been different. And then I was finished studying for an A level and had begun studying for the Open University, which meant that at the end of that first year there was the compulsory Summer School, a different summer to the one with a table in a pub garden and falling leaves. Open University Summer Schools had become known as a time and place for putting people together and fomenting relationships. People who hadn't had a chance at the age it was supposed to happen to behave like students now felt an excitement that was intellectual and physical, and probably appreciated it more because of the age they were. A week away from normality and being able to talk, write, argue, drink and expound. Alliances formed, heads were turned, trouble brewed. Old relationships foundered on these new rocks; fresh amities formed on these fete days. The characteristics of holiday romances were present, recklessness and innate possibility of emotional mayhem. For people however, who felt that they had been pressed to a life that had denied them the opportunity to be with someone sympathetic to an enquiring mind or formal study, they now had a chance, like Bob Dylan arriving in New York in the 1960th winter, to change everything, to feel that the world had moved in their favour. I can't say that I had ever felt thwarted by a person in that way, though I had felt all the What Ifs that arose when the prospect of going to university, and the life it might have brought into being, had disappeared. I was aware of currents moving, and thought, as Anthony Powell had, about how we make decisions and have no real idea what their result will be.

Had things been other than they were the married girl would not have been a married girl, and we would have found out what sort of partnership we could have made. But things are as they are and have to be your starting point. I met someone on that Summer School and paid a kind of court to her, almost laid siege to her, partly because I felt this kind of thing was expected, but also for reasons both more friendly and perhaps hidden from me. This boldness, I realised later, probably led to an attraction that was based on me being understood as something other than I usually was, which no doubt led to later disappointments when it became clear that my default personality setting was not quite the same as this week seemed to indicate, being nowhere near so capable of initiating change or controlling events. But then she had been drawn to me because of things that had happened to her in her immediate past that I had no idea about either. Perhaps something had ended for her, making me look like a possible, and like the girls who made the small profit margin of the pub punter worthwhile she thought, Why Not? I didn't know and perhaps she didn't either. The reasons why we do the things we do aren't always clear to us. We all oscillate and flicker, dials turning in varying directions and speeds, like orbits that sometimes match and sometimes go retrograde, and then we have to make the best sense of it we can later.

After the eventful week it turned out that in real life, back in the world as Vietnam soldiers said, she lived not far from where I lived. Continuing the relationship seemed an obvious choice, and besides I could feel an imperative on the move. I had already decided to leave the bedsit. It seemed an impossible and wrong way to be at the age I was. I didn't want any kind of alternative life or style. I thought of Stephen Stills line: I don't want no hot, dusty roads. No, indeed. I was a suburbs boy. The messy bedsit didn't mean I rejected order and comfort. My dad had some money put by and was prepared to help me with a deposit. So I had already started the process of buying a basement flat in a road near Twickenham station. Sometimes we do foolhardy things because something has to be done. Was it going to be an unwise choice, or worse, a mad thing to do? I didn't know if it was a good choice or not but it was an affordable choice. Besides, the couple who I was buying from lived there, proving it was possible to live there. I suppose no-one really wants to live in a basement flat. On the other hand it's a reminder that you're starting at the bottom. Someone always has to start at the bottom and so, unless there are faults out of all proportion, it should always be a saleable proposition. What can you lose? But now my time at the Nutshell became intermittent. I spent more time at my new girlfriend's place, a drive of a few miles away, and the sense of a kaleidoscope forming new patterns increased. I thought of some lines from a song by my teenage favourites The Lovin' Spoonful, already an old song when they sang it a decade before. "I'm getting tired of running round, believe I'll get married an' I'll settle down."

So the next year, 1978, having met in one summer and lived together on a part-time but increasing basis through an autumn and winter, lives were tidied up. We would get married and all would

be well. At the time of becoming involved with the purchase of a
basement flat down by the railway in Twickenham there had been no
sense that my circumstances would change substantially. Now they
had, which would change other peoples circumstances too. There was
no possibility, it was made clear, of beginning married life in a basement. I had to tell the young couple this, one of the most uncomfortable phone calls I'd made to that point. People explained that
this was what solicitors were for but I knew it would be the kind of
cowardice that would nag at me for some time if I didn't do it myself.
So palms cold and face hot I stumbled through it, and then we were
able to make other plans. My prospective wife already owned a proper
non-basement flat in a modern block, and knew about mortgages
and their brokers, being altogether more worldly-wise than me. The
outlines of roles began to emerge. I would allow her to be more silly;
she would encourage me to be more sensible. I settled the outstanding weeks rent that extended absences from my grotty room had
made it difficult to hand over; and where it was thought (as in the
Spoonful line, "It's okay to shoot the moon",) I'd run out owing it
all. We made plans to buy a house using the proceeds from her flat
sale and the money I was about to spend on a basement. It was going
to be a small house to be sure, but still a house. Something had
begun and something had ended. What I don't remember is how
they ended exactly, as I didn't remember what my last conversation
had been with the Paris girl, though the long aftermath, like a burnt-
out rocket taking forever to fall back to earth, remained clear. So now
I couldn't say exactly what words had passed between me and the girl
with sparkling eyes and a face that lit up, the girl with a husband;
or how I'd said, Hey, snap, I'm getting married too. But I remember how, not much later, there were lots of days as I drove to work
in one direction around Teddington roads, on certain curves near
the National Physical Laboratory, when her car would sweep in the
opposite direction, and we saw each other passing by under the great
trees and the green leaves, the sycamore and limes that thrive there

near Bushy Park. We smiled little smiles and shaped hello, goodbye, as our trajectories touched and separated, mouths and hair behind windshields. It was, I thought, like something from a French film, and then I realised what it was really like was Two For The Road, the screenplay I'd read and re-read not so long ago, and I felt too the little tug of What If, What If.

CHAPTER TWENTY-FOUR
THE ARITHMETIC OF MEMORY

Bob Dylan had come through a mirror when he had a motorcycle accident in 1966 that stopped one kind of life and began another. When he came back to public performing he'd changed and so had everything around him. I had felt that too, leaving school and not going on to university or college precipitated me onto a different path, one I'd followed until it led me here. A lot of the time in life you can feel you're somehow on the outside peeking in, as I had in and out of my tiny Richmond Hill room. With marriage you were always on the inside, mutually looking out for someone prejudiced in your favour. In the mid 70s I was discovering what kind of person I was, (a brooder on setbacks and issues arising it seemed, rather than someone temperamentally capable of saying, "I'm not thinking about that now,") but also finding what a pleasure it was to meet someone who would take you on. Now I had a chance to look back and see where I'd come from and where that had led. I thought about how when I'd first been in Richmond there seemed to be a world, some special time, I'd just missed, and how I knew that even if, at particular moments, it didn't feel like it, the days I was currently living through would be a missed age for someone coming along later, and now I had come through another mirror and was starting again, I remembered a specific memory picture I carried around.

There was once a party that took place in the grounds of the functional remains of a grand building, where the curving river, gleaming like silverware, was visible from the run of lawns, the light summer evening on the moving waters that Pope or Walpole would have recognised. Someone we knew walked on his hands down the lawns, upside down in his white suit. His knees pointed away from where he was going, and his feet, up in the air over his head, waggled to keep balance, pushed forward as a counterweight, and he stomped along on his hands down the grass, just to show he could do it; and the people laughing and drinking made room for him to pass. A little memory film that seems sometimes to stand for a kind of accidental splendour made of people and times of day, and therefore inevitably to dissolve except for the imperfect glimpses that can still come to mind. Sunlight turning to sunset: a short, stumpy blonde man but whose confidence and chest size always made you think of him as tall, dressed in his white suit, walks on his hands down a green lawn: the gathering of pretty young people, holding glasses and smiling, letting him pass and turning to admire his progress. Did it only happen once? Once is enough to keep forever. No matter that not much later he might be observed trying to persuade a girl to come with him somewhere more relaxed, where blouses didn't need to be quite so buttoned up, while his wife, not far away, trying to think of ways not to make a scene, fumed and gripped a wineglass stem so firmly it looked likely to snap. It was in any case just personal, as Gatsby observed, and his important work had been completed. All the people who came along later would have their own parties, their own golden age, but they missed this one and that image, and for once I didn't.

1978 and I was married and Bob Dylan came to England for the first time in 12 years and we were going to see him. All was activity around him. A new album was out, and a film was going to be released that featured material from his Rolling Thunder tour of 3 years earlier, following the pattern that Don't Look Back and the little seen documentary of 1966, Eat The Document, had set of being visible long after the events filmed, letting us see where he had been rather than where he was. The pattern too of reminding us how things change in short periods of time: atmospheres and the way life is and the way it seems to be. Married life. John Lennon seemed to think of it as an embarrassment, like having your flies open. One poet has said it's like promising to stand on one leg for the rest of your life. Their response was not mine. It felt to me like the situation I wanted to be in, one that I'd embraced. Some people are cut out for messy affairs and being chucked out of hotels, but I liked a pleasant domestic situation and having someone to love and care for. It also freed up something in writing. I started to do the weekly literary competitions in the New Statesman, something that required analysis of the style of well known writers, and then, in most cases, working the typical subject of one in the manner of another. This might be prose or verse but the idea was to be amusing while making a stylistic point. I took to this greatly and applied myself with focused industry, while also still trying to write original material. I came to think this was all to the good: the dissection required to write a parody, and the strict, tiny word length of the competitions, meant there had to be nothing extraneous. It let me acquire some objectivity, being less precious about what I did, trying to stand back and see it as other people might. Our situation provided subject matter.

> Favoured hour, lucky as clover
> secretly four-leafed all over
>
> the arable quilt of England. We
> chat after dinner with coffee
>
> and wine, watching the minute changes
> the texture of light arranges

upon the shifting leaves and grasses
and blossom. Blue air amasses

grace upon the world before us. The fence
is dissolving. There is silence ...

It might have been modern suburbia but the feeling evoked by evening was one I recognised from the psychedelic folkies of 1968, and
the bird clamour and activity of city roosts of that time. There was
a sense of a connection with England, and an older idea of England,
extending from this small house on a new estate of small new houses,
their roads too narrow and curving for all the cars that residents
seemed to need now, all the little houses with their new bricks and
tiny lawns and roads named after poets. In that respect only this was
like an earlier poet's estate I knew, the rougher 1930s houses near
Thames Road, where I could walk down Shakespeare Crescent to get
to junior school, but would usually try to avoid it. Here and now,
1978, I liked my poets' estate and felt lucky. The cost of the little
house at the time sounds as unlikely as the £5 rent of less than a
decade previously. £15,000, but then it seemed quite large enough. It
was from here I set off in the still operational fairground boy's car, to
pass someone from another time going in the opposite direction; and
from here too we set off to Earls Court to see the Bob Dylan who was
the one now in residence.

1978. What was on the charts and what did it matter? Punk
had come and gone. Its primitive, heartfelt simplicity and energy, its
noise, its need to gather together as many ways of outraging the bour-
geoisie, or anyone nearby, with piercings, bondage trousers, phlegm
and various offensive behaviours, had threatened to raze music to
Year Zero, but in the end failed to make other styles of music extinct.
Noise was still in, but complexity of various kinds returned. Different
styles blended and came to the fore. Synthesisers and David Bowie
descendants began to flourish. Dressing up returned, there always

being room for ridiculous hair and clothes in pop music, and called itself different things, New Romantics being one. Roxy Music made a kind of reformation and came out with a new album and more sober appearance. None of which had much to do with Bob Dylan, whose co-existence with the charts and their music is always going to be chiefly 1965 and 1966, and anything else is incidental. 1978. What did it mean, and when did it mean it? 1978. Punk had happened, and whatever happened next was happening. People were getting married and finding themselves in another lifetime. Bob Dylan had been getting divorced, editing a film from 2 years before, and thinking about the kind of music he wanted to make. The last album he had released was live songs from the later version of the Rolling Thunder tour, the one not judged to be of the same quality as the 1975 dates: old songs and recent songs rearranged, weight with guitars, and a cover picture loaded with the mascara and alarming thinness of face. The film, Renaldo and Clara, contained wonderful Rolling Thunder concert performances too, but he seemed to find them secondary to the am-dram acting out of symbolic and incomprehensible scenes usually alluding to what we knew, or thought we knew of him; all of it seeming to exist so scholars could go to work and tell us what it meant, or was likely to mean, with its moveable roses, white-face make up, and Les Enfants Du Paradis references. Besides, who got to see it? It didn't make your local Odeon, and featured only fleetingly at big city art houses.

What it did was show the parallel time tracks that operated around Bob Dylan. The film allowed those who got to see it a musical experience that was, it seemed, an attempt by him to bring to life aspects of a world he had been part of more than a decade before. Invoking carnivals and cowboys, the homespun theatricals seemingly spontaneous, (though actually quite staged), inventing their own folk tradition, where the Beats and the Western seemed to blend, where Greenwich Village folk, blues, gospel and rock dovetailed, doing their skilful, ramshackle work. What was on display in the present, though coterminous with interviews designed to publicise Renaldo and Clara, was an enterprise of a different order. The album Street-Legal was released in conjunction with the tour and the evidence of its photographs suggested a different sensibility at work. The back cover with its quilted sub-Elvis suit and eyeliner and *no guitar*, has over-tones of both the circus, as distinct from a carnival, and, more worry-ingly, a stuffed turkey somehow taking part in a variety show. It was the later-Elvis side of showbusiness, which was not exactly a business Bob Dylan had previously seemed to be in. Musically too the Rolling Thunder guitar-based ensemble deriving from Village days had been replaced. Now there was a much bigger outfit where saxophones and flutes were an important part of the sound, as were the girl choirs. The album didn't sound like anything he'd done previously in terms of the style of the songs, but it was generally agreed that its produc-tion was bad, marring the overall impression they made. There were long songs with lots of dense, rhyming verses, and melodies that seem to have begun life on a carousel or a barrel organ, up and down they went, round and round, repeating like revolving doors. There was a bright unrelenting quality present, directly related to the saxophones and the flute.

What would the concerts bring? After such a long absence what would he mean now? From the back of the vastness of Earls Court we saw him slow the tempo of I Want You right down to conversational speed. Unexpectedly it made perfect sense. It enhanced it. It made it seem French, and brought out the sadness of desire. The concerts didn't include many of the new album songs, but the unusual-for-him band allowed these different treatments of favourites from the well-known catalogue. Going, Going, Gone, from the Planet Waves album immediately prior to Rolling Thunder times, he sang with a hand mike, wandering around like a nightclub performer, like the Elvis or Neil Diamond his stage outfit with its sequins and quilts and flares now reminded us of. The girls' voices intensified the mood of the song, repeating the chorus as he moved to the back of the stage, disappearing in its darkness. Then there it was, the end of the first half, as if the song was partly about leaving a stage and existed to make such an exit, and this kind of slickness was what he had aspired to all his life. Hovering in the air were the words, Las Vegas.

All of this re-emphasised how the times were always a'changin'. That past, that reality, when Bob Dylan as a name, as a sound, as a collection of syllables juxtaposed with the early album cover images that evoked both the New York streets and the West, was like trying to recall a childhood or a dream. The world that had surrounded him early on, the one of traditional songs and then topical songs, of idealism, being for civil rights and against the Vietnam war, the heroism of students who were beaten and murdered in Mississippi while the mass of us were political only in the sense of being young and thinking in slogans, all of it had moved away like smoke. But gone too was the slightly later version that everyone attending Earl's Court would have carried in their heads: the 1966 dualism of slow, long, intense and excessively pronounced acoustic songs in one half, and the mad, loud, fast, enunciated intensity of him and the Hawks in the other. Because he still sang the way he did, he still had resonances and flavours of those earlier existences and meanings, but now he was an entertainer putting on a big show with a lot of crowd-pleasers in his songbag. What he had meant before, or what we had thought he signified, was always a kind of authenticity, one at odds with stage outfits and hand mikes.

There were more changes to come for both of us. The next year he took everyone by surprise, leaving no-one in doubt about his authenticity and intention to follow his own path. He became a Christian and evangelical to the extent of producing a whole album of songs whose subject was Christianity. He worked with a stripped-down guitar, bass, keyboards, drums group, including of-the-moment English guitar whizz Mark Knopler, that bore no relation at all to the recent touring band. He then played a whole tour where every performance had no old songs at all, nothing well-known for the crowd to feel pleased by, and all he did was the Christian songs from the album just released, and Christian songs from the album that was to follow. This divided opinion just as effectively as going electric had 14 years previously. While I, sharpened by literary competitions, continued to write poems and started to write stories. One of them I entered in a local competition judged by Jill Hyem, a writer for TV and radio. She picked it as a prize winner, surprised that a first person female voice story was written by a man. This hadn't been a deliberate or tactical choice on my part. It had all been more intuitive and spontaneous. When the story suggested itself it was as that voice saying the words and I tried to follow my nose and capture it. It was called At The End Of Lonely Street and connected the woman's sad story with the old Elvis hit Heartbreak Hotel, making a life connect with music, the way I thought everyone's did. Whatever the satisfaction I felt, and said that I felt, with my settled situation now, in my stories there seemed to be an underlying seed of unhappiness. I couldn't identify precisely why that was, but encouraged by Jill to write more, and to try submitting scripts to radio, I tried to be open to story ideas and send them off. Another story was accepted for broadcast on Radio 3. At the time even though such a story would only fill a 15 or 20 minute time slot and was no big thing, a writer was asked along to the recording. So it was that I was able to meet the actor chosen by the producer to read it. "Hello," I said to David Warner, as calmly as I could, "I saw you as Hamlet." "Did you? I can't believe it. You don't look old enough." This was better than any coincidence created by Anthony Powell. I was entirely happy, thinking how much time had gone by, and how unexpected it was, his reality was right there, the person who'd occupied my thoughts as Hamlet and Morgan not only was going to read my words, but we'd met, and as well as me knowing very well who he was, for a moment he knew me.

A little later I couldn't believe how an actor who could memorise all of Hamlet and act it easily, could stumble and trip over little sentences right there in front of him. Behind the glass the producer explained that this was how it was. Actors seemed to divide into those who sight-read scripts without fluffing, and those who though capable of memorising great chunks of text and delivering it onstage, found it more tricky to read from the page. I also saw that the work was done in removing from the tape any such stumbles, along with sentences that made the time slot overrun, and that anyone listening would only hear the finished product, a tape that sounded as if it had never been anything else. In the way I heard it, thinking, "It's David Warner. I know him and I've met him and he's charmingly polite and he's read my story on the radio, his voice has read my words." That may not sound like much, but the effect can be like following clues to a treasure. Every one chanced upon leads you further.

This connected with what had happened with poetry too. I'd met my wife during the first year of Open University, but that wasn't the end of studying. It continued, and being alerted to a national O.U. poetry competition in an O.U. newspaper, I entered. My tiny poem was one of the prize winners.

SUNDIAL

The brittle old lady in the white hat
is escorting invalid air. Her walk
hesitates, a memory jogged with a stick
white as her hat. Slow and slow in the heat

she pulls a dark shadow. It slides
smooth over flagstones, continuous
despite her deliberations, like years,
not to be eluded. The dark glides,

deferential waiter attending her hand and foot.
She stops to examine flowers intently
as if smell will ensure all petals fit. Her hat
is dazzling under the bright blue sky.

The real prize, as always, is finding out that you're not alone, not deluded when you think something you have written is worthwhile. That confirmation is very necessary and will last until someone rejects the next thing you do, though even then its power doesn't entirely disappear. The memory of it keeps you going on the same track until you happen across a like-minded person again. Around this time too there was a further development. Someone I worked with told me that he'd seen a small ad in something or other giving an address for some kind of Dylan newsletter, or something. He knew this kind of hard information appealed to me. "It should interest you," he said, "being a bit of a fan."

This was true and also a misconception. Yes, I'd had views and feelings about it all since at least 1964, and yes, I was what might be called a civilian Bob fan, owning the released albums, some Trade Mark of Quality or Swinging Pig bootleg vinyl, and the few published books that constituted the Dylan critical and biographical canon at the time. I was not, however, the real thing. I entirely lacked the industry, zeal, background knowledge, obsessive geekery and cassettes of live shows that being a genuine collector/fan demonstrated. But I found the address in the New Musical Express and sent off the small amount of money to be a subscriber, subscribing to what exactly? It was called The Telegraph and purported to come from the Bob Dylan Information Office, which was stationed, it seemed, in Radcliffe, Manchester. Less impressive than John Platt's Comstock Lode, which was an A4 size with photographs reasonably visible, and lots of long articles, this was an A5 hand-produced fanzine with badly photocopied photographs and various other Dylan-related, reproduced bits and pieces: Bob's birth certificate, Doonesbury cartoons, reviews from ancient Melody Makers, as well as a reprinted lyric or two of little known songs. What it also had a lot of was Dylan news items and stray mentions in newspapers all gathered together in a supplementary sheet that came posted with the Telegraph and was called The Wicked Messenger. The body of the magazine itself was mainly questions about Dylan material or events which were answered by an all-purpose identikit character called The Oracle, made up of the various people who put the enterprise together. What unnerved me was the feeling of having entered a room I had assumed was empty, only to find a party well under way. Here it was, issue 1, and already there were pages of questions from people. To whom had they directed their enquiries? What was happening here?

What was happening was that from this little black&white beginning at the start of the 1980s something was going to grow that I was going to be part of. Perhaps all decades are decades of great change, it's just that some you notice more because of the age you happen to be. It seems now that the 1980s were as tumultuous as the 1960s, in general and in relation to me personally. They began with riots in Bristol, Liverpool and London; the country went to war with a foreign country and its own miners. The government was more ideologically driven than any in recent memory, determined to reshape the nature of the relationship between the public and private sectors, central and local government, between unions and employers, self-interest and altruism. There were sharper dividing lines between the haves and have-nots. For younger people though, whatever the politics or economics, it was still, as it always was for young people, a time when pop music, clothes and hair were at their peak of excitement and interest. If you were a bit older, in employment, married, living on a modern estate, obviously you would be, whatever your political views, counted among the haves, as comfortable and as at ease as you could recall. The Telegraph was going to be part of that for me.

I had my Bob memories and my Sixties schooldays but I'd never written about him. Who would I be writing for? Seeing the Letterbox column in The Telegraph however, I began to write to the editor, long, chatty, ornate letters, and liked seeing them printed in the next issue. I became a pen pal and intermittent phone pal of the man who was The Oracle more than most, and whose idea it all had been. John Bauldie was the man responsible. Almost exactly my age he had been a Bob fan as I had, but was a good deal more enterprising, striking up a postal relationship with Greil Marcus when he first read him in Rolling Stone, and getting to know how he could get hold of those bootleg records himself. Liking what he read in my letters he eventually asked me to write reviews, and that was how my published writing about Bob Dylan began. I had parallel writing tracks. One was in writing poems that I hoped would be published, along with little stories and, eventually, plays, which were accepted for radio production. The confirmation that I wasn't deluded and was on the right track was reinforced here by being paid what seemed to me reasonable amounts of money for them, something I couldn't say was true of poems. Parodies for the New Statesman had fallen away now because that magazine, along with its literary section, had changed. I didn't fit. In this it was simply following the normal pattern. What you believe to be life and absolutely the case turns out to be a phase. Everything is a phase of some kind. The other writing track was reviews for the Telegraph, and that too didn't stand still. From being a college lecturer in English Literature, John Bauldie moved into magazine production with a job on the music monthly Q. With his acquired knowledge and some of his new colleagues he set to work improving everything about The Telegraph's production. From a scrappy, stapled fanzine, it morphed into something still A5 in size, but now a sturdily-spined, perfect-bound, professionally produced, glossy magazine, with colour photographs on the cover, and perfectly produced colour and black and white layouts inside. It looked impressive, and for me even more so because a lot of the time there were pages I'd written inside it.

What Bob Dylan did during the 1980s didn't greatly matter to the world at large. He seemed confused about what he was or wanted to do. There was a three year period after 1981 when there were no tours or albums released. The Telegraph bravely carried on, gathering its news scraps and creating articles out of thin air. The albums that eventually appeared were usually reported as being far from their original intent. Impressive songs were rumoured to have been recorded during protracted sessions and then left off, or inferior versions included, as if second-guessing himself didn't allow an original vision to emerge, or he wasn't able to judge accurately what made one song more worthwhile than another. Then came a release that was an indication of what the future might hold though it was all about the past.

In the middle of the decade a boxed set called Biograph was issued, a handsome production containing 3 LPs and two thick booklets, one of which had new Bob Dylan comments on each track chosen and a whole raft of new information, including family photographs, on what he made of these pieces of his life. The point about the collection was that it was more than a Greatest Hits: it was a retrospective to show what he had been capable of and created over the previous almost 25 years, including items collectors like us had previously only been able to find on bootlegs. CBS opened up its archives to put out live versions of songs recorded at concerts by them, and also outtakes from recording sessions of known songs, and first releases of songs never officially released before. In its rag-bag of contents, its hotchpotch attempts at thematic tracking, (major song nuzzles against minor, screaming electric against wistful folk) it was like experiencing the random nature of memory. It was a reminder too that in the past everything is right next to everything else. It helped too that everything had been remastered to improve the sound. To alert people to it there were interviews with Bob Dylan in various publications, where he said he hadn't chosen the songs on the albums, or been involved, nor was he excited about it. Nevertheless the sheer number of interviews seemed to indicate that he wished the enterprise well.

There were different ways to think about *Biograph*. It raised the issue of what it is to be an admirer, a fan, a critic, a collector, and how that sensibility could be transferred to the wider audience. After all the size of the package, and the enclosed booklets, were there to tell people that this was a cultural event and an important artist. The idea was to make this clearer to a bigger crowd than Telegraph subscribers, who would have had most rare items and would only argue about the songs they would have preferred included. Although Bob Dylan had toured and released a new album that same year, 1985, his best reviews were for Biograph. The sense of parallel worlds operating, his past usually being easier to understand and like than his present state, received new focus here. In fact the man who had put it together, a Dylan office lawyer called Jeff Rosen, who seemed to hold a wider brief than simply being a lawyer, had created a business model that was going to be become an important part of the future for Bob Dylan. Whatever new songs and albums he later created, there was fresh appreciation, and profit, to be mined from material that already existed, if it was re-presented and packaged in the correct way.

The constant rolling background of the 1980s happened outside and inside the bubble of my life, my marriage. There was my Bob writing, and other writing. There was being part of a community library, and living in a different house, a 1930s one in the kind of suburban street that my heart opened up to. Its price, £35,000, also seems like toy money 30 decades on, but that's an illusion, the translating value of money and what it could buy being not only one of the most difficult feats of memory but of true comparison. Of course money was a theme of that decade, performed by synthesisers, though I was far from the excess so mythologised then and later. Being employed throughout, however, did mean as a couple we had enough to feel at ease in a modest, public sector way, although like all people who depend on salaries, we were only ever a couple of months from disaster should the worst happen. In the meantime we had enough for holidays, where the hours are always an unhurried advance on or retreat from meals, with detours into beaches or siestas; holidays on Mediterranean or Aegean islands whose history may have been violent and bloody but whose present was all sun and pleasure: the waves and the light, glasses of water and milky ouzo, beer bottles golden and sweating in the afternoon. At home there was a kitchen extended and a dishwasher installed, thus necessitating a duplicate set of plates and cutlery, and still the glasses became scored and cloudy under the novel, scouring machine efficiency; and sometimes we had two cars and sometimes one; and we had a lovable Labrador on which we could pour love and affection as well as on each other. All was well, and all was well and all manner of things was well. Wasn't it?

What you believe to be life and absolutely the case turns out to be a phase. Everything is a phase of some kind.

CHAPTER TWENTY-FIVE
BLUE LAWN

During that decade my parents died, my mother at the beginning and my father around halfway through. My mother died of cancer that went away then came back, or perhaps never went away, as it is for most people. One of the things she had said in hospital, my dad told me, was to look after her slippers, because she would need those when she came out. I remembered her crying at the back kitchen table when I'd first left home, and all of the love and affection she'd poured on me, and how poor a son I felt I'd been.

She knew, as I didn't, that once you leave it doesn't matter how many times you come back, you never actually return.

Kitchen taps when I grew up always had a small rubber nozzle attached to direct the flow. People put them on so you could sluice out the sink in its corners. Everyone had them. You could see them from the table where a mother sat crying if you looked over to the sink through the open doorway. What happened to them? Did they make them anymore, the nozzles that directed the flow? Perhaps I couldn't ever have paid her back directly, but I wanted to pass it on somehow. Parents raise you so that you can leave, that's the pain of it. Perhaps part of the way to paying them back is to love other people the best you can, passing it on the way songs are.

Half a decade later, on the day my father died, that same afternoon we drove up the back roads and the motorways, all the bits that
connect into a journey, loading the agreeable hound and bags and
bundles and pieces in with us, leaving the day life behind, and by
evening were able to sit in his empty house, the one I'd grown up in,
watching the local news and seeing his slippers waiting for him by
the fireplace, as my mother had wanted hers to be. Part of me felt that
he might come in at any moment, and part of me knew that the house
was empty now and had a life of its own. The slippers like every other
thing there had a meaning drain away from them, and were, despite
being quite still, like wild, whirling things, all of which would be
dispersed, handed on to a person or persons as yet unknown. Sitting
in the room that he wouldn't return to, I also knew after this time
of arranging and funeral, it was the room I wouldn't come back to
either. We would salvage some things. Watches. Money. The little
green imitation-safe money box. The little brown suitcase which contained wartime bits and pieces and the few family photographs that
had accumulated: me when I was young; my parents when they were
young; people I didn't know. Almost everything else, every possession that was no longer possessed, would be given away or stay if
the next occupant wanted it. Furniture. Lawnmower. Garden tools.
Council houses get handed over and there would be no-one here I
knew to visit then. I sat on the sofa in the living room and thought
about those times I'd sat and slumped next to him, bunked comfort-
ably against his small, round-shouldered shape, while we watched
whatever we watched, Top Cat or Tom and Jerry, and he commented
on how sunny and open it looked in the background of Laurel and
Hardy films, or how American kitchens seemed to have better taps
and fridges in 1930s gangster films than England did in the 1950s,
or how Westerns hopelessly over-romanticised reality. "They were all
petty criminals and bad 'uns, Billy The Kid, all of 'em. No different
from the fingers around today"

And I thought, as everyone does at these times, how you grow confident that life is a certain way and then have to deal with a shock when it isn't. I looked at his slippers and all the things he'd walked out on that morning in the kitchen, even a dish with the frozen peas he'd left on the side near the stove, persisting in his belief, no matter what the packet said, that they had to be thawed before you could heat them through. The kitchen, like me, was expecting his return, wanting him to walk in through the door and say it had all been a mistake. We slept in my bedroom, the bedroom I'd slept in all the time I'd lived in the house, and I looked through the window out onto the same view of grass and line posts and paling fences where the gardens all ran together. The grass was even wilder and less tended now. I didn't want the time back when I'd looked at it 20 years ago, but I did want him to reappear. When I was growing up I'd felt, quite keenly sometimes, that he was less of a figure than other boys' dads. He didn't go to work: small: deaf, (an inheritance he'd handed down to me); but because he was always around, and because he read and talked and was intelligent and wrote me a letter every week I was away in London, I knew he'd shaped me forever. Inadequate son though I often felt myself to be, I was *his* son and he was my father, and this event, this sudden, permanent disappearance couldn't mean that he wouldn't always be within me, part of my texture, whether as thoughts or fibre of flesh, blood and DNA. There is something so at odds with the balances and time scales of death. A moment in a day, which engenders other moments on that day when things are said, unplanned and then unremembered, little memory flashes that may or may not be clear again. But the results of that instant last forever, never go away, sometimes appear once more in dreams, or passing thoughts, not necessarily sad thoughts but, like Chekhov, saturated with the sadness that past happiness can make you feel even as you remember how the happiness was true.

The next day we went to the hospital mortuary, which may have been to identify him or may have been to confirm it for ourselves in view of the ambivalent living room and the contents whose purpose derived from him and now was taken away. I don't know what I thought I would do. In films and stories people lean forward and kiss the brow of the departed. The body looked somewhat like him, but not really, like an inadequate effigy, rolled out like frosted turf. He looked so small, and his face without false teeth so hollowed. I put my hand out to touch his cheek, extending my finger and trying to keep it back at the same time. His face was surprisingly cold and solid, like touching a stone kept in a freezer, so that I knew kissing him would be pointless and also that I was scared to do it. No doubt he was cold because bodies are kept refrigerated, but that's not how I understood it. What I understood was that death transforms the warm, living person into this little strange statue that won't know whether you kiss it or not, and which wouldn't make you feel any better if you did. And the only thing Bob Dylan had to do with it was my knowing that all I could do was experience it, and later perhaps write about it, but not in the way he would. I had to use my own voice; no-one else's would do.

He fell down in the street. He fell, his heart
attacked by silted arteries. He fell
and turned bright red, then blue, as people do
whose blood is thick with waste and lipid gel
and insufficient oxygen: the blue
features darkening as blushes depart.

But a whole man, not witless with disease,
not senses dwindled in a feeble frame
leaving him unaware of memories
of Lil, or me, or knowledge of his name.
Surname: Kelly. Forenames: Sidney Arthur.
Neighbours knew him. He was identified
by those who were close at hand. My father
who fell down far away and later died.

And later still I touched his cold repose
and was frightened, knowing then where pride goes;

touching his stiffened cheek, shaved spick and span,
understanding what blood is thicker than.

The year after my father died I had a book of poems published, and that was in it. I thought about John Lennon before his first book appeared all those years ago, in an early interview I'd gobbled down, being asked if he would publish a book of his writing, and his reply-ing that he might if he could gather together the scribbled-on scraps and cigarette packets. Mine too was like a selected from all the ones I'd written, back 16 years to the bedsitter, but not quite beyond even though I'd been writing them from the schooldays time of absorbing Beatle interview. I thought about how unlikely my having a book of poems published had seemed over the years when I was trying to create them and sending them out and getting them back, and how fantastic a book was. In a year of unexpected conjunctions personal, universal and bathetic I also had a radio play broadcast, and a hur-ricane swept through Britain, bringing trees down across cars and into roofs all over the place, including the streets next to ours, and the park next to them where I exercised the golden hound. It was all very dramatic and all about change. The following night Bob Dylan played at Wembley Arena and I couldn't help being reminded of a line in a song from Infidels, an album of not long before, about how trees that stood for a thousand years could suddenly fall. I had to admit to myself it was perhaps the only way that he now seemed of the moment.

If he had seemed adrift at the beginning of the 1970s with inactivity, now being active was equally culpable. The previous couple of years had brought one album that was over-produced in the then modish-contemporary manner, with synthesisers and pro-grammed drums; followed by a slapdash, cobbled-together album of co-written songs and old songs by others; as well as his participation in a film that was an embarrassment to all concerned called Hearts Of Fire, which produced dyed ginger hair for him, along with a bad soundtrack. It was always possible to find something that gave heart, a glint that showed some diamond quality was still present, but the albums lacked an innate coherence, and the thing that had set him apart and drew you towards him was a ghost and a memory. He had become disconnected from the need and then the ability to write songs, but not the necessity of performing. He had undertaken a tour backed by Tom Petty and the Heartbreakers, and then one with the Grateful Dead, and was now back to Tom Petty again. This was the kind of event the Telegraph was made for: the circulation of news, of cassettes of albums to come, reports of shows that had been, everything culminated in this purpose: being at a Bob Dylan show. John Bauldie even managed to connect with the promoter to get tickets to sell, so like-minded fans could be there to enjoy a concert in a continuing series of concerts. Except that I didn't enjoy it much, and my mind didn't seem to be like that of the delighted fans all around.

What Bob Dylan had meant, the feelings his songs aroused, was about as absent as my father. Who was up there wearing his current disguise, this grouchy Mr Pouchy, wearing market-trader, fingerless gloves while playing guitar? He'd still been able to sing in 1980 and 1981. There had been deterioration in 1984. Now we were in another zone, pushed way beyond parody, affectation, or mannerism, and described, accurately, by John Peel as a "dying murder's last gasped confession." For the most part travesty seemed to be his chief interest. He had always been praised or excused for doing old songs differently, unrecognisably sometimes, on the grounds of artistic endeavour and keeping it fresh. Now he didn't seem to care what they meant. His past achievements became obligations, the audience adulation an albatross rather than a garland. If he didn't respect the songs how could he respect the audience? What did we come to him for if not to hear some kind of truth, even if we couldn't explain it logically. And what was the means of conveying that truth except for his voice? His throwaway delivery, harsh and hawkish, threw his gift away too. And yet there I was surrounded by rows of people who seemed to be eating it up with a spoon.

I was driven to examine what I saw and what I used to see and later worked it into a review of Down In The Groove, the album released the next year. I imagined what the Bob who had sung Positively 4th Street all of 22 years ago would make of this figure before us who went by the same name and was in roughly the same line of business. Might it be, You got a lot of nerve to say you are my future. His voice had never been better than on that record. It may not be his greatest song but usually I believe it is his greatest record, and because I loved it when it first appeared I love it the more whenever I hear it, and each time his current voice so changed, so damaged by comparisons. Positively 4th Street will never change but comes alive, anew, whatever the hour or season. Let you be in my dream if I can be in yours, he had once sung, and all of us out there in the 1960s had wanted to be in his, and had felt that in some way we were, enveloped and surrounded in times into which we all were woven. Now he seemed to want to be in ours. He needed the audience who wanted to see a man putting on a show of songs they had known and loved. He no longer even had to do them well to gain a rapturous reception. Simply being in his presence was enough for them to love him, and the merest use of a harmonica would intensify it. Not that he seemed to like the audience for this. He had to perform, and they would applaud, but the only opinion he trusted was his own. And he seemed to like himself no better than the audience.

This year of my unexpected writing successes, the more lucrative had been the radio play. In it I had used interlocking monologues for three characters, using the example of Michael Frayn's play Benefactors, which I'd seen more than once, and Robert Patrick's play Kennedy's Children, which I'd read many times. It was a form that appealed to me. Instinctively I knew it suited the internal voice

I had, and that if I was going to write a play that worked I had my best chance using it. I took aspects of myself and things I'd observed and scattered them among the three, a married couple and a teenage girl they tried to help towards an A level. Remembering the would-be beggar from 16 years ago, and how surprised I had been that an annoyed look from me had been enough to repel him, I remembered too how bad I had felt. So now my female character said:

I was furious. Furious for being caught by his polite begging, for being made to reject what he represented, for being exposed.

And she remembered:

Looking down the length of me like a fallen tower. I used to do that when I was a teenager. Lie there, moving one leg from the horizontal to the vertical and back again. Thinking how far away my foot seemed.

But, as well as remembering, writing can also be a kind of unintended prophecy. A few years before, I had not been any kind of writer about Bob Dylan. Now I tried to do it as seriously as any other writing I did notwithstanding absolutely no money being involved. The prophecy for the Dylan article was in clearly establishing a stance and a character for the kind of Bob Dylan writing I was going to do from now on, making a lens through which I tried to see him and me as clearly as I could. Writing about Bob Dylan would be a way of writing about me, and it was always likely to involve the past. The prophecy for the play was in more obscurely forecasting that a relatively short time after this successful year, fault lines would break up my marriage, nobody's fault lines intensified by the death of Sadie, the canine sponge that absorbed love and oozed it out again.

The decade travelled towards its turning point. Wembley, large scale, mass venue though it was, had been smaller, one Dylan scholar noted, than some of the arenas and stadiums his tours took in. Now he was scaling down further and playing theatres, real theatres seating hundreds rather than thousands. He was Bob Dylan and not Bob Dylan. Following the example of the Grateful Dead he'd had a conversion, less dramatic than being Born Again, but long lasting. He'd realised that he had to be someone who went out there and played regularly, going out across America but also through Europe and back again, following the seasons like a carnival. Summer would find him in one place, Fall in another There were various ways of viewing this, but one was that increasing his visibility had to lessen the rarity value, that special charge of seeing Bob Dylan. He went out there, country to country, town to town, with his stripped-down three piece group and played songs from the range of years, and though some would work better than others, and it was exciting because it was a live show, what I'd felt at Wembley stayed true. The rarity value decreased in the way bad money drives out good. He had become what perhaps he'd always wanted to be since a teenager: a working musician in a rock and roll band, drawing from types of American music many and various, including his own, but still loving traditional songs. The Civil Rights Bob, and even the 1966 Bob, were the equivalent of trying to recall a dream when watching this performer, though sometimes he sang their songs. Nevertheless it was from these earlier personae that his power and authority came. The people who came to see him had, like me, fallen under his spell then and felt themselves intertwined with his progress. Or they were younger and had missed those times, but believed that in going to see him they were making a connection: that some of the nimbus of myth, legend and history he carried would be accessible for the duration of the show, no matter how far away he was.

Time was the subject of his songs and his performances. In our lives it speeded up and slowed down, behaving in a contradictory manner. I was a Telegraph writer, which meant nothing to the world at large but increasingly more to me. That, and money from another radio play, gave me the chance to see Bob Dylan in New York, in a theatre and for more than one night, on a Telegraph organised outing. New York was the town where Scott Fitzgerald and Bob Dylan became themselves, the town where they found a constituency and a mirror, seeing who they were in the recognition of others. But it's also everybody's town. Everybody who ever read a crime novel or saw an American movie or even uttered the word "skyscraper" and built an inner vision as the syllables rose on the tongue. Inevitably one goes to New York with expectations. To see Bob Dylan is to have expectations both confirmed and confounded usually. What made these concerts of more interest was that after half a decade of unfocused albums that seemed to have no compelling reason to exist, Bob Dylan released Oh Mercy that offered a dark distillation of themes, vocal and musical, that he had dealt with over his whole career. There is a unity of mood, a despair and resignation everywhere in the songs, and Dylan's desperate need to sing them. Most of the songs could be about a broken romance. They could as easily be about a break up with God. There is in any event a loss of faith. In What Good Am I? one hears the sound of What Can I Do For You?, (from his second, all-religious album, Saved) but with an obverse meaning. There Dylan was full of hope and purpose, aching to be directed and made use of. Here he is so worthless that it's a wonder he can even write a song about it. It is a seriously sad album whose bleakness is disguised by the slow easy pace of the arrangements and unusually careful production by Daniel Lanois, who even if he didn't have an easy relationship with Bob Dylan always had a clear idea in mind about how the songs and the album should sound.

Anyone going to see Bob Dylan, no matter how awful his performance, will always think it was good if they were very close to the stage. Seeing him in a theatre where the foyer is all red and gilt and mirrors intensifies this. The first night he gave every indication of being drunk He stumbled back and forth from the mike to his harmonica collection by the drum kit. He stomped off to the side to scratch vigorously at one arm while the band grooved for a while. He clawed irritably through his hair in what seemed to be thwarted displacement activity. He fluffed instrumental breaks. He fitted and re-fitted harmonicas in his holder. In some songs he struggled for minutes and then decided not to play after all. Towards the end in Like A Rolling Stone he wandered up and down the diatonic scale until he settled on a child's attempt at playing one hole. Blow suck blow: tuneless, loud, squawking. But having stumbled into this he displayed that contrary Bob Dylan-ness that marked him out from normal rock tours. He stayed with it. He played it over and over until the guitarist picked up on it too. It was like a mantra where repetition goes beyond embarrassment, beyond boredom, beyond the normal, and enters somewhere else, somewhere existential.

Not all his shows were this strange. Even on the short sequence that we saw there was nothing so near to being out of control again, though with him one felt the possibility was always there. I was seeing him now more than at any other time, being part of that pre-Internet Telegraph collective, actually comprising genuine collectors, not writing imitators like me, though allowing me to be part of the phone messages, letters, and cassette packages of live shows from the other side of the world, or songs left off albums long ago that "you really should hear". Bob Dylan was riding a wave with an album that had made him visible by its good reviews, and by his taking part in the Traveling Wilburys. That had seemed almost an exercise in marketing and demographics for baby boomers: a group made up of an ex-Beatle; an ersatz Beatle whose career was founded on the sound of I Am The Walrus; an early 60s pop hero who had influenced the Beatles, Bob Dylan who had influenced everybody; and a Bob collaborator who could sound like him or the Byrds and was therefore perfect to help them all create a relaxed, let's have fun like we did in the Sixties, vibe. But it seemed to free up something in Bob Dylan, bringing him back to writing, even though its mood was nothing like Oh Mercy. Besides, the sheer unexpectedness of this supergroup sold albums.

He carried on carrying on. The tour now referred to as Never Ending went around the world with him torturing, travestying and transforming his songs, sometimes in the space of one verse. He wasn't in the business of perfection but of experience. The decade was coming to its end, and so were other things. The underlying cracks in my marriage prefigured by my earlier play grew wider. The fridge wasn't the only cold thing at the heart of the kitchen. After the New York trip there was a year getting used to the idea that whatever had joined us seemed to have severed. Why this was is tricky to be precise about. It might have had a specific cause, like my wife falling in love with someone else, or believing that I was no longer the same character that she had wanted to be with; but it's just as accurate, and fruitless, to say it was the result of both of us being the people we were. At one time we'd suited and been a match. Now we weren't, whether that began with one person or the other. What did it matter how it began? Now we were in this different terrain.

HANGING

In fitted wardrobes the orderly clothes queue,
contemplating the future, quiet days
waiting their turn, not knowing what to do
as time hangs heavy. A steadfast gaze

considers what's new. Is this the real thing
or a phase to go through? On the wall blouses
and neat shirts, crisp displays of ironing
view constancy in opposite houses,
dwelling on perfection, the correct setting
for appearance, the turnout of spouses.

That darkness when light leaves, when spark goes out,
makes itself at home, settling on sleep,
on two separate and intimate with doubt,
the racked and silent counsel clothes must keep.

There was an odd interlude of being in the same house and trying to
be as close as we could to companionable, while knowing that this
gulf existed. Morning tea was still made to greet the other person
into the day. We walked around in the shared loneliness not knowing
what to do next, or scared at the implications of what a logical next
move had to be. There is a turmoil of not knowing what you actually
think, of being so confused that you can't honestly say what things
mean, whether choices are good or bad. *Nothing either good or bad but
thinking makes it so.* Except that it's as if you can't think. You behave
as an animal seems to, by instinctive, unanalysed judgements. It's
not that things and situations aren't clear, simply that they make no
sense. Your head doesn't work. Up and down you go, like little blue
Shreddies frogman, pressures exerted by forces outside your control.
Later, when you're back in the world it's impossible to have access
again to the degree of bewilderment let loose. There's a memory of
what it was like in general terms, but not, fortunately, the sensation
itself. I have to say too that whether Bob Dylan had passed through
similar states of mind before he managed to write the songs on Blood
On The Tracks, about his own marriage troubles then, or the miseries
that later created Oh Mercy, was not uppermost in my considerations.

Two are glass-bound, desperate, asleep,
quiet as the watch that bookshelves keep.
Shrunken jonquils emit a tiny perfume
into the silent, pane-limited room,
their miniature, shrivelling petals
yellow as the beams where dust settles.
Rousing, predictive, a small scent floats

among swarming shiny motes.

Elsewhere music, sunlight-golden oldies:

Hank, foretelling how cold a heart that's cold is.

A script editor I'd met, someone used to examining plots and loose ends and sorting them out, – though her own life was a mess – said that I had to admit that it was over in order to be healthy and to be alive: to be or not to be in short. The iron consequence, I knew, was that the dear wife who had helped me so much when my mother died, then when my father died and I felt that sense of being an orphan out in the world, would not be part of my life. All of the things that had knitted us together over 12 years, were we saying they didn't matter? The settled house and life and happiness we seemed to have gathered so steadfastly about us, – which had become unhappiness, – all would be ungathered, and we satellites would orbit in different directions. 12 years wouldn't be wasted. They had to be honoured. Whatever was valuable then would be carried forward somehow.

Perhaps part of the way to paying it back is to love other people the best you can, passing it on the way songs are.

At that point the idea that I would be starting again other than by myself seemed impossible. Perhaps though the decision to do it, to say something had ended, seemed to make a new thing happen. In any event over that summer of 1990, with a new decade well underway, I met up again with Jo whom I'd worked with and known intermittently over the previous ten years, and who, as in the Paris time, was also absolutely involved with someone else, but that too was going wrong. If I'd been given away, now I was being claimed. Only Love Can Break Your Heart the high-pitched, whiney but tremendously moving Neil Young had sung in the little Richmond Hill eyrie 20 years before. It was true, but fortunately what made you sick could also, like Sixties alchemy, make you well. What else could heal your heart but love?

Towards the end of the year, in the week I was going to move out of my marital home, (accidentally, but bizarrely on the day after my wife's birthday,) Margaret Thatcher resigned in an example of symbolism that couldn't have been more apt. If further proof that the times were a' changin' were required this was certainly it. If you believed that all decades are decades of change, the proof, personal and general, was going to be plentiful. The 1990s were underway and now, definitely, the 1980s and its figurehead, were over. I was in a relationship that was going to save me but that didn't immediately mean doubts and pain were over. Marriage break-ups, like wounds, cause grief and confusion. But I was started into a direction that was going to take me somewhere new.

Bob Dylan, by contrast, was investigating the past twice over. The success of his last album of his own songs, produced to a level he wasn't normally accustomed to by Daniel Lanois, was two years behind him. He'd followed it with a scrappier affair, Under The Red Sky, where the songs seemed to be left overs, or throwaways, or reworkings of nursery rhymes, recorded piecemeal over a long period, with a shifting cast of walk-on people adding their tiny contributions. Some people preferred the result of this looser arrangement, not made under Lanois's very identifiable sonic imposition, finding it more enjoyable and, regardless of drawbacks, more authentically Bob Dylan. For the moment however he seemed to have given up on writing, or writing had given up on him. Acknowledging this he released an album of American and English traditional and folk songs, the kind he had been doing in the sections of his shows when the band moved away and it was only him for two or three numbers. The album was called Good As I Been To You, and consisted of the old songs, him, his guitar and harmonica, as it had been when he started out. The problem was he had to do it with the voice he had now, not the one he'd had at the time he started out.

Around the same time the idea that had underlain Biograph, of making a collection that was more than a greatest hits because it included songs not previously heard, whether because they were from live shows or from takes not used on albums, was taken to a level of richness that showed how long it had been in the planning. It seemed to mark his 30 years with Columbia, and also his now being 50 years old. The Bootleg Series, volumes 1 to 3, a rather confusing title that simply meant there were 3 discs in the box, was a masterstroke not by Bob Dylan but by Jeff Rosen, the man whose title is vague but who seems to be responsible for running the business that is Bob Dylan. Having seen how bootlegs were essential to Dylan fans, he acknowledged it by using the resources that bootleggers wouldn't have access to, in, of course, first generation quality. 30 years of Bob Dylan, but not the Bob Dylan that most people knew. There were rarities the most assiduous collector of Trade Mark of Quality albums, or the copied and passed on cassettes, didn't have; some whose very existence had been doubted. Farewell Angelina was present, a song there had never previously been proof that he had even recorded, and whose appearance was equivalent to someone finding a Shakespeare sonnet in William's own hand. 3 discs of songs that hadn't been included on albums, or were different versions of those that had, or were live recordings, all to show the range of what he had done in writing and singing over his life so far. For Telegraph people a major excitement was that our own John Bauldie had written informative background notes on each song for the booklet included with the package, an acknowledgement from the inner Bob sanctum of the importance of our enterprise.

For everyone, Telegraph subscriber, fan, or passer-by that happened to come across this boxed set, what it allowed, if he had ever been to your taste at all, was an appreciation of Bob Dylan's greatness as a singer. Inevitably this led to a comparison with his latest album, where his voice sounds like he looks on the cover, rough-edged and rheumy, the shape of tunes discernible as if through cross-hatchings of vocal cords. Inevitably too, with Jeff Rosen's Series meaning exactly that, further instalments and periods of time being prepared, Bob

Dylan's career now existed on parallel tracks. He was always assured of respect and praise for the shadow Bootleg life, while performances on his Never Ending tour, and responses to a current album were always likely, with good cause, to be grudging. Struck by the success, and the imitation and co-option of illegality by The Man, bootleggers hit back. A beautiful, plush and luxurious package of 3 other discs of other, non-official Bob cast-aside gems, from recording sessions or live shows, and again covering the whole of his career to date, and also with an informative booklet lavish with rare photographs, appeared under the title The Genuine Bootleg Series. You think you can steal our thunder, it seemed to say, just see what we can do. And this too promised to be a continuing enterprise, always more of the past's treasures to discover. Of Bob's past riches there seemed to be no end.

CHAPTER TWENTY-SIX
FANTASY AND TRICK OF FAME

By contrast I'd started again and my mind imagined it as a drive through a town where there's a main street that you know well, the shops are familiar, but then the road lifts up a hill to a plateau and a roundabout, and then you see that there's another part of the town. Now you're going down the other side of the hill into unfamiliar territory, town Part 2. That's where I was travelling. I was with someone, Jo, who saw me differently and valued me differently. I had the chance to be, depending on the way you viewed it, a new, perhaps different, person; or to become again the me who was always present, but had been overlaid by the need to be in tune with my first wife and the way she related to the world.

RE-RUNS

There was a long-gone segment of NYPD Blue
when it used to feature wannabe film star David Caruso,
the partly Irish-American actor who
years before played a Shamrock on the previous top cop show

Hill St Blues – the Shamrocks being a murderous
teen gang of guess what nationality?
This shared presence, foxy with greased, ferrous
oxide hair, sharp nose questing the Naked City

for spoils or clues, separated by a decade
more or less, seemed a semiotic sign
that progress of some kind was being made.
And his detective, same surname as me, said a line

that has played in my mind ever since.
Asked by some concerned girl if he was happy
he paused, eyes and mouth pursed to a wince.
No, he said, but he felt eligible now. He could be

if ever the circumstances were right.
Now another decade or so keeps now and then apart,
and all the husbands and wives are still fighting the good fight,
trying to be true citizens of the heart,

reviewing their lives like they happened on TV,
channel hopping between happiness, unhappiness and eligibility.

I had a chance to start again. For Bob Dylan, as he had made clear, the past was close behind. Having made one album of old songs, he did another along the same lines, this one being called, intriguingly, World Gone Wrong. Between the two he had given a long interview to the songwriters' journal Song Talk, in which he alluded to his not writing, or not being able to write, new songs by saying it wouldn't matter if no more songs were written. There were already enough songs in the world. As if to prove it scads more of the sessions that produced the Basement Tapes appeared on their covert cassettes, copied and passed on amongst the fans. There were many more songs than had previously been known or released, officially or unofficially, increasing the ways one could speculate about them and spin out articles. I wrote quite a long one myself.

None of this was new, and this shift away from what he was usually valued for – his ability to write – didn't uplift Telegraph people necessarily, though we thought that he needed people like us doing what we did, making it clear for civilians to whom he was a name and not much more. So there we would be when the Never Ending tour swung by Hammersmith Odeon, swapping one Broadway for another, meeting up in the bar of the Novotel, knowing that reassuring, odd feeling of being surrounded by the same faces, people who are involved in the same thing and who briefly gather down at the front at the end of the show. Sometimes I felt that this is what it must have been like to be a Yul Brynner admirer attending one of the performances of The King & I which were his sinecure in the last years of his life. Not that one could be unaware when a Bob Dylan show was terrible. Or at least, I couldn't. Others seemed to find it easy enough.

Amongst the Telegraph crowd I'd become a heretic, foremost among those who found him disappointing, or worse, wilfully wrong-headed and wasteful as he growled and grumbled through the grind of a concert, insulated, apparently, from normal perception of how he sounded. But if Bob Dylan was a role model in any way at all his mission had been to tell you to see what was in front of you as accurately as you could. This put me at odds with people who will always, whatever the current state of Bob's voice and performance, say he is singing better than ever. But I'd sat there, and more exhaustingly when it became a fad for people to stand throughout an entire show, stood there, when he had been beyond parody, laughable and indefensible. It made the toes curl. It made me very sad. Whether it was an excess of drink, cigarettes or concerts, or some kind of deliberate choice on his part, the expression, the tone I'd loved, had disappeared. The power he'd had to reach out and touch you with a fingertip was no longer present. Sometimes it was as if someone who was intermittently Bob Dylan was up there, going through the perpetual motions. The audience didn't connect to him. The songs, for the most part, didn't connect to him. All that mattered was getting through the time. It was as if the creativity of his spirit was blinded by sleep, the treadmill of the touring he elected to persist in. In Biograph, he says, "Sometimes you feel like a club fighter ... he punches his way through 10 rounds ... vomits up the pain in a back room ... and gets back on the bus, heading out for another nowhere ..."

What was surprising and wonderful about World Gone Wrong was that it seemed that he knew all of this. The distance and the decline, what he had been and what he was, the value of songs and singing, all of it was present or alluded to in this collection, particularly because he added sleeve notes on what the songs meant, or appeared to mean to him. And now when he seemed so far from 1965 and 1966 the colour cover of the album, so much more interesting than Good As I Been To You, had him appear in a top hat, his face once more halved by light and shade. The song notes too were in Tarantula's style precisely, so much so that sections written decades apart could be placed next to each other and look identical, even to subject matter. He may not have been able to write songs but there was nothing wrong with his verbal facility as such.

it means nothing so wear a top hat – travel on a slow ship back to your guilt, your pollution, the kingdom of your blues.

the roar of our engines promises us love – we wear choking pants and are a slave to appetite.

mystery on the rails – the train of love, the train that carried my girl from town – The Southern Pacific, Baltimore & Ohio whatever.

Delia, who's called Debra when she walks around in her nurse's uniform, she casts off pure light in the cellar & has principles.

Delia herself, no Queen Gertrude, Elizabeth I or even Evita Peron, doesn't ride a Harley Davidson across the desert highway, doesn't need a blood change & would never go on a shopping spree.

He had wanted to be a performer when he was a rock and roll teen-ager but circumstances meant he lost his heart to folk and traditional songs and started to be noticed there. But, as he said, it was because he sang folk with a rock attitude that he was noticed. Then he began to write and before he knew it was pegged as a certain kind of writer and person, someone concerned with social and political issues. He'd become that cartoon a protest singer. He'd started with a dream, but dreams have the potential to become traps. Weary, flat, stale and unprofitable as Hamlet at that point he went to the past, as he had done many times, as he was doing right now with this album, but he had remade his 1950s rock and roll past with the kind of songs he began to write, free from overt issues, and the band he gathered about him. Now with this new album of ancient songs, an album whose title seems the very summary of a protest stance, with sleeve notes in the Tarantula style, he was again making something old his own. He was passing on stories compacted and compressed into a few verses, the outline of a journey we all take, looming behind the darkness always waiting beyond lamplight, the experience of rooms and seasons changing.

In concert Bob's rough and gruff shadowing of traditional tunes left shreds and shapes of melody rising like spirits from the creased textures of his voice. In a recording studio he could bring a closer and more careful sound, tender, intimate and conveying much emotion. Delia is a long song, and much of it is repetition of the chorus, whose most affecting line is "All the friends I ever had are gone". He sings the line many times. Each time it's different. In his voice one hears, passing through, shifting, modulating, like a parade of ghosts, bewil-derment, pride, awe, regret, compassion, hurt, acceptance, blankness, all of it achieved with the tiniest movement of tones, silences, pauses within the syllable, the guitar too sometimes lapsing into silence. On The Lone Pilgrim, a song about dying and the necessity for belief in a better world than this one, he breathes it more than sings it, like a hymn, confession, and a prayer at bedtime. He makes the words resonate in your imagination, even in his raspy, cracked and frazzled vocal state. "And kindly assisted me home," is the last line, and on "home", the album's last word, he brings many resonances to what it might mean: the sweetness of childhood's location, the comfort of Heaven, the resting place of the grave.

World Gone Wrong was inescapably about mortality and growing old, death being its constant backdrop. But the experience of the album was heartening rather than depressing. The reason why was the control it exhibited, the fact that it seemed a coherent, whole, artistic experience made by someone who within his new, restricted vocal range was still able to conjure the ability to make a song true, and to make its truth matter to a listener. It seemed to me that his future lay in records and what he could do with their attention to fine details. It was clear however that he thought the point of being a performer was to be out there performing. This had its excitements, but for the most part, though the spirit could fly in the moment of creation, the result could be broad, crude, misguided or bizarre on various levels. The album lifted your heart with the knowledge that he was still a real artist capable of great work, what might he do next? The answer emerged day by day, the way we lived our lives. He kept on doing what he did, and no new albums were made, and I had my new life and happiness to think about. There were always bootleg cassettes and CDs to consider. Some of these things I reviewed, some I only thought about.

And before we knew it was 1996, which as John Bauldie pointed out to me at the end of 1995, in pursuit of an article, would mean soon it would be 30 years since, well, everything: the mad rock tour, Blonde On Blonde, the whole Bob deal. The Telegraph had to take note of this situation. There had been a time when being a fan of music, and therefore usually a teenager, had had nothing at all to do with noting the generation of anniversaries. Now it seemed inescapably linked. We'd somehow become involved with notation and statistics, like a branch of Wisden. I started writing what became a long piece in the Spring. That summer Jo and I had the chance to go to New York because we had enough money, and wanted to see it together, and now too we could visit John Platt who lived there with his American wife. He'd experienced a Bob Dylan fairy tale too, travelling from suburban South West London to the country where what he dreamed and wrote about had happened. He'd gone to New York, like George Segal in The Owl and the Pussycat. He actually lived on the street in Greenwich Village where the Lovin' Spoonful's John Sebastian had been brought up, as well as where John Lennon had had an apartment when first moving to New York: the Village that had a domain in all of our imaginations. I wrote my fantasy/memory/Ron Bobfan character piece at home, and there, and at home again, making notes and changing things as people gave me useable words and reactions. And it went into that late Summer's Telegraph, then at its glossiest and thickest, marking 30 years that had evaporated in a way that moment by moment seemed inexplicable. How could it be so, and how could we be the age we were? How did we get here?

There's always disappointment after a big article appears that you believe you have poured everything into. The reaction is never what you expect or want. A few friends may be nice, but you realise the vast majority of people, even these self-selected subscribing Bob Dylan fans, read what's in the magazine and have no desire to comment on it. Weeks elapsed. Autumn approached. The writing of the article seemed distant now, but not so distant as World Gone Wrong, and still no new album, although hearts had quickened with the appearance of the most highly praised bootleg CD for awhile. Guitars Kissing & The Contemporary Fix, a title using a Tarantula section heading, was a 2 disc representation, the acoustic and electric halves, of the 1966 concert most bootlegged in the early 1970s, called The Royal Albert Hall, but apparently in reality recorded in the Free Trade Hall Manchester. Why it was of extra significance was because in addition to being the best bootleg sound quality available, it was supposed to derive from Columbia's tapes, a preparation for the next instalment of the Bootleg Series. So the most famous absence was about to be corrected. This seemed of a piece with 30 years disappearing too. No-one would have believed that it would take 3 decades for a record company to release something that was so obviously important, or that an artist's own reluctance might be behind it.

As it turned out the official 1966 Bootleg Series didn't appear that year, Columbia being piqued perhaps by the bootleg version's emergence, and so the world missed out a while longer. What did come back into focus for me was World Gone Wrong's tender and apocalyptic intimations of mortality. There was a helicopter crash and all the people on it died. It had been travelling back from a football match, a helicopter commissioned by a millionaire football club owner to take him and his friends to see an away game. John Bauldie loved football probably more than he loved Bob Dylan. He had said that if he was forced to choose he would have to choose football and forego Bob. He had been one of the millionaire's friends and so, like a thunderbolt, he died and for a time it seemed that everything had changed. We were only separated by a month in age and I had come to think of him as a smarter and more worldly-wise version of me. Through him I had come to see that I had views about Bob Dylan, and not just teenage memories, although the views were inescapably formed there. These views were capable of being spun out into words and John gave me the space to write as many as I wanted. Where else would I have been able to write 14,000 words in a kind of meditation on what it meant to be a Bob Dylan fan 30 years after Blonde On Blonde, refracting what I knew of myself and him through a jokey character name whose intent was entirely serious. Now, a friend pointed out, it had become an involuntary memorial for him, concerning as it did all John and I knew about Bob Dylan, and concluding with the protagonist listening to I'm Not There, a song that had surfaced from the enlarged, and not officially released, Basement Tape sessions, and something John had written and lectured on, whose title now was all too apt.

Everything had changed, I told Jo through tears, nothing would be the same now.

Of course this turned out to be true and not true. You are the same person and have the same character, but something has gone from you and possibilities have closed down. Distance had meant that in a time before widespread email John and I had always been phone friends, but in the last year he had moved from Essex to Richmond, not far away. Of course we may have remained mainly phone friends and not become visiting friends, but proximity had at least made it feasible, and it had happened. It could never happen again. I thought about David Blue whom John had liked very much, using him rather than Bob as a model for his own attempts at guitar playing and songwriting; and how on David Blue's unexpectedly, ridiculously, early death John had put his photograph on the cover of the next Telegraph, unprecedented and unrepeated. The Telegraph too, even with various stalwart helpers, was inescapably his vision and creation. It was unthinkable without him. There were more tears to come. At John's funeral, instead of hymns or other expected funeral choices, a selection of his favourite records were chosen. Because he liked a range of people these weren't all Bob Dylan, but one of them was Mr Tambourine Man, the version we all knew from the album Bringing It All Back Home, released in 1965 when he and I had both been 16. I cried throughout, feeling that the song, every sound and nuance of it known so well, went through my life like an embroidery stitch. Later, talking with fellow mourners, peculiarly cheered, an effect funerals have, we started almost a parlour game of what songs we would want played as people watched the coffin leave. "Mr. Tambourine Man, yes," said novelist, screenwriter and Bob fan Nigel Hinton, "but which version?" And we thought about all the early and late ones that existed out there on the cassettes and CDs and coloured vinyl. I thought too of Lorraine Ellison's great single Stay With Me Baby, the definition of a one-hit wonder, but of such quality it was inexplicable that she hadn't had sustained success. Her great, lavish, tearing, extreme exposure of loss and grief was a wonderful record but, I recognised, might be cruel for any mourners to deal with.

The death of friends of your age makes you think about death, but also the pattern of life, what you have done and what you might do. In the manner of the old songs on World Gone Wrong, and the older ballads Bob Dylan had started out with, there were elemental details in the intertwining sequence of our foreground and background lives. In 1964's Hollis Brown Bob had sung of seven people dead on a South Dakota farm, and in the distance seven new people being born. The year after John's death Bob Dylan had a brush with an illness that had the possibility of being fatal, and was also distinctly American. It was called histoplasmosis, caused by fungal spores found along the Ohio and Mississippi river valleys. The swelling and inflammation of the pericardial sac around the heart gave symptoms like TB or pneumonia, and though being treatable with antibiotics and anti-fungal drugs caused pain and distress severe enough for anyone to think they might die. On leaving hospital Dylan famously remarked that for awhile he had thought he was about to meet Elvis.

Before his illness he had been preparing a new album, resuming his earlier collaboration with Daniel Lanois. His hospital treatment had focused people's minds on what it might be lost if he weren't around anymore, and so the range of what he had achieved, and the distance we had all travelled, was still part of assessing what a new album would mean. Although it had been written and recorded some time before the illness, its bleak subject matter was as if he too had been considering death and the absence of purpose. The songs are about love going wrong, and more than love going wrong. Nothing gives pleasure, no enterprise is worth tackling, and yet what else can he do but keep on keeping on. The sound was as if almost a decade had been skipped and the electrically-mutated air that conveyed Oh Mercy, altering voice and instruments, was in use again. It's an air thick with mortality and the sense of growing old, with all the regrets that gives access to.

Though this was a return to a producer and his idiosyncratic sound there was something new going on. The songs he had written had stopped being ambitious in an obviously literary way. His approach had changed. Throughout the album songs are studded with well-known words or phrases, some from common speech, some literary, as if universal terms of reference can express his personal poetry. "You got the silver, you got the gold," he says, along with "That's all right mama." He quotes an old joke, "I'm looking for a janitor to sweep me off my feet." What hadn't changed was his ability to sing a song, even with this changed voice, in a way that touched you. His own song Not Dark Yet had everything that he had brought to The Lone Pilgrim., an evocation of mystery and meaning, almost entirely based on the sound of his voice: not bitter, accepting, grained with regret. His voice sounds like smoke looks, disintegrating from white to blue. The melody, the loveliness, is in the micro adjustments of tone and emotion. The hairs on your neck prickle a little. "It's not dark yet, but it's getting there"; and his voice falls gently on "there", and you know he's talking about more than the sky.

It was from this point that Bob Dylan's star began to rise again. The Bootleg Series recommenced with the Live 1966 double set, along with booklet, and reviews were ecstatic. Everyone now knew what previously had been privileged to the thousands of insiders. This, along with the thought that it wasn't inconceivable that he could die, and that he was capable of producing an album of original songs so good that it won not one Grammy but many, selling more than he had for years, marked a change. He was engaged in something that might look the same from the outside but was now a revitalised enterprise. So were we. In the summer of the year, against various odds and somewhat unexpectedly, Jo became pregnant, giving us a different stake in the future and drawing forceful comparisons between death and life. More verses were to be added to the ballad we were living out, and that autumn we merged them with Bob's tour arrangements. We chose to go to Bournemouth for the weekend to see him at the

Conference Centre there, not far from the seaside theatre decked out
with posters for the Sixties Revival tour of a gang of erstwhile B List
top pop beat groups that had been rounded up and wheeled out to
go through those 30 year old Top Ten hits one more time for several
nights in a row. That was an instructive contrast to what Bob is always
up to. At the end of the show he did something that changed my way
of regarding him. He'd finished the last encore. He walked off to the
back of the stage. He had a jacket whose sleeves were way too long and
as he turned to disappear he jiggled his wrist within them slightly, in
a gesture I interpreted as one of signing off, a "that's another one over
with" movement. With that and his height and his posture, stiff and
remote, he looked like a little old workman, a plumber say, someone
hired to do a job of work, putting in the time and occasionally making a standout effort, but mostly getting through what had to be done
as professionally, which is to say as impersonally, as possible.

The next year, in February, the bump that had shared Bob's concert emerged to share our world, revealing himself in all his minute
individuality as Louis, one of the names we had considered if we had
a boy – having tried hard not to know the gender beforehand – and
somehow declaring to us that that's who he was. Even people who
think they aren't religious are forced to consider what existence means
when a baby appears. Thinking about sperm and eggs and gestation
doesn't seem adequate when faced with the specific and there quality
of that small package of flesh and character who wasn't in the world
and now most assuredly is.

My blue-eyed boy, not figuratively
but absolutely. Not the passing hue
of babies: a fixed and permanent blue
clarity, wide-open, looking at me

unsullied by knowledge or subterfuge
or anything which is not as it seems.

His eyes find me, pure and simple gleams
of light and mystery, clear and huge

and endless, looking out into my face.
One sea-blue, sky-blue iris flecked with brown,
a tiny inlay like a skew-whiff crown,
brown and blue and white, like the world from space.

Heart-shaped, world shaped, his face opens a grin,
toothless and sincere. His merry eyes
sparkle with the novelty of surprise
occasioned by the face above my chin.

An Atlas, I raise him to my shoulder,
holding my own, my sea-and-sky-eyed son,
symbol and actual, my darling one
growing with the days that turn us older.

As a death can make you feel that everything is irrevocably changed, so too can a birth. And in the same way it is true and not true. You are still the person you were, with all those flaws and merits, but now you are opened up because more than simply another person, you have another life to consider, a life you will shape knowingly and unknowingly. Now you have the chance to be a better person. Not that it was something I considered at the moment of Louis's birth, but it turned out that both Bob Dylan and I were beginning a new productive era in our lives. Moving to part-time hours to help take care of Louis, to be around him and see him grow, I found that I had the subject matter for poems. I was opened up to what I felt and saw in this daytime world away from work, the realm of love and parks and seasons and time. I had written a poem Sundial 20 years previously, and now I saw how a child was like a sundial too, their height markers on bedroom walls always showing us where we are.

Of course we still behave as if each night helping children achieve sleep only counts towards their tally of years and not ours. Meanwhile Bob Dylan was a sundial and a mirror, inevitably showing where we were, but also how time had changed us and him.

With the next decade underway he released another album. His wave of acclaim following illness and the Grammys, and an Oscar-winning song called prophetically, Things Have Changed, was still potent. Having previously had years of not being of great importance to anyone outside of a relatively small circle of friends, his status as a national icon was newly reasserted. But again the birth of something new coincided with death. John Platt having achieved the life he had wanted was not allowed to enjoy it very long. He contracted cancer, whose effects were slow to appear, but then speeded dramatically, and he died in May of 2001. I remembered our first meeting and the long-gone lunch café; how he'd loved the Grateful Dead and Love and that mythical California sunshine, but felt blessed to be ensconced in New York, New York. Someone I had known off and on, near and far, for 30 years, and I thought how like fiction it would have been at that first lunch for either of us to imagine his living and working in Greenwich Village, curating film festivals, writing books and TV programmes. How inconceivable that I would be writing his Guardian obituary, as I had for John Bauldie too, fearing that a millionaire might obscure him. In an odd and fitting coincidence worthy of Anthony Powell, the duty obituary editor was Penny Valentine, light years from the radiance she had once brought me, helping to say farewell to an era she had been such an important part of. Why them, and why me left behind to tell a small tale? I thought how not only a 30-years-ahead future is unknowable, but even the next day, the next moment. Who knows what's lying in wait or about to emerge. When I rang his widow, Mary Lou, sometimes I would get the answer machine, and still hear his cheerful voice asking me to leave a message, because, she explained later, she didn't feel she could delete him yet. She told me too that all of the music he had spent his life listening to, thinking about, writing about, lost its appeal. In the end times he lay listening to BBC comedy programmes on the World Service, or the birdsong he could hear out of the window.

LIVE/DEAD

i.m. John Platt 1952-2001

If I ring the transatlantic number
of his apartment I will hear his voice,
upbeat, as if nothing could encumber
his good cheer; as if there was no choice

other than optimism in this world
where messages greet an absentee's return.
I hear him now, telephone wire curled
about my finger, knowing there's more to learn

about finding someone not there, knowing
we are kept apart by more than an ocean,
remembering laughter and hours flowing
through beats per second, music in motion.

Now you are forever changed and always gone
I keep composing messages to leave.
You lived and loved half a world away John
and I still think of you there. I believe

you live in music we share, words in my head,
when I'm in the presence of Love and the Dead.

Other deaths had a world-wide repercussion. Only a few months after John's death Bob Dylan's new album was set for release on September

11th 2001, the day the planes hit the Twin Towers. What it was to be American or anti-American became an urgent topic. Coincidentally, the subject of his album was intimately related to being an American. Musically and lyrically Bob Dylan looted, plundered, reworked made over and alluded to all kinds of American musical styles, while extending his magpie lyric method used on Time Out Of Mind, taking wholesale, or minimally adapting, words from all kinds of literary and other sources everywhere. He made his manifesto fairly clear when he puts into one of the songs the Gatsby quote, Can't repeat the past, why of course you can. On Bob Dylan sites the song words and all their provenances were tirelessly tracked and noted. Listening to the album however, a duty that the DJ John Peel wisely noted could not be "accelerated or delegated", I found its reality separate from the one in the intense considerations of fan sites.

There were two broad groups into which the songs fell and both were exceptionally well-produced and played. One was blues-based riffs and patterns; the other was softer, slower, slyer pastiches of 20s or 30s tunes that seemed to have Bing Crosby or Hoagy Carmichael as subliminal presences. There were also, as the fan sites showed, lots of words. The odd thing from my point of view was that no matter how much interest these might have onscreen, or how they might be analysed as to indications about Bob Dylan's sensibility now, such analysis would only be writing about writing and not their existence as songs. When listening to the album the words became subordinate to the overall sound produced on each track. This seemed to be a result of two things. One was his voice making it tricky to be precise about what the words were, especially on the energetic bluesy songs, where he pushes too hard, and his catarrhal crackle sounds as if actual flesh might tear. The other was that because the words had an assembled character rather than being written out of an individual, they lacked, for me, a personal touch. That seemed to be his intention. The sons were anthologies rather than testaments. By taking from old jokes, old songs, old books perhaps he wanted to show that everyone has a similar experience, what's universal is personal too. The cost of this is that nothing, even if there are great lines and deadpan humour, (*My father was a travelling salesman, I never met him*), can move you with what you take to be the autobiographically-based, experienced truth of Not Dark Yet. Songs could go by and I would have no clear idea what they were about, or whether I'd just heard a joke or not, or whether Bob Dylan cared one way or the other. The words weren't the point it seemed. Making the *music* was Bob Dylan's purpose now, American continent music, losing himself in the band and what it could do. This seemed to require the dissolving of the characteristics of the artist we thought constituted Bob Dylan, and changing our expectations of his song writing.

CHAPTER TWENTY-SEVEN

DEFINITELY UNFAMILIAR & VAGUELY RECOGNIZABLE

As you watch a child grow you see the shape and form before you, the way a face will change as teeth and hair make themselves known, as they grow and walk. But you remember their earlier incarnations, or compare them in photographs, knowing that this person, this little human, is the same as the one who once could fit along your arm from elbow to wrist. They will always be changing but you will think of them as the same essential individual. If you're a Bob Dylan fan this has its symbolic aspect, and you've already received some useful training. Like a fish inhabits water a Dylan fan lives in the world of comparisons, aware of the past and where we now are, trying sometimes to imagine the album after next. Children, obviously, are always a link with the past and the future, the past that doesn't exist except in you, the future that can only be imagined and wished for. The Telegraph had died but a new and similar magazine now replaced it. This gave the opportunity to be a father to a toddler, then a little schoolboy, then a taller one, while plaiting together the writing of poems and Bob Dylan articles at a time when he was in one of the most productive and praised times of his career. I was aware of this, though also discovering for myself that old songs I thought I knew could speak with a newly revealed truth or authority simply because my situation had changed. I spent some time thinking about

Forever Young but more time playing Young But Daily Growing, a traditional English song transplanted to America, also known as The Trees They Do Grow High, a lovely arresting title and first line reminding me of those that grew and arched in the lane behind our school. It was a song that non-official bootlegs revealed had been captured for us to enjoy 3 times. Two of his versions came from the early 1960s, before he was even protest Bob Dylan; one was from the enlarged Basement Tape. No version was sung with precisely the same words though of course they were similar, none of them delivered in quite the same way; none ever studio-recorded or officially released.

What the song demonstrated to me, by insinuating itself into my thoughts, – its words, tune and the texture of his voice, particularly his voice in the version he sings into a friend's home tape recorder back in Minneapolis in the May of 1961, – was how the traditional, the ancient, can be as contemporary as each dawn. What the song is about, aside perhaps from child marriage in mediaeval times, is how fast time can seem to pass, or how there can be left-over oceans of it that you're marooned in. And it's about the constant presence and possibility of death confiscating what is precious to you. If you're a new parent these subjects are never far from waking considerations. Meanwhile, as revealed in the latest biography, with new details acquired from court records and published the year of "Love And Theft"'s release, this wouldn't have been a revelation to Bob Dylan. He was grandfather to some, father of many, married more than once, and in and out of relationships.

"Love And Theft" showed what would be the template musically in forthcoming new releases, but the Bootleg Series also continued, highlighting former glories and incarnations, – a Philadelphia Halloween from 1964, a shuffling together of Rolling Thunder from 1975, – with their illustrated explanatory booklets. But as I watched the days add up into a decade, measuring the months in changing shoe sizes and outgrown toys, the Bob Dylan brand was diversifying.

Books of photographs taken in previous times were published, one by John Cohen, one by Douglas Gilbert, both reminding us how striking he had been to look at, and reminding us too that whether they are artfully arranged or snapped on the fly, grave, beautiful, profound, throwaway, pointless, disappointing, misleading, photographs are always about themselves. This world, the one where they are taken, no matter how it seems mired in boredom and endless repetition, is forever one of flow. Youth is always leaving, age is always arriving, and we look at photographs of ourselves and others in the way we regard the cards or a crystal ball, seeking clues. No matter how appealing his photographs may be however, what Bob Dylan is about is fundamentally at variance with them. Photographs are a dumb show of silence and stasis; the live show of performance is evanescence and movement. Moments aren't frozen: they dissolve or evaporate on the fountainhead of the spring they rise from and ride upon. You can make notes. You can record it. You can get hypnotised to recall every last detail and the order in which they appeared. And none of it will ever come back again, and what you have captured in whatever format, labelled with dates and places, will not allow the re-experience of the flow that unreeled before you and came to an end.

Not that this stops him from trying his hand at other artistic endeavours. A book of drawings he had published back in the 1990s, the world as pencilled by a touring musician, became, when encouraged by a German gallery owner, the basis for paintings achieved by colouring in these outlines in different ways. An exhibition followed, and eventually another book, this time of those paintings beautifully printed and produced. Soon the paintings seemed to be on their own tour, popping up in galleries large and small in different countries, allowing reaction to move between the two poles of, He's a charlatan, or, They're a refreshing change.

He wrote a book of memoirs, Chronicles Volume One, a title promising more to come, and had an unexpected critical and popular success with his apparent photographic-memory command of detail, and lavishly personal tone. He co-wrote, pseudonymously, a feature film called, very characteristically, Masked & Anonymous, and starred in it with a slew of well-known faces. There was also a huge documentary directed by Martin Scorsese, called No Direction Home. This skilfully and evocatively blended still photographs, all kinds of old footage, and music, and interviews, not only with Bob Dylan but also the musicians and characters who had been part of his story. It had clearly been in preparation for years awaiting artful assembly, and was another aspect of the purpose animating the Bootleg Series. The intention was to alter people's perception of what Bob Dylan meant, what in terms of soft drinks or magazines would be called shifting the market position. It did much more than that, succeeding beautifully, being a picture of a gone American world that could interest people who may never have been Bob Dylan fans. For those who were the riches were without end, all of the film never seen of the 1966 tour, Bob and the Hawks in his mad, wired, shouting splendour in colours as vivid and bright as stained glass.

One of his most successful performances was also as unexpected as him writing a memoir. He became a radio dj for an American sat-ellite station, but by the magic of the internet and the expertise of obsessives, the shows rapidly became downloadable zip folders, and then homemade CDs, and soon were out there in the world well beyond the range of the original radio station subscribers. The shows were called Theme Time Radio Hour, allowing each show to have records that had some connection with whatever the subject might be (Cars, Dreams, Night California) along with snippets of old radio ads, film dialogue, telephone calls, corny jokes and deadpan summaries of factual information, either about recording artists, or aspects of the subject in hand. The conceit of the enterprise was that it recre-ated what a radio station might have been like in the mythical 1950s, beaming out at night from Studio 2 in the fictitious Abernathy Building, Downtown USA., the kind, in fact, that had meant so much to Bob Dylan when he was a teenager. You couldn't say that he had a natural ease reading things out, but you could say that everything about his voice and delivery, awkward and stiff though it could be, was attention-grabbing. If you ever wondered why he couldn't sing as he used to, listening to his speaking voice made all clear, though clear was not the word that sprang to mind to describe it: so mannered, so much calling attention to itself while studiously ignoring how odd it might appear, a dandy's hip joke, as cracked and black as the shellac that appeared to be the source for much of the music. There was the definite suggestion that his voice was like a physical phenomenon rather than existing as vibrations in the air, the way it produced the hallucination of some physical thing, like wood, or charcoal would be a closer comparison, a sweet core but eroded, all kinds of damage flaking and wearing away at the edges, all crackles and abrasion.

It became clear too that the show was a working model of Bob Dylan as an artist now. In creating illusory Fifties radio it was as modern as it could be. Everything was a collage of taped or digital sounds made by different people at different times and places. His own contributions might be taped anywhere on his tours with only a playlist in his hand. Then, assembled later to give the illusion of one time and one place, we had the fictitious or pseudonymous staff; his between disc capsule histories of performers, written by diverse hands, often Wikipedia contributors; strands of music commenting on a mood; and the comforting, rich tones of the final announcer crediting all the diverse hands involved in its creation over Top Cat's theme, which for me was a Madeleine cake all by itself. Everything was an exact analogue of the way "Love And Theft" had been made, an anthology the guiding principle. His presence was what gave everything its authority. The tone was that of a jokey, sly, grandpappy who'd been around the block, but as he was one who'd changed the course of popular music during the last half century, we listened that bit more receptively because these records were his choice and his enthusiasms.

But were they? The question merged with similar considerations. There had always been latitude about the authorship of songs, even if some people fell foul of legal action in taking someone's tune without

credit. Bob Dylan came from the folk and blues world where ownership was often blurred or imprecise because tunes were recycled to
give a starting point for something new, and blues verses existing as
a floating cache to be taken from and put into some other context.
It was only with the advent of Google, and its digitisation of thousands of books, thus allowing rapid searching for words and phrases
in all those texts, that it became possible readily to check if they
were original or not. I have no idea why anyone began to check up on
Chronicles, probably because their own memory showed that some
of its striking phrases came from elsewhere. In any event further
checking was now easily done. So I came across blog evidence of the
widespread and systematic interpolation of passages from all kinds of
authors – Jack London, Robert Louis Stevenson, Sax Rohmer, Mezz
Mezzrow, a 1959 New York Guide book – that Bob had carefully
stitched and embedded in what was supposed to be his memoir, and
was surprised and shocked, and further surprised by my own surprise.

There were a couple of reasons for it. One was that I had loved
Chronicles for what I took to be its *personal* idiosyncrasy. These revelations made me feel foolish and cheated. The point about Chronicles
and its style, –heightened, artificial, self-conscious, extravagant, moving between a poetic representation and what appeared to be a more
deliberately artless, homespun, clichéd usage, – was that you wondered how much was true and how much improved upon. I found
that I could accept that in pursuit of a larger truth he might exagger-
ate, but that this was quite distinct from copying out other people's
words and passing them off as your life. His attitude to songs – that
he could be a vehicle through which assemblages would pass and
thus become his – seemed now to apply to all he wrote, including
Chronicles and Masked & Anonymous. Whether the thoughts and
fine phrases he used originated with him seemed to have become
irrelevant. As he had sung in I Shall Be Free No. 10 from far off
1964, but also ever since, "It ain't no good talking to me, it's the
same as talking to you," as if this was a democracy where everyone

was equal. Except of course they were still copyrighted as Bob Dylan songs because that's where the money and creative credit resided. What praise was due these days? Is being a conduit or a maker of collages worthy of the same reverence as writing Mr Tambourine Man? Apparently so in the world of American popular song. But a memoir, I found I believed quite firmly, had to be what *you* remembered of *your* life. Anyone else's words should play a minor role, and if there was reason for them to be used they should be duly credited.

There was a cloud across my appreciation of Bob Dylan now. Odd how words can change their meaning. I had come to love clouds when Lou was a baby and we went through the days together. Something about their size, movement and textures moved me in ways I couldn't always transform into words. Jet trails too seem to stand for and actually be another dimension of existence.

> except for drifts of cloud banks
> heaping against a proliferation of jet trails,
> newly minted and ancient evidence,
> thin scars of white outpourings laid down
> like tread marks, tyre tracks in the snow,
> scoring the clear and blue bell of sky,
> silently disintegrating, broad, snowy ripples
> that warp along a thermal faultline
> like a flourish under a fading signature

When you're in the world away from work, you're in the seasons and repetition, occupying the days, pushing the buggy along the streets or visiting a great park, on the way to or from daytime sleep. Park and streets will show, turn and turnabout, cherry blossom, or the fallen hulls spiked like maces that split to reveal the glossy brown burl of chestnuts within. Each season coming back again seems like a repetition, but of course is not the same, and would be different even if there was no growing child to measure it against. So you experience how repetition of the same thing changes because you change. Singers have to sing the same song, and parents have to watch the same DVD or read the same story and we are what we bring to it. It's from Lou that I learned the connection between repetition and the past and experiencing it afresh; and then saw how it related to Bob Dylan and what I already knew.

GEESE

The air and the light
tasting of the time to come,
sweet and heartbreaking.

The sky suddenly
tracked with the pattern of geese
and the noise of geese

at July's ending,
rehearsing change and return,
the oldest surprise.

"Look," I say, "darling,
look. They're geese. Can you see them?
Can you see the geese?"

And I hold him high
against the sweet mortal sky
to see their beauty,

seeing in his face
my face, and my father's face,
and the time flying.

CHAPTER TWENTY-EIGHT
DOWN WHERE ITS ROOTED

A kind of epiphany came listening to my Fabs tape in the car when he was aged around four. So recent, and yet still far enough away for tapes rather than CDs to be played, and tapes that were carefully made from records I owned, vinyl records that is, the ones that travelled down to be with us, carrying their clicks and tiny scratches with them. The Fabs, of course, are the Beatles and the albums they released in a particular time period, as people who shared it recall. It can be precisely limited to Beatles For Sale, Help and Rubber Soul, and they all fit onto the C100 rather than C90 cassette, which sounds antique now, like the years, 1964 and 65 that they are encapsulating. Before those comes the nutty upsurge of wacky Beatlemania. Afterwards is the onset of English psychedelia. So the pure heart of Fab is those albums, when every little thing they did was a kind of perfection in pop songs that sounded like nothing else previously created, and Lou could sing along to them with heartbreaking accuracy, having received no more coaching than being around in the backseat when I was playing the tape. Sometimes in the garden in the capricious warmth of the English sun I heard him quietly mouthing to himself: "You're going to lose that girl, you're going to loooose that girl." Compared to Bob songs of the same period the Fab songs are almost free of content, incapable of précis, have no poetry that an academic would recognise, but nevertheless are drenched with meaning.

That meaning is in the sound and shape of tons of guitars, in a drum-beat and silence, in the splash of cymbals, in the harmonies of three permanently young voices, in the short, odd, indelible melodies. Here are songs exactly as they were in the mid 1960s. They are repeated over and over on a tape in a car. No creative rearrangement occurs and never will occur and for Lou they existed in the here and now. Like Tom and Jerry cartoons from the 1940s, or Top Cat from 1962, that we watched leaning together on a sofa, as my dad watched with me, they have no connection with the past for him, are not a symptom of nostalgia or a yearning for earlier times. They are alive in his head every day, memorable not because they signify an earlier time, simply in and of themselves.

What's the lesson that Lou demonstrates to me? Well every day we get older and can never go back. But the things from the past can be rediscovered and have meaning without wanting to return there. For Lou everything is in the present. Rearranging a Beatles song wouldn't make it fresh for him, it's already brand new. He reminded me that it's always the present where I am. Which doesn't mean that the past is without its powers. In the next couple of years, under the Beatles spell, we went to Liverpool, wandering around the Penny Lane area, standing outside the grim gates of Strawberry Field, and booking the John and Paul houses tour, both now being National Trust properties. I hadn't expected where they came from to remind me so much of where I came from, even to Paul's council house, though not looking exactly like mine, *feeling* exactly like mine, the surrounding streets like those I walked. The rooms, the kitchen looking out on the garden, the fireplace and settee in the front room, all of it as familiar as the dreams you have when your body feels as if it will wake in the house where you were a child. Whereas John's house and situation was a reminder of the posher, private homes in Smithfield Road I'd walked past on my way to and from school. Between them the two locations were evoking the life I'd lived. In a crowd of tourists from all over the world, countries that were simply places on a map when John and Paul had lived here, or when I had been at school, I felt that I knew and understood this better than anyone present showing due awe or reverence or trooping around looking non-plussed. "You don't understand," I could feel the sentence forming in my head, "This was my life too, I lived in a place like this at the same time, exactly like this."

Melvyn Bragg once wrote a biography of Richard Burton, who came from a poverty more or less unimaginable for most of us, and moved to a luxury similarly improbable. It's not where you come from, Bragg said, but the journey you take. All over Liverpool the tag associated with the Beatles is Four Lads Who Shook The World. Being in Paul McCartney's little front room, or John Lennon's tiny bedroom, you had to think about how far they had travelled and what had propelled them. I did that, and because I recognised so intimately their beginnings, felt how fantastic what they had done was all the more. What I hadn't expected was the uprush of emotion all this released. I was in a spin for days, never far from tears it seemed, almost in the way I was when my father died. I was steeped, saturated, in memories that didn't feel like memories exactly, as if my actual tissues were loaded with them and not only my mind. And my mind was overlain with transparencies of those Liverpool streets and my streets, memories of my own childhood and what I'd imagined of theirs, what the Beatles meant as I listened and read all about them in those early days of 1962 and 1963, and what I'd thought about them ever since.

It all made me think about Bob Dylan too. I knew in my heart that although visiting any hero's childhood home would have its effect – and later I completely understood when he went to visit Neil Young's home, to stand in the bedroom, look out the window, and see what Neil had seen – in the improbable event that I ever saw it, I could never have the same reaction to Bob's house. The Beatles were part of me because their background was mine. There used to be so many associates named as The Fifth Beatle, but going to Liverpool I understood that any of us who were alive with them from the start, and came from the estates we did, might claim the status. It was odd that I'd spent decades writing and thinking about Bob Dylan, and none about the Beatles when I was capable of this reaction. It seemed that he was an external love I applied myself to, while they were an intrinsic part of my DNA. It wasn't that I wanted to live in the past; the past was alive in me and needed only to be summoned. The Beatles, as a band, could never make people feel bad because their legacy was perfected and complete. It was as later individuals that dissatisfaction set in. Bob Dylan had made people feel bad because he'd been human, because he had been going for such a long time, inevitably he'd produced bad work as well as good. That didn't matter now because he'd moved to a point where, after bleak times when the world at large hadn't cared whether he was around or not, essentially he'd become unassailable, inhabiting his various parallel worlds of recorded music, repackaged older recorded music, and the continuing tour.

Now he is seen as some kind of living museum artefact coming to a town near you, a genuine moving exhibit of musical Americana, whose reception seems to be grounded in the idea that when he goes a whole slice of musical and social history goes with him. Here plagiarism isn't seen as a debar to that status but part of it, because he is a living Magimix who blends what he sees and knows, what he's read and heard about, into a new fusion whose value is that it has issued through his nervous system and faculties. What other people have suffered and thought and loved, well so has he; and it's what you and you and you will too. That they may be other people's words is somehow a testament to the authenticity of general human experience, as well as, paradoxically, a confirmation of his personal creativity. A memoir that consists in large part of other people's words is to be regarded as a new art form, a shadow story within the one we see. Standards of judgement that might be applied to others are suspended. He becomes all the Bob Dylans there have ever been, and always referred to as an icon of the Sixties generational politics he repudiated even at the time he was acclaimed for it, immediately following the short while it seemed to be true. The odd, cranky, impenetrable, frequently disappointing performer has to be valued because of what he achieved in the past, but also because he still seems to be someone who is doing exactly what he wants on his own terms, a prickly individual genuinely not caring about what reception he gets, though apparently driven to go out and perform for audiences without connecting with them in any more relaxed way.

Praised for making things new by reinterpreting and rearranging the old repertoire, the result is that though everything will sound different from the original (except songs from the last decade where a ravaged voice can still replicate a ravaged voice) it will sound very similar to the song just played. Invariably, fans, no matter how long-term, will have trouble identifying anything from its introduction, or even long after the singing had begun. What he seems to enjoy are the bits between the singing, as if getting through the words with his bark and rasp, banging out phrases like a short-order cook, is the price he has to pay so that he and the band, – skilled, well-drilled and knowing him very well – can cut loose and make music that he gets lost in. This is the time he seems to live for. The sound levels go up and up, and the bass and the drums grow thunderous as children and, inevitably, grandchildren when you have fans as old as Bob's, put hands over their ears and bow their heads against an adult chest. At the end of the show he will stand in his Western suit and hat, alongside the cowboy businessmen band, and he'll hold up a harmonica perhaps, in a kind of salute, acknowledging the crowd now by introducing the musicians and where they are from, his voice in identifying the American place names making the syllables sound like a Basement Tapes fragment, more lyrical than most of the songs he chopped through. What he reminds you of then is a boxer at the end of a bout, receiving the plaudits and letting the audience know that he knows that they appreciate the pound for pound effort he's exerted. And you think of the boxers he's sung about and compared himself to, and remember Muhammad Ali and all the boxers who went on too long.

Against this rough magic that rouses him and the crowds who come to see a legend boogie, one can place the way he is capable of delivering a song on an album even now. His voice is still a constricted wreck compared with what used to be, but not having to force it to be out there in an arena or a stadium, having the intimacy of a studio, he can bring his powers to bear. His chief power, surprisingly, is of delicacy. There are different ways to visualise his present voice. It can remind you of a pane of crazed glass thick with cobwebs and dust, a gargle of ashes, the action of a cheese grater on petrified chamois leather; but his control of a micro pause between words, the shift in the load of meaning that an individual sound can bear, continues to be unrivalled. He can make the air around a syllable indicate his attitude to what lies behind the song, particularly when a chorus line comes back and back and he works tiny variations, like thoughts registering their minute changes across someone's face, even when lyrically the song is as negligible as Huck's Tune, for a film people won't be able to place. The repeated line "I'm gonna have to put you down for awhile," though nothing in print, can suggest reserves of pain and regret when he sings it, perhaps even more so with his voice in the state it's in.

CHAPTER TWENTY-NINE
ANOTHER WORLD

There's no end of parallel worlds. Someone who was always keen to be part of the present and not dwell on the past, fronted 100 radio shows designed to evoke a mythical radio experience, playing and paying tribute to all kinds of music from long ago, or not so long ago because, as he pointed out, there's always more of the past than the present. On record although he can and does reproduce the blues-based riffs and chugging power of live performances, his band can casually and precisely create any style or era. On Waiting For You, another film song whose home will elude you, the music behind him goes on with a dreamy formality that he is barely part of. There are suggestions and elements of 20s music, of Western Swing, of cowboys, of formal dances, of the sounds you heard behind the lighted windows in John Ford's Calvary Trilogy. On Return To Me, the Dean Martin favourite, unexpectedly featured in The Sopranos, his worn voice is also warm and affecting, even retaining the Italian words, and, with a 1950s accordion of the kind seen and heard in Lady and The Tramp, his band is pointillistically perfect.

Once again having a child helped me to understand about the past and the present. Having been in a house with Bob Dylan music around but ignored all his life, Lou began to take a more direct interest, the kind he'd taken in the Beatles. Initially won over by songs on the Watchmen soundtrack he moved to playing the Greatest Hits in the car, hearing them over and over, as, of course, did I. We were both involved in the terrain that's a combination of space and all times, where everything is available if you want it to be: the past as one place, not a succession. Listening with Lou I felt some kind of shift occur in me. Bob Dylan cannot be faithful as James Taylor or Paul Simon can be to their songs, because their voices are largely unaltered, and besides, they don't see singing something as they used to as a betrayal of artistry, or the hell of being reduced to a jukebox. To be true to how he sees himself he has to be his more elemental character, not faithful exactly, but true like ice, like fire. For people like Lou who don't necessarily know what songs were on what albums, or the order they came out in, all they require is a surrender to the excitement of someone alive now who was alive then, before them, this person touched by history thundering and growling and making something come into existence loudly and at length.

I knew too much to be ignorant, but I could choose to take a different attitude. There would be no point in me going to a Bob Dylan concert now, but it was similarly pointless to rail about it. This is what he does; but nothing else he had ever produced has gone away. It's all still in the big house that contains all the connecting rooms. I could prize many aspects of Bob Dylan now, or regret them, or feel that someone had become someone else. "It's like *he* wrote it," he said, pointing to a sleeping Hawk when taxed with some tall-tale early programme note then 4 years away from being written.. We all have people we used to be, that succession who can come alive over and over in the continuum and separation that make our memories and perceptions cleave together and asunder. A record will always reanimate them, and it doesn't have to be Bob Dylan.

THE SIXTIES

She would be well over sixty now,
obviously, the same year at school

as me, if she's still alive,
and there's no reason why she shouldn't.

Except of course there's friends younger
no longer with us for one reason or another.
I was thinking of her the other morning
sawing slices, some breakfast deejay yammering

before the blessed sound of the Byrds.
She was saying how her mother
had seen her and her boyfriend kissing.
"And you couldn't get a knife between you,"

her mother said, shocked apparently.
"But mother, why would you want to?"
she replied, laughing then and now.
This, naturally, was the middle 1960s.

It's the journey you take, but not everyone can go from rags to riches, or from riches to rags; the journey most of us take is the one where we have to leave the home where we were loved and shaped into who we are, in order to make our own home, to find someone to recreate our own ordinary, unextravagant love and kindness. The home where we grew will disappear like days, but it will be within us still, and aspects of its spirit will be in the home we are now part of, regularly altered and decorated, never quite as it should be and always perfectly imperfect. The journey we all take is growing old and having songs and singers remind us, as children do. Our dream lives, like the transparencies of the Liverpool past and my past, or like separate Windows resting on a toolbar to be maximised as required, overlap the time we inhabit, called up when required.

One myth or dream of the 1960s was that of youth being enough to change the world. It was a dream that wasn't new, though most of us weren't sufficiently aware of that. Scott Fitzgerald, in his crack-up 1930s, had written of the early 1920s

> ... and it seemed only a question of a few years before the older people would step aside and let the world be run by those who saw things as they were – and it all seems rosy and romantic to us who were young then, because we will never feel quite so intensely about our surroundings any more.

Anyone who was a teenager in the middle 1960s, no matter how far from drugs or politics, would have recognised this, and known too the illusions, delusions, and idealism that fuel that dream. Running the world, it turns out, is a million times more difficult even than getting along with your family, all most teenagers have to worry about; and there are always a lot more horrible people out there to deal with than your family is likely to accustom you to. John Lennon had begun his 1970s, as I read in a silent staff room, by telling us that the dream was over. The Sixties, the Beatles, what we had thought it all meant was over. All it had meant was dressing up a bit, he said, and people had to be aware of the Capitalist dream they were enslaved by, keeping them in their place with consumer goods. The next year he sang that we might think he was a dreamer because he still believed in peace and love and everyone being, well, what exactly? Free and happy apparently, realising that there was no God or Heaven, and we were all responsible for ourselves. He was as naïve and simplistic about politics as most of us were, but a good deal more forthright. Not too long afterwards he retreated into the private happiness of a very rich person, fulfilling himself by raising a child, living in the daytime world, owning some of it, and occasionally flying or sailing about it. He'd discovered what most of us already had: that the only way the majority express themselves politically is not by becoming activists but in how they live their lives.

The world so wrong for young and rosy 1960 romantics seemed, after the changes of the 1970s and 1980s, to be an enviably fair and cooperative arrangement of society. I'd directly benefited from it and wouldn't be who I was unless I had been nurtured by council housing, universal education, nationalised healthcare; none of it run to fit market forces, and all interlocking parts of an attempt to make a new, responsible, and optimistic society after the destructive effects of war. Now it's another dream that we recall with varying degrees of accuracy. It blended and blurred too with that other constant background dream: Wanting to be with one person and sharing a life, as I'd seen in the bedsit times, muddling through the difficulties of living with someone else's, possibly oppositional, needs and desires. It's the journey you take, and only love can break your heart. Having sustained a broken heart is probably a working definition of what being adult means. Adults don't have the same hearts they began with. Broken hearts knit back into a different shape which you must grow to fit. I used to be someone else, and so did Bob Dylan. We both almost know the words to a lot of Bob Dylan songs. Those times are dissolved in me, the tissues of my consciousness, accretions of memories and forgettings, things I remember and things I'd like to remember.

The days come and go, delivering us to the repetition of seasons that will come round with the same name, but won't ever be quite the same. I hadn't sinned but I had been redeemed by finding not just love, but the right kind of love, and then the chance to pour some back into Louis. My parents were gone but when you raise a child, method acting your way out of ignorance, you find yourself saying things they said that you didn't even remember you remembered. They are returned to you. That post-war dream society came round again for me even though the country since had been transmogrified under the rigours of Margaret Thatcher, and then the strange blend of ideologies and chicanery that was New Labour. Walking down to school with a child makes you feel part of a bigger enterprise than simply going to work, or watching the news. They walk and run in front of you in shoes that have built-in lights in the sole, flashing with the vibrations as they hit the ground. Or they skip all the way, bouncing up on one foot and then the other down all the streets, until there you both are at the school gate. Then one day you see they don't skip any more, though they still run, and you realise you never noticed the exact day they stopped, and it's hard to say why that gives a pang of regret, but you know it does, even in this happiest decade, the one that runs concurrently with Bob Dylan's most productive, packed and praised one. I think about Bob Dylan's passages about his father in Chronicles, and hope that, unusually, they are his words and emotions; and remember too his line in one of the "Love and Theft" songs – "I wish my mother was still alive" and want that too to be genuine. I think about me and my dad on a sofa together and how that's being passed on.

> Sprawling on the sofa as we watch TV
> I feel the round hardness of his shoulder
> dig into my ribs, and my hand lies at rest
> along his slim and limber, lovely arm:
> this magic in disguise as normality
> and little things; ...

> the softened marble, warm and rounded, of his smooth shoulder,
> a silent happiness that increases as I get older.

You live through the days one at a time, like words in a sentence, and the months become paragraphs. You live in prose, but you remember in poems, with editing and highlights

SANDFALLEN

From behind, his heels
lifting and falling in a neatness

of motion, red sparkles flash
in his shoes of light,

his shoulders and jogging limbs
rolling in small harmony.
Running and running ahead
tireless as a dog soldier,

Cheyenne was it, Comanche, Sioux?
Under ancient skies like this one,
the mile-eating pace of a warrior
tackling any terrain that comes

in Western annuals that consumed me
as a boy, older than this boy,
my son, jinking and trotting
away from me, school and home,

back and forth, alternating worlds
on standby, his economical
always stamina carries him forward
into each sphere of knowledge,

towards unknown books he will hold
hidden in his thoughts forever.
Running and running before me,
sparkling and unshowy, natural

and unlettered, moving away
from me at roughly the speed
of sand pouring, falling and falling
from one glass bulb to another.

There was no society, Margaret Thatcher had said, there was only the family. But down at the school gate and on into the yard, all milling children and watching parents, you saw how all those conflicting views and temperaments, all those people who may not think like you but are part of the same experience, had to work together, how families had to be a society. I had travelled from one society where you could still touch remnants of the nineteenth century: little lamp standards that had started out with gas fittings were still standing; horses and carts moved on streets with cobblestones; houses had mangles, wash tubs and poshers. Technology changed everything, technology and its becoming affordable. From a childhood house where television was absent, I was in this world where most people are never more than a few feet from a screen of some kind, and can't imagine it otherwise.

Everything we know, can go away, will go away no matter how one feels that they will go on like this forever.
Even videotapes are symbols of the fate we are moving towards, clogging the charity shops, shelves of them, all made undesirable by changes in the way new machinery comes into existence and people are persuaded. Cassettes too, once so important to Telegraph readers and writers, proof of Bob Dylan's other life beyond released albums, all the outtakes and alternative versions from recording sessions, and the live shows from every phase of his career. Of course his career had fewer phases at the time. Outdated now, they are to be found in bent cardboard boxes on landings or in the loft. Unclear, scratchy plastic cassette cases, no longer played, still not quite thrown away, their inserts foreign with runic handwriting, except where the meticulous wasted work of a ballpoint or felt-tip has faded with sun and time, "Hobart" or "Jones Beach" possibly discernible in John Bauldie's handwriting, no year given and several elapsed since they were last played, little scaled down miles of tape still representing

the miles Bob twirls about the turning world. Books, which fill a house as a child grows, can't escape either, the charm of acquisition weakening in their slow, long-term dance of possession and loss. They start to migrate back towards places where they were found: charity shops in general, second-hand bookshops, book fairs, jumble sales, car boot fields.

Things change and leave, but the nineteenth century hangs on in different ways. Here I am in a small nineteenth century house its original tenants wouldn't recognise, working men's houses not as large as the ones I knew in the Smithfield Road of my childhood. Nevertheless I'm here owning one, having somehow been transported into the kind of life I could only imagine for other people in the bedsit times. Those happy families I saw around Richmond Park's Pen Ponds 40 years ago, eventually I joined them, scarfed and warm-coated, hooped and woolly; or bright in the summer on bikes to the children's playground; all of us living in the seasons of the daytime world, and school. Like traditional ballads, schools are shaped by seasons and festivals: Easter and Halloween, Leavers Assembly and Christmas. It's a phrase worn out by use that Christmas is for children, but it's true that having a child, and making your way from the baby years upwards, when Father Christmas and parents share the same wrapping paper, lets you experience again Christmas feelings that were implanted when you too were a child, before it became a teenage boredom or an opportunity to arrange drinks appointments. Christmas is about looking forward until the day arrives, children ticking off the dates and counting; but it's always inescapably about the past, previous Christmases. Who would have thought that Bob Dylan would have anything to do with it?

It seemed so unlikely when it was rumoured that there was a Bob Dylan Christmas album to be released, only a couple of months after his then most recent one Together Through Life. That gave us the mixture as before but in a more lively, hard-edged fashion: excellently produced, everything loud and clear, from a band that could play anything, and nothing that wouldn't prompt a feeling you'd heard it before somewhere. Most of the songs were co-written with a former Grateful Dead lyricist and credited as such, rather than being ghost composites, but it hardly mattered. The words were so universal, such familiar recycling, as to be impersonal. It was enjoyable enough if you weren't expecting important statements, or Bob Dylan as he sounded 30 years ago. As no-one did any more, not even me, it could be enjoyed within its playing time constraints for its expertise in creating riff-based, accordion flavoured, genre exercises, for exhibiting Bob's contentment with his role in life, then returned to the shelf and not necessarily thought about for awhile. No-one, therefore, had high hopes for a Christmas album, particularly because it was to be released in October well before anyone had a chance to build up the necessary emotion, and some people, like those in my house, have rules as strict as the pheasant season, but much shorter, for when Christmas albums can be played. There was also, and permanently, the question of his voice.

I suppose I counted myself chief amongst the doubters and expected to listen and find more evidence that the disintegration of Bob had continued apace. It was a real surprise then, and a terrific pleasure, when breaking my 1st December embargo on any Christmas music being played, I sat down to listen to the album to review it. Anyone who had read Chronicles knew that he had written about Christmas in the most affectionate and detailed way (and in words that some of us now fervently wished were *really* his), so we knew that, unexpectedly, it was dear to him. We knew too that he would be singing the songs in the voice he now had. Sometimes this was exactly the right voice to convey the emotions he now seemed to excel at: tenderness, regret, wistfulness, a sense of the irrevocable transience of all things but the necessity for always trying to do your human best. That was what made even an old light entertainment hit like Return To Me such a moving, rewarding (and entertaining) experience, when the title itself seemed to be a plea to the past. But what would he sound like on standards and familiar favourites? And what would the music be?

Gloriously, and happily, what was immediately striking was the quality of the sound as a recording, and as arrangements. All of the instruments are pitched to be just so, to play exactly the right role in the enactment of each song. The perfection and precision and expertise of the musicians and the singers is like a Christmas chamber group, while from the first song onwards what the detail and the general feel reminded me of, surprisingly, was Self Portrait, that often unregarded album, where throughout there are examples of beautifully recorded instrumental elements. What he had done, as I understood it, was try to recreate the kind of Christmas album that he had grown up on, and so had my generation of Bob fans just that little bit later. Dickens has a claim as the prime inventor of Christmas as we now understand it, but so does the entertainment industry of America after the Second World War and on into the 1950s. With this album Bob Dylan recreated as faithfully as one could wish the choirs, the strings, and the implacably non-ironic, absolutely sincere approach that one heard and expected from Bing Crosby or Perry Como. His voice of course couldn't be changed. Before the album appeared it was clear that there couldn't be the deconstruction of melodies to suit limited singing abilities, the kind of mangling hailed as brilliant artistic choices by some. No, if you choose to do Christmas songs you have to honour them and your audience by doing them as they are, and as well as you can. You sing them and become part of the tradition just as much as if you sang Barbara Allen.

The good news was that Bob did just that, though anyone who had never been any kind of Bob fan would be impregnably immune to his virtues. There were times that he sounded as if he was trying to free his throat from a waffle of catarrh, and on occasion his nose sounded as if it had been plugged, but from the first song we know, we hear, that this enterprise is no joke, hoax, throwaway, or postmodernly ironic. What you hear emerging from the perfect storm of torn charcoal textures is his knowing, eccentric phrasing, his idiosyncratic pronunciation, his humour and sincerity, and all of the resonances and associations that are generated by placing him against that pristine choir and master small group context. On songs where he doesn't have to push or strain, like The First Noel or the Little Drummer Boy, the result is more obviously pleasing. On the latter he drops in at the end "me and my drum" in a child-like tender way that fits wonderfully. In fact throughout there are examples of gentleness beneath which is a wistful and sad quality. There's no way that he or we can't hear what he sounds like now, but he steps up to the plate and lets the recording spotlight pick him out. You have to do them as well as you can, we know it, but the humanity of Christmas, the Christmases he and we experienced as children, permeates the album. There are great imperfections in his voice and a great desire to do the best he can with no hiding place. It's a lovely and brave thing to do. His voice is mostly not beautiful but his intent always is. It's a reminder that anyone can want to sing at Christmas, any dad or uncle, but he brings something else that's emotional too. He used to be a great singer, and now he isn't, but you still hear at times another voice hidden inside what he has now. At the end of Do You Hear What I Hear on the final line "He will bring us goodness and light", on the extended last note he starts in a blur of voice wrack and then the note emerges clear, fittingly like a light breaking through a cloud. Of course there's a special pleading involved in finding something emotional because you're listening to someone who was once remarkable now having to do their best with what they've got, but the merits of the album aren't falsified.

There were a couple of other elements that I found pleasing too. In addition to Christmas songs being part of the tradition we all shared, so that Bob was reaffirming his link with what was of value in a general way, without having to claim or fake writing credits, these commercial products he was now singing, odd as it sounds, connected to the protest and civil rights ethos of almost 50 years before. The songs exist to show us the wider possibilities of amity, co-operation, looking out for each other, and that it doesn't necessarily have to be restricted to one time of the year. Of course this sounds grandiose, pretentious, wishful thinking, and Christmas is ever a puzzle of schlock, base motives, and idealism. But when artists make a Christmas album, and many make more than one, they're making a statement, and standing up to be counted.

By chance and fluke and happening upon an internet link in the year or so before Bob's Christmas album, I had been able to download an album, never released in Britain in 1959 when it was made, tracks converted to mp3s, front and back covers obligingly scanned, and all generously provided for strangers simply because it was possible. The major Warner Brothers TV stars of that year had been corralled together to make a Christmas album and they had had the benefit of a full film studio orchestra whose sound is wonderfully lush and impressive, and so different from rock or blues. The Western stars and the detective stars I had loved then were there with this encapsulation of the exact year when I had first seen the Western Film and TV Stars annual, those pre-Christmas Saturday afternoons in the darkness and shop lights all permeated by Christmasness. Bob Dylan's album reminded me of that, acting as both a closing of a circle and a mirror to show me where I had come from, and what I could now pass on, what Christmas makes you part of: a family of course, but the society that families form and the values we hope it shares. Christmas is the absolute summation of seasonal repetition, the past, the present and the future as one; the proof of events coming round and being the same and not being the same because they happen to older, different people, the lesson that school teaches us, and teaches us all over again when we are lucky enough to be parents.

CHAPTER THIRTY
A SERIOUS DREAM

John Fuller, the poet and academic, said once that his University career ran on the equivalent of two-star petrol. I hadn't had what I thought of as a career as such, but I had done library work all my adult life, fuelled perhaps by something closer to the pink paraffin lugged to the door for people with those odiferous heaters when I was a child. Sometimes my lack of ambition embarrassed me, particularly if I felt obliged to explain it. Mostly however I felt that being engaged in work that existed in order to bring people gradations of knowledge, information, wisdom and entertainment couldn't be other than an honourable thing to be involved in, at whatever high or low level it took place. Asked by Lou what I'd done that day I could say, "I helped somebody," and mean it in a specific, concrete way, and mean it day after day. A small thing compared to grand offices and responsibilities, but not a negligible one. It was also indisputably a service to society, a public service, an organised community kindness, at a time when the nineteenth century is making itself known by means other than old lampposts or cobblestones. The reliance on philanthropy, charitable altruism and profit rather than local government to sort out people's lives is touted once more. The 1980s are back in their remastered, expanded edition. Local government becomes the enemy as the unthinkable gets thought again by people who think that word means desirable. The work I've done and the world I came from may come to seem like a story or a dream, like the Sixties. Thinking about library services in practice however makes me consider that, though it may not have been expressed in quite this way, in terms of communal care and looking out for people they have always been a continuation of what people believed the Sixties stood for, no matter what peripheral youth nonsense and delusion also floated free then, however unhip and unlikely libraries might seem as a descendant.

So here we are, every season a beginning and a demise, always existing in the days that become years and the anniversaries keep coming and what does Bob Dylan have to tell us now? Well, it's no surprise that as with most people regarded, or once regarded, as oracles, it's all in the interpretation. Tim Hardin once asked how can we hang onto a dream, but there's always been a thriving industry concerned not with hanging onto them but working out what they mean. After the Christmas album I came to an accommodation with Bob Dylan and the dream he let me be in almost all my life. He had spent much of his life in specific opposition to repetition whether it be record takes, rehearsals or performances. Some song lines dwell on it:

> *sick of all this repetition,*
> *what price to get out of going through all these things twice,*
> *Oh no, no, I've been through this movie before.*

making the basis of his career his need to keep things fresh, spontaneous, off the cuff and rearranged. He changes styles, appearance, bands, and this is thought to be a good thing, compared to most of us who plug along and are changed only by being worked over by Big Daddy Time and his henchmen. Against this is the fact that far from being unpredictable, almost anyone can predict that his shows now will consist of unrecognisable songs delivered, rather than sung, in a ruined voice; everything going on too long, too loud and hardly any variety with regard to tempo or arrangement; and looking much as he did over the last decade, this stern little fellow with the Western suit and hat, the faintly ridiculous moustache and haggard features, propped behind his small keyboard making faces and gestures but otherwise ignoring his crowd. He doesn't consider himself part of the consciousness that so attracted us in the 1960s, and yet every stage announcement and campaign for new records explicitly, ruthlessly one might say, evokes that former life because that's why people pay for tickets and albums. His latest releases are remastered mono versions of the earliest albums, along with another Genuine Bootleg instalment consisting of early 60s demo recordings. Over the years he's become a different product with the same brand name.

Listening over months to Lou play Bob's Greatest Hits in the car, as he had once had the Beatles on heavy duty rotation every journey, then James Taylor, I realised it didn't matter. What did it matter what I thought about where he was now? Unlike the past of most people his was always there, endlessly accessible. When asked by Daniel Lanois if he would sing a song onstage now the way he had on its original album, he is said to have replied, "You don't wanna live the same day over and over do you?" Actually most of us do want something like that, the good bits still operational, the bad in recess. The message of Christmas albums is the same as that of the film Groundhog Day: the protagonist, Bill Murray, gets exactly the same day to live over and over, an endless repetition to realise gradually what he's doing wrong, what his faults as a person are, and given the endless vista he's offered for correction, to become a better one. We think that it's a fantasy because he gets the same day with the same incidents that he can adjust to or change, and nothing like the real world. But then in 1965 Bob Dylan in interview said: "realising in terms of really hard reality that tomorrow never comes. You always wake up and it's today. Tomorrow just never seems to come. And there is no yesterday."

Like Bob we're all on a Never-Ending Tour and travel doesn't have to be involved. We all get to do our best one day at a time between the arrival of the light and the drawing of the curtains. Each day, no matter how apportioned in seasons, in weeks and months, we will enter as we did the one before; until suddenly, unexpectedly, or all too predictably, we won't. Meanwhile the family factory goes on. The supplies come in: the food, the clothes, the shoes, the books, the newspapers, the framed posters, the dishes, the cutlery, the tins of paint; and every week out go the bags and boxes and caddies stuffed with the remain of things the house has digested, in time to meet, moving like mechanised locusts slowly through the streets, clearing as they go, the guys in refuse and recycling. The houses will get cleared eventually; everyone will face those wild, whirling, motionless slippers. The jazz records I bought in a spirit of altruism from Potter's 30 years ago were sometimes the result of a widow clearing out a collection that probably had been built with love over a lifetime. Once, casually, inadvertently cruel, Lou said to me about Bob Dylan: "I tell you what; I'll miss him when he's gone." Bob Dylan started young and his first album was already haunted by death. We have been catching up ever since.

In quantum physics light can be discerned as a wave or a particle depending on the context. Sometimes I think deciding on Bob Dylan's state is a little like that. Once he seemed to signify a heightened present and a better world to come. Now it's difficult to say exactly what he does tell us, but I think it has something to do with the past and how it can help us if we understand it aright. From teenage bedroom listening and reading of record sleeves, to toe-curling attendances at 1990s Hammersmith Odeon shows, to looking bemused at You Tube clips of shows on the other side of the world so current they only happened the night before, has been part of the journey taken. Inevitably the distance he travelled was greater, which might please Melvyn Bragg, but all of us make some movement. A three hour journey to bedsits and alone; married; separated; unexpectedly loved by someone wise; divorced; married; and, to someone Bloxwich born, a child whose birth took place in the colourful, photogenic modernity of Chelsea and Westminster hospital. This may not seem like much when others have gone from council house living rooms to shake the world, but we all do the best we can. Helicopters don't have to fall out of the sky, or babies be born, to indicate what's important in the world, but every little helps.

The Sixties had hardly finished when John Lennon proclaimed the dream to be over, something that was flat wrong because the whole world ever since has been dreaming about that dream, remembering it, living in the reality informed by the dream that never went away. There are industries making books that shuttle the words together to chronicle every detail, day by day; big, art object books collecting photographs of the buildings and the streets where things occurred. Reality seems to have shifted, so that time now exists most solidly, most reliably, within the accumulating library of text and glossy illustration. One's own memories can seem, by comparison, insubstantial and sparse, elusive and thin. Begin at the beginning, Alice is advised, and go on until you have reached the end. Deciding what makes a beginning or an end is what can preoccupy us, wondering where the exact start of something is. Sometimes, walking along a river bank in dazzling morning sunlight, or at the other end of the day, in sadder evening brightness, you see a figure ahead of you, clear in silhouette. As you look you can't tell immediately if it's coming towards you or going away. The past can look like that.

Time has passed, Bob sang, and now it seems everybody's having them dreams. The typography, designs, fashions, invented and made popular in the 1960s are still a big pattern book that people can loot or use for inspiration over and over. Sixties songs act the way old folk and blues did for Dylan, giving a vision and a version of another world, one that gives a clue as to how one might behave in this one. Go to Brighton or Camden and you see a kind of outpost of what some might think a Sixties sensibility is. Organic and vegetarian are mantras and watchwords in the way macrobiotic used to be. Market stalls and fairgrounds seem to infuse the atmosphere of streets, and all the people walking by are in a clothes museum, taking styles from everywhere and all times. The beliefs that people have, or live by, are blurred with appearance, and appearance seems to be crucial in whether they are judged good people or not. The chief reminder is in how the world seems to be made for young people, but the old people want to share that look, despite the evidence of their bodies. It's always the Sixties for teenagers, busy creating their own golden age to look back on. And into my mind comes a picture Joan Baez made, though it feels like something I dreamed or lived myself, the way Bob's creativity works perhaps: brown leaves falling all around and snow in his hair, their vulnerable breath mingling and hanging in white clouds, those young lovers who aren't any more, who pass by and move on and can no longer do distance and close simultaneously. And with every day's greeting and farewell we find that no matter how many far away decades have disappeared like dreams, it's all a little time.

We were children, and now we are not, and we dreamed childish dreams, believing in change, the double helix of politics and virtue, as we had once believed in Father Christmas, wanting to be good so that the rest would follow. We were innocent, some of us more than others, and believed, as Bob Dylan did, in the songs and the music more. Bob Dylan was part of it, then not part of it, and has been what he wanted to be ever since, committed to the succession of recording and shows; a series of dissolves between rehearsals, soundchecks, working up new songs, breaking in new band members; versions tried and dropped, unreleased songs performed over and over and then put away; like a whaler on a tour of duty, American as Melville, travelling and travelling across countries he sees through a window and draws when he can, his personality like a core of smoke inside him, nebulous, modulating and shifting, as if he feels most real only when he is out on stage undergoing that discipline and further degrading his vocal cords.

The concerts were once admired for changing set lists, melodies, words, and often short-changing audience expectations. Now they are a planned theatrical experience, and though there may be some song order changes, for the most part the content stays fixed, and concentrates on the most recent albums, the ones whose songs are the apogee of the method he uses now, where lines can come from anywhere, will usually remind you of something else, can turn weirdly violent or brutal in a moment, and surprise you mainly in that he can remember them all, and deliver them with an authority the same as if they had the deep personal meaning that I hear, and prize, in Not Dark Yet. The excitement that was once part of Bob Dylan concerts isn't present in the same way. As the songs have come to consist more of lines that anyone, but not necessarily him, might think or feel, his stage demeanour becomes more and more undemonstrative, his physical unease when singing only slightly less than when he seems redundant between verses; and all punctuated by sub-OCD flicks and gestures at cheeks or brow. He stalks the stage with a stern manner, looking as if he might reprimand the vintage stand-up microphone, or is contemplating wringing its neck. A concert from this side of the stage looks more like a duty he has agreed to undertake, one that will be meted out and paced song by song, but not necessarily one he takes pleasure in. Now that he doesn't play guitar his main emotional expressiveness, when he really seems to connect, comes when he plays mouth organ, when words and a voice aren't necessary but we can believe we are glimpsing something heartfelt in him. People can watch him for real or on You Tube in those European cities that could be locations for thrillers and film noir, the kind he likes too. The excitement will come because he is like a famous museum in such a town, or a gallery, or an historical monument under threat, a tourist's must-see, and he means and has meant so much, and so much of people's emotional lives are invested in him that often they offer the tribute of tears. All the images, memories, album covers and ghosts have been precipitated and solidified into this remote person in the draped and swaying trousers, the man in a hat and a storehouse of earlier meanings and values.

Nevertheless, he is attempting to make something come into existence and, difficult though it is to believe it sometimes, to share that with us. Popular music constantly changes and stops being about what you are, or what you like, because now it's not made or meant for you; but whatever was once important always maintains a relationship. Bob Dylan changed so that now one may not always want to share what he creates, but he remained a constant through all the shifts that happened, even in a fan's largely uneventful, normally momentous life. Winners need to be defined, given existence, by losers. Stars can't shine without fans to notice. Being a Bob fan is a little like going to a cinema in the days when there weren't programme times. You went in while a film was on, wherever the story happened to be, and watched until it was where you came in. Then you could choose to leave or stay until the end you had already seen. Here, where I sit, thinking about time all the time, and "you've got yesterday, today and tomorrow all in the same room" like the Tangled Up In Blue tenses Bob described, I can regard the shelves where CDs weave their lines, and the shelves where books are constantly on parade, and think Bob thoughts I may have thought before, or new ones I may not remember. I can ignore the various wholly-owned subsidiaries of the Bob Dylan Corporation, the touring art prints, the sad paintings, the meticulously timed and tooled marketing campaigns and IT mastery that will unleash a new record or a Bootleg Series unto the world. I can ignore this and put on any Bob Dylan voice I want to hear. He created and discarded voices, the way he sounded, with no trace of sentiment or regret well before the mid-1960s hits that make anniversaries and get radio play. And I may put on Corrina, Corrina, those six versions he did in 1962, in two months, April and October, separated by a long season. Six performances and all different, and the song not done since, and the one on Freewheelin' is still the most perfectly affecting. He may never have sung like this again, and certainly couldn't now, but of course he doesn't have to. It's here, in this room all the time, all the times. And looking up I think, "Isn't this where I came in?"

...

Let him be the Bob Dylan he is in all his dualities: duplicitously truthful, old and young, now and then, his heaping work flawed and generous, this Pat Garrett and Billy The Kid carrying his aura of possibility, the possibility of the past. Let him be the man who is and isn't Bob Dylan, that freak and force of nature, the living chip off Mount Rushmore, who is always judged by standards applicable only to him, holder of a never-ending special pass, producer of these offerings: amped up, pumped up, loud, lively, weird, bracing, mad, odd, irradiated with latter-day darkling delights, intermittently dreary, repetitive and finally sad because though this may surprise us it will never be the surprise he made the gift of when he was young and we were younger. And let me be all the me's I have access to, overseeing the preparation of school bags and homework, polishing shoes, sending my son out to face the world the way my parents did for me, with whatever dreams they had, a continuity of recurring dreams in the smoke of voices, the reflection of mirrors, all under the drift of clouds, all of us in the serious business of being surprised by happiness and treasuring contentment.

We come into existence out of absence: not there, then there, like songs. When we disappear what remains is in the memories of other people, who will also vanish, and from these and whatever kind of lyric sheets survive, we might come to some kind of life again, as the old ballads do in later voices. The mystery of time is that things happen once only, and yet for many reasons, – dreams, memory, imagination, film, writing – they seem to happen over and over. So I think about the Sixties, and the perfection of The Beatles and what they created; thinking how wonderful it must be to conflate a confection out of nothing, out of thin air, scattered files and filings away and footnotes lying around in your head, forgetting what it was you started to look for then finding things you had forgotten; from facts and fancy and whims and prejudice; from what you know and don't know, quotes you can check and those you put in anyway; from what you suspect and from things you simply like the sound of; from ancient memories or hallucinations you'd like to remember; and all of it from love, willpower and a desire to entertain. How wonderful it must be. And so it is

DREAM JOURNAL

for Jo, with love for the dream we share

It's not just a song Charlie,
it's a place in your heart.

Doc Pomus

Sometimes when I go in to rouse my son in the morning,
on those days when he doesn't visit us first,
I make a space and lie there, putting my hand
around his ribcage, as I did when I nursed

him as a baby, that ever-present age ago,
feeling the warm, breathing, moving solidity,
holding the evidence, commonplace and startling,
of another person, so separate, so much entwined with me.

Light comes around the curtains, illuminating his softened
sleep-pout,
his mashed hair, and I lean in to see how close he is to waking,
brushing his ear with my lips, watching eyelids
dream-flicker, twitching indications of breaking

consciousness. One night as a baby, the first
he was home, he spent entirely on my chest
as I cupped him fore and aft, smaller than my arm, on the settee,
knowing the weight of him as his mother got the rest

she sorely needed, allowing this close separation,
never closer. And I was nervous and blessed, knowing
I would hold this in my memory all my life, as I held him
now,
his cheek against my chest, the moments going

from darkness to light, travelling through
the strangeness of the hours, the cool gloom
of the night time house that makes all objects
unfamiliar, and we are awake in the living room

aware of breathing transformed into time.
Years of days and nights have brought us here, to the pleasure
of sleep's smooth warmth,
the arms and legs that measure

how far we have come. Stretched alongside me,
his head reaching my chest now, more than half my length,
a beautiful compendium of powers
increasing in everything all the time: size; strength;

the ability to annoy; the sense of being completely himself
and right that bursts out of him like energy
from a star. Except when he sleeps, as he sleeps now,
my hand light on his ribs, next to me.

Do you know when a song comes on the radio,
a song you love, a song on a record you own and play
but it being on the radio verifies individual experience,
makes it more obviously so; the happenstance day

confirming and authenticating what you know
by the charm of serendipity,

revealing the personal to be universal too
in all the broadcast waves through village, town, and city.

Sometimes when I go in to wake my son
and lie quietly near, my memory
and that moment reality are like a radio soundtrack,
a reminder of an epiphany

which passes and endures. Like the sound the Beatles made
and will always make, inexhaustible streamers of song filling the car
wherever we go, the mythical Sixties we're singing together in
these confines,
reality, imagination and memory fused, light from a star

still radiating generations after the fact.
Shadowing his position I lie waiting for the time it will take,
immersed in the seasons that led to now, right now.
Night lights and night terrors; sore throats and tummy ache;

birthdays and counting charts; nursery rhymes and Christmas;
the pushchair afternoons moving in succession through the great
park
in the river's bend; its sunlit mowers, its heaping leaves;
the bath that signals bed no matter or not if it's dark;

the sleeping story ritual whose simplicity grows more complex.
Eight winters and eight springs and the splendid gift of cherry
trees,
and always returning to this lovely island and boat,
our refuge of rest and comfort and ease.

Lying close and separate as voices rising in harmony,
curled against increasing light,

FOR JO, WITH LOVE FOR THE DREAM WE SHARE

feeling moments arrive and leave like prayer beads,
the abacus of day and night

counting for and against, the movement of planets
in complementary orbit, sunshine and moonbeams,
my mouth touching his head, my hand cradling his breathing,
the intense reality of moments that drift away as dreams.

ACKNOWLEDGEMENTS

Remembering John Bauldie, mastermind of The Telegraph, the Bob magazine where all my first Dylan essays and reviews appeared, thus transforming me from someone who liked Bob into a writer about Bob Dylan.

With thanks for his kindness to Tony Lacey, Penguin Books editor, who read my Bob essays and suggested I contact literary agent David Smith.

Thanks too therefore to David Smith who thought the essays could become an autobiography, persuaded me to write it, and tried to convince editors to take on the result, and then did so himself.

Nigel Hinton who responded enthusiastically and encouraged me when that meant a great deal.

Terry Kelly who requests Bob reviews and essays for The Bridge, oversees them cannily, and who will recognise poems and reworked text included here.

Michael Gray, my pen pal and occasional poem subject supplier, who put me in his Bob Dylan Encyclopedia and has a sharp eye for everything literary and Dylanic, and whose praise therefore means a lot.

And to Hugo Williams, whose poetry books I read in a nutshell abode and who decades later accepted my poems for publication in The Spectator, another kind of dream.

16035959R00250

Printed in Great Britain
by Amazon